Political Map of the World, January 2015

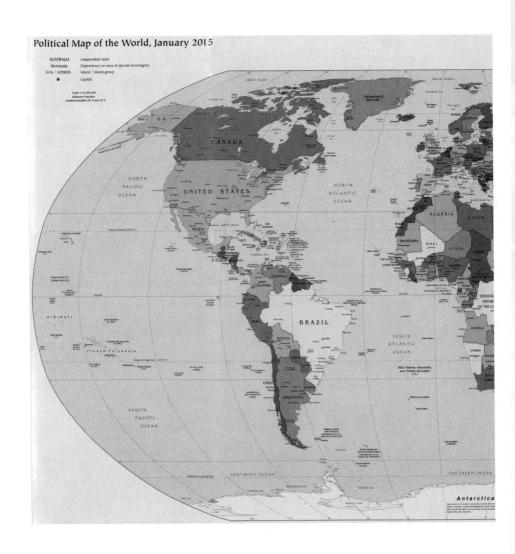

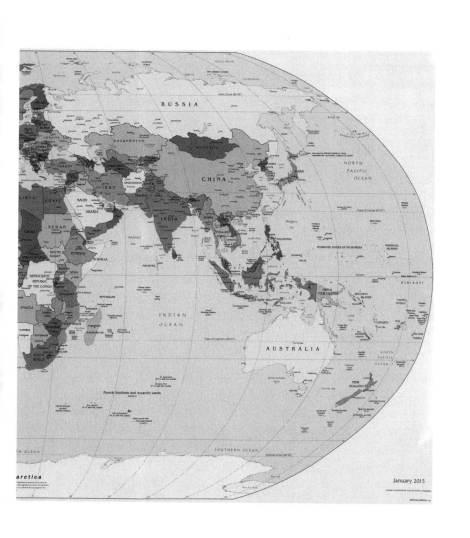
January 2015

BORDER POLITICS

IN A GLOBAL ERA

Comparative Perspectives

Kathleen Staudt

University of Texas at El Paso

Foreword by Tony Payan

ROWMAN & LITTLEFIELD

Lanham • Boulder • New York • London

Executive Editor: Traci Crowell
Associate Editor: Molly White
Assistant Editor: Mary Malley
Senior Marketing Manager: Karin Cholak
Marketing Manager: Deborah Hudson
Interior Designer: Ilze Lemesis
Cover Designer: Sally Rinehart
Cover photo provided by Kathleen Staudt

Credits and acknowledgments for material borrowed from other sources and reproduced, with permission, in this textbook appear on appropriate page within the text.

Published by Rowman & Littlefield
A wholly owned subsidiary of The Rowman & Littlefield Publishing Group, Inc.
4501 Forbes Boulevard, Suite 200, Lanham, Maryland 20706
www.rowman.com

Unit A, Whitacre Mews, 26–34 Stannary Street, London SE11 4AB, United Kingdom

British Library Cataloguing in Publication Information Available

Library of Congress Cataloging-in-Publication Data Available

ISBN 9781442266179 (cloth : alk. paper)
ISBN 9781442266186 (pbk. : alk. paper)
ISBN 9781442266193 (electronic)

∞™ The paper used in this publication meets the minimum requirements of American National Standard for Information Sciences—Permanence of Paper for Printed Library Materials, ANSI/NISO Z39.48–1992.

Printed in the United States of America

Dedication

This book is dedicated to my now-grown children, Mosi and Asha

Brief Contents

Contents

Abbreviations

ACLU	American Civil Liberties Union
ABORNE	African Borderlands Research Network
ABS	Association for Borderlands Studies
ASARCO	American Smelting and Refining Company
ASEAN	Association of Southeast Asian Nations
BCCs	Border Crossing Cards
BCIM	Bangladesh-China-India-Myanmar
BSF	Border Security Force
BECC	Border Environment Cooperation Commission
BID	Border Inequalities Database
BNHR	Border Network for Human Rights
BRIT	Border Regions in Transition
CIA	Central Intelligence Agency
CEC	Commission for Environmental Cooperation
CILA	Comisión Internacional de Limites & Aguas
CEDAW	Convention on the Elimination of All Forms of Discrimination Against Women
COLEF	El Colegio de la Frontera Norte
DACA	Deferred Action for Childhood Arrivals
EU	European Union
EEZ	Exclusive Economic Zones
GDI	Gender Development Index
GDR	German Democratic Republic
GII	Gender Inequality Index
GATT	General Agreement on Tariffs and Trade
GDP	Gross Domestic Product
HBI	Hope Border Institute
HDI	Human Development Index
HDR	Human Development Report
IACHR	Inter-American Court of Human Rights
IAUS	Israeli Association of United Architects
IBWC	International Boundary and Water Commission
ICAO	International Civil Aviation Organization
IR	international relations
IS	Islamic State (also called ISIL, ISIS, Daesh)
ISO	International Organization for Standardization
IOM	International Organization for Migration
IMF	International Monetary Fund
IMDB	Internet Movie Data Base
I-2	Inequalities and Institutions

JBS	*Journal of Borderlands Studies*
LOC	Library of Congress
MERCOSUR	Mercado Común del Sur
MDNER	Ministry of Development of Northeastern Region
NADBank	North American Development Bank
NAFTA	North American Free Trade Agreement
NASA	National Aeronautics Space Administration
NATO	North Atlantic Treaty Organization
NBI	National Bureau of Investigation
NGOs	non-governmental organizations
OFW	Overseas Filipino Worker
PBS	Public Broadcasting Service
POEA	Philippines Overseas Employment Administration
PPP	Purchasing Power Parity
SAARC	South Asia Association for Regional Cooperation
SPP	Security and Prosperity Partnership
TEA	Texas Education Agency
TTIP	Transatlantic Trade and Investment Partnership
TTP	Trans-Pacific Partnership
UN	United Nations
UNCLOS	United Nations Convention on the Law of the Sea
UNDP	United Nations Development Programme
UNEP	United Nations Environment Program
UNHCR	United Nations High Commissioner for Refugees
USSR	United Soviet Socialist Republics
US	United States
US CBP	United States Customs and Border Protection
US DHS	United States Department of Homeland Security
US DEA	United States Drug Enforcement Agency
US ICE	United States Immigration and Customs Enforcement
US NIDA	United States National Institute of Drug Abuse
UTEP	University of Texas at El Paso
UICAI	Unique Identification Authority of India (also called Aadhaar)

Foreword

Kathleen Staudt is one of the most qualified academics I know to write a book about borders. She has spent four decades as a keen observer of border phenomena and traveled around the world comparing border processes, peoples, and flows. But Kathy is not just a scholar, studying the border as an object of science. She has lived the border. She has worked on the border. She is, as she says, a *fronteriza* by adoption—a true borderlander.

Border Politics in a Global Era is, thus, the culmination of four decades of work. It is vast in its coverage, drawing from Kathy's decades of accumulated knowledge, a massive bibliography in border studies, and from firsthand observations of borders around the world. This important book also draws from the social sciences and the humanities. Her inclusion of films that visually portray a variety of different borders adds a dimension rarely seen in academic books—the day-to-day impact of borders on human lives everywhere. I have never read a scholarly work with this multidisciplinary breadth, from film to political science to cartography to history to cultural studies to economics to sociology to anthropology and international relations.

Besides this marriage of science and humanities, *Border Politics in a Global Era* moves us through history, including the Border War between the United States and Mexico, colonialism, as well as postcolonial Africa and Asia. It offers critical perspectives on gendered borders, socioeconomic barriers in the form of hardened inequalities, inhumane securitization processes at borderlines, and cultural divides that discriminate and exclude. Throughout the book, Kathy exposes the distortions of border life through the art of cartography and the way it draws our attention to the center, while it marginalizes the periphery. She lays bare the power structures—bureaucratic and otherwise—built to keep the "undesirables" out and shelter those deemed worthy of protection. And she unmasks the sheer artificiality of borderlines as drawn by the colonial powers in the Middle East and Africa.

Kathy carries the reader across the globe, from North America, with its always-controversial US-Mexico border; to South Asia, which bears the lines of colonialism like scars on the earth; to Europe, with its borders reemerging, threatening the very viability of the union; and to the high seas and the grab for maritime resources from fisheries to mining. Her comparative approach is truly born of a lifelong study of borders everywhere. Besides the impressive geographical scope, Kathy's work also highlights key topics through the lens of border studies. One of these is security. The increased securitization of our lives has found a welcoming environment at borders. Borders, because they are the "skin" of the nation-states, are seen as highly vulnerable, and we have stripped borderlanders of their right to make their spaces inhabitable and safe according to their own designs.

This innovative text not only gives us multidisciplinary, critical, and broad theoretical perspectives on borders, it also suggests that borders can be transcended, regardless of political conditions. Kathy argues that we need to stop "seeing like a border" and explore more deeply democratic processes to escape state-centric analysis and find common solutions to our cross-border problems. Ultimately, we are in this together, and the time has come "if we do not wish to perish" to "set aside our ancient prejudices [which include borders] and build the earth," as Pierre Teilhard de Chardin warns us.

I am aware of no other text in the literature that offers a broader perspective on borders. *Border Politics in a Global Era* awakens our moral conscience to the kinds of discrimination, exclusion, injustice, inequality, and repression that occur at borderlands across the globe every day. Reading this book is not only an academic exercise; it is a spiritual exercise, because it gives us the facts but it also calls us to act morally upon our surroundings.

Tony Payan, PhD
Director, Mexico Center
Rice University's Baker Institute for Public Policy and
Universidad Autónoma de Ciudad Juárez

Preface and Acknowledgments

I have crossed many borders in my life, both literal and metaphorical. Because of this, I have many people to thank.

Above all, I treasure the opportunity to live, teach, and pursue research in the central Mexico-US borderlands at the University of Texas at El Paso (UTEP) for over thirty-five years. At least 10 but as many as 20 percent of students are border crossers, either as commuters or as students who have lived for part of their lives on the "other" side of the border. My lived experience at and in borderlands grounds me and sharpens my border lens.

Throughout history, the region has been called the "Ellis Island of the Southwest" for the many migrants from the north, south, east, and west who have passed through or settled here. I teach in a political science department but have always packaged my courses in interdisciplinary ways: women, power, and politics; politics of developing countries; nonprofit organizations; public policy analysis; and, of course, border politics at the undergraduate, master's, and doctoral levels. I like to teach with visuals, so this book contains suggestions, even a whole chapter, on films and documentaries that offer multiple insights about borderlands for international and comparative classes.* The borderlands have not only immersed me in the so-called in-between, hybridized spaces and places but also with border people for both everyday and momentous experiences and events. Like my colleague and near-favorite novelist Benjamin Alire Sáenz says: "The border has given me my voice."

The opportunity to cross borders, near and far, has extended my insights and comparative perspectives with grounded experiences, using all the senses. Those insights have often come from different world regions in the South, including Asia, Africa, and the Americas. As an undergraduate student, I minored in Latin American studies (thank you for your inspiring teaching, Howard Handelman!) and traveled through Mexico and Central America. As a graduate student, I specialized in African studies, conducting my dissertation research in western Kenya in 1974–1975. On my return journey, I was able to spend time in Tanzania, Malawi, Botswana, Ghana, and Spain. I was also a Peace Corps Volunteer in the Philippines for two years, an experience that internationalized me. In the 1980s, I did research in the eastern Caribbean. These lived experiences have offered new lenses in and across borders, while giving me broad vantage points with which to comprehend our changing global economy.

I always appreciate scholars who reflect on their backgrounds before moving on to their books. Permit me to indulge in this practice a bit more, for I have much and many to thank for my professional work and research agendas. Racialized political economies have always caused me to wonder and ponder *why*, even as a child, possibly because of the rigidly class- and race-segregated urban area of Milwaukee, Wisconsin, where I grew up.

As for most people in the United States, immigration was also part of my background with German-speaking parents and grandparents. While agricultural mechanization in Prussia drove migrants on my mother's side to the United States in the distant mid-19th century, the immigration experience was closer on my father's side. My grandmother's stories told of Germans in earlier centuries sent to clear swamps south of Budapest in central Europe. I always wondered: Did "sent" mean they were forced to resettle? Heralding from the declining Austro-Hungarian Empire before and after World War I, my grandfather came first (scholars call this stepwise migration) before war broke out, then my grandmother and her two boys after the war ended. Both grandparents made separate, harrowing journeys on ships, out of Hamburg and Amsterdam, respectively, with my grandmother and her sons quarantined in a warehouse for two weeks before departure. After passing through Ellis Island, they met brokers who negotiated in German and English languages, then put them on a train for the Midwest. We all lost touch with relatives in Hungary except to hear that after World War II those who remained were sent to East Berlin to work in factories. With Hungary's ethnic cleansing to rid the place of Germans, they had a day to pack one suitcase with belongings before embarking on a train northward. That is more time than 21st-century mass deportations from the United States that allow people little but the clothes on their backs.

My research interests have always gravitated toward marginalized people and places. As a woman, I too was marginalized in graduate school at the University of Wisconsin, finishing my PhD in 1976 when only 13 percent of PhDs in the discipline went to women. My dissertation research focused on the delivery of agricultural services to farmers—women and men—at a time period of high male out-migration from rural Kenya when most farming was not only typical "women's work" but also required female management of small farm holdings despite women's lack of control over land title deeds and other resources. In graduate school, I was fortunate that committee members supported this focus on "gendered" research (though gender was not part of 1970s social science discourse). I also had the opportunity to take courses with political anthropologist James C. Scott who made enormous theoretical contributions to many disciplines including anthropology for what he called "weapons of the weak" and "everyday resistance." I now think of another professor, Africanist M. Crawford Young, as a border scholar because African politics seminars puzzled over the artificiality of colonial borders and assigned readings addressed to "nation-building" in new postcolonial states.

I have lived in the borderlands since 1977 and complemented my specialization in comparative politics and international development with interdisciplinary border studies. In so doing, I initially focused on the US-Mexico border region and have many colleagues, some of them former students, to thank for their friendship and co-authorship: Irasema Coronado, Guadalupe Correa-Cabrera, Pamela Cruz, Sandra Deutsch, Timothy Dunn, Azuri González, Manuel Gutiérrez, Nuria Homedes, Cheryl Howard, Jane Jaquette, Vanessa Johnson, Jesse Kapenga, Z. Anthony Kruszewski, Oscar Martínez, Zulma Méndez, Tony Payan, Gregory Rocha, David Spener, Beatriz Vera, Gay Young, and Jakub Zajakala. Jakub and I developed the approximate 300-state Border Inequalities Database, their numeric economic indicators, and various tables referred to in this book. I have long been part of the Association for Borderlands Studies (ABS), served on its Board of Directors for two years, and appreciate its welcoming and scholarly home to people from many places. I owe thanks to several people for pictures they gave me permission to reprint: Fred Cady, Asha Dane'el, Manuel Gutiérrez, Luis Pablo Hernández, and personnel at the *Texas Observer*. Thanks also to the reviewers and especially to the wonderful editor and staff members at Rowman & Littlefield.

My research agendas have also provided opportunities to interact with other border people and scholars in other parts of the world: the BRIT (Border Regions in Transition) conference in Fukuoka that involved crossing the maritime border of the Sea of Japan into Busan, South Korea (my third trip to Japan); the ABS/World meeting in the Russia-Finland borderlands; and an ABS co-sponsored conference that began in northeastern India, specifically Guwahati, then involved travel to the Bangladesh border, and concluded in New Delhi. There, I much appreciate colleague Mirza Zulfiqur Rahman, his organizing skills at the conference, and his expertise on transboundary water systems. Many thanks also go to colleague Tony Kruszewski, for his introductions led to the opportunity for me to develop a higher education partnership with the German-Polish border university, European University Viadrina. There I met historian Beata Halicka with whom I co-taught a political geography course for part of a semester when she became a visiting professor at UTEP. They both shared many, many insights and conversations about European borders with me.

I mention these places and borderlands because my grounded experiences informed my rationale for selecting the in-depth cases in part II of this book. To my university, I appreciate being named Endowed Professor of Western Hemispheric Trade Policy Studies for it funded some of my travel to conferences related to this book and my research assistant. My trade policy research ranges all the way from informal economies in the borderlands to the voluminous and profitable but violent transnational drug trade to supply US consumer demands, and finally the tensions between the border business community's desire for efficient cross-border trade and the heavy state security apparatus. I work with many community organizations in and across the border. In fact, when I prepared the TEDxElPaso talk entitled "My Border: Gateway to the World," organized by the El Paso Community Foundation, I became determined to write this book.

For too long, research in border studies has relied mainly on generalizations from cases in the US-Mexico borderlands. I have participated in extensive field research on those borderlands for, to me, it seems like the center of the world, where the global meets the local. From North America, border studies subsequently burgeoned in Europe, fueled with generous funding from the European Union and its Euroregion projects. This book offers a pioneering approach, attempting to include the postcolonial South in comparative border studies, using critical and gendered lenses in the process. The book advances border categories and theoretical perspectives to include the South and maritime borders with a focus on reducing inequalities and building institutions with border voices in the common grounds of borderlands.

The challenge we face in interdisciplinary border studies is to explore borderlands in many contexts, with and across a variety of states, some of them in the so-called developing, postcolonial states of the South with little more than a half-century since independence. Most of their territorial lines were drawn by distant colonizers and make little geographic or identity sense, but once constructed and fixed, people learn to live with, or get around and through, those borderlines.

My broad comparative project in this book is found in cross-regional comparisons of borderlands regions. With border eyes, and the multiple lenses of different world regions, I hope to challenge and stretch seemingly familiar concepts about territory, trade, security, and migration toward less familiar understandings. In so doing, an additional hope is to stimulate attention in international studies, political science, and sociology to border studies and thereby make their analyses more complete.

*Please send names of more suggested films and documentaries to me at kstaudt@utep.edu.

PART I

Conceptual Framework and Historical Backgrounds

Part I sets the stage for the book: first, an introductory framework that looks with a critical eye through the borderlands lens; second, historical and map imagery perspectives that help explain the "Othering" processes; and third, some conceptual, numeric, and theoretical foundations that build inequalities and institutions (I-2) into understanding borderlands.

The foundation—advancing the work of previous historians, political scientists, geographers, and gender and border studies specialists—brings a normative dimension to analysis in trying to forge answers to questions: Can we move toward a more equitable world, starting with the borderlands? What sorts of institutions, governmental and nongovernmental, can facilitate that process? In analysis thus far, we also see the importance of democracy and good governance, including the reduction of "rent-seeking" policies and border bureaucrats' practices in the borderlands.

Chapter 1

Introduction

The history of the world is best observed from the frontier.

Pierre Vilar (1989: xv)

People and goods move constantly in our bordered world, some legally and others illegally. In a world of over 300 land borders, approximately 200 sovereign states, and many more maritime borders, such mobilities are contentious and value-laden in these obscenely unequal, polarized, and fear-mongering times.

Many contemporary issues and conflicts in 21st-century global politics are connected with territorial borders and borderlands wherein power is asserted and resisted between states of asymmetrical dimensions in income, size, and population—the essence of broadly defined "border politics." Globalization compresses time and space in so many ways, from trade to social media, but borderlands, their people, and the places themselves are central to global trade and production. The global economy produces some winners and all-too-many losers, if we define loss as perpetuating or aggravating relative inequalities.

Borders range from obvious territorial lines on artifacts like maps, to defensive security lines that powerful states draw well beyond their own land and territorial waters, to hardly visible borders at internal checkpoints such as those at airports or in clerks' offices where work authorization documents are verified. This wide range of borders could be expanded to include the lines drawn around individuals and groups based on their identity and language, or on reactions to bodies, their color, hair, and gender, or on designations assigned by law enforcement officials in and away from borderlands. In this book, however, we focus on spaces around international territorial lines, using borderlands and critical lenses. Less commonly addressed in academic disciplines and even in traditional border studies, we highlight this perspective in three regional borderlands and in maritime borders, bringing postcolonial states of the South into the discussion for comparison. In so doing, we disrupt some of the usual perceptions about states and their borders, including those of Mexico and the United States in North America.

My vantage points in this book are several. First, I analyze borderlands spaces and their people, sometimes called *borderlanders* in English (*fronterizos* and *fronterizas* in Spanish). The width of such spaces ranges from 100 kilometers (62 miles) on each side of the US-Mexico border (based on the La Paz Agreement of 1983) to 100-mile distances from US Border Patrol checkpoints and the border to a variety of spaces elsewhere, including those within the confines of villages or in cross-border twin towns in European regions. Border people live in *hybrid* zones, often speaking multiple languages and frequently crossing cultural and national identity lines. All too commonly, as we shall see, border people's voices go unheard in capital cities located far from the border periphery although they often bear the brunt of decisions subject to the political whims and viewpoints accepted there.

This book is a critique grounded *in* the borderlands perspective, rather than in the state-centric or international relations (IR)-centric perspectives that have long dominated political science. Thirty years ago, analysts encouraged those in the discipline to bring the state back in;[1] here I ask analysts to bring the borderlands into focus. My critical vantage point incorporates alternative ways of examining borders and borderlands, with more emphasis on postcolonial states of the South, especially Asia and Africa, rather than drawing conclusions based on information about borders from North America and Europe.

Critical studies necessarily involve bringing the *body* back in to analysis, specifically including gendered social constructions that vary across eras and places. The experiences of and hierarchical power relations between women and men have heretofore been less visible in border studies. Gender interacts with nationality, ethnicity, income, and other factors in ways that illuminate comprehensive coverage of power in space. Moreover, gendered social constructions have been used to characterize institutions and policies as hegemonic and hypermasculine.[2]

Based on over 35 years of lived experience teaching and researching in the borderlands, I favor practices that move societies toward more open and cooperative borders as metaphoric *bridges* rather than closed and conflictual borders as *barriers*. Nearly two decades ago, David Spener and I wrote about the constant dynamic of respective *de-bordering* and *bordering* or *re-bordering* processes that have come and gone.[3] These terms form part of the way border studies scholars analyze change.

Borders and borderlands figure prominently in world politics, conflict, media, and popular culture, such as films, television programs, and novels. In international politics and public affairs, one frequently hears and reads the words "border" and "borders," whether in the context of territorial conflict, occupation, and invasion or in the mobility of goods and people. Hardly an issue of the weekly news magazine *The Economist* emerges—complete with maps—without coverage of border issues regarding migrants and refugees, territorial and maritime conflicts, national and regional trade negotiations, or inequalities between nations in the global economy.

Despite the high visibility of borders, analysts in the disciplines of political science and international relations seem wedded to national "containment" models: people, power, and politics, such disciplinarians write, are to be studied *within* nation-states rather than at or across borders and in borderlands. Even in IR and global studies, many scholars identify the primary units and actors as states, nations, or the people therein. Here, my focus is borderlands and regions. Transnational border politics and power inequalities affect mainstream polities and economies, as do the reverse relations—states and capital cities affect borderlands. John Agnew famously portrayed state-centrist analysis as the "territorial trap."[4] In this global era, people travel across borders, they do business across borders, and they engage in virtual communication across borders via electronic mail, social media, the Internet, and diaspora networks.

Part I and this chapter frame the book with its broad border lenses, critical perspectives, and inclusion of postcolonial border regions and states. For sovereign countries, I usually use the word *state* rather than the more emotive words *nation* or *nation-state* to avoid the often-problematic assumption that people fully identify with the place. While sovereign states aim to control territory, people, and territorial boundaries, and exercise a monopoly over the use of force, such aims are neither universally realized in practice nor respected by other states. Part I, chapter 2 focuses broadly on geographic and historical perspectives on borders and the "Othering" processes of people outside borders. Chapter 3 reviews border theories on which I build, particularly drawing on my theoretical framework based on the Border Inequalities Database assembled for this analysis, and on income *inequalities* and *institutions*, discussed later and sometimes referred to as "I-2," before comparing regions and thematic issues in parts II and III. I begin by discussing the book's purposes and approaches, including key questions that make the book cohere in this interdisciplinary field of border studies.

Purposes, Methods, and Approaches

This book broadly covers borders—territorial and maritime—in contemporary world politics from the geographic "South" of Asia, Africa, and Latin America–Caribbean to the "North" of Europe, North America, Japan, and (admittedly) southern locations of Australia and New Zealand. I use the word *broadly* because the book draws on multiple disciplines, first and foremost on the disciplines of history and geography, particularly its map constructions, to explain the roots of border conflict and cooperation today.

My own discipline, political science, provides key concepts and tools for analyzing comparative and international politics, but I also make use of ideas from the disciplinary subfield of public policy and public administration, such as the model of ground-level state agents—or what Michael Lipsky calls "street-level bureaucrats"[5] that I alter slightly with the label *border bureaucrats*—who interact with borderlanders and often operate at their own discretion with impunity. Another advantage to using public policy analysis involves the inclusion of ethical and principled rationales, such as equity and liberty, for critiquing existing policy and for proposing policy change. I pay attention to discourses in official documents and in everyday life, including not only "Othering" (see chapter 2 and elsewhere capitalized in the book) but also camaraderie and cross-border interaction and solidarity. As a closet political anthropologist, I appreciate and cite how sociologists, anthropologists, and women/gender/feminist scholars often challenge territorial confines by attending to experiences and to identity groups that *transcend* borderlines. Literary, philosophical, and popular cultural studies add conceptual insights and yet more nuance in the use of metaphorical approaches to border studies, though I prefer the grounded evidence of empirical observation and data more than philosophical assertions.

The methods and sources in this book are drawn from my own original empirical field research and observations in the US-Mexico and Paso del Norte central borderlands, on syntheses of secondary academic and credible journalistic sources, on figures from the database, and on narratives. I complement these materials with visuals, including films, and many links are included to bring the content to life and to augment readers' understanding. Moreover, I call upon my many years of grounded experience living in the borderlands and on border-crossings I have made in Asia, Africa, Europe, the Caribbean, Mexico, and Central America.

Disciplinarians tend to analyze borders, borderlands, and border peoples from a state-centric perspective, yet most countries share international borders with multiple states—for example, China, Russia, Brazil, the Democratic Republic of the Congo, and India each share borders with seven or more states. The complications of multiple borderlands should be obvious, yet we need some comparative conceptual handles to move beyond singular case studies of each and every borderland of the more than 300 in existence and their changes over time, as I studied in the large Border Inequalities Database built in part for this book. (See chapter 3 for a description of some of the ways in which these data are unpacked.) The broad conceptual threads that link comparative border regions focus on inequalities, inclusive institutions (or the lack thereof), and the voices within them, as well as on the states and the length of time since their sovereignty, which is relevant for the majority of postcolonial states, independent for just over a half-century.

What makes this book new, different, and unique? While it will appeal to those who read comparative politics, political economy, and world politics, it also cuts into the territorial boxes of contemporary analysis by focusing on borderlands, borderlanders' experiences, state policies toward borders, and the mobility of women, men, and trade. The book also elevates the interdisciplinary field of border studies beyond a case study or a single region into a cross-regional analysis—somewhat unusual in our "area-studies" academic world. The Border Inequalities Database provides the broadest of global perspectives.

While I address many borderlands in all of the chapters, with attention to African and Western Asian borders in chapter 2, part II's focus covers the regions of North America (chapter 4), South Asia (chapter 5), Europe (chapter 6) and the maritime borders of East Asia and the South China Sea (chapter 7). The book also weaves substantive issues and public policies into part III, with chapters on security (chapter 8), migration (chapter 9), and trade (chapter 10). These essential themes are threaded throughout other chapters and parts of the book. With my anthropological bent and my appreciation of learning through experience, I include boxes of ethnography, observation, and case examples, using what anthropologists call "thick description." All in all, the book should be an interesting read.

States Still Matter

States confer rights and responsibilities on their citizens. Many millions of people experience statelessness with minimal or no rights, for international and national human rights depend on states' adherence to conventions or individuals' access to legal resources. While nationalism can draw incredible pride and sacrifice from inhabitants, nationalist loyalties can also rear their ugly heads, specifically for those initially forced into or held captive by the territorial cage. National identity becomes normalized over time, though occasionally it is resented and resisted due to long-term collective memories about the damages states impose upon people.

For an example in the newly independent Nigeria of 1960, people in the southeast attempted to secede and build a new nation called Biafra, recognized by few states as sovereign, which was eliminated after several years of bombing and starvation imposed by the Nigerian central government. Chimamanda Adichie's novel, *Half of a Yellow Sun*, offers beautiful but painful prose with the voices of many Biafrans in different life circumstances. Nigeria tried to deal with fragmentation through *internal* re-bordering by multiplying subnational states at its independence from 3 to 4, then 12, then 20, and now 36 in a complex institutional formula for elections that is currently beset by security threats from Boko Haram which kills or captures villagers and kidnaps and sexually assaults hundreds of schoolgirls, some of whom once freed have given birth to Boko Haram infants and face discrimination for raising "terrorist" babies. Mass rape is a gendered war crime, but it still continues.

Nationalism, learned at an early age and reinforced in school with rituals like flag salutes, national anthems, and routine pledges of allegiance, aims to instill a sustained, emotional, and loyal connection to the state. After time, nationalism often succeeds and normalizes the abnormality of artificially constructed borderlines drawn out of sync with people's former everyday lives. After centuries, the national loyalty may be strong, hardly affected by superstructure regional institutions like France in the European Union. When terrorists attacked Paris in late 2015, people evacuating one of the targeted public sites sang the national hymn, "La Marseillaise."[6] Although France is part of the European Union, the EU anthem, Beethoven's "Ode to Joy," was irrelevant.

Among the alienated and exploited, nationalist messages may backfire. In borderlands, the interplay of defensiveness by the colonized and state suppression of their language(s), repression, and control over their mobility through border crossing may be the first places where resistance to central governments occurs. In many states in Asia and Africa, where independence is only a half-century or so old, the colonial-driven border lines around their self-declared "spheres of influence" still wreak havoc on contemporary politics. For example, in the post–World War I era when the victors divided the spoils, the British and French "drew lines in the sand" with the Sykes-Picot Agreement and others in deliberating over strategic geopolitical considerations surrounding Syria and Iraq after the fall of the Ottoman Empire. The victors' lines left Kurdish people divided among Turkey, Iraq, Syria, and Iran in massive borderlands.

Walls have been built to keep people out or in, from the Great Wall of China to the Roman-built Hadrian's Wall, now a quaint tourist site. Despite such walls, ordinary people and warriors crossed walls, and for example, spread deep into China as the 10-part documentary series titled *The Pacific Century* makes clear from maps of a swollen and shrinking China over centuries. Since the fall of the Berlin Wall in 1989, some 40 states attempt to solidify their border territorial lines with walls and fences (see more about security in chapter 8).

Key Questions in This Book

We must begin to understand the world and its approximate 200 states using a border lens to discover what knowledge about borderlands and border people can offer to mainstream politics and policy development in this era of global flows of people and trade. The follow key questions are addressed in this book:

1. Is there a common core to border studies worldwide, a core that moves beyond approaches developed in the northern or western countries? After all, an understanding of particular border regions requires knowledge about place and context. Many edited volumes in border studies deal with case studies, albeit useful in examining single world regions, but more often applicable in the North (including Mexico as part of North America).[7] How do international borders compare across regions? Can we move from single cases to regional contexts in analyzing border studies? And what theoretical framework might tie northern and southern border areas in a unifying framework? In chapter 3, I propose a common-core theoretical framework with inequalities and institutions at its center.

2. How do border people work, trade, and socialize across territorial lines that divide once-shared linguistic and cultural groups or that resettle people in new lands? Despite the seemingly fixed lines of international boundaries on world maps, postwar and postcolonial territorial grids drawn in the last half of the 20th century may be understood as home to near- or newly stateless peoples, such as around northeastern India until recently, or as hybrid places of multiple cultures and languages, with mixing, border-crossing, dynamism, opportunity, and change. In the last centuries, international boundary lines have changed hundreds of times due to war, negotiation, and purchase. To what extent have states and transnational institutions facilitated or inhibited these cross-border connections, whether institutionally based in governments, in business ties so common in the global economy, or in civil society–based nongovernmental organizations (NGOs)?

3. How do border people cope with the state apparatus—which may range from their efforts to live with its aimed-for total control, such as fences, walls, and/or virtual technology, to their attempts to make use of its facilitation or even funding and endorsement of interaction, such as in European Union (EU) regions?

4. How do states deal with their frontiers, borderlands, and border people? To what extent do border people benefit from such state policies? To what

extent are border people's voices included in authoritative political decisions? For example, the US Homeland Security Council in 2016 appointed no border people as advisers but rather chose mostly border security officials and consultants in the Washington, DC, area.

5. Beyond case studies, what can a synthesis of border studies tell us at the regional or global level in an era that limits government and utilizes the comparative advantages of stronger states in less powerful countries to extract resources and the value of low-cost labor? Might regional policies or transnational nongovernmental organizations (NGOs) provide models toward more prosperous and cooperative borderlands? Might popular culture in the form of realistic, not only sensationalist, films and documentaries (see chapter 11 and selected commentary in other chapters) lead to greater understandings and actions on cross-border interaction in borderlands?

6. What, if anything, can be applied to action and practice to reduce hostility and increase shared prosperity at and across global borders? While I resist "seeing like a state," to draw on the warnings of James C. Scott's book title of 1998, I understand how states and policies shape border people's lives, opportunities, and burdens and therefore merit inclusion in the discussion.

Grounded border studies, covered in the body of this book with examples in each chapter, provide insights that complement our knowledge of national and global politics and policies. In many regions, people cross borders daily or frequently to work, to visit family and friends, and to shop. For example, the central Canada-US borderlands of Windsor, Ontario, and Detroit, Michigan, have a long history of people crossing for work, tourism, and commerce, both licit and illicit.[8] In addition to ferry boats, the bridge and tunnel built over and under the Detroit River in 1929 and 1930 facilitate interaction with more or less efficiency. During the US prohibition of alcohol production, distribution, and sale in the 1920s and early 1930s, residents on both sides of the border hardly respected or obeyed such laws but rather participated in a thriving beer and liquor trade. Today, in the eastern townships of Quebec Province, people cross borders into Kahnawake (Mohawk) territory to purchase goods like cigarettes at lower prices (a common practice in many borderlands, including on the Polish side of borderlands with Germany).

In still other borderlands, people have lived in both cooperation and conflict amid statelessness as James C. Scott so eloquently outlines in *The Art of Not Being Governed*.[9] While empires came and went, extracting tribute and resources from ethnic communities living in mountainous regions to varying degrees, these peoples often retained their own cultural and linguistic identities. However, in the colonial era and by the mid-20th century, statist projects began to envelop territory, border people, and resources under national control through the construction of roads, railroads, and communication technology. Such is the case in so-called Zomia in a region surrounding northeast India, Bhutan, Myanmar, China, and Bangladesh (see chapter 5).

Border Studies: A Half-Century-Old Interdisciplinary Field

As noted earlier, the field of border studies draws not only on political science and geography but also on sociology, history, and anthropology with occasional overlays or threaded connections with critical, cultural, and gender/women/feminist studies. Border studies began in the 1970s, growing by leaps and bounds to include various world regions, and is now part of the curriculum in many academic programs. The Association for Borderlands Studies (ABS), born in 1976, publishes the *Journal of Borderlands Studies*, one of many journals in the field such as *Political Geography*, *Geopolitics*, *Environment & Planning* (especially volumes *A* and *D*), *Gender, Culture, and Society*, *Eurasia Border Review*, *Progress in Human Geography*, and *Space and Polity* among others. It is time for other disciplines such as comparative politics, international relations, and area studies to add borderlands to their repertoire of scholarship.

As is the case in many fields, border studies have taken a postcolonial, postmodern turn which questions old paradigms and visuals like maps. The traditional state-centric, capital city–based models of comparative politics and international relations rarely do justice to the nuanced understandings that come to light when regions are examined with the border lens and a presence in the borderlands. I am less interested in attempting to fit philosophers' assertions into the study of borderlands than I am in analyzing the voices of scholars, everyday people, and field researchers who examine and experience them firsthand. I appreciate plain language so I consciously write in accessible ways rather than in academic abstractions, hoping to speak to a wide range of audiences. Because I treasure the visual and narrative images that popular culture can convey, I offer links and recommend films and fiction to extend insights for readers and viewers. Of course, I am keenly aware of the representational challenges inherent in when and where such images and storylines are developed and by whom.

In the United States, all too often border studies focus on the US-Mexico border and to a lesser extent on the US-Canada border. Each of these long borders, approximately 2,000 and 5,000 miles, respectively (to include the Canadian border with Alaska), is home to multiple key crossing points in the central regions (Great Lakes of the north, El Paso–Ciudad Juárez of the south); the Pacific US northwest and Canadian southwest, known as Cascadia; and the Pacific US southwest and Mexican northwest of the Californias, including Baja California. Each place has its own unique contexts. North American places may be quite familiar to readers, given the peaceful relations and extensive trade between and among Mexico, the United States, and Canada, enshrined in the still-controversial North American Free Trade Agreement (NAFTA), now more than 20 years old, and because of the various US "wars" against drugs, terrorism, and immigrants, as Tony Payan has analyzed so well.[10] However, my investigation of the region may make the familiar seem less familiar.

It is also extremely important that we become aware of borders in other world regions, comparing their similarities and differences. Rather than take a Western, Euro-centric, or northern country approach, my aim is to draw more fully on voices and studies from the South, without excluding the North, in part II's regional chapters and in four particular borderlands—land and sea—throughout the world.

Border studies scholars periodically come together in global meetings, among them the ABS and the BRIT (Border Regions in Transition), with presentations on both sides of borderlands. With its Secretariat now located in northern Europe, the Association for Borderlands Studies turned global, holding its first ABS-World Conference in the Russia-Finland borderlands (2014). Additionally, regional ABS meetings were conducted outside of Europe in the northeastern India borderlands with Bangladesh (2015) and in New Zealand (2016). Many European border conferences are convened in opulent settings; generous European Union–funded research encourages cross-border interchange in some areas. African border studies networks and associations also come together in the ABORNE (African Borderlands Research Network) and the African Union's border program. Japan has its own border studies network and programs at several universities.

How Many Borders?

With around 300 land borders, countless sea borders, and borders with unique multiple contexts, it would be impossible to write a sweeping narrative that does justice to every one of them. Moreover, borderlines and states undergo constant change. Viewing territorially based world maps of 1880, of 1920, of the years immediately before and after World War II, of the late 1990s during the breakup in the Balkans region, or of newly created states such as South Sudan in 2011, one can appreciate the continuous changes that reconstruct borderlines.

The less visible borderlines between cultural, linguistic, and ethnic groups also undergo redesign and reshaping by bordering processes. Administrative jurisdictions, like districts and provinces, may reshape identities. My dissertation research in 1975–1976 in western Kenya indicated that 17 linguistically related but distinct groups of people living in the territorial grid known as Kakamega District of Western Province gradually began to identify as Luhya people during the lengthy colonial era, eventually becoming the third largest group in independent Kenya by 1963 and beyond. Inside Kenya, district borders matter for traders; women farmers who take their surplus produce for sale across the district border to Nyanza are stopped by police officers who extract taxes or "rent," the euphemism for extortion.

States deal with identity groups in multiple ways, especially when it comes to political appointments to high-level positions, patronage, benefits, and inclusiveness. Political clientelism has become a tried and tested way to temporarily appease people and to govern without threatening the status quo. Border people often experience a "democratic deficit," as they have less experience with democracy than mainstream residents in the state.[11] While the United States has appointed "border czars," it lacks cross-border or transnational appointees except on river water matters,[12] although it can claim a robust group of NGOs, the most successful of which focus on business and trade.

UN Members and Indigenous Affiliations

The number of states affiliated with the United Nations has grown from 51 members at its founding on October 24, 1945, to 193 at present.[13] The UN website is available in six languages that transcend state borders, but this is only a fraction of the world's languages. At the close of World War II, victors redrew European borders (again, after World War I's re-bordering), and soon many formerly colonized countries achieved independence and sovereignty as states with their own territorial boundaries. Besides growth in the number of states, the number of international borderlands has increased exponentially, totaling thousands if one counts both the land and maritime borders of sovereign states.

Some identity groups gain recognition and voice with international bodies. On September 13, 2007, a majority (or 144 countries) in the United Nations General Assembly voted to support the Declaration on the Rights of Indigenous Peoples, as the UN Permanent Forum on Indigenous Issues posts on its website.[14] Long overdue, this action occurred after centuries of injustice and near-statelessness that indigenous peoples have experienced in some states (see chapter 2).

Disappearing Borders? Hardly Likely

Will state territorial borders disappear? In his futuristic fiction novel, *1984*, published in 1949, George Orwell projected shifting alliances among three regional groupings. In the real world, regional and defense pacts undergo periodic negotiation, not quite as quickly as in Orwellian fiction. But state borderlines are unlikely to disappear in our lifetimes.

Globalization, which connects people and goods worldwide via communication and trade, brings both positive and negative experiences. Strong free trade ideologies and regimes emerged in the 1980s, and the reduction of state tariffs as well as export and import duties gave rise to de-bordering. Business strategist Kenichi Ohmae, whose early book *Beyond National Borders* was published in 1987, followed with more startling titles with similar messages like *The End of the Nation State: The Rise of Regional Economies* in 1995. Soon thereafter, tragedies like the attack on the United States of September 11, 2001, led to heavy emphases on securitization and re-bordering processes. More states built border walls and fences, with rising fears over security.

In a world with a dominant neoliberal ideology—one that values marketplace, capitalist economies, and limited government and regulation—Ohmae continues to pitch his conceptions of "borderless" global production and consumption, opining that "nation-states retard economic development." He calls for regions to be open to the outside world, its capital, and people in order to find good places to do business, to live, and to work with "homeless corporations."[15] State-based regulations for health, safety, and minimum wages would perhaps, in his vision, also become homeless or figure into corporate cost-savings strategies. Corporate tax inversion practices ("tax dodges," in common parlance) of formerly US-based businesses that have gravitated toward lower-tax states seem to illustrate this trend; some nations seek to ensure the protection of citizens and territory from absentee corporations and to hold them accountable for their social responsibilities to the states in which they are headquartered and allowed to produce and/or sell.

Regionalism confers new, supranational identities that encompass people in wider spatial areas with multilingual communication networks. Whether analyzing the European Union and its Euroregions in borderlands or larger trade and security pacts, it is important to recognize that regional identities also matter, from the North Atlantic Treaty Organization (NATO), the Association of Southeast Asian Nations (ASEAN), and MERCOSUR (Mercado Común del Sur) in South America to efforts to build a Trans-Pacific Partnership.

Outline of Chapters

With four parts to this book, the reading pathway moves as follows. In part I, we cover history, maps, and "Othering" processes in chapter 2. I advance border theories in chapter 3, with a focus on inequalities and institutions.

Part II covers regional land and maritime borders. Chapter 4 examines North America with a special focus on the US-Mexico border and the central Paso del Norte borderlands. With states created in the 19th century and normalized nationalities, a hybridized borderlands has emerged in everyday life with cross-border cooperation in one of the most disparate and unequal borderlands in the world. The primary institutional focuses are security and, to a lesser extent, trade across fixed and fenced boundaries that comprise extreme wage differences.

I analyze the postcolonial South Asia borderlands in chapter 5. Once a borderless region, then scarred by colonialism and Partition in the birth of multiple nations, the Indian state and its Border Security Force seek to establish rigid controls to separate peoples of northeastern India, Bangladesh, and other states, but they lack resources and good governance and thus are unable to accomplish this in fully controlled ways.

Chapter 6 examines the integrated borderlands of the European Union, a large common market using a mostly common currency, where people and commerce enjoyed relative freedom of movement until the refugee crisis beginning in 2015. Scarred by World War II and the forced resettlement thereafter, the chapter questions whether EU investment in the German-Polish borderlands addressed the formerly glaring inequalities between West and Central/Eastern Europe.

I cover maritime borders in chapter 7, specifically focusing on contemporary conflicts in the South China Sea, on the UN Convention on the Law of the Sea, and on sea migrants seeking entry into Australian territorial waters. I also discuss the Philippines with its state-sponsored labor export program.

Part III contains chapters on major policy issues threaded throughout the regional chapters of part II and reintroduced in the big-picture terms of plural securities (to include and prioritize environmental security), migration, and trade. Each chapter offers conceptual insights that invite us to rethink how to view the issues.

Finally in part IV, we turn to potential ways to bridge borderlands in the wider world. Chapter 11 highlights popular culture in the form of films and documentaries in various world regions. In chapter 12, we examine policy and strategic actions at multiple levels to include governments, nongovernmental organizations (NGOs), and individual ethical choices. In the summary chapter of the book, the questions posed in this first chapter are addressed along with ideas for further research in borderlands studies.

Recommended Resources

Films and Novelists

The Pacific Century
George Orwell, British novelist
Chimamanda Adichie, Nigerian novelist

Notes

[1] Peter Evans, Dietrich Rueschemeyer, and Theda Skocpol, eds., *Bringing the State Back In* (Cambridge: Cambridge University Press, 1985). Historian Michael Baud and anthropologist Willem Van Schendel can be credited with a focus on borderlands worldwide. See their "Toward a Comparative History of Borderlands," *Journal of World History* 8, 2, 1997, pp. 211–42.

[2] Gay Young calls gender a hierarchical social construct that privileges the masculine and de-values the feminine, p. 5 in *Gendering Globalization on the Ground: The Limits of Feminized Work for Mexican Women's Empowerment* (NY: Routledge, 2015). Among many gender studies, see Joni Lovenduski, "Gendering Research in Political Science," *Annual Review of Political Science*, 1998, pp. 333–56; Karen Beckwith, "Introduction: Comparative Politics and the Logics of a Comparative Politics of Gender," *Perspectives on Politics* 8, 1, March 2010, pp. 159–68; and Judith Butler on the performativity of gender, including masculinity and femininity, in many books, including *Undoing Gender* (NY: Routledge, 2004). See Anna Agathange-lou and L. H. M. Ling, "Power, Borders, Security, Wealth: Lessons of Violence and Desire from September 11," *International Studies Quarterly* 48, 3, September 2004, pp. 517–38.

[3] Kathleen Staudt and David Spener, "The View from the Frontier: Theoretical Perspectives Undisciplined," in David Spener and Kathleen Staudt, eds., *The U.S.-Mexico Border: Transcending Divisions, Contesting Identities* (Boulder: Lynne Rienner Publishers, 1998), pp. 3–34.

[4] John Agnew, "Still Trapped in Territory?" *Review of International Political Economy* 1, 1, 1994, pp. 53–80; and "The Territorial Trap Fifteen Years On," *Geopolitics* 15, 4, 2010, pp. 779–84.

[5] Michael Lipsky, *Street-Level Bureaucracy* (NY: Russell Sage Foundation, 1980).

[6] These spontaneous songs can be found through searches on YouTube, which occasionally changes its numeric identifiers, but I accessed the following on December 1, 2015: (https://www.youtube.com/watch?v=4iQ2cHuZ0xE; https://www.youtube.com/watch?v=4K1q9Ntcr5g for a formal version).

[7] The question about common core was inspired by Anssi Paasi, "A 'Border Theory': An Unattainable Dream or a Realistic Aim for Border Scholars?" in D. Wastl-Walter, ed., *The Ashgate Companion to Border Studies* (Farnham, UK: Ashgate, 2011), pp. 11–32. Among various edited volumes, see Paul Ganster and David Lorey, eds., *Borders and Border Politics in a Globalizing World* (Lanham, MD: SR Books 2005); Emmanuel Brunet-Jailly, ed., *Borderlands: Comparing Border Security in North America and Europe* (Ottawa: University of Ottawa Press, 2007); Hastings Donnan and Thomas M. Wilson, *Borders: Frontiers of Identity, Nation and State*

(Oxford: Berg Publishers, 1999), with a rare focus on the actual *borderlands*; Nancy Naples and Jennifer Bickham Mendez, eds., *Border Politics: Social Movements, Collective Identities, and Globalization* (NY: New York University Press, 2014); and I. William Zartman, ed., *Understanding Life in the Borderlands: Boundaries in Depth and in Motion* (Athens: University of Georgia Press, 2010). Only one introductory book exists on borders: Alexander Diener and Joshua Hagen, *Borders: A Very Short Introduction* (NY: Oxford University Press, 2012). Indeed it *is* very short, with 4" x 6" dimensions and 124 pages of text on them.

[8] Holly Karibo, *Sin City North: Sex, Drugs, and Citizenship in the Detroit-Windsor Borderland* (Chapel Hill: University of North Carolina Press, 2015).

[9] James C. Scott, *The Art of Not being Governed: An Anarchist History of Upland Southeast Asia* (New Haven, CT: Yale University Press, 2009).

[10] Tony Payan, *The Three U.S-Mexico Border Wars: Drugs, Immigration and Homeland Security* (Westport, CT: Praeger Security International, 2006), 2nd edition 2016.

[11] Tony Payan, "Crossborder Governance in a Tristate, Binational Region," in Kathleen Staudt, César M. Fuentes, and Julia E. Monárrez Fragoso, eds., *Cities and Citizenship at the U.S.-Mexico Border* (NY: Palgrave USA, 2010), pp. 217–44.

[12] With one exception, the International Boundary and Water Commission; Mexico has a counterpart, the Comisión Internacional de Limites y Agua.

[13] United Nations history: http://www.un.org/en/sections/history/history-united-nations/index.html.

[14] United Nations Department of Economic and Social Affairs (accessed 11/1/15) http://undesad spd.org/indigenouspeoples/declarationontherightsofindigenouspeoples.aspx.

[15] Kenichi Ohmae, *Beyond National Borders* (NY: Richard D. Irwin, 1987) and *The End of the Nation State* (NY: Free Press, 1995), quotes on pages 87, 94–5, and 246, respectively.

Chapter 2

Geography, Maps, and the "Other" in History

To imagine communities, says Benedict Anderson in his magnificent work on once-imagined nations and their nation-building projects, founding elites use three strategies.[1] The first is demarcating border lines around territory. The second involves counting and categorizing people through censuses. The third is constructing traditional museums which display imaginaries of an often-idealized place, history, and culture. Anderson's insights can be applied worldwide. Imagining nations means imagining the territorial borders around states. It also requires that we consider social forces that affect imaginaries, including processes of political socialization, school curricula, and civic rituals that children and adults practice daily in many states, like singing national anthems, using "national currencies" (with some exceptions), and pledging allegiance to flags. Puzzlingly, Anderson did not examine loyalty-building education, rituals, and symbolic strategies in his analysis.

This chapter pieces together the artificial social construction of states, territories, and their borders, bound together by the tales of adventurers and travelogue writers who, during the colonial era, often created "Othering" images, particularly of places in the global South. There is more at work here than the imaginations of aspiring national elites. In this chapter, I provide coverage for regions in the world such as Western Asia (Middle East) and the African continent that are not addressed in part II (North America, South Asia, and Europe, in chapters 4–6).

European powers met in Westphalia in 1648 to settle the Thirty Years' War and to establish the state structures as we now know them, with the expectation that each state would recognize the sovereignty of the others over bounded territory and peoples. A variety of political systems existed worldwide at the time, and the world economic system was beginning to connect continents and peoples in uneven ways, including via the human slave trade and forced resettlement. We begin this chapter with brief acknowledgment of shifting and changing indigenous systems from small-scale, relatively nonhierarchical societies to kingdoms and empires. We then move to geography and map constructions, giving attention to early northern adventurers and travelers to places in the South and the way they and their successors in the 20th century produced "Others" through narratives and pictures. After that, the chapter turns to imperial empires and colonialism, the means by which mostly European nations sought to control over half of the earth's land and spawned settler societies, such as those in Australia, New Zealand, Canada, Algeria, Kenya, South Africa, Rhodesia (now Zimbabwe and Zambia), and (some would argue) the United States.

On Maps and Containment: Our Visual Pictures

Over centuries, mapmakers have designed various projections of spaces and places that shape our images and perceptions of other parts of the world: their size, their significance, and even their orientation or "right-side-up-ness." In the United States, we typically see maps situating northern countries in the top half and southern countries at the bottom. The United States is also usually positioned at the center rather than off to one side or the other. In Asia, not surprisingly, mapmakers position Asia in the middle, just as European-centric maps focus on Europe. No wonder many children grow up thinking that their country is the center of the world.

Seemingly technical and neutral technical graphics, all maps contain a "political" edge, "selective representations of reality" aiming to assert and settle territorial claims.[2]

During the continuing Cold War of the 1980s between the United States and the Union of Soviet Socialist Republics (USSR), I taught with transparencies of "politically threatening" maps: In one image, Soviet missiles pointed toward the United States; in another US naval operations and military bases surrounded the Soviet Union. Mapmakers may be handmaidens of the state (see the Nazi geography book cited in chapter 6). The political map of the world in the front cover of this book comes from the US Central Intelligence Agency (CIA) and is updated annually, available on the Library of Congress website.

With the global Internet, we now have many options for viewing maps including pictures from outer space, thanks to the US National Aeronautics and Space Administration (NASA) (see map links listed at the end of this chapter). NASA presents images of the earth with no land border demarcations (with a few exceptions: India's border wall, for instance, is eerily lit in orange at night). Rather, NASA's photos from space show shapes in the form of land masses, wild fires, bodies of water, weather patterns, and lights. Examples include astronauts' pictures of the "Nile at Night" and "London at Night," which offer breathtaking images.

With images from above the earth, airlines also project flight patterns across borders. Most airline flight route maps delineate territorial boundaries; however, traveling on Japan Airlines in 2013, I was astounded to see maps without territorial borders in the in-flight magazine.

In great contrast, the contemporary images we usually see of the world map are divided by borderlines. Freely available, through Creative Commons, one finds the Robinson projection developed in 1963. Check also (at the end of the chapter) the images of a blank map with only borders. In my teaching, I occasionally require students to identify 40, sometimes 60, countries on a blank world map (to audible groans). Elementary and secondary Texas education "standards" (see later section) do not require knowledge at those levels.

People learn about others in other countries from childhood onward in social studies and world history classes, and in literature, television, and films, for better or worse. Note that my intent in referencing popular culture in this chapter and others is to suggest *quality* films rather than stereotyped imagery perpetuated in numerous Hollywood Westerns, one of a number of film genres played and replayed on cable television.

Geography Education

As playthings, maps are available as puzzles for children. Geography is taught from elementary school onward. Children practice coloring "in the lines" using maps and their borderlines. As early as grade 4, Mexico's government-produced public school textbooks show images of the loss of almost half its land to the United States in *La Invasión Norteamericana*, conceptualizing the "colossus of the north," as some refer to the United States, and the Treaty of Guadalupe Hidalgo in 1848 after the Mexican-American War. One can see *National Geographic* magazines at home, in school libraries, and in various waiting rooms.

Texas, a former independent republic for almost a decade, is home to over 25 million people. The Texas commercial textbook market is so large that publishers develop their products for other states in the United States based on Texas "standards." In parts of the United States, geography is not stressed in the curriculum or even tested in the standardized assessment systems which place more focus on language and math skills. (School administrators assign lower priority to non-tested content areas.) In higher education, my students often must study hard to learn the names of less than half the world's countries correctly for political geography or world politics courses as noted, though my international students from Mexico and Europe seem to have an easier time with this.

The State of Texas uses "standards" called the TEKS (Texas Essential Knowledge and Skills) organized by grade and content area in the public accountability website of the Texas Education Agency.[3] The Texas State Board of Education, representing the second-largest state population in the United States after California) in partisan elections, makes textbook choices and sets standards. Wondering why students struggle with map quizzes, and thanks to the Ctrl+F function in Microsoft Word, I was able to identify when and how students learn the world map in the geography standards under the social studies TEKS—only in grade 6 does a standard exist to identify 26 countries. With a required course in Texas history, Texas standards-makers seem to put their state at the center of a small world—one which also has required students to pledge allegiance to the state flag since 2001.

Map Distortions

Maps are distorted in various ways: making round shapes flat, altering images in ways that reflect wealth, energy use, land and population sizes, and communicating politically-tinged assertions, claims, and names. Many coffee table–sized atlases and posters—some outdated as soon as they are published by changes to borders and the establishment of new nations—can be purchased online and from bookstores.

The US Library of Congress (LOC) has an extensive collection of a half-million maps from both contemporary and historical time periods, of which more than 51,000 can be found online. The LOC website includes world, regional, minuscule regions, and single-country maps as well as 298 border maps. The Library of Congress posts year-by-year world physical and political maps. Pursuing the theme that maps are political constructs, one can note changes in the names and shapes of countries over time. For example, the country now generally known as Myanmar is identified on some maps by its earlier (colonial) name "Burma." On another map, a differently colored but unnamed space (Palestine) is shown in its pre-1967 shape, the West Bank and Gaza, before Israeli settlers occupied parts of the West Bank near the Jordan River and split up the land into speckled shapes and enclaves divided by military checkpoints. The Islamic State (IS, also called ISIS, ISIL, and Daesh) claims territory in Iraq and Syria, but current conventional maps of the region do not acknowledge this claim.

Each map projection contains distortions because a round global shape is flattened to two dimensions. To what extent does that flattening process alter or misrepresent actual land sizes? The Mercator map projection, designed for sea navigation in 1569, flattened the world in ways that made land masses in the temperate zones and near the Arctic seem much bigger than they are in reality. (Fewer land masses near the Antarctic reduce that problem in the South.)

German historian Arno Peters corrected past distortions with the Peters' projection in 1967 (published in English in 1983); Peters built on the formulation of Scottish cartographer James Gall in 1865.[4] (See the map in glorious color in the link listed at the end of the chapter.) Greenland, on the Mercator projection, is seemingly bigger than China, but Greenland's land mass is only 0.8 million square miles and China's land mass is 3.7 million square miles. Europe looks gigantic on a Mercator projection, seemingly larger than South America, but South America's land mass of 6.9 million square miles is far larger than Europe's 3.8 million square miles. The continent of Africa is 11.6 million square miles, but the old Mercator projection makes it look smaller than the former USSR (once 8.7 million square miles). And overall, the Northern Hemisphere (north of the equator) at 18.9 million square miles looks larger on the Mercator projection than the Southern Hemisphere (south of the equator) at 38.6 million square miles. The Peters' projection corrects the centuries-old distortions of the Mercator map which, amazingly, still shows up on some televised news programs.

Alternative projections exist, and I list links at the end of the chapter. Some projections tried to build cylinder-shaped, structured images in order to feature countries in more accurate ways; one website suggests a hands-on way to see the distortions using an orange peel. Another website offers an image of the African continent with other seemingly large countries contained within it: the United States, China, India, and others. Still other projections turn maps upside down, placing continents and countries of the South in the top half.

Check the "Upside-down Map" in the link at the end of the chapter. And for the most creative cartography of all, see the website of the antiAtlas of borders, with alternative maps, pictures, exhibitions, and galleries.[5]

Some atlases incorporate socioeconomic, health, and democracy indicators. For example, see *The Penguin State of the World Atlas*, now in its 9th edition, Freedom House *Freedom in the World*, and *Women in the World: An International Atlas*. Various United Nations agencies also configure maps in these ways.

In his Radical Cartography project, Bill Rankin developed multiple maps—by territory, problematic theme, and genre—that move and flow. Consider his "One World II" polar-centered map depicting the "frenetic circulation" and the "intermodal donut of global capitalism" via international shipping routes and railway lines. Rankin captures the way the world economy condenses time and space. He also highlights efforts to claim space, such as in the Arctic. (See chapter 7 on contested sea space and attempts to control maritime islands and undersea rock deposits in order to exploit whatever treasures they may contain, either now or in the future.)

This section on maps, cartography, and their politics shows the graphic images that shape how we see the world. For many years, people viewed the world in a way that exaggerated the size and power of the North. Children seem less aware of the rest of the world in a state like Texas where the public educational system emphasizes state loyalty. Our world is crisscrossed with territorial borders that are rarely drawn by the people who share communities and identities in borderlands but rather by those who control powerful states. At each and every border, borderlands and border people exist. Keep in mind that the world was once borderless; indigenous people may well have lived together in these places that are now divided.

Indigenous Peoples

Indigenous peoples, whose ancestors predate those of foreign settlers, have histories that are not well-documented in most political and world historical narratives. One regional exception is Europe, which is generally included as part of "Western heritage." History did not begin with imperial conquest or colonialism. However, colonial powers narrated their conquests and, in so doing, attempted to portray peoples they hardly understood, thereby generating potentially misleading images of them.

European nations sent officials, explorers, and entrepreneurs who occasionally married or developed liaisons with indigenous women in colonies, resulting in the color-conscious, hierarchically organized societies of South America, the Caribbean, and elsewhere. Peter Winn wrote multiple editions of *The Americas* to accompany a fine documentary film series of the same name, both of which examine the impact and effect of this legacy in the region. An unusual and moving film, *También la Lluvia* (*Even the Rain*), uncovers layers of conquest and exploitation as a Mexican film crew attempts to recreate the Spanish conquest on Hispaniola (now the Dominican Republic), staging it in the Bolivian highlands where indigenous people, hired at very low cost, struggle against their own government which has privatized water to a foreign corporation, thus threatening indigenous people's ability to live (the latter based on the Cochabamba Water War of 2000).

As Europeans traveled, they colonized and settled among indigenous populations and often succeeded in usurping lands, instigating slavery or meager wage-taxation systems, and imposing their worldviews as a dominant ideology—one to which local people assimilated if they sought to advance in the colonial system. This is known as settler colonialism. Even elsewhere in nonsettler colonies, officials ruled with what has been called a "thin white line"—a minuscule number of European officials overseeing multiple peoples in their newly established boundaries. Most of the earth's southern surface—including Latin America–Caribbean, South Asia (minus China), and Africa—was once directly colonized by the North. (The British colonization of Ireland is a persistent geographic exception.) Indigenous peoples eventually acquired the language, culture, and partial education imposed by Europeans and to a lesser extent, US and Japanese colonizers. Tsarist and Soviet colonization of Western Asia (Eurasia) reflected similar dynamics (see later chapter section). Drawing on Antonio Gramsci and his discussion of dominant ideological hegemony, Edward Said says that initial force eventually gave way to a type of normalized "consent."[6]

European colonial settler societies, with foreign "invaders" in places like Canada and Australia, hardly understood the stewardship rights that indigenous peoples exercised over their land. Western individual ownership rights, imported and imposed in settler societies, undermined indigenous peoples' resources and identities. In what eventually became the Canada-US and Mexico-US boundaries, officials drew border lines through indigenous societies, splitting some between states and countries, such as the Tohono O'odham Nation which has members in both Sonora, Mexico, and Arizona, United States. Other non-Westphalian "nations" were contained in bounded native reservation systems. People maintain their identities amid numerous challenges, with one hand of the federal government supporting community development, but the other heavy hand requiring militarized presence in the name of security on their land (see chapter 4).

In South Africa, long-settled Dutch (called Afrikaners) and later English settlers established an apartheid system of separate, segregated development with enclaved pockets of "native homelands" between which indigenous peoples required official "passes" to move about or to enter "White" land. Some homelands consisted of large territories, like the Transkei, but other homelands were "Black" spots of tiny territories, even noncontiguous territories. Various films have been made of Nelson Mandela's life, such as *Long Walk to Freedom* based on his autobiography, including the contentiousness of early independence with sports (rugby) as a potential symbolic national integrator. In 1994, Africans became full citizens in integrated territory.

In Australia, a particularly brutal settler colonialism was established. Scholars estimate that people now lumped together as "Aboriginal" consisted of 500 nations before European settlers arrived, further divided by language, clan, and kinship groups.[7] As Sarah Maddison elaborates, the "lines that were drawn through Indigenous nations were not the borders of the nation-state, but rather of the states and territories created when the colonies federated in 1901" which carved up nations and divided families. In her words, policies sought to "contain" and even "eliminate" indigenous peoples. Australian states passed legislation between 1901 and 1946 in what was, ironically, called the protection era: "to control Aboriginal people's independence of movement, marriage, employment and association" and "that authorized the removal of Aboriginal children from their families." Forced resettlement to reserves and missions also occurred during this era.[8]

Several films provide visuals of and stories about this region. The evocative *Rabbit-Proof Fence* illustrates official policies to kidnap "Aboriginal" children, telling the story of three girls who escape time and time again to rejoin their family. At the moving close, the real siblings, now aged, are pictured. The Australian film *Charlie's Country* centers on an indigenous man who has become a stranger in his own land, beset by numerous white laws with controls and penalties that make no sense to him.

Laws and policies similar to these were also enforced in other settler colonies. In the United States, indigenous peoples ("Native Americans") were forced to move off their lands and resettle into government-designated reservations according to what some scholars describe as genocidal policies. There, too, indigenous children were forced to attend assimilation schools, thereby diminishing and undermining their language, culture, and identity. In legal policies of the time, traders captured indigenous peoples from the African continent, forcing them into slavery throughout the Western Hemisphere. Slavery, abolished in Mexico in 1829 (soon after independence in 1821) was only abolished in the United States after the Civil War in 1865, and still later in Brazil in 1888. An exhibit in São Paulo shows photographs of slavery in its last few decades.[9]

The African continent, now state-defined with recognized territorial borders, once had hardly visible boundaries before the late 19th century. Rather, as Paul Nugent analyzes, people of various ethnic groups and kingdoms across the continent used mental maps rippling from "centers of political power interspersed between no man's lands and scatterings of decentralized politics"[10] and common dialects, more fluid than any cartographic conception of their "territory" next to other territories.

In subsequent chapters, I analyze contemporary time periods in which indigenous peoples no longer occupy many places on internal or transnational maps. However, there are also efforts to form "pan-indigenous" groups on a national basis. See, for example, organizations such as the Assembly of First Nations in Canada and the National Council of American Indians in the United States.[11]

This overview is by no means meant to glorify or romanticize indigenous peoples. Centuries of occupation, assimilation, and other imposition have wreaked havoc on cultures. A compelling film situated at the Canadian-US border, *Frozen River*, shows the intersection of poverty, nationality, and gender as two women, one of them Mohawk, struggle to feed families and to generate income through work with smugglers, crossing Asian migrants over the St. Lawrence River that weakens under the weight of their vehicle. An historic film, *Last of the Mohicans*, based on the novel by James Fennimore Cooper, parts ways with the usual, earlier Hollywood depictions of indigenous peoples in the Americas confronting White settlers; rather, Mohican strategic agency is portrayed. They call themselves Kanienkehaka (also known by the Dutch name "Mohawk"), and are members of the Iroquois Confederation that later became known as the Six Nations.

Adventurers, Travelogues, and Pictures: Creating the "Other"

In his mammoth book, *Orientalism,* translated into 30 languages, Edward Said offers sweeping treatment of how Northern people in the Western world, historically, had the "intellectual power" to create representations and construct the images of people and places worldwide. Whether adventurers and travelers or consumers of popular magazines like *National Geographic,* those in the Western world imagined peoples in the South as different—as "Others," exoticized people who looked and dressed differently. The narratives often painted a picture of seemingly inferior people, less "civilized," who would benefit from European superior tutelage, development, and patronage. Social imaginaries in writing and photographs reveal not only a patronizing quality but also one we might now identify as racist in its stereotypes and sometimes demeaning language. Even academic international relations publications succumbed to the discourse and images. The journal that eventually became titled *Foreign Affairs* began as the *Journal of Race Development* in 1910. Frantz Fanon also wrote about colonial (especially in Algeria) and postcolonial experiences in his famous *Wretched of the Earth*. In the black and white film *Battle of Algiers*, which projects itself like a documentary, viewers can see the vicious circle of violence and terrorism on the parts of the colonizers and the colonized, still relevant with parallels elsewhere in the 21st century.

Travelers and Adventurers in the 18th–19th Centuries

As Said argued and others developed, the power to represent people in the South in word and photo rested in the North. A good source on representation and image-making comes from the writings of adventurers who "discovered" places in the vast South prior to colonial and modern map construction. Images and narratives of places in the South began to emerge that made civilizing missions appear benevolent rather than invasive. Mary Louise Pratt argues that this was "anti-conquest" writing that created a "utopian, innocent vision of European global authority."[12] Such writings helped stake out regions for possible settler habitation in now-independent Australia, New Zealand, Algeria, Rhodesia (now Zimbabwe), Kenya, and South Africa. Many overseas territories still remain, controlled mainly by the United States, France, and Great Britain in far-flung places around the globe. Some now-autonomous countries have or had semi-autonomous "dominion" status under the British umbrella, and to this day are connected in the Commonwealth.

Even in the late 20th and early 21st centuries, travel writing has the power to represent large swaths of people in a territory, and the popular reader audiences are huge. Paul Theroux has written not only many fiction novels set in various contexts but also 16 travelogues (labeled nonfiction). Some of his writing has been excerpted in *The New Yorker*. His books, with their large print runs and their reviews, gain extraordinary visibility in wide-circulation popular magazines and in national US newspapers with vast readerships. In other words, his writing reaches a much broader segment of the population than the specialized audiences of academic books or journals.

I have read several of Theroux's books, each of them about crossing borders—by rail, foot, vehicle, and air—from *The Great Railway Bazaar* to *The Tao of Travel*. Here I cite Theroux's latest book from 2013, one that updates his best seller, *Dark Star Safari*. It is titled *The Last Train to Zona Verde: My Ultimate African Safari*, useful here for he focuses on borders traveling from the South African former segregated internal borders of the apartheid era through the international borders of Namibia and Angola. In chapter 11, "The Frontier of Bad Karma," he writes evocatively of the road northward to Angola in an "ill-defined borderland, a zone of decrepitude and hunger."[13] He paints a borderland of fear with sweeping generalizations not only from that context but also with regard to global borderlands.

> All national boundaries attract temporary people, as well as rejects and immigrants and fixers. At this, the limit of the country, far from the capital, normal rules did not apply. People did whatever they could get away with. . . . Such a fringe area lacked any identity except its own fraying face, and attracted mostly fugitives and hustlers.

Border people live with the characterizations writers and filmmakers paint of them, whether accurate or not, in media and films (see chapter 11 on films).

To his credit, Theroux also contextualizes global historical greed and criticizes the Angolan elite who rule a wealthy country (with oil, diamonds, and gold), but his narrative depicts a place of hopelessness and misery, saying that he witnessed: "the mute and brutalized Angolans, ignored by the kleptomaniacs in power."[14] He cites the commentary on internal checkpoints from Karl Maier: "The [Angolan] checkpoint consists of two small red 'stop' signs facing opposite directions, two pieces of string" with arrogant "roadblock dictators" who decide who passes for how much money and who "would be at home in Liberia, Nigeria, Mozambique or a dozen other countries where the link between police work and banditry is very fine indeed."[15]

In later sections of this chapter and others, I synthesize contemporary research about world border regions, albeit from academic sources with smaller readerships. This section is designed to show the "Othering" processes in popular travelogues.

Magazines, Films, and Popular Culture

After the explicit rhetoric of "civilizing missions" and "racial development" diminished, other media took over for mass audiences. The 20th-century constructions of the "Other" in picture magazines and in Hollywood paint indelible images for readers: for East Asia, consider the many Fu Manchu films; for South Asia, Rudyard Kipling's books and the films made from them persist in 20th- and 21st-century imaginations.

Beginning in the early 20th century, Edgar Rice Burroughs wrote "adventure novels" of Tarzan, the (White) ape man. According to the Internet Movie Database, 48 Tarzan films were made;[16] readers can view pictures of the posters and DVD covers on the link and draw their own conclusions. Tarzan's always-clean-shaven whiteness, albeit swinging through the rainforest and doing the right thing, offered great contrast to the occasional appearances of Africans in the films, as drums beat in background music, showing traditional warriors or dancers yelling in unintelligible languages in these English-language films. Far too many Hollywood movies like this, replayed on cable stations like Turner Classic Movies, exist for me to list them all. The point here is that "Othering" processes took hold in popular culture.

Brazilian actress and singer, Carmen Miranda, who sang and danced with enormous hats of fruit, epitomized the sexy image of Latin America via 1940s Hollywood movies on the "happy tropics."[17] Feminist theorist Cynthia Enloe analyzes the politics of women's symbolic appearances in world affairs in a 1980 book, *Bananas, Beaches, and Bases*. During the interwar years, many Latin American states sought to alter their economies to reduce dependencies on the North and presumably to alter the ways in which films infantilized and sexualized the region.

Perhaps the most common early source of the "Other" came from *National Geographic* magazine with its stories and glossy photographs of people and places in southern countries. Victorian-era thinking might paint the material as soft pornography, but the magazine was about so much more than showing dark-skinned bare-breasted women. Geographer Tamar Rothenberg, taking a cue from Pratt, examines *National Geographic* as an "assertion of innocence regarding the larger imperial project and complicity with that project." She continues, noting how the magazine seemingly presented facts and images without any political analysis of colonialism and imperialism, yet it still conveyed a presumption of "white or Western superiority."[18]

Anthropologists Catherine Lutz and Jane Collins wrote a comprehensive analysis of the magazine, focusing on the way images of non-Western people were produced, in photographs and in content (600 randomly selected images from 1950 to 1986). They also analyzed how readers responded to randomly selected photographs. The magazine's viewership is huge: 37 million people worldwide. It has the third-largest number of subscribers (after *TV Guide* and *Reader's Digest*) and has been a significant source of Western (Euro-American) "appropriated" images and representations of the non-Western world in "contrastive and hierarchical" fashion.[19]

After a full century of disseminating misleading images of the "Other," the powers of the North have left indelible marks on people of both the North and South. With 21st-century social media technology, people from many places represent themselves in various ways, clashing and resonating with the multitude of images in virtual and physical spaces. Founded in Montreal and now based in New York, VICE Media news operation launched cable shows and a television network Viceland airing numerous sensationalist stories of conflict and savagery from around the world, taking the "Othering" process to a whole new dimension.

Imperialism, Empires, and Colonialism

The historical forces of empire have made a deep mark on territorial claims and borderlines, extending into the global era of the 21st century. Among the major forces, this section will examine imperialism, empires, colonialism, wars, and occupation in several border regions not covered in chapters 4–6. Foreign victors of war drew territorial boundaries around spaces that continue to offer challenges to democracy and good governance.

About the size and scope of empire, once covering 85 percent of the world's surface,[20] the oft-quoted sentence provides a sense of its expanse: "the sun never sets on the British Empire." To this we could add the earlier Spanish, Dutch, and Portuguese Empires in the Western Hemisphere and Asia and the French Empire, mostly in Africa and Southeast Asia but also in the Caribbean. See the list of maps posted in the "map room" on a thorough and comprehensive website by S. Luscombe.[21] Once again, note the size distortions from the Mercator map projection, particularly showing India as tiny, though India was what Britain called its "jewel in the crown."

Many European nations used both trade and direct colonial control to establish their spheres of influence in the South. Among them, one can count Belgium, Britain, France, Germany, Italy, Portugal, Spain, and in other parts of the North, Japan, Russia/USSR, and the United States. Some granted control and tax-collection rights to what (in a "long read" with video) *The Guardian* calls the "original corporate raiders," such as the British East India Company which for a century was responsible only to its shareholders.[22] (See chapter 5.)

A single chapter in a contemporary book can, by no means, outline the whole of world history over one or more centuries. However, it is possible to highlight bordering practices in several Southern regions. This chapter will not cover the other empires, such as the Austro-Hungarian, Mughal (Moghul), Chinese, and Ottoman (except for the latter, at its close). Roots of late 20th- and early 21st-century border conflicts can be traced to century-old history. The famous, if not tragic "line in the sand" comment about Middle East boundaries is eloquently explained by Robin Wright:

> Borders were determined with a ruler—arbitrarily. At a briefing for Britain's Prime Minister H. H. Asquith in 1915, Sykes famously explained, "I should like to draw a line from the 'E' in Acre to the last 'K' in Kirkuk." He slid his finger across a map, spread out on a table at No. 10 Downing Street, from what is today a city on Israel's Mediterranean Coast to the northern mountains of Iraq.[23]

She says that nine years of deals, declarations, and treaties "created the modern Middle East out of the Ottoman carcass."

Western Asia and Eurasia

The Ottoman Empire grew from a tiny spot in 1300, near Istanbul, to a huge expanse which included central Europe, northwest Africa, and the Arabian Peninsula, until World War I ended with the victors partitioning it among themselves. The Republic of Turkey was established in 1923, with a neat set of borders with Syria and nearby states in crisis. A website shows a progressive display of the empire's ascendance and decline over centuries.[24] I provide only brief coverage of postcolonial Western Asia (or what the United States calls the Middle East), through its closing documents. The famous film, *Lawrence of Arabia*, covers the life of T. E. Lawrence, a British geopolitical strategist in Western Asia, about whom an autobiography and biographies have been written focusing on his alliances against the Ottoman Empire (which would soon be recolonized).

World War I produced a convulsion of border changes as the victors continued to divide the spoils. European national interests—including geopolitical concerns about access to the sea, economic or military advantages, and the balance of power—influenced these negotiations. Of key importance was the division of the Ottoman Empire and its outposts of Palestine, Syria, Mesopotamia, and other communities. During the war, the Turks had aligned with Germany, giving rise to a victorious alliance in which they acted together to divide far-flung territories in the empire.

The Sykes-Picot Agreement, signed in May 1916, was a secret agreement between the British and French which divided much of Western Asia between the two into their "spheres of influence." The next year, the Balfour Declaration was made expressing support for a "national home" to be established "in Palestine" for the Jewish people.[25] Documents like these lie at the roots of conflict, initially relating more to land than to religious issues, and are a source of lingering tensions in the region a century later. (See the fine set of late 2015 articles and interactive maps from the *New York Times* in the list of maps at the end of the chapter.)

With the legacies of a lengthy colonial autocratic Tsarist empire and Soviet state, the postcolonial Eurasian states and their former "subjects" suffered decline and stagnation related to the Russian economic meltdown of the late 1990s.[26] The film, *Prisoner of the Mountains*, takes place in the Caucasus between mutually suspicious Russian soldier captives and remote villagers. The film was based on the historic Leo Tolstoy short essay of the 19th century, "The Prisoner in the Caucasus." Border conflicts linger over centuries, with autonomous communities seeking relief from empire builders. Tensions linger elsewhere, to which we now move.

Bordering the African Continent

As in India, European traders initially interacted with coastal traders on the continent of Africa after the rise of navigation and the world economic system. At the instigation of the Germans, however, world powers of the time met in 1880s Berlin to plan how to divide and rule their spheres of influence on the African continent. Although some country names now differ, many of the current territorial borders were established then and in the next 40 years. The boundary lines showed little respect for people, physical barriers, and bridges. Paul Nugent cites an economist who found that 44 percent of border lines in Africa are meridian parallels, 30 percent are mathematical arcs and curves, and only 26 percent are based on geographical features.[27]

Prior to but codified at the Berlin Conference of 1884–1885, European powers took approximately four months to divide the continent among them (with the exception of independent Ethiopia and Liberia). Those present included representatives from Belgium, Britain, France, Germany, Spain, Italy, and Portugal whose interests included containment of the Boers (people of Dutch ancestry in South Africa). Obviously Africans' interests received no consideration.

From Creative Commons, see maps of the claims Europeans made to the African continent in 1914. In that section of the list, there is also a series of maps covering the 20th century as well as a map of the world in 1945 from the United Nations.

The named territories and their borders became fixed, creating artificial divisions among and between groups. Examples include the pastoral Maasai people whose homeland straddles now-named Kenya and Tanzania [formerly named Tanganyika] and the Yoruba kingdom whose people live in both Nigeria and Benin [formerly named Dahomey]. Nigerian historian A. I. Asiwaju, a pioneering border analyst, focused on the human factors associated with the establishment of these international boundaries. He calls people on the continent *Partitioned Africans*, to use the title of his book. For him, the "political surgery" that divided indigenous peoples involved not simply socially constructed identities, as abstractly conceived by academics, but "common ancestry . . . strong kinship ties, shared socio-political institutions and economic resources, common customs and practices, and for some, an acceptance of common political control."[28] In some cases, he says, borderlines separated worshippers from their shrines and sacred groves. William Miles, in his 1994 book *Hausaland Divided*, analyzes the contrasting national differences for Hausa people in Nigeria and Niger with a marker of the international boundary in "desolate bush . . . a monument to the splitting of a people, a symbol of colonialism, an ideology of 'national sovereignty.'"[29]

Africanist and political scientist M. Crawford Young names Bula Matari ("crusher of rocks") to frame his magnificently detailed book on the brutality of the colonial state. The name comes from Bakongo people and their language to refer to the "alien superstructure of rule." The legacies of colonial states, Young argues, go a long way toward explaining the failures of independent states in contemporary times. The reason of state, in Machiavellian terms, is to reproduce itself over time, caging society in a territorial or bordered grid.[30]

Young divides changes in the colonizing state into several stages that consolidated, then expanded rule. Historians distinguish between so-called French centralized "direct rule" and the less centralized British "indirect rule," but the nature of rule varied more with the presence or absence of White settlers. Mahmood Mamdani is frequently quoted as calling all this colonialism "despotism," no matter the despot, though the legacies of French and British traditions have consequences for the contemporary era and internal identities, as the Mauritius case demonstrates.[31] As in India, the British delegated sovereign authority to private companies in some territories. Once the foreign rulers contained and repressed African resistance and rebellion, officials imposed head taxes (compelling labor) and utilized indigenous leaders (such as chiefs) to collect such taxes, providing them with a share or commission in the process but ultimately undermining their legitimacy for their subjects.[32] "Othering" processes permeated European thought. Young describes how "the conviction of African 'savagery' . . . [gave] rise to the conclusion that the new colonial regime, no matter how harsh and extractive, was axiomatically beneficial to the African subject."[33] Colonials also imposed forced labor upon subjected peoples to build roads and to serve in world wars. Selections from the BBC-PBS documentary series, *People's Century*, show colonial propaganda films (news shorts shown in between films at old-style movie theaters) with narratives about their supposed benevolent rule.

By the late 1940s, as Europeans recovered from war and acceptance of the UN principle of self-determination spread, the decline of imperial rule set in with an urgency pressed from people in territorial colonial cages. From 1957 onward on the African continent, decolonization and nationalist movements moved over 50 states toward independence, or at least independence in name with continued ties to the North. After World War II, former French colonies (French West and French Central Africa), were renamed and reterritorialized in smaller units with straight-lined and river-based territorial boundaries. As Young eloquently concludes, "the constitutional apparatus of representative democracy was grafted onto the robust trunk of colonial autocracy."[34] This conclusion vividly resonates with Frantz Fanon's book discussed earlier in the chapter.

Wherefore civil society in the partitioned continent? Nationalist movements morphed into political parties—often reduced to a single party—aimed to structure representation with enclaved women and youth wings. Ethnic identities sometimes mutated into identities based on administrative units. In some cases, with the politics of ethnicity, opportunism and ethnic cleansing took hold, with tragic consequences in places like Rwanda. As Frantz Fanon analyzed, the postcolonial rulers internalized the practices of former rulers. Military coups occurred in scores of states, some multiple times in a single state like Nigeria. Yet borders became sacrosanct, even in the Organisation of African Unity (OAU) (later morphed to the African Union), for fear that numerous secessionist movements would occur.

However, in Judith Vorrath's comparison of 13 case studies in African borderlands, taking a view from the periphery, she finds that borders have become more permeable since independence. She uncovers several themes, among them that borderland identities emerge and that borderlands become economic arenas where locals take advantage of opportunities in price differences and product availability to generate income informally through cross-border trade and smuggling.[35]

Box 2.1

Farmers in Western Kenya

Villagers remembered the British colonial legacy in Idakho Location of western Kenya where I lived during the mid-1970s for my PhD dissertation research. Written in 1974–1975, with distinctive chapters published in many peer-reviewed academic journals over the next decade, my participant observations highlight features covered in this chapter, illustrating the arbitrary nature of colonial, then independence agricultural policy, the way borders hindered trade, and the gendered economy.

Situated at about 5,000 feet in altitude, people enjoyed two growing seasons per year with plentiful rainfall, but on ever-shrinking plots of land, divided among sons, shrunk to the equivalent of 1–2.5 acres. In the later colonial era, British agents ordered that land be consolidated and titled in men's names from the former system where people grew food in multiple plots of varying soil quality, some close to the river and some not.

Women farmers grew food crops, like maize (corn), sorghum, and vegetables to feed their large families, selling surplus for cash or for brewing and selling local beer. Working-aged men migrated to the (formerly called) White Highlands or to Nairobi to work for cash wages in order to pay taxes and fees associated with schools.

The railroad connected the Highlands, capital city, and coastal region quite well. Those men that stayed in the village tended the few, if any, cattle they owned and conversed about public affairs. Local headmen collected taxes, and if villagers had no cash, headmen took blankets and any over movable property they could find to resell. It was impossible to know how much of that money went for taxes and how much was simple extortion.

During the late colonial era, British colonial officials decided that men should grow cash crops to sell through colonial marketing boards. On the east side of the paved road from Kisumu to Kakamega, tea was to be grown, and on the west side, coffee. If farmers did not follow directions from the agricultural extension agents on the proper ways to plant and tend coffee trees (I interviewed 212 farmers on the west side of the road), they could be fined and jailed. One coffee farmer I interviewed was fined and put in jail where they shaved his head, a humiliation he could never forget. Most women farmers sold food crops locally because even if they managed to get enough cash to transport produce on buses to the paved road and then south to Kisumu, they would cross a district boundary where local agents might confiscate their goods if they paid them no fees.

Concluding Reflections

In this chapter, I developed broad historic and representational themes about the shaping of borders, borderlands, and conflicts in our world today. The narratives of indigenous peoples, along with those of the colonized, have been clouded by Northern voices exercising representational power to categorize many people of the South as "Other." These "Othering" processes have been achieved through the publication of travelogues, popular magazines, and stereotyped commercial films, and even via maps which portray the size of countries in ways that exaggerate Northern spaces. The chapter also covered the colonial-driven bordering processes in Western Asia and on the African continent, drawn primarily to serve colonial interests. Artificial borders undermined local communities and economies. Colonialism was a force that shaped the postcolonial world, and it cannot be undone. In the next chapter, we turn to border typologies, theories, and the Border Inequalities Database for a global overview that may provide clues for answers to the questions posed in chapter 1 and action strategies for the future.

Recommended Resources

Links are listed in the order they are discussed in this chapter.

Maps

NASA

https://www.nasa.gov/topics/earth/index.html (the earth without borders)
http://earthobservatory.nasa.gov/IOTD/view.php?id=86725 (India's border wall)

The Robinson Project, on Creative Commons (blank map)

https://commons.wikimedia.org/wiki/Category:Maps_with_Robinson_projection#/media/File:Political_Grey_Map_World.png

U.S. Library of Congress Maps (and border maps)

http://www.loc.gov/maps/
http://www.loc.gov/maps/?q=borders&st=gallery

Peters Map Projection

http://www.petersmap.com

Alternative Projections

http://www.science4all.org/scottmckinney/non-euclidean-geometry-and-map-making/ (cylinder)
http://livelearnevolve.com/peters-projection-worldmap (countries packaged in continents)
http://www.flourish.org/upsidedownmap/ (upside-down map)
http://www.radicalcartography.net (Bill Rankin's radical cartography)
http://www.radicalcartography.net/index.html?one-world-II (frenetic circulation in globalization)

S. Luscombe's "map room" of the British Empire

http://www.britishempire.co.uk/maproom/maproom.htm

The moving map of the Ottoman Empire link, also found in note 24

http://cdn3.vox-cdn.com/assets/4224911/ottoman_empire_gif.gif

New York Times on Iraq and ISIS

http://www.nytimes.com/interactive/2014/06/12/world/middleeast/the-iraq-isis-conflict-in-maps-photos-and-video.html

Africa in maps (various sources)

> https://commons.wikimedia.org/wiki/File:Colonial_Africa_1914_map.png
> http://www.nationalarchives.gov.uk/cabinetpapers/documents/maps-in-time.pdf
> http://www.un.org/Depts/Cartographic/map/profile/world45.pdf

Films

See chapter 11 for fuller details and years released.
The Americas
Battle of Algiers
Charlie's Country
Embrace of the Serpent
También la Lluvia (Even the Rain)
Frozen River
Last of the Mohicans
Lawrence of Arabia
Long Walk to Freedom
People's Century
Prisoner of the Mountains
Rabbit-Proof Fence

Notes

[1] Benedict Anderson, *Imagined Communities: Reflections on the Origin and Spread of Nationalism*, 2nd ed. (NY: Verso, 1991).

[2] Jeremy Black, *Maps and Politics* (Chicago: University of Chicago Press, 1997), pp. 9, 11.

[3] The huge Texas Education Agency website can be easily navigated to identify standards, pass rates by grades, and content areas for every campus, district, and region in the state, http://tea.texas.gov. In the United States, education is far more decentralized to the states and local school districts compared to the centralization model in many other countries.

[4] Black, *Maps and Politics*, p. 31.

[5] http://www.antiatlas.net/en/.

[6] Edward Said, *Orientalism* (NY: Pantheon, 1978).

[7] Sarah Maddison, "Indigenous Peoples and Colonial Borders," in N. A. Naples and J. Bickham-Mendez, eds., *Border Politics* (NY: New York University Press, 2014), pp. 153–76.

[8] Maddison, "Indigenous Peoples," quotes, pp. 457, 172.

[9] From National Public Radio, http://www.npr.org/sections/parallels/2013/11/12/244563532/photos-reveal-harsh-detail-of-brazils-history-with-slavery. Accessed 7/1/15.

[10] Paul Nugent and A. I. Asiwaju, eds., *African Boundaries* (London: Pinter, 1996), pp. 39, 36.

[11] See also Colombian film, *Embrace of the Serpent* (2016), on two scientific travelers' encounters with indigenous peoples of the Amazon in the 19th and 20th centuries, using nine languages. Websites for Assembly of First Nations (Canada), http://www.afn.ca/Assembly_of_First_Nations.htm, and National Congress of American Indians (United States), http://www.ncai.org/. Accessed 2/1/16.

[12] Mary Louise Pratt, *Imperial Eyes: Travel Writing and Transculturation* (NY and London: Routledge, 1992), p. 39.

[13] Paul Theroux, *The Last Train to Zona Verde: My Ultimate African Safari* (Boston: Houghton Mifflin, 2013), quotes from pp. 201, (indented quote) 204.

[14] Ibid., p. 215.

[15] Ibid., p. 219.

[16] Tarzan movies on the Internet Movie Database at http://www.imdb.com/list/ls058415951/.

[17] Carmen Miranda photos on National Public Radio website, http://www.npr.org/sections/parallels/2015/04/22/401467980/of-fruit-hats-and-happy-tropics-a-renaissance-for-carmen-miranda. See Cynthia Enloe, *Bananas, Beaches, and Bases: Making Feminist Sense of International Politics* (Berkeley: University of California Press, 1980), for one of the first feminist critiques of IR literature and its exclusionary packaging of the world without gender.

[18] Tamar Rothenberg, *Presenting America's World: Strategies of Innocence in National Geographic Magazine, 1888–1945* (Hampshire, England: Ashgate 2007), pp. 7, 9.

[19] Catherine Lutz and Jane Collins, *Reading National Geographic* (Chicago: University of Chicago Press, 1993), synthesis of methods, pp. 2–3, and discourse used throughout.

[20] Said, *Orientalism*, p. 41.

[21] Recommended by Martin Jones, et al., *An Introduction to Political Geography: Space, Place and Politics*, 2nd ed. (London: Routledge, 2015). Luscombe's website is dated 2012, http://www.britishempire.co.uk/maproom/maproom.htm.

[22] William Dalrymple, "The East India Company: The Original Corporate Raiders," *The Guardian,* March 4, 2015 (accessed 11/1/15), http://www.theguardian.com/world/2015/mar/04/east-india-company-original-corporate-raiders.

[23] Robin Wright, "How the Curse of Sykes-Picot Still Haunts the Middle East," *The New Yorker,* April 30, 2016 (accessed 5/2/16), http://www.newyorker.com/news/news-desk/how-the-curse-of-sykes-picot-still-haunts-the-middle-east.

[24] http://cdn3.vox-cdn.com/assets/4224911/ottoman_empire_gif.gif.

[25] http://www.jewishvirtuallibrary.org/jsource/History/balfour.html.

[26] Mark Beissinger and Crawford Young, "Convergence to Crisis," in their coedited *Beyond State Crisis?* (Washington, DC: Woodrow Wilson Center Press, 2002), pp. 16, 23.

[27] Nugent and Asiwaju, *African Boundaries*, p. 41.

[28] A. I. Asiwaju, "The Conceptual Framework," in A. I. Asiwaju, ed., *Partitioned Africans* (NY: St. Martin's Press, 1985), p. 2.

[29] William Miles, *Hausaland Divided* (Ithaca; London: Cornell University Press, 1994).

[30] M. Crawford Young, *The African Colonial State in Comparative Perspective* (New Haven, CT: Yale University Press, 1994), p. 19.

[31] William Miles, *Scars of Partition: Postcolonial Legacies in French and British Borderlands* (Lincoln: University of Nebraska Press, 2014); Mandami quote from M. Crawford Young, *African Colonial State*, 1994.

[32] M. Crawford Young, *The African Colonial State*, synthesized from pp. 78, 126–8, 140, 174.

[33] Ibid., p. 98.

[34] Beissinger and Young, "Convergence to Crisis," p. 38.

[35] Judith Vorrath, "On the Margin of Statehood? State-Society Relations in African Borderlands," in I. Zartman, et al., eds., *Understanding Life in the Borderlands* (Athens: University of Georgia Press, 2010), pp. 85–104.

Chapter 3

Global Inequalities and Local Borderlands

Conceptual Foundations

This chapter analyzes theories about a global world with both border and critical lenses. The particular focus synthesizes work on economic inequalities and power asymmetry at borders from an historical perspective and posits theories regarding categories or stage-based transitions toward cross-border cooperation. Note that these models address neither variations among states nor the length of time that they have existed, which are especially important considerations in the postcolonial world. We also cannot assume that states operate with legitimacy, consent, and/or relative democracy for those in the mainstream or for border people.

Political scientists bring keen awareness to differences among states—strong and weak, federal to centralized, even quasi-states and failed states—classifying them on a spectrum from so-called good-to-bad governance.[1] The glories (or horrors) of state variations deserve a place in border studies due to their impacts on borderlands and border people. I have spent my professional lifetime teaching courses on the politics of developing countries, most of them postcolonial states in the South, with a focus on governance, so I bring a global geographic lens to border studies as well.

This chapter moves from global inequalities to local borderlands, challenging existing measurements that are locked in state-centric units yet acknowledging that such data offer the only currently accessible means by which to examine South and North for analytic purposes. I thread the chapter with a preview of the regional borderlands examined in chapters 4–7. For this book, I guided the building of the Border Inequalities Database using multiple measures of gross domestic product (GDP) per capita (i.e., per person) income gathered over several decades that, alas, hardly capture informal earnings, transnational money shelters for the wealthy, cross-border trade in regions with porous borders (some of which is state-defined as illegal trade), and/or internal inequalities, particularly between borderlands and the mainstream or within states. Until such time as scholars and states take the study of borderlands more seriously, these data with their limitations are the best available to us. First, however, I synthesize multiple conceptions of borderlands in size and senses, that is, in their cultural landscapes.

Borderlands: Spatial Size versus Identity

Examining territorial and metaphoric borders may lead readers to conclude that the world and everything within it is a borderland. In this book, however, we will focus primarily on the territorial landscape of borderlands within the spaces near international boundaries and borderlines. Depending on context, the size of that space varies. First, it is important to say something about borderland identities.

With the flowering of border studies in the humanities and literature, some scholars have questioned whether and where borderlines stop—especially those relatively invisible borders of color, dress, and language—given the "Othering" processes that occur in law enforcement, surveillance, and similar monitoring methods (see chapter 2 on "Othering"). For example, will an Algerian-heritage French citizen be questioned by surveillance authorities on a Paris street or will a Mexican-heritage person switching traffic lanes without signaling be detained by immigration officials in an era of mass deportations in the United States? What are the implications for soldiers at the large US military base in Okinawa, Japan, or at the hundreds of other US bases, and in US preclearance zones located in the sovereign space of other countries? Constitutional scholars might differentiate between the rights and protections available to citizens and residents where "border exceptions" do not operate, such as away from airports and territorial borderlands. One critic of US border policy argues that the whole country has become an extraconstitutional zone, with the spread of surveillance to the mainstream.[2]

How wide is the space around territorial lines? Some border theorists provide a fixed figure of 10 kilometers on either side,[3] while others focus on local government jurisdictional lines around territorial borders, such as those defined by counties in the United States and *municipios* in Mexico. Most states with land borders do not make data available about these local jurisdictions, their formal incomes, or local cross-border trade; indeed, some states have no credible national data (for example, Myanmar, as noted in chapter 5). However, exceptions exist such as at the US-Mexico border; see the quantitative comparisons of Anderson and Gerber.[4] Nevertheless, one wonders about the quality of these data. For example, the size of Ciudad Juárez, one of Mexico's big cities in the north-central borderlands, has been officially stuck at 1.3 million people—both *before* the period of extreme violence (2008–2011), when local planners estimated the population as hovering around 2 million, and *after* the violence, from which many residents fled (perhaps some returned?), the exact estimates for which will never be known. Population size variances alter per capita income figures for the *municipio*, that is, the total income divided by the number of people (of course, money earned through drug trafficking, hidden tax shelters, and other crimes goes uncounted).

Using local government units, one would estimate about 14 million people living on both sides of the Mexico-US border. Moving to the next highest unit of government, if border states from Texas to Baja California were counted as the borderlands, the population of all 10 states would total over 80 million, but places like San Francisco and Sacramento, California, hardly seem like border cities.[5] In the Mexico-US La Paz Agreement, an environmental document signed in 1983, the borderlands were measured as 100 km (62 miles) each way, north on one side and south on the other, to deter negative environmental impacts near the border. Yet environmental damage regularly features in nongovernmental organization (NGO) struggles to address issues that affect land and people on "both sides," such as the ASARCO copper-smelting plant which spewed lead into surrounding border soils, which will contaminate them for over a century, and the post–La Paz efforts, with Texas regulatory approval, to spread east-coast sewer sludge in Sierra Blanca, Texas, 30 miles from the border. Another unit of measure is the US Department of Homeland Security's established checkpoints up to 100 miles from the border along Interstate Highways 10 and 25 going north, west, and east. Southern New Mexico is home to six checkpoints, fewer than those of the Israeli military in Occupied Palestinian Territories, but operating with profiling barriers and delays just the same.[6] The size of borderlands is a slippery one, depending on varying local perceptions, government agency rules, and governments.

Anthropological definitions, according to noted border scholars Hastings Donnan and Thomas Wilson, focus on people's perceptions of a border identity, that sense of cultural or linguistic difference from the mainstream or everyday where territorial lines and border policies affect people living in those spaces.[7] In some borderlands, cultural and linguistic heritages span territorial lines and people cross or seek to cross regularly to visit relatives, to shop for price advantages, or to work on the other side. In times of heightened or artificial fears about security—seemingly permanent in some countries—national border control policies stall, delay, or prohibit such everyday crossings, subjecting people to long waiting lines or even fences and walls. Border studies scholarship has only begun to accumulate information about perceptions, cultures, and changing identities in everyday lives in the widely varying spaces around borderlands. Given all these ways to define borderlands, I focus primarily on units of space that approximate 100 km or 62 miles on each side, following the La Paz Agreement.

From the local view, we now move to the global—with my Border Inequalities Database and its state-centric methodological challenges—ultimately advancing theories about cross-border institutions and inequalities over historic, postcolonial times while examining a wide variety of state types, from relatively democratic to authoritarian and from strong to weak.

Global Inequalities

In 1992, the United Nations Development Programme (UNDP) published a widely reprinted graph in its annual *Human Development Report* (HDR) that illustrated economic inequalities in our world at that time. The graph, shaped like a champagne glass with a very narrow stem, showed how most of the world's wealth (82.7 percent) was concentrated at the top, among the top fifth of the population.

At that time, the UNDP pioneered a fine index, still in use, of human development—the Human Development Index or HDI—to include a composite of education, health, and income indicators, with a rank ordering of countries. Over time, the UNDP infused a gender-sensitive HDI into indexes, moving

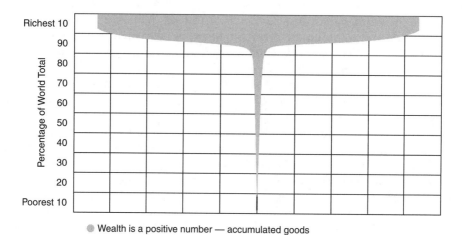

● Wealth is a positive number — accumulated goods
● Wealth is a negative number — debt

FIGURE 3.1 Distribution of Economic Wealth in the World, 2015.

Source: Based on a design by Jakub Zajakala, Research Assistant. Data from Border Inequalities Database, compiled from World Bank and International Monetary Fund figures.

on to the Gender Development Index (GDI) and the Gender Inequality Index (GII).[8] International organizations, like the UNDP and the World Bank, also calculate the absolute and proportional numbers of people living on US$2 or less per day, down to one in eight compared to two in five in 1990.[9] However, *absolute* numeric changes need to be examined with *relative* changes.

Because I have yet to see the UNDP update of that global inequality figure, I had another such graph prepared using current 2014 data from my Border Inequalities Database, using deciles. It is shown in figure 3.1.

As the figure shows, inequalities continue but wealth is more concentrated at the top, in the top decile. In spite of these extreme *relative* inequalities, Human Development Index (HDI) figures in many countries have improved since 1991, a quarter-century ago, in *absolute* terms. UNDP annual *Human Development Reports* and charts can be easily accessed online, though the rank-ordered list is state-centric.

In the late 20th and 21st centuries, a mixed process of economic growth and poverty-reduction policies emerged selectively around the world. The development process hardly produces a fair distribution of growth with equity everywhere, within and between countries. Rather, economic growth occurs amid glaring inequities in state-driven strategies shaped by the global economy. It is important to emphasize that, in policy and practical terms, a good place to begin addressing inequalities is in the borderlands. Below, with the Border Inequalities Database, I examine binational pairs and ratios of inequality.

Border Inequalities Database

In late 2015 and early 2016, research assistant Jakub Zajakala and I planned and developed the Border Inequalities Database. We used the latest figures from the World Bank and the International Monetary Fund (IMF) from 1975 through 2014 with multiple indicators. We opted to compare the strengths and weaknesses of gross domestic product (GDP) per capita income based on purchasing power parity (PPP) (as opposed to based on per capita income alone) due to the way it adjusts for price differences within states. We also used constant 2005 dollar terms. For a full explanation of the various options, see table 3.1.

TABLE 3.1 Border Inequalities Database

The Border Inequalities Database was built using public figures from the World Bank and International Monetary Fund. Research assistant Jakub Zajakala, MA located and entered the figures. He and I will develop other analyses from it and then post it on my university website. His glossary on the Excel file reads as follows:

Term	Meaning
GDP Per Capita	A measure of the total output of a country that takes the gross domestic product (GDP) and divides it by the number of people in the country. The per capita GDP is especially useful when comparing one country to another because it shows the relative performance of the countries. A rise in per capita GDP signals growth in the economy and tends to translate as an increase in productivity (*Source:* Investopedia).
Purchasing Power Parity (PPP)	An economic concept that estimates the amount of adjustment needed on the exchange rate between countries in order for the exchange to be equivalent to each currency's purchasing power (*Source:* Investopedia).
1990 International GK Dollar	The Geary–Khamis dollar, more commonly known as the international dollar, is a hypothetical unit of currency that has the same purchasing power parity that the US dollar had in the United States at a given point in time. The years 1990 or 2000 are often used as benchmark years for comparisons that run through time.
	It is based on the twin concepts of purchasing power parities (PPP) of currencies and the international average prices of commodities. It shows how much a local currency unit is worth within the country's borders. It is used to make comparisons both between countries and over time. For example, comparing per capita gross domestic product (GDP) of various countries in international dollars, rather than based simply on exchange rates, provides a more valid measure to compare standards of living (*Source:* Wikipedia).
Current International Dollar	Reflects the current year's exchange rates and current PPP adjustments—SHOULD NOT BE USED TO BUILD COMPARISONS OVER TIME (JUST WITHIN THE SAME YEAR) (*Source:* Building the Business Case Analysis).
Constant 2005 US Dollar	Similar to "1990 International GK Dollar" with the exception that here the benchmark is the value of the US dollar during the year 2005.

My inspiration for looking at border inequalities came from Iñigo Moré in his book, *The Borders of Inequality*.[10] He ranks the *most equal* and the *most unequal* borders for 197 countries, using 2004 GDP per capita income data. Moré uses both the regular and GDP PPP income data which offer slight contrasts in rank ordering. Thus, looking comparatively at border inequalities, thanks to Moré, I realized that over 35 years at the US-Mexico borderlands situated me in the 17th and the 26th most unequal borderlands, respectively, in the entire world. And this poor ranking emerged and continued in a regional economic community participating in the North American Free Trade Agreement (NAFTA).

Because of the dated nature of 2004 figures, I resolved to update Moré and also complement a longitudinal dimension to the comparative analysis. Thus, the idea of the Border Inequalities Database was born. We listed far more borderlands (approximately 300, not a fixed figure, since borders and states vary over time) than those in Moré's book, and we inserted figures in cells from 1975 onward to obtain longitudinal insights. Our list contains only states with *land* borders, not island states separated by seas and oceans and in constant tension over boundaries around the world. We calculated inequalities in terms of "ratios" between bordered states.

We expected to find considerable changes over time in the degrees of inequalities between two-state pairs, stated as ratios of richer-to-poorer adjacent states. Why? For starters, the world in 1975 was more fully postcolonial, though many countries then and now continue to bear the weight of colonialism and neocolonialism, as might be expected from the analysis in chapter 2. Also, former satellite states behind the borders of the "Iron Curtain" and the "Bamboo Curtain" made their way toward autonomous, sovereign statehood in the early 1990s. Some politically authoritarian states, such as China, now produce under state-owned enterprises and welcome foreign firms and capital to compete in the global economy, with skyrocketing growth rates and advances in workers' wages. Additionally, the globalized economy took hold with the implementation of "free trade" regimes, treaties, and regional organizations that allowed businesses to take advantage of more open borders and lower costs associated with the comparative advantage of transnational production and trade. In the 1980s and thereafter, the raison d'être for a whole host of regional and global organizations was to promote policy changes to enable freer trade. One might imagine that more countries in the South would benefit from free trade promulgated by international institutions such as the World Bank and IMF. A few clearly did and still do: Brazil, India, China, and the East/Southeast Asian states that moved away from dependency on export-processing production toward greater diversity in their exports.

Figure 3.2 provides bar graphs for the numbers of ratio categories for border inequality pairs at different levels along with how those ratios changed over time for all the states in the database. We found states with tenfold differentials, such as Afghanistan and its surrounding states, but decided to treat them as outliers in the last (F) category. We settled on five ratio categories and *graded* them to show the number of states in the spectrum from relatively equal

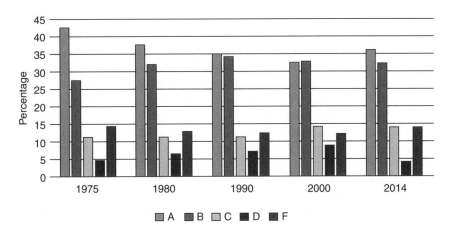

FIGURE 3.2 Percentage of Borders by Category and Year, 1975–2014 (Graded A, B, C, D, F).

Source: Based on a design by Jakub Zajakala, research assistant. Data from Border Inequalities Database, compiled from World Bank and International Monetary Fund figures.

to unequal: A = 1–1.49; B = 1.5–2.49; C = 2.5–3.49; D = 3.5–4.49; F = 4.5+. Surprisingly, with a few blips in specific years, the longitudinal global perspective shows that the proportions of equal to unequal state neighbors changed little over decades. Yet the figure also shows that the majority of border pairs (graded A and B ratios) reflect somewhat similar wealth *or* poverty.

Upon examination of the Border Inequality Database list of states, it became clear that some regions showed low while others showed high numeric ratios. The regional approach, I believe, is necessary to flesh out understandings and action strategies; chapters 4 and 5 contain longitudinal data and/or narratives for most states mentioned in those regions (chapter 6, by narrative only, given the large number of countries). To preview those results, more equality can be found *within* Europe, for example (though not at its external borders). Internal European equality reflects relatively shared prosperity, partly produced with decades of institutional, cross-border attention. Equality can also be found within areas of lower GDP per capita. For example, South American states show relative equality in GDP per capita among pairs, but it is an equality of unrealized prosperity. Finally, considerable equality can be found in impoverished regions. Such is the case in the postcolonial regions of Sub-Saharan Africa and parts of South and Southeast Asia (with China increasingly exceptional). These regions exemplify shared poverty and, at least for India, extensive preoccupations with security. They also lack institutional investments and cross-border attention to land and river systems. Whether China's ambitious Silk Road and sea *trade* agendas move toward border institutional cooperation is a question for the future.

Occasional outliers can be found in regions of shared poverty. Countries with precious minerals or oil (called the "resource curse") such as in Angola show higher GDP income per capita than surrounding nations, but when compared with HDI or inequality indexes (such as GINI), it becomes clear that

the wealth is hardly distributed fairly within countries. One of the most striking features of measures of inequality, like GINI, is extensive missing data for
most countries.[11] During this book's preparation, oil prices fell enormously, so
time will tell what happens with resource-cursed and other outlier countries.
Measures of internal inequality rarely reflect realities in many countries due
again to informal economies and foreign money shelters for the rich. We await
the analysis of documents hacked in the 2016 Panama Papers! Numeric indicators like the GINI index, GDP per capita, and purchasing power parity are
flawed and do not capture the informal economy, including both illegal and
illicit trade. (See chapter 10, on trade, for a conceptual discussion of goods that
some states and/or people deem legal and licit but others do not.)

Below, I develop further the many caveats to accepting international institutions' figures as an accurate reflection of income within countries and for
border comparisons.

Caveats in Numeric Narratives: "Numeric Metaphors"?

Deborah Stone, whose insightful analyses on policy paradoxes get more coverage in chapter 8 on security, warns about the reliance on composite numeric
figures in understanding reality.[12] Her book covers the United States, that is,
the North, but such problems are magnified in postcolonial developing countries that may lack resources to generate the sorts of data that numerically
obsessed countries collect and use. After a chapter analyzing the political uses
of discourse and rhetoric, her chapter on numbers characterizes singular quantitative snapshots as "numeric metaphors." A numeric figure stands for or substitutes for a fuller description and interpretation of reality behind a singular
number. Readers should think critically about what they see, count, and read,
whether content appears in stories, films, cases, or data-driven numeric metaphors. Here I am reminded of the numbing effect of violence as told in the
numeric metaphors of mass murder and death, whether in relation to the Holocaust, genocide, Partition, and/or *feminicidio* (femicide). In the famous words
of tyrant Joseph Stalin: "The death of one man is a tragedy. The death of millions is a statistic." As Deepti Misri analyzes, the reasons and stories *behind*
the numbers may be most crucial but can be missed in the descriptive statistics or closed-ended surveys from which researchers and bureaucrats solicit
information.[13]

Many caveats exist about full trust in income figures reported to or by
international institutions such as the World Bank, UNDP, and International
Monetary Fund, particularly in postcolonial developing countries. Indeed,
working with such figures—as many do—could be called a leap of faith for the
quality of data is uncertain and, at best, provides only probable estimates. Gross
domestic product is a construct invented in 1940 as a summary statistic and
thereafter has been used by most states, but with troublesome methodological
adjustments, such as Nigeria's bump up by 89 percent as *The Economist* points
out in a special section on this misleading measure, "The Trouble with GDP."[14]

First, as is most obvious, GDP per capita is a measure of central tendency,
an *average* figure which does not provide the range from rich to poor or the

proportion of earners at polar opposites of poverty and wealth. The GINI index of inequality seeks to provide such measures, but no credible figures exist for many countries, especially in the South. Besides internal income inequality, data hardly capture gender-disaggregated differences in income, although the UNDP's annual *Human Development Reports* contain tables of the Gender Development Index (GDI) and Gender Inequality Index (GII) as noted above. With critical attention to ethnicity, regional space, and race, analysts could better ascertain the situation (or predicament) of people inside states. Consider examples of Africans in South Africa with its long historic tradition of institutionalized White privilege or Palestinians in Israel and the Occupied Palestinian Territories. Moré identified an outlier ratio for 2004 in Spain's enclaves in Morocco (15—far worse than an F grade in figure 3.2), but in my Border Inequalities Database, the highest ratios existed in Palestine-Israel and Yemen-Oman (17).

Second, many people earn income outside the formal economy in what is called the informal economy of unregulated, usually uncounted, and untaxed economic production and trade. In early United Nations reports from decades past in places like Ghana and Kenya, the term "informal work" was coined to conceptualize the ways that people supported and sustained themselves in subsistence agriculture in unmeasurable ways (sometimes producing surplus crops, sold for cash, bartered, or traded). Pockets of informality exist in the North as well. Consider the informal sector in the US-Mexico borderlands in box 3.1.

Box 3.1

Informal Economies in the US-Mexico Borderlands

My 1990s original research, conducted with a full faculty and student research team and supported by the National Science Foundation, documented informal economic activity on both sides of the central US-Mexico borderlands of El Paso, Texas, and Ciudad Juárez, Chihuahua.* We drew a random sample of 600 households in six neighborhoods, three in each city of the central borderlands, each spatially distinctive: near the border and downtown, at the old periphery of the city, and at the new periphery outside city and municipal boundaries. We also sampled hundreds of obvious informal street-vendor workers, interviewed local government officials, and read policy documents.

Literature in the United States tends to treat informal earnings as crime or tax evasion, while in Mexico, as many as a third of economically active people work legitimately and informally (including microenterprises with five employees or fewer) according to both government and scholarly reports. Among major findings, we documented that cross-border informal workers earned three times the earnings of export-processing factory (maquiladora) workers, though they worked in a potentially risky atmosphere given border crossings that might result in officials confiscating their goods, in fines, or even in capture by the US Border Patrol. In other words, the borderlands provided people with economic opportunities.

However, tighter border controls occurred after the September 11, 2001, terrorist attack on the east coast of the United States, thus undermining the ability of Juarense border crossers to support themselves with higher earnings as traders and service workers.

*Kathleen Staudt, *Free Trade? Informal Economies at the U.S.-Mexico Border* (Philadelphia: Temple University Press, 1998).

Some trade is dangerous. For example, cross-border transnational criminal organizations ship or smuggle illegal drugs into the lucrative US commercial market. However, it is inaccurate to characterize the sum totality of informal activity and borderland exchanges as "smuggling," with all of the negative connotations the word implies. As *The Economist* notes about Nigeria's trade with countries on its borders, "at least 70% of the trade. . . . goes unrecorded."[15]

State-centric figures do not envelop the whole of everyday life and earnings *in* borderlands, however wide or narrow their spaces. In the central and eastern US-Mexico borderlands, the Texas border is relatively impoverished compared to other parts of the state, while the northern Mexico border states of Chihuahua and Coahuila have higher per capita incomes than other parts of Mexico. In some countries, the central government neglects the population at the border, perceived as peripheral in space and political loyalty, while in other borderlands, the state security apparatus creates formal jobs in borderlands to police and surveil the border. As box 3.1 describes, border people themselves develop ways to generate incomes using the border and its price differentials as an opportunity.

From here, we move to consider ways that border scholars have categorized borders and developed theories about increasing cooperation at borders. Amazingly, beyond the use of phrases like "power asymmetries" in the context of foreign policy or with regard to income and other resources, few scholars (save Moré) focus on wage and income inequality. This book aims to alter that silence in theoretical perspectives.

Building on Border Theories: People's Livelihoods

Until now, border theories have been developed by Europeans and North Americans about the North and its historical experiences of once-imagined nations (recall Benedict Anderson). Of course, conflicts have arisen and the victors have re-bordered space, even as recently as the post–World War II era, but colonial pasts are distant—in the 18th and 19th centuries for the United States and Mexico.

Some theorists began by categorizing different types of borders, then others posed interactive models for border integration, and still others considered sequential movement among the factors in those models that might foster cross-border institutions. In focusing on borderlands, theorists may miss variations among states and postcolonial states that emerged in the latter half of the 20th century, and as late as 2011 in South Sudan. There is a tendency to assume the constant of a strong "state," with the semblance of democracy and good governance, rather than to evaluate the reality of strong to weak, failed, and/or absent states. While gaps exist to understanding borderlands worldwide, the theoretical pioneers offer an informed foundation on which to build—my intent in this book is to add considerations of income inequalities and institutions to the whole picture.

My interest lies in border people's income and everyday lives. Curiously, no models put wages and income inequalities into their analytic puzzles or equations. With a critical lens applied to these theories, we cannot assume that cross-border trade volume and interactive processes alone will prompt shared wealth or a lessening of inequalities (lower ratios, discussed earlier) or that wealth that will trickle down to the wider society, especially in borderlands. Borderlands can be places of shared prosperity, but they often operate with an apartheid-like segregation and huge income differences with business boosters packaging regions as globally competitive in order to induce more investment and perpetuate profit incentives. Indeed, business leaders who benefit from the labor of people trapped on the low-wage side of a border may seek to protect their investment stakes with the security fences and walls built by their government allies rather than foster cooperation and shared prosperity, a circumstance common along the US-Mexico border. Those with short-term visions to protect low-labor costs fail to challenge wage inequalities in the borderlands. Those with long-term visions promote shared prosperity.

With this book's critical perspective, I hope to take borderlands theory to the next level by building on Moré and my Border Inequalities Database with a focus on inclusive cross-border institutions. These two words beginning with "I"—Inequalities and Institutions—are the focus in the I-2 perspective. As noted earlier, Moré produced a path-breaking effort to document and rank countries in *The Borders of Inequality*. Besides ranking borders from the most unequal to the most equal, one of his chapters compares three case studies of declining income inequality over time, a potentially useful application to the real world and to the final chapters in part IV of this book on NGO action and policy change to induce proactive investment in reducing inequalities and building democratic institutions. Yet the flaws of state-centric orientations obscure a comprehensive approach to borderlands, so I make reference to legal minimum wages as well to address the tenfold differences at the US-Mexico border (~US$60 per day, at $7.25/hour compared with ~US$4–5 per day, at 80 *pesos* daily in 2017; but exchange rates further reduced the *peso*'s value from 16 in mid-2016 to 21 to US$1 in 2017), the fluctuations of which aggravate uncertainty for border people. In the South Asian borderlands, in contrast, informal workers may earn more than those in the formal sector, where minimum wage figures offer little relevance, but the states stifle trade.

The theories synthesized below provide useful building blocks to develop a more comprehensive theoretical model—one with the potential to incorporate more borders in the world, including the postcolonial South. Below I outline features of previous models, in their chronological order of publication, and then propose my Inequalities and Institutions (I-2) model as a guide for the

Currency fluctuations: Mexican peso to the US dollar. Sign on restaurant door in Ciudad Juárez.

Source: Photographer Kathleen Staudt.

regional and issue chapters in this book along with the closing chapter with connections to practice and policy.

Categorizing Borders

The best and pioneering categorization of borders comes from Oscar Martínez in his book entitled *Border People,* published in 1994. Historian Martínez attends to power symmetry and asymmetry, terms which could include income inequality but also other factors like military strength, both binationally and internationally. Many theorists use power asymmetry to explain geopolitical dynamics and by extension border politics, but these categories may not fully cover the border regions analyzed in this book, as comments below and subsequent chapters outline.

The four categories of borderlands and their descriptions in Martínez's work[16] include the following:

Alienated Borderlands: "where routine cross-boundary interchange is practically nonexistent owing to extremely unfavorable conditions."

Co-existent Borderlands: "where their respective nations reduce international border-related conflicts to a manageable level. . . . or where unfavorable internal conditions in one or both countries preclude binational cooperation, when such problems are resolved to the degree that minimal border stability can prevail."

Interdependent Borderlands, asymmetrical and balanced: "when a border region in one nation is symbiotically linked with the border region of an adjoining country [with the result of] a mutually beneficial economic system."

Integrated Borderlands: where "neighboring nations eliminate all major political differences between them as well as existing barriers to trade and human movement across their mutual boundary."

Martínez, based at and specializing in the Mexico-US border and in Mexico itself, labels the region "interdependent" but with asymmetrical power relations. His most recent book examines uneven development in Mexico and the United States and its causes. While geography fits squarely into the explanation, embedded therein is also the historic fact that the United States took approximately half of Mexico's territory (now the US southwestern states) in 1848 (and later with the Gadsden Purchase of 1853)—territory that included coastal regions and deep-sea ports around which grew large cities such as San Diego, Los Angeles, and San Francisco.[17]

Using the US-Mexico border as his vantage point, Martínez outlines these categories before the tragedy of 9/11 and the US border security regime which followed. While migration and transnational criminal organizations existed in the 1990s, the upturn in transnational organized crime and murder from 2008–2011 in Ciudad Juárez changed the US public's perceptions and increased their fears about borderlands. The Hollywood movie industry aggravated those fears with tales of macabre people who had a seeming taste for violence and brutality, aggravating the "Othering" processes.[18] Many factors combine to create simultaneously inconsistent categories at the US-Mexico border.

Martínez's categories seem mutually exclusive, yet along both interdependent borders—the 2,000-mile US-Mexico border and the 5,000-mile Canada-US border—there are differences significant enough that analysts have used phrases like "the multiple US-Mexico borders" to distinguish between areas in the Pacific Coastal regions, the central arid deserts, and the tropical river system near the Gulf of Mexico.[19] In the vicinity of the Arizona-Sonora borderlands—with the exception of friendly relations between "Ambos Nogales" (twin-named towns Nogales, Mexico, and Nogales, Arizona) through which the US government built a wall—the two states are "alienated" from one another, marked by the presence of vigilante groups called Minutemen, criminal gangs, US Border Patrol officers, and Mexican Grupo Beta officers who assist migrants.[20] In metropolitan areas like Tijuana–San Diego or El Paso–Ciudad Juárez, extensive, legal, daily interaction occurs—with economies dependent upon one another—for family visits, shopping, manufacturing, and support services. It is the border *people* who make the region interdependent, not the *state*. San Diego's economy is diverse, and thus less dependent than El Paso on Mexico. El Paso and Ciudad Juárez share Mexican heritage and Spanish-speaking population majorities. Surely big differences also exist along Russia's lengthy borders. India's militarized Border Security Force patrols very different borders with Pakistan, Bangladesh, Myanmar, China, and in the Kashmir region.

These myriad categories in multiple locales along binational borders can change rapidly, but for how long or short a time, or whether or not conditions might foster change, we cannot know. From an interdependent, relatively porous border during much of the history between Mexico and the United

States, periodic military-style "operations" stalled people and commerce at the border: Operation Gatekeeper, Operation Hold the Line, and others. The US border agents check and delay not only northbound but southbound traffic at some ports. The US security apparatus imposed after September 11, 2001 (9/11), created an alienated border for some, delays in trade for others, and family separations for many. *Who* imposes these characterizations—border people or the federal government and its policies? In South Asia, one might categorize borderlands as alienated or coexistent from the state's perspective, but the people living there would not, at least not yet and probably not for another generation or more.

Ultimately, we must determine from whose perspectives they are developed and for what reasons these categorical labels exist. Does the alienated border emerge from border people or from state policies, and policies against whom—the other side or distant migrants? The categories describe consequential processes in the borderlands.

Thanks to Martínez's innovative historical-cultural approaches, we also learn about the variation in border people's identities, from "national" to "binational," at least at the US-Mexico border. Whether or not borderlanders in other world regions identify with people living on both sides of any particular border space requires investigation. In the Bangladesh-India borderlands, for instance, some people simply identify by community (as Bengali, for example) or by caste or according to linguistic commonalities. In the chapter on Europe, with a special focus on the German-Polish border, fewer bilingual Polish-German speakers live on the German side. The recentness of forced relocation and a changed territorial line (1945) may account for the lack of a binational identity, despite all the money the European Union pours into its Euroregions, including twin cities at the German-Polish border.

At the US-Mexico border, one finds a good share of formal dual citizens (which Mexico has allowed since 2000) and informal binationals (born on one side and raised on the other), creating intriguing third and fourth identity group boxes to tick in interviews and surveys about the region—an opportunity heretofore missed in most US-Mexico borderlands research.

Do binational identities exist in other world regions or do people simply identify in communal, caste, or linguistic identity groups rather than in "borderland" identities? If such border identities once existed, one wonders about the conditions under which they persist or decline, particularly with the emergence of walls, fences, and harsh migration policies such as those enforced by India's Border Security Force. Among Bengali-speaking people, divided by Partition and then by fences and the Indian Border Security Force, contemporary alienation may be imposed by their own government as well as from the other side of the border.

Political science perspectives on strong-to-weak states and statelessness also add nuance to border categories and their critique. The United States celebrates well over 200 years of existence, while Mexico will soon celebrate 200 years (1821–2021). Each operates with the trappings of democracy, though with considerable flaws in governance and corruption. Relatively recent "statelessness" characterizes many border regions in the postcolonial world, as was the case in India, Pakistan, and Bangladesh until a half-century ago with the construction of roads and new forms of communication. India has been called the largest democracy in the world, given its regular elections, but border people's experience with democracy is an empirical one, likely to raise questions about the extent of democracy in distant frontiers. Consistent democracy and good governance are dubious prospects in postcolonial Bangladesh and Myanmar, the first born in civil war and the second existing under long-term military rule. One wonders how many generations it takes for national identities to sink into people's hearts and souls, particularly when some communities are ill-treated by an authoritarian state.

Even in contemporary times, people may be ambiguous about the state in which they live. In Japan's outlying islands with US military presence, as a survey study of residents on one of them shows, a large percentage of islanders are uncertain about their state affiliation. Many states in Africa are weak and hardly able to police their borderlines. In failed or weak states, border people may resent or resist government interference with borderland economic opportunities or they may ally with state agents who eagerly augment their earnings (euphemistically called rent in political science).[21] Thus, Martínez's categories may be less relevant to postcolonial countries where governments assert but do not fully control their territorial borders. Presumably, some degree of state presence should exist if cross-border institutional presence is to be developed. In my I-2 framework below, inclusive institutions are a core component of healthy and prosperous borderlands.

Another core component, the other part of I-2, includes an examination of income inequalities and wage differences. Thinking about figure 3.2 and the graded, less equal C, D, and F borderlands in ratio terms, interdependent borderlands are quite common but need to be unpacked and historicized as to the degrees of inequality in people's livelihoods. Interdependence has long been the label for US-Mexico metropolitan regions that transcend the border—an interdependence built for over 50 years on low-cost labor and transportation of goods manufactured in Mexico for a US market which has barely changed the living standards for Mexican assembly-line workers, even after a two-decade-old free trade agreement. Mexico's so-called democracy does not attend to working people's interests in higher legal minimum wages, for its elite and political machinery have been captured by political parties that serve a neoliberal economic development strategy. Interdependence presumably begins with considerable wage inequalities, but a normative focus implies a move toward reduced wage inequalities rather than a continuation of the apartheid-like containment of hundreds of thousands of Mexican factory workers in Tijuana and Ciudad Juárez alone. Despite use of an upbeat word like "interdependence" to describe the relationship, surely the persistence of aggravated wage inequalities cannot be a model for other border regions in the world.

From borderlands categories and the ways they might be adjusted to cover a post-9/11 and postcolonial world of multiple states of extreme inequalities in people's everyday lives, we move to North-based models that posit movement beyond interdependence toward integration. Such models seem to assume democracies and good governance. Such assumptions exclude a majority of states and borderlands around the world. Curiously, the models say nothing about wage inequalities.

Toward Integration

Several theorists pose models outlining multiple processes that, once strengthened, would presumably move borderlands toward equitable interdependence and greater integration. Integrated borderlands represent an optimal category in normative perspectives. Integration stage theorists make key factors visible: border political voices, coordinated policies, cultures, commerce, and trade. But theorists say little about triggering moves toward shared prosperity and greater wage equalities. Unless wage inequalities are addressed, in democratic institutions in which multiple stakeholders have voices, integrated borderlands could perpetuate hypersegregated wage structures to maintain a so-called globally competitive economy. In most of Europe or at the Canada-US border, the vantage point for some of these theories, greater equality already prevails (graded the A ratio of figure 3.2), but this is not the case at the US-Mexico border.

Canada-based geographer Emmanuel Brunet-Jailly posits four "concurrent and essential roles" toward border integration, in no particular sequential order. Arrows go in both clockwise and counterclockwise directions without a starting point. These roles include "local cross-border culture," "policy activities of multiple levels of government" to link vertically and horizontally across specific issues, "local cross-border political clout," and "market forces and trade flows." He gives us conceptual language on the tools and cues for these processes. If roles straddle the border, integrating effects occur.[22] Brunet-Jailly's model includes a much-needed emphasis on institutions, including presumably nongovernmental institutions covered in the "political clout" process. Such clout should include the voices of multiple sectors, not only the already-powerful stakeholders like business groups and local government.

The inclusion of culture and political clout also offers useful counter in a world of "Othering" (analyzed in chapter 2), in popular culture (chapter 11), and in what has been described as the "democratic deficit" at the border.[23] In many regions of the world, except perhaps Euroregions (see chapter 5), decisions about borderlands are often made in distant capital cities with national or other foreign policy interests at heart. To the extent border leaders activate processes, Brunet-Jailly's inclusion of cross-border political clout opens the opportunity for both local officials and nongovernmental organization (NGO) leaders to make or influence decisions about the borderlands. All too often, current NGO leaders with cross-border power come mainly from the trade and business sectors, such as chambers of commerce; voice is muted for working people and residents affected by externalities (such as pollution and additional taxes to reduce trade flow times). Presumably, they would articulate a need for living wages, among other issues. As such, the model needs a *democratic* injection to include multiple stakeholders in the cross-border clout of institutions. Few, if any, scholars address the nature and composition of these institutions except to differentiate those operating in coordination, cooperation, and collaboration from those with a mutual understanding to "stay out of each other's way."[24] For this reason, we must also plug institutions and their composition into models that represent more diverse border people and sectors.

In yet another theoretical development toward border integration, Canadian geographers Victor Konrad and Heather Nicol build on Brunet-Jailly's model. Their construction derives from the Canadian-US context of two strong, democratic states rather than creating a model for the whole world with its varied types of states. For Konrad and Nicol, cross-border political clout becomes a catalyst[25] that influences—in their circular, counterclockwise diagram—"socially constructed and reconstructed identities" that in turn influence "multiple levels of cross-border culture," that influence policy activities of multiple levels of government, and ultimately that influence "market forces and trade flows." Conceivably, interventions could occur at any point to reinforce the integration tendencies.

Konrad and Nicol are to be applauded for advancing, strengthening, and clarifying existing models. For them, political clout is a driver. Yet I would ask again about local clout: by whom, advancing which interests, and in what kinds of institutions involving and representing multiple stakeholders in the borderlands? While trade potentially fosters interaction and integration, business alone cannot and should not be the only voice in cross-border political clout.

The neoliberal era, emphasizing limited government and maximized market forces, is a shroud that shapes the possibilities of local border clout and trade. In many parts of the industrialized world, trade union membership is on the decline. The emergent tendency is toward new localism, heretofore used within states in the context of a neoliberal global economy. In that model, national and regional governments downsize and devolve responsibilities onto local governments which subsequently rely on NGOs to provide services previously supplied by the state. Without sufficient resources or subsidies from the states, impoverished localities race to the bottom in the provision of services and support.[26] At the US-Mexico border, new localism or urban growth machines, coupled with extremely low voter turnout rates on the US side of the border, add up to a system that burdens local property taxpayers for enhancing border trade flows through their communities. While such concepts are not part of the Konrad-Nicol model, nuance could be drawn from it.

Konrad and Nicol acknowledge that political clout at an asymmetrical border has usually emanated from the powerful side. Also useful is their emphasis on reconstructed identities, for the "Othering" processes require adjustments on both sides in everyday life and in popular culture (see chapter 11; for example, films affect not only the mainstream population but also border people's perceptions of their region). However, as noted above, theorists make positive assumptions about market forces and trade, presuming shared prosperity for many, but the US-Mexico border shows no compulsory move in that direction or toward the reduction of wage inequalities. Of course, the Canada-US ratio from the Border Inequalities Database shows it to be among the more equal in the world (i.e., A grade). But if this model is to work elsewhere, we cannot assume that trade volume and growth will lead to trickle-down benefits for border people working on the other side, the less powerful side, in institutions that represent the whole community.

In an early volume that put cross-border regions on analytic maps, Bob Jessop lays out multiple trajectories of cross-border institutional development that could possibly be generalized to other parts of the world.[27] In other words, borders begin at different points. In chapter 12, I will apply his ideas to the content in the body of this book, for he reveals historic trade networks, supranational bodies that stimulate trade, and exploited, uneven development models.

Border theorists with a normative agenda to move toward integration make valuable contributions to Martínez's categories of borders and border identities. Namely, they highlight processes, culture, and institutions with a special focus on trade. Yet there is still room in future border theorizing to push for a reduction in wage inequality and to promote shared prosperity. Institutions, NGO and governmental, represent official and business interests, but the voices of working people and everyday borderlanders also need to be heard.

Reducing Inequalities: Wherefore Institutions?

Until Spain-based economist Iñigo Moré did so, no attempts had been made to build incomes, equality, and inequality into models. In his ranking of 197 country pairs from the most unequal to the most unequal, he uses 2004 data of both gross domestic product (GDP) per capita and in purchasing power parity (PPP), the latter to "eliminate distortions caused by the relative differences in prices measured in foreign currencies." In chapter 5 of his book, *The Borders of Inequality*, he takes three cases using data from 1970 to 2004 to show the rapid upturn in inequality in Spain-Morocco, the downturn in inequality in Germany-Poland, especially since 1992, and erratic turns in the unequal USA-Mexico pair.[28] Not unexpectedly, he found 7 of the 10 most *equal* borders in the world, with near 1:1 ratios, in Europe. Of the 20 most *unequal* borders, only 2 are found with at least one side of the pair in Europe (Norway-Russia; Spain-Morocco) and the rest are found in countries of the South. As others have noted, walls and fences tend to be built in unequal borderlands. Counting 25 barriers (walls or fences) built since the fall of the Berlin Wall, Reece Jones contrasts per capita GDP in US$ 2010 figures: the average for wall/fence builders was $14,067, while for countries on the other side it was $2,801.[29] Chapter 8 on security contains a section on walls and fences.

Although Moré is the only theorist herein who covers northern and southern countries with income data, he covers policies but not specific cross-border institutions that may produce upturns, downturns, and erraticism in changes for country pairs. Furthermore, Moré says nothing about categories of borders, whether they are alienated, coexistent, interdependent, integrated, or something else altogether. For all the valuable contributions Moré made, his database from 2004 needs to be updated and, like the North-based theorists above, he seems to assume that people are state-identified or state-contained. For countries in the South, the size of the informal, illegal, and illicit economies may not even be counted, as I have indicated earlier.

Clearly, a good place to begin addressing inequalities is among binational border pairs and regional borderlands, many of which may be identified as alienated, coexistent, or interdependent in Martínez's terms, or they may be assigned other terms and placed in categories yet to be named. This is my aim in building a model on existing theoretical foundations. However, harking back to global inequalities and the champagne-glass-like graph, much still needs to be done to move toward a world of greater shared prosperity.

Concluding Reflections: Building the I-2 Model

We have examined inequalities from global to local borderlands perspectives. Using the Border Inequalities Database, we see a range of country pairs with ratios of more-to-less equality and their persistence over time.

The chapter analyzed existing border theories, categories, and process models that give us conceptual tools to forge ways of understanding borderlands worldwide and the political, cultural, and commercial moves toward more balanced interdependence and integration. Theorists assume relatively strong states and good governance, although the near-200 states in the world vary enormously in these regards. To their credit, theorists highlight political clout. However, in a neoliberal economic mode, with new localism and near-total focus on trade alone, the powerful stakeholders might be limited to business organizations and local governments propelled toward urban growth. The theories say little to nothing about people's livelihoods *in* borderlands, such as their wages in regional spaces of shared prosperity and comprehensive institutions of inclusion. For these reasons, inequalities and inclusive institutions must be core concepts.

With the examples threaded throughout the chapter, I have previewed the historical, postcolonial, state, governance, and wage issues highlighted in regional chapters that follow in part II of the book. The issues put inequalities and institutions at the center of the ways we understand borderlands and the processes toward cooperation and integration.

The I-2 model focuses on two key issues. The first is *reduced inequalities* in incomes and wages in borderlands as an investment strategy, a condition or standard, or a priority of regional institutions and supranational institutions. Shared prosperity norms and standards should govern the political clout and culture in borderlands where human security prevails. The second is the construction of inclusive *cross-border institutions* with border voices from more than just the business and trade sectors. As some models of interdependence show, business may have stakes in maintaining low-cost labor and hard borders for short-term profit advantages. NGOs, states, and international bodies ought to highlight borderlands as a focus rather than relying on territorially trapped state-centric models.

We ought to move toward a world in which graded country pairs reflect more equal A or B levels rather than C, D, and F levels (or the inequitable stains of border pairs on a world map, the outliers noted in this chapter). Global inequality graphics ought to be shaped more like a normal glass instead of a champagne glass that symbolizes institutionalized privilege and capital for the few. In such a world, better governance and democratic norms would prevail, providing the context in which to put I-2 and implied changes into practice.

Notes

[1] Adrian Leftwich, "Theorizing the State," pp. 179–95, and Lise Rakner, "Governance," pp. 225–40, in Peter Burnell, Lise Rakner, and Vicky Randall, eds., *Politics in the Developing World* (London and NY: Oxford University Press, 2014; 4th edition).

[2] Todd Miller, *Border Patrol Nation: Dispatches from the Frontlines of Homeland Security* (San Francisco: City Lights Books, 2014).

[3] M. Foucher quoted in Willem van Schendel, *The Bengal Borderland: Beyond State and Nation in South Asia* (London: Anthem Press, 2005).

[4] Joan Anderson and James Gerber, *Fifty Years of Change on the US-Mexico Border: Growth, Development and Quality of Life* (Austin, University of Texas Press, 2008). In *The Economist's* Special Report on India, May 23, 2015, internal state GDP is provided, p. 4. In my introduction to *Cities and Citizenship at the US-Mexico Border,* Staudt, César Fuentes, and Julia Monárrez, eds. (NY: Palgrave USA, 2010), p. xv, I apply Saskia Sassen's phrase of "methodological nationalism" to challenges in borderlands studies. In the *Free Trade? Informal Economies* book, Staudt (Philadelphia: Temple University Press, 1998), research illustrated those challenges, for example US census reports of per capita income versus Mexico census reports of 1 Minimum Wage, 2 Minimum Wages, 3 Minimum Wages, and other examples.

[5] Kathleen Staudt and Irasema Coronado, *Fronteras no Más* (NY: Palgrave USA, 2002).

[6] American Civil Liberties Union (ACLU) Regional Center for Border Rights, *Guilty Until Proven Innocent: Living in New Mexico's 100-Mile Zone* (Las Cruces, NM: ACLU, 2014).

[7] Hastings Donnan and Thomas M. Wilson, *Borders: Frontiers of Identity, Nation and State* (Oxford: Berg Publishers, 1999), p. 8.

[8] See the UN Development Programme's calculation notes at http://www.undp.org. (Accessed constantly.)

[9] World Bank, http://www.worldbank.org/en/topic/poverty/overview.

[10] Iñigo Moré, *The Borders of Inequality* (Tucson: University of Arizona Press, 2011).

[11] See the World Bank chart: http://data.worldbank.org/indicator/SI.POV.GINI. Based on OECD data for its affiliates, inequality increased from 1985 to 2013, with the highest increase in the most unequal of the bunch, the United States from .34 to .40, with Britain and Japan next, and the least increase in Australia and Canada, but the greatest equality in Norway and Denmark, around .25. *The Economist,* "Sighing for Paradise to Come," June 4, 2016, p. 22.

[12] Deborah Stone, *Policy Paradox* (NY: W. W. Norton, 2012), chapter 8.

[13] Deepti Misri, *Beyond Partition: Gender, Violence, and Representation in Postcolonial India* (Champaign-Urbana: University of Illinois Press, 2014), p. 15.

[14] *The Economist,* "The Trouble with GDP," April 30, 2016, p. 10.

[15] *The Economist,* April 30, 2016, p. 46. In Andreas's first chapter of his 2000 book *Border Games* (Ithaca, NY: Cornell University Press), the word smuggling and linguistic derivatives are mentioned over 100 times in 11 pages.

[16] Oscar Martínez, *Border People* (Tucson: University of Arizona Press, 1994), pp. 6–10. On power asymmetry, also see David Newman, "The Lines That Continue to Separate Us: Borders in our 'Borderless' World," *Progress in Human Geography* 30, 2 (2006), pp. 143–61.

[17] Oscar Martínez, *Mexico's Uneven Development* (NY and London: Routledge, 2016).

[18] Kathleen Staudt, "The Border Performed in Films: Produced in Both Mexico and the US 'To Bring Out the Worst in a Country,'" *Journal of Borderlands Studies* 14, 4 (2014), pp. 465–80.

[19] Guadalupe Correa-Cabrera and Kathleen Staudt, "An Introduction to the Multiple US-Mexico Borders," *Journal of Borderlands Studies* 29, 4 (2014), pp. 385–90.

[20] See a fine documentary about the Arizona-Sonora borderlands by Luis Carlos Davis, *389 Miles* with interviews from a variety of voices (available on YouTube); and Cari Lee Skogberg

Eastman, *Shaping the Immigration Debate: Contending Civil Societies on the US-Mexico Border* (Boulder: Lynne Rienner Publishers, 2012).

[21] Rakner, "Governance," section on corruption, pp. 231–6. On the Japanese island research, see Yuki Sato, "Exploring 'Borderlity' on the Ogasawara Islands," *Journal of Borderlands Studies* 26, 3 (2011), pp. 327–44.

[22] Emmanuel Brunet-Jailly, ed., "Introduction: Borders, Borderlands, and Porosity," in his *Borderlands: Comparing Border Security in North America and Europe* (Ottawa: University of Ottawa Press, 2007), pp. 9–10.

[23] Tony Payan, "Crossborder Governance in a Tristate, Binational Region, " in Kathleen Staudt, César Fuentes, and Julia Monárrez, eds., *Cities and Citizenship at the US-Mexico Border* (NY: Palgrave USA, 2010), pp. 217–44. Turnout in *local* government elections in El Paso and other Texas counties typically is limited to about a tenth of registered voters.

[24] Payan, "Crossborder Governance," pp. 230–31.

[25] Victor Konrad and Heather N. Nicol, *Beyond Walls: Re-inventing the Canada-United States Borderlands* (Hampshire, England; Burlington, VT: Ashgate, 2008), pp. 54–5.

[26] From Martin Jones, Rhys Jones, Michael Woods, Mark Whitehead, Deborah Dixon, and Matthew Hannah, *An Introduction to Political Geography* (London: Routledge, 2015; 2nd edition), chapter 4.

   On global neoliberalism, it should be noted that the meaning contrasts sharply with the peculiar US use of the word liberal for proactive government policies generally associated with the Democratic Party. Before the "new localism" model, Harvey Molotch and others emphasized cities and their productive space as "urban growth machines," though border metropolitan regions were not part of analysis. For a volume that treats two cities in the large Paso del Norte metropolitan area as a region, see Kathleen Staudt, César Fuentes, and Julia Monárrez Fragoso, eds, *Cities and Citizenship at the US-Mexico Border* (NY: Palgrave USA, 2010).

[27] Bob Jessop, "The Political Economy of Scale," in Markus Perkmann and Ngai-Ling Sum, eds., *Globalization, Regionalization and Cross-Border Regions* (NY: Palgrave Macmillan, 2002), pp. 25–49.

[28] Moré, *The Borders of Inequality*, p.12 quote and p. 118.

[29] Reece Jones, *Border Walls* (NY and London: Zed, 2012), pp. 10–11.

PART II

Regional Case Studies

In part II, three chapters cover borderlands in different world regions of the North and South, tapping histories, concepts, and images introduced previously in part I. Part II's final chapter covers maritime borders.

Chapter 4 examines North American interdependent borderlands, with a special focus on the United States–Mexico borderlands and its fixed territorial lines set in 1848 and 1853. Border people there live and work in some of the world's most unequal borderlands, with GDP per capita figures showing little dent in the inequality since the North American Free Trade Agreement despite enormous increases in the volume of trade.

Chapter 5 moves to the seemingly coexistent, partially alienated South Asian borderlands, with a special focus on northeastern Indian borderlands with Bangladesh, Myanmar, China, Nepal, and Bhutan. Most of these countries underwent the ravages of colonialism and neocolonialism, with territorial lines drawn in Partition and conflict, only partially halted in the mid-20th century. GDP per capita figures show relative equality, but in comparative poverty from world perspectives, though more recent economic growth put China and Bhutan on different pathways. Cross-border institutional activity is nearly absent, even for shared transnational waterways. A securitized state, India stifles informal licit trade which has an historic base and would be a good place to generate more interaction and interdependence.

Chapter 6 analyzes the integrated European region, one bordered after World War II's post-conflict and until recently called borderless for Schengen Area countries but now challenged with the influx of over a million refugees from war-torn, re-bordered areas of the postcolonial western Asian world. The supranational European Union is institutionally complex and envelops nations of more democracy, equality, and human security than most parts of the world thanks in part to peaceful cooperation going back a half-century.

In chapter 7, we move back to Asia again with coverage of maritime borders and their many conflicts and tensions partly addressed in an institution and its rules of recent vintage, the United Nations Convention on the Law of the Sea (UNCLOS). The chapter considers whether powerful states like China, the distant United States, and Australia can deal with simmering and continuing tensions over the South China Sea with respect and acknowledgment for other states in the region which have legitimate rights and claims to the seemingly borderless seas.

After part II, part III will examine issues and policies that address three major concerns threaded through the regional chapters: security, migration, and trade. I plant kernels for possible solutions in these chapters, but part IV contains explicit action-oriented strategies for dealing with popular culture, advocacy, and policy changes.

Chapter 4

The Americas
Interdependent
US-Mexico Borderlands

Indigenous people, as in most other parts of the world, resided in lands now called the Western Hemisphere or the Americas for short: North America, Central America, and South America. While many people refer to the United States as "America," identifying themselves as "Americans," these terms also resonate with people in *all* of the Americas—north, central, and south. This chapter focuses on bordering processes in North America—Canada, the United States, and Mexico—with a special focus on the latter two countries. North America's southern border, once at the boundary of the southwestern United States, has become the Guatemala-Mexico border since the North American Free Trade Agreement (NAFTA) was implemented in 1994, south of which we find Honduras, El Salvador, and Nicaragua.

The US-Mexico borderlands, called an *interdependent* borderland for many decades, is among the more unequal borderlands in the world, according to the work of Moré and as analyzed in the previous chapter. Figure 4.1 contains data on per capita income inequality for the countries mentioned here, making obvious one of the main drivers of northward migration. In this chapter, we ask whether these unequal borderlands, with the absence of comprehensive cross-border institutions, have the potential to become more balanced or even integrated borderlands. Despite extensive trade, constrained by US border security apparatus, the low wages, human *insecurity*, and poor governance in countries to the south propel migration in people's search for work and shared prosperity.

Enshrined in NAFTA, the three peaceful neighboring countries of North America have become even more interdependent since 1994. North American states trade extensively with each other, but the movement of people is complicated, certainly for those without authorization, but also for those with documents who must pass through the complex machinery of the largest US police force (agents affiliated with the Department of Homeland Security) and its bureaucratic apparatus (customs) at border ports of entry positioned between approximately 800 miles of fences and walls and the Rio Grande. The *legal* movement of people and goods is enormous in numerical terms. Combined totals of pedestrian, automobile, and truck travel at the land borderlines

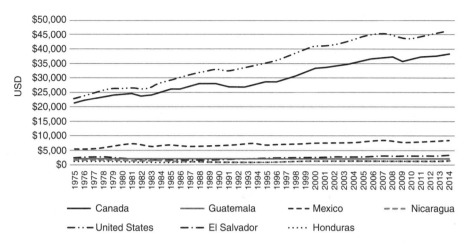

FIGURE 4.1 Comparative GDP Per Capita Growth, North and Parts of Central America, 1975–2014.

Source: Based on a design by Jakub Zajakala, research assistant. Data from Border Inequalities Database, compiled from World Bank and International Monetary Fund figures.

between the United States and Mexico are measured at approximately 150 million *legal* crossings per year,[1] down just after 9/11 and during periods of high criminal violence in northern Mexico but over decades on a steadily upward trend. Much of this legal crossing occurs daily and weekly in interdependent economies.

To examine North America with a border lens, my overview begins in the 19th century—a longer historical period than other border regional chapters—in order to cover the US annexation of half of Mexico's territory in 1848 and 1853, the redrawn boundaries in Texas (and Mexico), and US designs on parts of Canada. The chapter also analyzes the plight of various indigenous peoples who lost their lives and lands except for the territorially bounded "reserves" (in Canada), "reservations" (in the United States), and *"reducciones"* (in Mexico, a term which perhaps comes closest to describing the process of land reduction). Historical memory must also include the forced resettlement and sale of enslaved people from Africa, some of whom escaped to cross borders "illegally" into Mexico and Canada via the Underground Railroad.

For much of history, the North America borders were relatively porous. However, studies on the low-intensity conflict and militarization of the border became prescient predictors of the deepening and hardening re-bordering processes reinforced with the growing border patrol apparatus throughout the United States.[2] The Canadian-US border is the longest international border in the Americas, extending over 5,000 miles, and includes Alaska (purchased from Russia, with boundary demarcation decades later), the 49th Parallel, and the Great Lakes. Most Canadians live just north of the border, with relative equality (graded A level, see chapter 3) to the United States in economic terms, from the Pacific region through the Great Plains and Great Lakes.

In contrast, the US-Mexico border stretches for nearly 2,000 miles, comprised of various types of terrain from deserts to mountains to tropics as well as 14 interdependent twin cities. It is inhabited by approximately 14 million people (adding both US border county and Mexican *municipio* populations).[3] A bit more than a decade ago, depending on which economic indicator is applied to 2004 data, Iñigo Moré called it the 17th and the 26th most unequal border in the entire world.[4] According to my Border Inequalities Database, it has been consistently graded at D to F levels over the years. Based on *minimum wages* in 2016, the ratio is 10:1, given US minimum wages of $7.25 per hour or approximately US$60 per day, and Mexican minimum wages of 73 *pesos* per day (recently raised to 80 *pesos* per day), or approximately US$4–5 per day (with currency devaluations, the *peso* fluctuated from US$12–21 in the 2014–2017 period). Canadian legal minimum wages vary by province from C$10–12 per hour (hovering about 80 cents to the US$1 in 2015–2016). Trade since NAFTA has grown rapidly, making its multiple borders and ports of entry highly interdependent but well-monitored and controlled, complete with homegrown binational institutions that facilitate movement under heavy US security apparatus.[5] The Cascadia region of Seattle and Vancouver represents a well-developed border region, yet the area has no supranational institution like the European Union with regional border funds. The Bush-era Security and Prosperity Partnership, with only government and businesspeople on its advisory boards, was short-lived. The volume of crossing is staggering—as shown in the official data for 1995–2015 on the Bureau of Transportation Statistics website—from trucks (counted in the hundreds of millions) to pedestrian vehicles (counted in the billions) to every conceivable figure one might desire.[6]

In 1848 and 1853, after the Mexican-American War, the Treaty of Guadalupe Hidalgo, and the Gadsden Purchase, the border was redrawn and Mexico lost nearly half of its territory, just over 550,000 square miles. With the Chamizal Treaty in 1963, the United States returned one square mile of land to Mexico to channel a meandering river with different names in each country, the Río Bravo/Rio Grande. In historic and contemporary times, the central region served as a major gateway for south-north/north-south migration and trade, known as the Camino Real (from Santa Fe to Ciudad Chihuahua)—a name still invoked by binational businesspeople in the border region. As I unpack the local to global dimensions of the region below, historical perspectives reveal deep roots of foreign direct investment and large mining operations, joined by a binational elite, which add more than a century of global economic complexity to the interaction between two asymmetrical powers.

History Matters

As it did in other parts of the world, European colonialism shaped the people, territories, economies, and the land that subsequently became the contiguous states of the Western Hemisphere. The broadly defined Americas experienced colonialism longer than any other world region with a massive shift of 7–9 million Europeans, especially in the late 19th century and thereafter, who imposed

Spanish, Portuguese, English, French, and Dutch languages on a hemisphere that once was home to speakers of 2,000 indigenous languages, now reduced to 800.[7]

Treasure-seeking conquerors (*conquistadores*), missionaries, and settlers also made their mark on peoples and lands before nationalism and national identities took hold. Peter Winn analyzes the rush for gold and silver in brutal mining conditions that led to a large number of deaths—sometimes within weeks—from poverty, imported diseases, and forced labor.[8] He says Spaniards imported a caste-like social hierarchy, with whites at the top and people of color at the bottom, and people of mixed race somewhere in between. In addition to chapter 8 of his mammoth book, part 4 of his documentary series *The Americas* covers this well. Until colonialism on most South American contiguous lands ended in 1825, with legacies of centralized rule yet inevitable local autonomy, neither imperial rule nor Simón Bolívar's dreams of a united region could be achieved. Colonial viceroyalties re-bordered the land into eight republics, then 12 states, and finally multiple states with lingering border disputes. Even the Central Americans left Mexico two years after its independence in 1823 to form a federation.[9] Indigenous people lived on land with porous borders, but when settlers, fur traders, and others arrived, they gradually lost their way of life, becoming trapped in new borders.

In the transnational slave trade, women's offspring became part of the human trafficking market, central to the economic foundation of plantation economies. While Mexico abolished slavery in 1829, US abolition happened only after Lincoln's Emancipation Proclamation of 1863 and the end of the Civil War in 1865, with the addition of a constitutional (14th) amendment requiring that citizenship be automatically granted to all those born in the United States. The historic roots of citizenship are relevant because the definition of "citizen" is contested in contemporary US immigration debates. In some US states, including Texas, legislators recently introduced bills that challenge citizenship based on US birth, an issue that affects the children of noncitizen adults. Despite constitutional guarantees of freedom and due process of law, legacies of slavery and colorism in the Americas instigated and perpetuated racism against and segregation of persons of color, relegating them to second-class citizenship whether native-born, immigrant, or descendants of immigrants.

Looking northward in the late 18th century, Valentine and McDougall analyze how US and British treaties in the "Old Northwest" (Detroit, initially a French, then a British settlement) drawing borderlines through the Great Lakes imposed a new reality and undermined a way of life for indigenous peoples (initially named "Aboriginal" peoples in Canada, but now called First Nations). Settlers and traders exchanged "gifts" (including weapons) with indigenous leaders who sought to maximize benefits with their potential foreign allies, including some who even shifted their settlements. With an established border in 1796, Indian confederacies moved back and forth across the border to try to maintain their resource base. "The border offered the opportunity to choose between state regulatory systems, but in both cases, [European] settlement eclipsed their traditional lifestyles."[10]

As US settlers moved west, the borders shifted along with how and where the United States conceptualized the frontier. Re-bordering occurred by conquest, payment, and negotiation. Nowadays US schoolchildren read about the Louisiana Purchase of 1803, a huge swath of land once conquered by both Spain and France, but before them, inhabited by indigenous peoples. Once colonized by Spain, when Mexico achieved its independence in 1821, its territory included not only the area we now know as its sovereign state but all of the land bordering it to the north in what is now the Southwestern United States—California, Nevada, Arizona, Colorado, New Mexico, and Texas. With a new and weak central government, Mexico's loss of Tejas in 1836, when it seceded as a separate republic (later annexed by the United States), dealt a blow to the fledgling new state. Mexico lost not only land but also California's deep-sea ports at Los Angeles, San Diego, and San Francisco, and natural resources like gold, copper, and silver. Oscar Martínez asks and answers the question about Mexico's uneven development compared with that of the United States, focusing on the territorial loss and the remaining geographic challenges in what is now Mexico.[11] Mexico's geography consists of rugged mountain ranges and limited waterways (including deep-sea ports)—geographic advantages that have historically served to facilitate long-distance internal and external trade.

Indigenous or Native American peoples, some settled and others nomadic, resisted incursions on their spheres of influence but gradually succumbed—at least those remaining after massive loss of lives—to re-territorialized, shrunken, bordered spaces. The plight of indigenous peoples shows parallels throughout North America.

When the Spaniards first came to the State of Chihuahua (in what is now a border state with Texas and New Mexico) in the 16th century, they anticipated riches and used violence to establish themselves, but initially they focused on mining and converting people to Christianity. As historian of Mexico's northern region Mark Wasserman writes,

> The native tribes stubbornly fought *conquistador* and friar alike. Indian rebellions racked seventeenth-century Chihuahua. The Tarahumara [now known as Rarámuri people] rose in bloody revolt four times between 1647 and 1697; each time they were crushed, but at terrible cost to the victors. The Indians revolted because the Spaniards stole their lands, herded them into settlements (*reducciones*), and enslaved them for arduous work in the mines. As it did for all the indigenous peoples of America, Spanish rule brought only misery and death for the Indians of the North.[12]

Wasserman said that Apache forays continued into the 19th century, with the national and state governments unable to restore peace, but also in conflict with the liberal federalists who preferred weak central authority. He said that in the 1830–1840s, Chihuahuenses offered bounty "for Apache scalps" financed by tax revenue and private entrepreneurs, but "the scheme failed . . . because bounty hunters killed Mexicans, whose hair was indistinguishable from that of the Apaches and who were easier prey."[13] Clearly, the brutalities produced treacherous and insecure times in the fluid borderlands.

Both massive in size, Mexico's northern states of Chihuahua and Coahuila became economic powerhouses and engines of economic growth. Yet the semi-arid climate, mountain ranges, and lack of rivers limited their prospects. In the 19th century, large landowners (*hacendados*) ruled economic empires in regions with considerable autonomy from the capital, Mexico City. Even the Mexican Revolution of 1910 offered variations in regional resistance and leadership to the dictatorship of Porfirio Díaz. The rigid economy, inequalities, and outcome of Mexico's revolution prompted people to migrate northward to the United States, which was hungry for their labor, especially since they were willing to work for lower wages than their US counterparts at higher pay than offered in Mexico.

Settler-imposed boundary lines created problems for indigenous peoples whose formerly porous land boundaries transcended the new US borders. Along the now-familiar 49th Parallel border with Canada—the former Montana territory, which later became a state within the United States—tense relationships developed with the Cree and Chippewa peoples who, prior to European-heritage settlers, crossed northward in summer and southward in winter to replenish their stock. Analyzing the unease during the early 1880s, Brenden Rensink reveals Montanans' discourse of "foreign Cree" and "domestic Cree" or even "our Cree," with territorial settlers viewing the foreigners (actually, the original inhabitants) as illegal (on their former land). The perception of legal and licit behavior varies with vantage point as analyzed in this book's later chapter on trade. As Chippewa Chief Little Shell pronounced: "We recognize no boundaries, and shall pass as we please."[14] Montanans periodically called on the federal government for help; Montana finally became a state in 1889.

Moving southward to the Arizona, United States–Sonora, Mexico border, the Tohono O'odham people lived for centuries on both sides of what was to become the US-Mexico border. First under Spaniards' heavy-handed rule, the ancestors rebelled in the late 17th and 18th centuries, but gradually retreated to a type of resistance that involved as much avoidance and withdrawal as possible.[15] Their land once stretched over vast territory to the Gulf of California, but shrunk to perhaps a fourth of its size in a 1919 reservation at the US-Mexico border on land that neither railroads nor settlers wanted. More recently, the US border security apparatus imposed a heavy hand on the inhabitants. Until 9/11, Tohono O'odham could freely cross the border, but increased security and staff in the US wars against drugs, immigrants, and terror have led to the border patrol's visible presence and authority. Desperately poor, with a per capita annual income of $8,000,[16] some people became involved in illegal trade, such as smuggling, while others did not, in a community divided over the extent to which they should cooperate with the federal government. The area is beset by division and contradictions amid poverty that security equipment hardly addresses.

This historical section shows continuous re-bordering as the United States and its settlers moved into Mexican and indigenous people's lands and developed economies linked to the national and global economy. The process had consequences for migration northward.

Migration for Work and Security

Mexicans moved northward largely for economic reasons. Although wage data from a century back prove difficult to verify, Mexicans who migrated to the United States could earn at least twice as much or more than their counterparts (now perhaps 5 to 10 times as much, year-round), yet got paid lower wages compared to Anglo counterparts in the United States. Detailed historical studies of the central borderlands, namely the border states of Chihuahua and Texas, document these crossing processes.[17] Mexican elites also moved northward, bringing their capital, given the political and economic instability of the 1910 Mexican Revolution and thereafter. El Paso may have the only street in the Western Hemisphere named after the dictator around whom the revolution was fought, Porfirio Díaz, with an Interstate 10 exit, the street then runs through a once-elegant and increasingly gentrified neighborhood of mansions near downtown where people say residents watched the Battle of Juárez from their balconies.

In a regional 19th century history of the wealthiest extended family in the Mexican State of Chihuahua, unparalleled in prerevolutionary Mexican history for its control, historian Mark Wasserman details how their empire expanded through marriage, business, and blood kinship and in collaboration with foreign (US) investors. He documents regional and export-oriented entrepreneurialism that approached, as he says, the tycoons and robber barons of the comparable US industrializing era. Luis Terrazas became the "world's largest landowner and cattleman"—controlling over 15 million acres for the extended family of the "most fertile and best watered" land with a hand in banks, transport, industry, and of course political offices.[18] The elites, who held state and municipal offices, concentrated their control over lands and indebted peons and "disgruntled" peasant laborers, offering refuge and protection from bandits and Apache raiders who, too, resisted the loss of their territory.[19]

Wasserman analyzes how the foreign-owned mining industry drained the state of natural resources, and how workers chafed under exploitation, paternalism, and the monopolization of most opportunities by the privileged political-economic elite. Scores of thousands of Mexicans migrated northward around the turn of the 20th century for higher (noted as "double" or "twice" the wage in an era of poor recordkeeping) though still-exploitative wages. Under conditions like these, most remaining small landholders (*rancheros),* miners, and a small but growing middle class eventually threw their support behind revolutionary forces in 1910 and thereafter.

Informally, binational business collaboration continued. Terrazas family members also moved northward, fleeing across the border with their capital, starting new business enterprises in the United States, and even getting compensation from the postrevolutionary government for expropriated land. One might call these businesspeople interlocking binational elites, both then and now. Border and national elite Terrazas family members cooperated with US border businesspeople binationally, serving on boards and enjoying investments in their enterprises.[20] Wasserman assesses that "The native elite-foreign enterprise system hurt the other sectors of Chihuahuense society and economic development."[21] The historical pattern of uneven development and binational cooperation among elites continues with the Border Industrialization Program and NAFTA.

Ciudad Juárez, named after the beloved indigenous president Benito Juárez, spurred growth on both sides of the border as a bigger city with its duty-free, free-trade zone in the years 1885–1905. According to historian Mario Garcíá, the policy hurt El Paso businesses which pressed to remove the zone. El Paso, Texas, also developed on an economy based on mining, ranching, the railroads, and cattle imports in an eastward-oriented "export" economy. Another of El Paso's crucial dependencies, he also says, involved its demand for and reliance on low-cost Mexican labor.[22] At that time, people moved relatively freely across the border, and Mexican labor recruiters facilitated the process.

Later, Ciudad Juárez developed economically with an infamous reputation for vice. During the US Prohibition of alcohol era of 1920–1933, people crossed the border to drink and bootleggers to buy liquor in Mexico to sell across the border in the United States. In South Texas, historian George Díaz documents the cross-border entrepreneur *tequileros* with their thriving businesses, illegal in the United States due to (with historical hindsight) misconceived prohibition law, but probably not illicit in the eyes of buyers and sellers (drawing on conceptual distinctions developed in chapter 10 on trade).[23] These practices paralleled the historic trade in Detroit-Windsor, where beer and other alcohol was illegal during Prohibition in the United States but not in Canada. Current parallels exist in the marijuana prohibition era.

US Immigration Policies: Increasingly Difficult Journeys

US immigration laws, complex and ever-changing, posed obstacles for people seeking to work and improve their livelihoods by crossing the border. The border "crossed" many Mexicans who lived in sparsely populated Tejas/Texas (once part of Mexico, then a nine-year independent republic, then annexed as a state in the United States, as noted earlier). Depending on the extent of labor demand, many Mexican migrants would cross in a pattern that migration scholars call circular; that is, crossing to earn money and then returning to Mexico. Legal or illegal? Demand for labor mattered. It is beyond the scope of this book to cover full details of US immigration reform; however, a summary is provided to show the widely variant reforms, confusing even for lawyers to follow but much more so for workers.

Mae Ngai's comprehensive overview of US immigration policy is useful for historical understanding. The United States maintained a relatively open-door policy to migrants from 1880–1920, with an influx of eastern, central, and southern Europeans. She notes that non-English-speakers were named "lesser whites" or "lower races," especially those from peasant backgrounds. Only in 1924 did Congress pass the first comprehensive immigration policy with ceilings and national-origin quotas in an era of nativist and antiradical fears.[24] Race, a constructed social category then and now, referred to national origins such as the "Romanian race," despite the ever-changing borders in Europe (illustrating the folly of such constructed categories). Unwanted migrants included those with diseases or who were likely to become "public charges." The complexity of law gave way to loopholes that lawmakers eventually tightened with more and more restrictive regulations. For example, migrants could go to no-quota Canada, live for five years, and then be admitted from there. Only in the 1920s did inspectors begin to require documentation from Mexico when, not surprisingly, deportations skyrocketed for what had suddenly become a chargeable offense: entry without a visa.[25]

At ports of entry in earlier eras, immigrants would present documents and pay fees for inspection. At the New York/New Jersey coast, Ellis Island remains the most famous of these port-of-entry places. But the desert region of El Paso–Ciudad Juárez has been called the Ellis Island of the Southwest as another huge entryway.

In 1917 and thereafter, inspectors required working-class Mexican crossers to submit to humiliating and dangerous chemical baths and delousing sprays, a supposedly public health–inspired practice not utilized in other border entry points. Historian David Romo documents these practices, their authorizations, and pictures in his detailed 2005 book about the region from 1893–1923. He and John Burnett of National Public Radio (NPR) narrate the practices, with pictures, in an eight-minute video entitled "Indignity on the Border."[26] The number of premature deaths and health problems caused by this multi-year practice will likely never be known.

Already-settled people faced insecurity. Seasonal migration from Mexico was common, but with the economic downturn during the Great Depression in the 1930s, deportation increased, even of US-Mexican American citizens and of children born US citizens. The United States "repatriated" (deported) more than 400,000 ethnic Mexicans, despite their jobs, property, and families.[27] By World War II, just as the United States declared Japanese Americans to be Japanese and a threat (which offered another opportunity to grab property) and resettled families into desert camps, the US economy continued to require more labor.

The era gave birth to the Bracero Program between the United States and Mexico from 1942–1964 in which recruiters went to Mexico to recruit labor for mostly seasonal visas (in circular-return migration), then inspected workers just across the border and loosely monitored their placement. The complex regulations deterred both US ranchers/farmers and Mexican "*braceros,*" so unauthorized workers, nearly a half million people annually, also moved northward at the height of the Bracero Program.[28] Roundups in the 1950s in the demeaningly named Operation Wetback resulted in nearly a million "repatriations" (deportations) at their peak in 1953.[29] In a major change to immigration law in 1965, the old quota system was not only eliminated but so too were exemptions from the most likely sending countries—mostly in the Western Hemisphere—and especially Mexico. Because of new forms of politically constructed illegality (that is, changes in the law), Mexicans found new obstacles unless the new openings for family, talents, investments, and technical skills could accommodate them.

Contemporary Immigration Practices

Two more path-breaking immigration laws, in 1986 and 1996, simultaneously loosened (for amnesty) and tightened the process for migrants and their ability to get jobs. The Immigration Reform and Control Act, signed by Republican President Reagan, allowed unauthorized migrants with proof of residence to apply for amnesty and provided a pathway to citizenship to approximately three million people, a majority of them of Mexican heritage. Moreover, under the employer sanctions provisions, employers could be held liable for hiring people not eligible to work—a common practice then and now but one which previously resulted in punitive consequences only for employees, not employers (though scantily enforced then and now). Widespread US popular opinion has been that this policy induced more migrants to move northward in the hopes of a new amnesty. Drawing on the US Census, the Pew Research Center (Hispanic Trends), and other agencies and think tanks, an estimated and widely accepted number of 11–12 million unauthorized people live in the United States. They come from a variety of world regions including Asia and Europe, many of them parents of US-born children who, as noted earlier, are citizens at birth. Most residents pay taxes, social security, sales and property taxes; various studies in Texas and the United States show net gains and economic growth from their presence. The implementation of NAFTA in 1994, which undermined small-scale agriculture in Mexico, also pushed people to migrate in search of a livelihood.

The 1996 immigration law tightened restrictions and made deportation easier. Unauthorized immigration gradually shifted from civil to criminalized offenses (expanding the penalty for infractions once considered misdemeanors, transforming them into "aggravated felonies," or retroactive deportable felonies).[30] With heightened polarization between Republicans and Democrats, even an immigration reform advocate like Republican president George W. Bush could not convince Congress in 2004 to support a bipartisan immigration reform bill.

Currently, immigration reform is at an impasse, with stiff and expensive border barriers such as a physical and technological *fence* (named by proponents) or *wall* (named by opponents) and huge increases in border policing. A failed bipartisan immigration reform bill in 2013 which prioritized high-cost border fencing and unrealistic apprehension goals was named with the evocative political phrase "border security," despite the fact that nearly half of the unauthorized people in the United States are those who have overstayed visas and likely travel via airports.[31] In one of the rare, large surveys to tap borderlanders' voices, a vast majority of the 1,427 respondents abhor the prospect of border walls. They seek more binational coordination among sister cities to deal with policy issues.[32] While the United States, with more than 300 million people, is not aging with a declining birth rate as quickly as many European countries—presumably incentivizing the acceptance of more immigrants there—such patterns loom in the future, albeit in a changing economy with unemployment rates that hover between 5 and 10 percent but one that also requires tax payments and mass consumption (whether people are here legally or not). Historically, the United States has not only needed Mexican labor, but has recruited it vigorously. The new security regime renders these economic forces less important or at least operates in tension with such forces.

Meanwhile, deportations continue with great vigor and speed, given ever-increasing technology and collaboration with local police and sheriffs' departments under the Secure Communities program. As DHS and legal experts testified in the 2011 PBS documentary *Lost in Detention*, the congressionally imposed deportation quotas represent "enforcement on steroids." Under the Obama administration, as figures and charts show, annual deportations increased to approximately 400,000 annually to meet these quotas in order to avoid putting new Department of Homeland Security (DHS) budget requests at risk.[33] The combination of these processes results in deportations for trivial traffic offenses, thus separating families.

Another part of the immigration picture involves legal permanent residents, who number almost a million people.[34] The figures classify people by age, marital status, employment, and category of admission, with family and employer sponsorship among the largest, respectively.

More recently, long-standing violence in Central American countries has prompted people to migrate northward in the hopes of seeking asylum and refugee status. Many NGOs in US border communities step up to shelter and feed migrants, often mothers and children who, once they are registered with "credible fear" documents and released to shelters, then contact relatives in the mainstream United States to whom they go, awaiting hearings. Others who are not so fortunate are sent to public and private, for-profit detention facilities that operate like jails, as the fine PBS documentary *Lost in Detention* shows. The US government is under no obligation to supply lawyers to these adults or children—many of them destitute—so their prospects for success usually depend on nonprofit, low-cost, or pro bono lawyers who can represent them in complicated hearings with politically appointed judges. The percentage of seekers granted asylum from Mexico and Central America is extremely low. Foreign policy alliances, rather than evidence of credible fear, seem to drive the low rates.

The Security Regime: Imposed on Borderlands

US fears about drugs and immigrants, later terror, has produced a security regime that constrains border life and crossing. Politicians often augment such fears during election times, as has been obvious during the 2016 presidential campaign. While Timothy Dunn analyzed the low-intensity conflict practices beginning in the 1980s, based on US–Central American strategies in El Salvador, Honduras, and Nicaragua, the US federal government's security apparatus imposed both Operation Gatekeeper (San Diego) and Operation Hold the Line (El Paso) in 1993 and 1994, around the time of NAFTA,[35] thus setting the stage for the ongoing tension between trade and security. The language itself—gatekeeper, line—evokes border barrier metaphors. One architect of El Paso's strategy, Silvestre Reyes, former US Border Patrol sector chief in the region who ran for elected office, co-constructed the architecture of militarized border control, and served in Congress for eight terms.[36] The blockades in heavily populated urban areas channeled migrants to less populated desert regions where the heat and aridity result in the deaths of up to 400 people annually (at least, based on the skeletal remains located).[37] The costs and the dangers of the journeys have increased,[38] and several films vividly convey the dangers from bandits, extortion, and sexual assault along the way, such as *Sin Nombre* and *7 Soles*.

Douglas Massey analyzed the escalating militarization of the border with a graph and numeric chart, showing the number of US agents growing by 600 percent since 1986 and the budget increasing by 24 times.[39] The costs have become a boon for border security industries, who occupy a business-government contractual market niche threatened with the return of US military troops from Afghanistan and Iraq.[40]

This section shows how immigration has become extraordinarily more complicated and dangerous over the years. The US government has built a huge bureaucratic apparatus to deal with border control, though its effects have spilled over into the entire country.

Everyday Life in the Borderlands

Local governments and grassroots participation in NGOs, including business, generate much of the cross-border cooperation, or lack thereof, given the federal government's preoccupation with national security and its various declared "wars" on terror, drugs, and immigrants. The US national security apparatus hinders timely crossing; and surveillance and checkpoints have become almost normalized except for periodic complaints about racial profiling and verbal and physical abuses, though official oversight focuses primarily on corruption and conflicts of interest. Wage inequalities require border control in which some businesses have stakes, yet the extremely low minimum wages in Mexico reduce retail sales on the US side of the border. Popular culture emphasizes difference and "Othering," though this backfires to some extent given that the majority of border residents share Mexican heritage and speak Spanish. Films like *The Global Assembly Line* and *Maquilopolis* provide perspectives on assembly-line workers not generally covered among the business boosters of the global economy. "Othering" films about the borderlands are plentiful, whether produced in Mexico or in the United States.[41]

When US policies that hardened the border went into effect, after the tragedy of 9/11, everyday life in the borderlands underwent change. The material below illustrates life in the contemporary central borderlands.

Like borderlands elsewhere, the majority of people view their twin cities and towns as single communities where issues are understood far better than by federal governments in capital cities. As the large survey cited above reveals, border people seek bridges, not barriers or walls. Their lives are interdependent, woven together, no matter what the state-centric discourse and polarizing politicians impose. They seek easier, efficient, and less time-consuming ways to cross the border and to work. The section below is divided into several sections on border life.

US and Mexican flags, with Texas in the background. Park in McAllen, South Texas.

Source: Photographer Fred Cady, used with permission.

Income-Stretching and Price Differentials

With interdependent economies in all fourteen twin cities and towns, changes on one side invariably fostered changes on the other. As a past Mexican President once said, when the United States sneezes, Mexico catches a cold. The reverse also occurs, for the local economies depend on shoppers going in both directions and on extensive crossing to visit relatives and friends. Each year, Mexican shoppers in both El Paso's downtown shops and high-end malls spend over US$1 billion for retail goods.[42]

Shopping in asymmetrical borderlands can offer opportunities for consumers seeking lower prices on the other, less prosperous side of the border. In the US and Mexico borderlands, many US residents pursue income-stretching activities. They get prescriptions filled at pharmacies, which often house doctors who can diagnose and administer injections. Dentists and eye doctors in Mexico offer health services at a fraction of the US cost. Mexico appears to be a partial solution to lack of health care for impoverished residents in the United States.

In an environmental health survey of just over 400 individuals conducted in a US border *colonia* (unplanned settlement), one respondent told his story of a near heart attack. He went to nearby US clinics and they brushed him off. He continued having symptoms, crossed the border, and saw a doctor at a pharmacy in Ciudad Juárez who told him a heart attack was imminent. He was given an injection, told to wait a few hours for observation, and paid his bill equivalent to US$20.[43] Mexico offers universal health care, of uneven quality and largely in urban areas. US insurance companies and medical providers do not support coverage in Mexico, with the exception of California. Binational border businesspeople have been developing a new economic niche of medical tourism to private hospitals in Ciudad Juárez that escorts US patients via a security corridor. Wealthy Mexicans cross for private hospital services in the United States, complete with hospital staff who tend to the needs of accompanying family members. Both sides of the border would do well to widen access for larger numbers of people.

Schools and Education

People spend part of their lives working or attending school on one side of the border or the other in cities all along the US-Mexico border. US citizen children, for example, may live on the Mexico side. Some US citizen children, who have never lived in Mexico or learned Spanish until they are deported with their parents, face hardships in Mexican schools, given the language challenges. The number of US citizen children now enrolled in Mexican schools is large, estimated at a half million. In the United States, the children of sales and property taxpaying residents with proof of residence, for example utility bills, have the right to attend public school as determined in the 1982 Supreme Court case, *Plyler v. Doe* 457 U.S. 202.

The US government imposed policies on border people that fostered tension and alienation well before 9/11. In early September 1993, it came as a great surprise to El Paso's Mayor, Chamber of Commerce, and others, on the eve of NAFTA (effective January 1, 1994), when the US Border Patrol blockaded the borderline. Border patrol officers sat in their vehicles within sight of each other, aiming to prevent unauthorized crossing outside the ports of entry. Before the blockade, people would sometimes cross surreptitiously; US Border Patrol officers drove around the city and county of El Paso, stopping people who "looked Mexican." Such a policy might border on ludicrous in a region where more than three-fourths of the population shares Mexican heritage and speaks Spanish. Essayists and novelists have written compelling and insightful analyses of this surveillance (as have academics), among them Benjamin Sáenz's "Exile: El Paso, Texas" and Debbie Nathan's "The Eyes of Texas Are Upon You," noting dress-code advice for those who want to "look US."[44]

US Border Patrol officers' harassment was common, especially in impoverished neighborhoods close to the borderline. At that time, few mechanisms existed for complaints against border patrol impunity, and besides, older people felt intimidated, worried about deportation. Timothy Dunn's book and documentary *The Time Has Come* analyzes the early 1990s era, focusing especially on heavy surveillance on and around Bowie High School close to the border named, ironically, after a Texas mainstream hero of the Alamo (Jim Bowie) enshrined in state folklore.[45] Over 95 percent of Bowie's students are

"Hispanic" and "economically disadvantaged" (in Texas government record-keeping parlance), and its traditions celebrate both Mexican and US heritages in song and dance at extracurricular events. US Border Patrol officers used binoculars to study girls' legs, pulled weapons on football players and their coach at morning practice, and assaulted students on their way to prom and graduation. Young residents became ready to challenge impunity, trying first to meet with the US Border Patrol Sector Chief who did not believe the reports. In the documentary, people's testimonies offered insight into federal police impunity. School principal Paul Strelzin, originally from the East Coast, said he could not believe these activities were happening in America. Amparo Woo, a student who after graduating with higher education degrees became assistant principal, recounted how during her youth, her US citizen brother was taken across the border, dropped off east of Ciudad Juárez, and then had to sell his shoes in order to pay for a bus to take him to the city center where he could call his mother. In alliance with the small and fledgling local Border Rights Coalition, students learned their rights (which when exercised, sometimes induced beatings) and eventually filed a lawsuit which was settled out of court. The Border Rights Coalition eventually grew into one of the largest human rights organizations in the region, the Border Network for Human Rights.

Many border teachers, on both sides of the border, have enriched classrooms with insights about the binational border region. While civic rituals, such as flag and song ceremonies, remain national in their respective languages, along with each state's versions of their histories and relations with the "Other," everyday classroom dramas in primary/elementary schools reflect the interaction of border people who frequently cross, celebrate holidays binationally, and eventually acquire bilingual skills.[46] Yet standardized testing regimes in each country have assumed greater importance, likely undermining some of the ways teachers incorporate context-rich curriculum at secondary school levels and above. The inclusion of North American, binational, or cultural heritages is poorly reflected in the "standards" developed (see chapter 12, "Toward Solutions"). Yet as Timothy Cashman documents in a small sample, high school teachers discuss binational issues and students appear hungry for more relevant curriculum.[47] More research is necessary in this and other borderlands with potentially conflicting or resonating curricula about the "Other" side.

Business and Labor

Binational business has long taken advantage of US and Mexican policies to facilitate cross-border trade that utilizes low-cost labor on the Mexico side and transportation via truck or rail to consumers on the US side. In 1965, Mexico created the Border Industrialization Program for foreign firms in the United States and elsewhere to establish export-processing manufacturing and to create jobs. However, most assembly-line workers earned the low legal minimum wage. Initially, around 80 percent of workers were women, thought to be not only nimble-fingered but also compliant to authority. In the 1983 documentary, *The Global Assembly Line*, Lorraine Gray compares the Mexican and Filipino export-processing industrialization strategy with foreign-owned factories. The documentary also features NGOs seeking to improve wages in accordance with skills or training for those forced to leave their factory jobs once they are in their 20s and 30s.

By the late 1980s, a gender-balanced labor force grew in electronics, garment, and automobile and harness factories as Detroit and surrounding cities obtained auto parts via subcontracts outside the United States.[48] NAFTA accelerated business interest in this "globally competitive" region in which maquila-connected employment reached a quarter-million in approximately 300 factories. Still, wages did not keep up with the cost of living, so real wages did not increase. Despite new buildings, comparisons of factory discipline and employment treatment are reminiscent of 19th- and early 20th-century industrialization. Convincing evidence comes from a large sample of women workers who experience "wage penalties" and continuing disempowerment.[49] (See details in chapter 10 on trade.)

When the Border Industrialization Program began, then and now, migrants moved northward from central and northern Mexican states for year-round employment. But the minimum wage of US$30 weekly, plus bonuses for punctuality, food coupons, and perfect attendance raising that weekly wage to US$40 or $50 weekly, could not adequately provide a decent standard of living for workers. Workers shop around for better subsidies, creating periodic turnover crises for management, or they simply quit. Of course, some migrate northward, as low wages impelled many of them to move to northern Mexico in the first place.

The Economist has criticized Mexico for its low legal minimum wage compared to other developing countries and for its slow-to-no increase over a decade compared to China.[50] At least a third of Mexico's labor force works informally, outside the regulated economy and in microenterprises. A comprehensive study of both a random sample of 600 households and samples of street vendors in the central borderlands shows that those able to cross the border could triple their earnings compared to assembly-line minimum-wage workers. However, those stuck on the Mexico side of the border earned extremely low wages. Of course, the border-crossing risk (without documents) and the "rent" paid to officials at the border who might also confiscate goods like clothing and toiletries present challenges to people seeking to support themselves.[51]

The drug trade has also made its way through the central and other borderlands. Once supplies from South America through maritime routes reduced, traffickers shipped goods through land routes and often used ruthless means to control their space, usually negotiated as secure with municipal and state authorities. Drug production and shipping became a sophisticated yet brutal business. Criminal organizations create earning opportunities that range from lucrative to paltry pay, including those for assassins and lookouts, which can be especially enticing to those who neither study nor work (*ni estudian ni trabajan,* or the so-called *ninis*). Mexican municipal police and some border agents on both sides of the border are tempted with bribes or threatened with harm into disregarding legality. During a violent time period of four years in Ciudad Juárez (2008–2011), when two transnational criminal organizations competed to control the space, murder rates skyrocketed tenfold from approximately 300 to 3,000 in a city of approximately 1.3 million where some residents fled northward or to other parts of Mexico. Yet on the US side of the border, big cities like El Paso and San Diego continue to be on the US top-10 safest list. Violence in northern Mexico has moved to the northeastern border of the State of Tamaulipas.[52]

As the 40-year-old, costly US War on Drugs continues, approximately half of states in the US federal system have regulated or legalized marijuana for medicinal or recreational use. If and when those state policies result in changed US federal policy away from interdiction toward prevention and treatment, the borderlands will gain relief from the heavy surveillance and profitability of underground criminal shippers in markets selling goods of questionable standards and quality.[53] (See chapter 10 on trade.)

Many Security Issues in the Borderlands

Tony Payan analyzes the three border wars: against drugs, immigrants, and terrorists.[54] To address these violent problems, the solutions of "border security" and border walls are often articulated, especially around election and legislative budget-making time. With the impasse on immigration reform, various security policies have been put into place which frame everyday lives at the border. For example, the US Congress passed a law authorizing an extension of the border fence in 2006. In some places, the obstacle is mere blockage to vehicle crossing; in others, it is a fence including mesh and chain-link material; still others are 16-foot steel walls, such as those that extend into the Pacific Ocean off Tijuana and San Diego County. The fence/wall is expensive to build and maintain, though it is a boon to business contractors.[55] Land confiscation for fencing has led to conflict between the federal and local governments along the border, the latter seeking to encourage legal cross-border business with fewer obstacles. Lawsuit successes inhibited some confiscation of private land, but in other places, the fence separated farmers' lands from the Rio Grande into a no-man's land of no-longer valuable property. Among the more ludicrous sites I have observed is a mile-long wall surrounded by open space; all that is achieved by such extensions is longer fencing to report completed to Washington, DC—particularly when the barrier is not even contiguous.

There is more to security than keeping out drugs and immigrants. In the discourse about border security, little attention focuses on human security, that is, the everyday ability to live inside shelter with adequate food and wages or to expect everyday public safety from abusers, predators, and thieves. The extreme inequalities at the US-Mexico central borderlands put human security in jeopardy for approximately *half* of the population whose earnings fall below the equivalent of the Mexican poverty line standard of three minimum wages.

In Mexico generally and Ciudad Juárez specifically, police are not trusted to solve crimes; the general population is afraid to report crimes to the police for fear of getting into further trouble. Government provides few resources for investigating, much less prosecuting crimes, so most (97 percent is the typical scholarly figure) rest in "impunity." When comparing murder rates, a solid figure reported to numerous agencies, Mexican border cities count higher numbers than US border cities. But when comparing theft, the US side appears to be a land of thieves, not necessarily because of more actual theft, but because people *report* crimes more frequently and trust the police at higher rates. In a 2004–2005 study about violence against women, 75 percent of the 400 women surveyed said they did not trust the police, a comparable figure to those who said they would not contact the police if physically abused.[56]

Police impunity, the critical cry of Ciudad Juárez and other major cities, inhibited the investigation of the disappearances and murder of women, named *feminicidio* by mothers, feminists, and human rights activists in the city. From 1993–2003, Amnesty International counted and named 370 such murders, approximately a third of them preceded by rape and torture.[57] The sexualized nature of many killings, seemingly driven by misogyny, sets these crimes apart from other murders, homicide (*homicidio*), and is among many reasons why border studies should be "gendered," with specific attention focused on gendered experiences and impacts.

Juarenses, known for pioneering activism that inspired other parts of Mexico to follow suit, organized protests, rallies, and marches that took on a cross-border and transnational focus. At its height, a cross-border march in 2004 attracted an estimated 7,000 people. The government at municipal (local), state, and national levels, sought to quiet the activism for the shame incurred that might deter investors, but this had little impact on the crimes and their solution. After the high-visibility activism, a women's network of lawyers and human rights activists developed and took the case of three murdered young women to the Inter-American Court of Human Rights. This activism shows the promise of international legal bodies. After assessing the evidence, the court held the Mexican state responsible and ordered changes, but the state offered mixed compliance.[58] Other international and cross-border pressure came to bear on police and government impunity, but different official priorities surpassed those relating to stopping femicide.

Mexico's own version of the "War on Drugs," coupled with US support through the $3 billion Mérida Initiative, led to the militarization of the border on both sides. The Mexican government sent military troops and federal police to occupy the city. While both men and women continued to be killed, men's murders predominated and activists allied to counter the national security strategy with a counternarrative critical of militarization.[59] With print news media and journalists under threat, social media operated by both criminals and ordinary residents seeking information about security became the default communication strategy.[60]

Meanwhile, workers (including underage children), asylum seekers, and refugees lack public safety on their journeys northward not only from Mexico but also from Central American countries where inequalities, civil wars, and extreme criminal violence propel people to move for their everyday safety. Beginning in 2014, US agents saw a rising number of Central American families who presented themselves at the South and West Texas borderlands ports of entry with "credible fears" and the search for asylum.

To gain asylum, seekers must present evidence of their credible fears. They may be processed in either "affirmative" or "defensive" procedures, the former an interview with DHS officials and the latter with a hearing in immigration court. Due to backlog in the system and the large number of cases, the wait may take 1.5–2 years, while asylum-seekers wait with US-based relatives, but the chances of success are low, especially without a lawyer. From all countries, approximately 7 of 10 cases are denied. The DHS judges in El Paso have exceptionally low rates of granting asylum, with Judge Roepke's record of hearing 196 cases from 2009–2014 and granting only 2,[61] according to information drawing on sources from DHS, Refugee Processing Center, the United Nations High Commissioner for Refugees (UNHCR), the White House, and the Syracuse University Transactional Records Access Clearinghouse. (See also chapter 9 on migration.)

Faith-based and nonprofit organizations in El Paso have longed stepped up to assist asylum seekers who are temporarily housed and fed while volunteers contact relatives elsewhere in the United States and transport people to bus stations or to the airport. Other NGOs, for the larger immigrant community, empower people with leadership skills, training on their rights, and opportunities to voice their concerns in DHS enforcement advisory commissions. Two border US Congressmen repeatedly introduce a bipartisan bill to strengthen human rights and accountability in border communities, but it has not passed yet.

Historic re-bordering, global economic linkages, and migration are constants in the contemporary everyday life of borderlands. Binational elites continue to work together to make the region more globally competitive, and both the federal government and polarizing politicians evoke controls, fears, and barriers. Without revisiting marijuana prohibition policies and the problematic lack of police professionalism in northern Mexico, barriers persist but the sense of everyday community and camaraderie makes this hybrid region a creative, resilient place.

Concluding Reflections

In this chapter, we began by focusing on the history of a region of older states, with long-recognized borders (at least since 1848), that are now called interdependent. Re-bordering, migration, and global connections have been hallmarks of development for more than a century and a half. North America's settler colonies displaced indigenous people.

The interdependence of Mexico and the United States, both in terms of labor and capital, began more than a century ago as binational elites cooperated over mining, marketing, and ranching, using low-cost labor. Some Mexicans chose to vote with their feet before and after a revolution that promised land and liberty, but which did not deliver fully, instead resulting in a political system of questionable democracy and poor governance. US immigration law and practice varied with the need for labor in complicated legal reforms. Most short-term temporary migration on the scale of the binational World War II–era Bracero Program ended in the mid-1960s, just when the Mexican

Border Industrialization Program began offering the prospect of *containing* low-cost labor in the territorial trap of the state.

The contemporary analysis in this chapter contextualized policy issues that will be threaded into chapters of part III. Everyday life in the US-Mexico borderlands involves crossing and exchange. However, such crossing has been hindered with both violence from drug suppliers to US consumers and the US national security apparatus that fences and militarizes this increasingly controlled borderlands.

Recommended Resources

Films

7 Soles
The Americas
The Global Assembly Line
Lost in Detention
Maquilopolis
Sin Nombre
The Time Has Come

Notes

1 Carlos Vélez-Ibáñez, "Another Way of Looking at Things from the Prevailing Prisms," in Carlos Vélez-Ibáñez and Josiah Heyman, eds., *Anthropological Visions of the Mexico-US Transborder Region* (Tucson: University of Arizona Press, 2017).

2 Timothy Dunn, *Blockading the Border and Human Rights* (Austin: University of Texas Press, 2009); Todd Miller, *Border Patrol Nation: Dispatches from the Front Lines of Homeland Security* (San Francisco: City Lights Books, 2014).

3 See the US-Mexico border region of 14 major cities and towns along the border on page 2 of the Pan American Health Organization 2012 publication: http://www.paho.org/salud-en-las-americas-2012/index.php?option=com_content&view=article&id=63&Itemid=63&lang=en. Kathleen Staudt and Irasema Coronado, *Fronteras no Más: Toward Social Justice at the US-Mexico Border* (NY: Palgrave USA, 2002), chapter 1, on census figures.

4 Iñigo Moré, *The Borders of Inequality* (Tucson: University of Arizona Press, 2011), pp. 25, 145.

5 Emmanuel Brunet-Jailly, "Toward a Model of Border Studies: What Do We Learn from the Study of the Canadian-American Border?" *Journal of Borderlands Studies* 19, 1 (2004), pp. 7, 9.

6 US Department of Transportation, Bureau of Transportation Statistics, http://transborder.bts.gov/programs/international/transborder/TBDR_BC/TBDR_BCQ.html http://transborder.bts.gov/tbdr/bc_tsatableprt.jsp/. Accessed 6/1/16.

7 Peter Winn, *Americas: The Changing Face of Latin America and the Caribbean* (Berkeley: University of California Press 2006, 3rd edition), pp. 19–20, 24. Also see Alejandro Lugo, *Fragmented Lives, Assembled Parts* (Austin: University of Texas Press, 2008) for detailed and lengthy historical material on indigenous people of north-central Mexico.

8 Winn, *Americas*, chapter 2.

9 Winn, *Americas*, p. 84

10 Lisa Philips Valentine and Allan K. McDougall, "Imposing the Border: The Detroit River from 1786 to 1807," *Journal of Borderlands Studies* 19, 1, 2004, pp. 13–22.

[11] Oscar Martínez, *Mexico's Uneven Development: The Geographical and Historical Context of Inequality* (NY and London: Routledge, 2016).

[12] Mark Wasserman, *Capitalists, Caciques, and Revolution: The Native Elite and Foreign Enterprise in Chihuahua, Mexico, 1854–1911* (Chapel Hill, NC: University of North Carolina Press, 1984), p. 12.

[13] Wasserman, *Capitalists*, pp. 13–4.

[14] Brenden Rensink, "Cree Contraband or Contraband Crees? Early Montanan Experiences with Transnational Natives and the Formation of Lasting Prejudice, 1880–1885," in Elaine Carey and Andrae Marak, eds., *Smugglers, Brothels, and Twine* (Tucson: University of Arizona Press, 2011), p. 28.

[15] Miller, *Border Patrol Nation*, chapter 5, pp. 124–5.

[16] Ibid., p. 131.

[17] Mario T. García, *Desert Immigrants: The Mexicans of El Paso, 1880–1920* (New Haven: Yale University Press, 1981); and Mark Wasserman, *Persistent Oligarchs: Elites and Politics in Chihuahua, Mexico, 1910–1940* (Durham, NC: Duke University Press, 1997).

[18] Wasserman, *Capitalists*, quote p. 27, also pp. 43, 48.

[19] Ibid., chapter 1, p. 3.

[20] Ibid., p. 92.

[21] Ibid., p. 94.

[22] García, *Desert Immigrants*.

[23] George Díaz, "Twilight of the Tequileros: Prohibition-Era Smuggling in the South Texas Borderlands, 1919–1933," in Elaine Carey and Andrae Marak, eds., *Smugglers, Brothels, and Twine* (Tucson: University of Arizona Press, 2011), pp. 59–82. Also see Oscar Martínez, *Border Boom Town: Ciudad Juárez since 1848* (Austin: University of Texas Press, 1978).

[24] Mae Ngai, *Impossible Subjects: Illegal Aliens and the Making of Modern America* (Princeton, NJ: Princeton University Press, 2004); and Mae Ngai, "Undocumented Migration to the United States: A History," in Lois Lorentzen, ed., *Hidden Lives and Human Rights in the United States* (Santa Barbara, CA: Praeger, 2014), Volume I.

[25] Ngai, "Undocumented Migration," p. 13.

[26] David Romo, *Ringside Seat to a Revolution* (El Paso: Cinco Puntos Press, 2005); *Indignity at the Border* can be inserted into the You Tube search engine: https://www.youtube.com/watch?v=3Nz-253RaQo.

[27] Ngai, "Undocumented Migration," p. 15.

[28] Douglas Massey, "Why Migrate? Theorizing Undocumented Migration," in Lois Lorentzen, ed., *Hidden Lives and Human Rights in the United States* (Santa Barbara, CA: Praeger, 2014), vol. I, p. 63.

[29] Christine Wheatley and Nestor Rodríguez, "With the Stroke of a Bureaucrat's Pen: US State 'Reforms' to Manage Its Undocumented Immigrant Population," in Lois Lorentzen, ed., *Hidden Lives and Human Rights in the United States* (Santa Barbara, CA: Praeger, 2014), pp. 162–3.

[30] Miller, *Border Patrol Nation*, pp. 214, 222.

[31] Alan Gomez, "Study: Nearly 500K Foreigners Overstayed Visas in 2015," *El Paso Times*, from *USA Today*, January 21, 2016, p. 3A. President Obama signed an executive order that would temporarily legalize undocumented children who came with their parents (DACA), but an executive order that would have given parents a similar reprieve (DAPA) is still contested in the courts.

[32] Molly Bilker, "Border Residents: Don't Build a Wall between Cities," Cronkite News, Arizona PBS, http://cronkitenews.azpbs.org/2016/07/17/border-poll-overview/. Accessed 7/18/16.

[33] Wheatley and Rodríguez, "With the Stroke of a Bureaucrat's Pen," pp. 168–9, on numbers. Also the documentary by María Hinojosa's *Lost in Detention* provides enormous insights into the human costs along with political and bureaucratic processes behind the deportation-immigration reform impasse. I show the PBS film regularly in border politics classes.

[34] The figure was 990,553 with DHS reporting the latest figures (from 2013): https://www.dhs.gov/profiles-lawful-permanent-residents-2013-country. Accessed 5/1/16.

[35] Dunn, *Blockading the Border*.

[36] Kathleen Staudt and Zulma Méndez, *Courage, Resistance, and Women in Ciudad Juárez: Challenges to Militarization* (Austin: University of Texas Press, 2015), chapter 5.

[37] Massey, "Why Migrate?" 66; Joseph Nevins, *Dying to Live: A Story of US Immigration in an Age of Global Apartheid* (San Francisco: City Lights Open Media, 2008); Moré, *The Borders of Inequality*, using figures from El Colegio de la Frontera Norte (COLEF), a think tank and graduate school, p. 107. The Border Patrol runs a Search, Trauma, and Rescue operation, BORSTAR https://www.cbp.gov/document/fact-sheets/border-patrol-search-trauma-and-rescue-borstar.

[38] David Spener, *Clandestine Crossings* (Austin: University of Texas Press, 2009); see selections in Staudt, et al. eds., *Human Rights along the U.S.-Mexico Border* (Tucson: University of Arizona Press, 2009), especially by Olivia Ruiz, Anna Ochoa O'Leary.

[39] Massey, "Why Migrate?" pp. 64–6.

[40] Miller, *Border Patrol Nation*, chapter 2. Kathleen Staudt, Tony Payan, and Timothy Dunn, "Closing Reflections: Bordering Human Rights, Democracy, and Broad-based Security," in Staudt, et al., eds., *Human Rights along the US-Mexico Border* (Tucson: University of Arizona Press, 2009), pp. 185–202.

[41] Kathleen Staudt, "The Border Performed in Films: Produced in Both Mexico and the US 'To Bring Out the Worst in a Country,'" *Journal of Borderlands Studies* 14, 4 (2014), pp. 465–80.

[42] City economic development figures cited in Kathleen Staudt and Beto O'Rourke, "Challenging Foreign Policy from the Border: The Forty-Year War on Drugs," in Tony Payan, et al., eds., *A War That Can't Be Won* (Tucson: University of Arizona Press, 2013). Also see chapter 10 on trade.

[43] Kathleen Staudt, Mosi Dane'el, and Guadalupe Márquez-Velarde, "In the Shadow of a Steel Recycling Plant in These Global Neoliberal Times: The Political Economy of Health Disparities among Hispanics in a Border *Colonia*," *Local Environment* 21, 5, March, 2016, pp. 636–52.

Also see price differentials from the 1990s on prescribed drugs and hospital procedures in Kathleen Staudt, *Free Trade? Informal Economies at the US-Mexico Border* (Philadelphia: Temple University Press, 1998), chapter 3.

[44] Benjamin Sáenz, "Exile," in *Flowers for the Broken* (Seattle: Broken Moon Press, 1992); and Debbie Nathan, "The Eyes of Texas Are Upon You," in her *Women and Other Aliens: Essays from the US-Mexico Border* (El Paso: Cinco Puntos Press, 1991).

[45] Dunn, his book and documentary, *The Time Has Come* (which is now available on YouTube).

[46] Susan Rippberger and Kathleen Staudt, *Pledging Allegiance: Learning Nationalism in El Paso–Juárez* (NY: Falmer/Routledge, 2003).

[47] Timothy G. Cashman, *Developing a Critical Border Dialogism: Learning from Fellow Educators in Malaysia, Mexico, Canada, and the United States* (Charlotte, NC: Information Age Publishing, 2015), pp. 88–9.

[48] Lugo, *Fragmented Lives*; see also chapter 10 on trade.

[49] Gay Young, *Gendering Globalization on the Ground: The Limits of Feminized Work for Mexican Women's Empowerment* (NY: Routledge, 2015); selections in Kathleen Staudt, César Fuentes, and Julia Monárrez Fragoso, eds., *Cities and Citizenship at the US-Mexico Border* (NY: Palgrave USA, 2010). Also see Martínez, *Mexico's Uneven Development*, on stagnant wages.

[50] *The Economist*, "Stingy by Any Measure: In the Name of Curbing Inflation, the Government Is Hurting Workers," August 16, 2014, http://www.economist.com/news/finance-and-eco nomics/21612255-name-curbing-inflation-government-hurting-workers-stingy-any. Accessed 7/1/15.

[51] Staudt, *Free Trade?* chapter 4 especially. Also see box in chapter 3.

[52] Guadalupe Correa-Cabrera, "Drug Wars, Social Networks, and the Right to Information: Informal Media as Freedom of the Press in Northern Mexico," in Tony Payan, et al., eds., *A War That Can't Be Won* (Tucson: University of Arizona Press, 2013), pp. 95–118.

[53] Tony Payan, Kathleen Staudt, and Z. Anthony Kruszewski, eds., *A War That Can't Be Won* (Tucson: University of Arizona Press, 2013).

[54] Tony Payan, *The Three US-Mexico Border Wars: Drugs, Immigration, and Homeland Security*, (Westport, CT: Praeger Security International, 2006; 2nd edition, 2016).

[55] Staudt, Payan, and Dunn, "Closing Reflections." Reece Jones, *Border Walls* (London and NY: Zed, 2012).

[56] Kathleen Staudt, "Violence at the Border: Broadening the Discourse" in *Human Rights along the US-Mexico Border*, Staudt, et al., eds. (Tucson: University of Arizona Press, 2009) on Mexico-US differences in what constitutes crime; Kathleen Staudt, *Violence and Activism at the*

Border (Austin: University of Texas Press, 2008) on lack of trust for the police. While border people in both Mexico and the United States had similar opinions, reported in the largest-ever border people's survey cited in note 32, one big difference was trust of their own police. While over 80 percent of Mexican borderlanders did not trust their police, about the same number of US borderlanders trusted their police.

57 Kathleen Staudt, *Violence and Activism at the Border* (Austin: University of Texas Press, 2008) cites the Amnesty International monograph 2003 and many other sources.

58 On judicial approaches, see selections in William Paul Simmons and Carol Mueller, eds., *Binational Human Rights: The US-Mexico Experience* (Philadelphia: University of Pennsylvania Press, 2014). Staudt and Méndez, *Courage, Resistance, and Women in Ciudad Juárez*, chapter 2 especially.

59 Staudt and Méndez, *Courage, Resistance, and Women in Ciudad Juárez*.

60 Guadalupe Correa-Cabrera, 2013.

61 Chris Hooks, "Closing our Doors, Closing our Minds" (with accompanying Chart, "How to Get Asylum or Become a Refugee")," *The Texas Observer* 108, 1, January 2016, pp. 6–7. See chapter 9 on migration.

Chapter 5

From Borderlessness to Partition Scars and Border Fences

Postcolonial South Asia

The South and Southeastern Asian region is a place to rethink border theories and categories developed in the North and Western world. Each world regional context adds complex layers to border studies. While the construction of borders was often a violent process here and elsewhere in the world, large swathes of space with now-bordered people remained stateless until the mid-20th century. What does border studies in the South add in this global era? Crucial factors influence border theories, illustrated in this chapter: (1) relatively recent statelessness, (2) shorter length of time under state governance, and (3) shared poverty across borders until the late 1990s when economic growth in China growth outpaced the rest (see figure 5.1). Assumptions about state-norming lives could and should be questioned, given the range of good-to-poor governance in this region. Whether living in state-imposed or stateless spaces, potential opportunity or damage exists for border people, survivors, victims and/or active agents in borderlands. A central dilemma involves whether recent states born in violent partition can move away from their hard-border approach and narrow security strategies toward more cooperation, trade, and freer borderlands life.

The history of the region—now cut across by the 20th century borders of Pakistan, India, Bangladesh, Burma (Myanmar), China, Bhutan, and Nepal—is a grand one. The grandness, coupled with periodic suffering for many, covers multiple empires, such as the Mogul (also referred to as Mughal) Empire and its iconic Taj Mahal visited by millions. The region's global trade dates back a millennium to when Northern ancestors lived in caves, but in now prosperous regions with relatively open movement across borders. Two thousand years passed without regard for borders; traders forged the Silk Road, now under revival as a China-led collaborative effort to foster cross-border regional trade and to access the sea via its southwestern province Yunnan. Yet less prosperous and unstable states seem wary of China's intentions, given suspected official, business, and criminal designs on water, forests, and other natural resources in a still-porous border region, nicely illustrated in over two centuries of historic maps until 1905.[1]

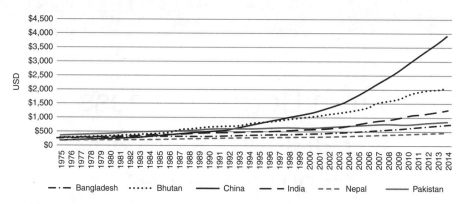

FIGURE 5.1 Comparative GDP Per Capita Growth, South and East Asia, 1975–2014. Based on a design by Jakub Zajakala, research assistant.

Source: Data from Border Inequalities Database, compiled from World Bank and International Monetary Fund figures.

Despite extensive reading, my grounding in the region is less deep than my lived experience in the central US-Mexico borderlands for over 35 years. In 2015, I attended border studies academic conferences in Guwahati, Assam, traveled through Meghalaya to the Bangladesh border, and attended more academic meetings in New Delhi. In so doing, I interacted with colleagues and students from the South Asian region. Borders divide an entire region with recently drawn external and internal borderlines at international and subnational (state) levels. The newest state in the region was born in Bangladesh (1971, with minor border adjustments in 2015) and India's division of federal states, divided into eight subnational territories in the northeast with their different indigenous communities that Britain and India call "Scheduled Tribes."

This chapter begins by highlighting stateless people (that is, borderless peoples) and then moves on to the British "Raj" and Partition of 1947 which carved merciless scars through the lives of many peoples. With an eye on gendered borders, the chapter makes clear how the constructions of gender in symbols and law reveal different life experiences for women and men whose lives are shaped by class, caste, and other factors. Gendered violence occurred in and during border scarring, such as Partition and India's walls and fences around territory. The chapter's primary focus is the India-Bangladesh borderlands.

Historical Perspectives

The section begins with the meandering process, back and forth historically, of stateless societies. After that, we move to the sort of pure global capitalism that befell India, followed by direct colonial rule and Partition.

Stateless Societies?

With South and Southeast Asia as his analytic spatial setting, James C. Scott turned both the traditional state-centric political science and international relations subfields on their heads with transformative ways of thinking. Scott's focus is "ground-up," including the lived experiences of people's selective participation in and resistance to top-down overtures in subtle and overt ways. Scott's initial work (to paraphrase parts of three book titles) named heretofore hidden individual and collective participation as "weapons of the weak," followed by an ambitious cataloging of the "arts of resistance to domination," and warnings to analysts against "seeing like a state," published in 1977, 1990, 1998, respectively. Scott's more recent book analyzed in this chapter is titled *The Art of Not Being Governed.*[2] The book's focus is upland southeast Asia to include what is now northeastern India, separated from the main expanse of India by a thin 13-mile wedge, drawn in the fluke demarcations of Sir Cyril Radcliffe's territorial line in the 1947 Partition. In India, people call the shape the "chicken's neck," the resemblance of which anyone can see on a map.

Scott analyzes a nonstate multibordered region called Zomia which, until the post–World War II era, consisted of mountain and lowland peoples. Willem Van Schendel was the first academic to name this 15-million kilometer region with a population of over 200 million. Zomia once had its own website, a celebration of culture and resistance, with pictures that I studied before my visit in early 2015, but the website has come down, either for lack of resources or for its role as a thorn in the side of India (a "security threat") and perhaps nearby states. In the meantime, Zomia has acquired a near-mystical quality with blurs over other maps (for the demarcation of a border does an injustice to the concept and place).[3] Scott argues that various mountain peoples shared common characteristics, one of which was behavior to evade empires and states and their revenue generation, land grabs, conscription, and forced labor. They did so by retreating into rugged terrain.[4] Gradually by the late 1940s, with the extension of technology and road construction, states reduced the distance between their center and periphery. Later in the chapter, we cover the complex and contradictory ways in which border peoples negotiate the state to extract benefits and to provide leverage in local struggles while simultaneously asserting their agency and resistance—part of the normalizing process as generations of peoples adjust to the political structures imposed upon them. However, territorial borderlines do not always resolve conflicts but rather magnify and increase them in hard-line border security approaches.

"Othering" and imaginary processes took hold in the colonial era with officials, their anthropological handmaidens, and adventurers that classified and attempted to pacify people they called uncivilized, backwards, and violent. Such is the case of Naga Hills people who resented intrusions into forest lands and their resources.[5] Zomi people live in the current Indian federal states of Manipur and Nagaland, next to Myanmar, Bangladesh, Bhutan, China, and Nepal, but the place Zomia has a far wider reach and incorporates other peoples. And more current studies of Manipur and Nagaland show divisions among groups and the perceived "occupation" by the Indian Army (protected from impunity charges by the 1958 Armed Forces Special Powers Act) and the Naga peace process. Duncan McDuie-Ra analyzes antimilitarist civil society women's groups, some that use the discourse of and respect for motherhood.

Others use a more radical approach—between mountain-based Naga communities, some of them secessionists and expansionists (into Nagalim, an imagined larger homeland)—and the valley-based Meitei ethnic group. Gender-based violence is a common casualty of intergroup struggles.[6]

British India's borders were carved, becoming the larger shroud, and drawn right through these peoples who lived in mountains and hills. Later after border changes, the area multiplied into internal states that drew their own multiple territorial lines and restrictions, complete with military and border bureaucrats to enforce laws. In his book on the postindependence Bengali borderlands transcending India and Bangladesh, Willem Van Schendel poses questions about 4,000 kilometers of international and binational borderlines drawn through local cultural groups, their multiple identities, and economies—even farms, divided by border fences or meandering rivers. What was local became international, he says.[7] We return to his work in a later section of the chapter.

Savage Capitalism, Colonialism, and the Partitioned Borders

British colonialism began formally in 1857, but for two centuries before, London granted unusually extreme authority to the British East India Company to divide and rule in accordance with the then-globalizing world economic system. According to Alex von Tunzelman, King Charles II

> would turn the East India Company into a monster. With five acts, he gave it an amazing array of rights without responsibilities. By the 1670s, the company could mint its own coin, maintain its own army, wage war, make peace, acquire new territories and impose its own civil and criminal law—and all without any accountability, save to its shareholders. This was pure capitalism, unleashed for the first time in history.[8]

Compared to this description of "pure capitalism," contemporary neoliberalism seems almost tame. On the ways Britain profited from India, Dr. Shashi Tharoor, Member of Parliament in India, gave an eloquent Oxford lecture to argue that Britain owes reparations to India.[9] Reparation claims often fall on deaf political ears.

As covered in the earlier historical chapter 2 about colonizers' abilities to create representations and images for peoples of the South, "Orientalism" captured many imaginations as representations of peoples in exotic places where fortunes could be made. British imperial writer Rudyard Kipling wrote books and poems contrasting the "real native" and deprecated the "inauthentic hybrid."[10] Later, films like the Hollywood-produced *Gunga Din* (1939), based on a Kipling poem, ended with the loyal and faithful underling (called a "blackface" "native water bearer") who saved British soldiers by sounding the alarm to warn of approaching Thuggee cult enemies (~1830s) at the cost of his own life. These sorts of images, whether on movie and television screens, leave impressions on viewers. I have far better films to list than this one at the end of this chapter and in chapter 11, "Borderlands in Films."

British India, the largest empire worldwide, became known as "the Jewel in the Crown" given its enormous resources coupled with its huge market for

British products. The lengthy period of colonial exploitation stimulated resistance and the rise of nationalist movements, nongovernmental organizations (NGOs), and political parties seeking independence. The Indian National Congress Party was born in 1885, long before pro-independence parties in other European colonies and perhaps accounting for its jumpstart on state-building activities, despite the tumultuous violence after Partition in 1947. Few other postcolonial states had the same institution-building advantages, though good governance is still problematic in this, the second-largest population of over a billion people in the world, with huge absolute numbers of impoverished people.

Resistance to colonialism and independence movements took many forms, with multiple leaders vying with one another to protect "their people," divided into Muslim, Hindu, Sikh, and other communal groups. Religious and cultural identities did not begin with colonialism, but colonial rule typically foments categories and divisions in overt and subtle ways, such as in censuses (noted in the earlier chapter citing Benedict Anderson's work). In everyday life, cultural identities display a complex variety of forms, from language, to clothing styles, head coverings, male circumcision (or not), and food consumption traditions, such as vegetarianism.

Partition: A Border Horror Story

After World War II, the near-bankrupt Britain was hardly in a position to maintain the costs and complexities of its empire. Birthed in 1945, the United Nations had established principles of self-determination and human rights. After many decades of Indian nationalist pressure and struggles, Britain finally acquiesced to independence, but responded to divisions among nationalist leaders with Partition: the creation of two separate states that would seemingly divide people in territorial spaces based on Hindu (and Sikh) or Muslim identities into India and Pakistan, respectively, with Pakistan divided by 725 miles between West and East Pakistan. Of the British, Edward Said cynically called Partition the "parting gift of empire,"[11] as a bordering practice not only in India and Pakistan but also elsewhere: Ireland, Palestine, Cyprus, and much of Africa.

Partition based on religious affiliation became a near-impossible task in areas where both Muslims and Hindus lived together, whether living in past harmony or in underlying tension. Delhi, for example, was home to Muslims as a third of its population, yet as readers know, it became the capital city of India, an imagined Hindu nation. At midnight on August 15, 1947, authority changed hands from the British to the leaders of both respective countries, with India's Prime Minister Nehru's famous declaration: "At the stroke of the midnight hour, when the world sleeps, India will awake to life and freedom." These inspirational words would belie the tragedies that had begun affecting many millions of people. "When India was partitioned, some 60 million of her 95 million Muslims (one in four Indians) became Pakistanis; some 35 million stayed back in India."[12]

Decisions about where to draw Partition lines rested with Sir Cyril Radcliffe, a British lawyer operating with a six-week deadline. He had never even been to India until assigned the task to determine boundaries between Muslim and non-Muslim areas, beginning June 30, 1947.

With people's uncertainty about where borderlines would be drawn, tensions mounted with murderous results. People of one faith sought to flee from areas deemed likely to be assigned to the nation of the other faith, on foot, by train, as kidnap victims, and/or with the always-ready smugglers who move people for a price, whether safely or not. Horror stories emerged, with trainloads of murdered, tortured, and sexually assaulted victims: the so-called trains of death. Angry mobs of one faith or another, to which thugs contributed their own opportunistic violence, left scores of thousands of victims on roadsides during the exodus. Others died from epidemics. The British offered little protection from the lawless mayhem. Some people sought to stay alive through changing their religion and names or even getting circumcised. Although numbers cannot be certain, most sources claim that one million people lost their lives, and as many as 12 million fled—land and property confiscated—to areas deemed safer to start new lives.[13]

Like other countries in the post–Berlin Wall (1989) world, India built fences (walls) with the grand aim of sealing the entire border. Securitization processes took hold inside the country and at borders. At one of the borders with Pakistan, both Indian and Pakistani troops routinely perform daily hypermasculine behaviors in the openings and closings of the gate, which can be viewed on various websites.[14] To this day, India and Pakistan, two nuclear powers, continue to exhibit tensions over the division of Kashmir, in the north with its bordered "Line of Control," and border security in the territorial divide of borderlands. The documentary *Inshallah, Kashmir* (2012) offers painful testimonials on the militarized border and disappearances in that region.

Gendering Border Conflict

Many studies on the Partition focus on the Punjab regions of what is now northwest India and eastern Pakistan. The gendered dimensions of exodus, murder, torture, and capture have been well documented and continue to be remembered. Partition also revealed unequal gendered, rather than equal, citizenship rights. History can hardly be understood without reference to these still-remembered gendered experiences. In South Asia and elsewhere, women and their bodies often symbolize a communal group, its honor and dishonor.

Many historians have taken up the task of reconstructing memories, but one book stands out. Ritu Menon and Kamla Bhasin have unearthed documentary and testimonial sources to provide the most thorough accounting of women's experiences and agency during and after Partition: oral histories, social workers involved in rehabilitation, legislation, and documents in government archives about the post-conflict experiences of women refugees. Contemporary feminist scholars like Deepti Misri[15] laud their pioneering work. Menon and Bhasin focus on Punjab, the site of maximum relocation. Their research forms clusters of relationships, "between women, religious communities and the state, both within and across the two new nations; between women and their families, 'real' and 'acquired'; between women and their men, women and their country." The Partition produced "mass widowhood," they say, "on an unprecedented scale." After mass abductions and conversions, governments sought to recover women and "restore them to where they 'rightfully belonged' "[16] revealing gendered statist assumptions of the era. In later chapters, they document from legislative records and ministry files how adult women could not choose where to stay after "recovery," even if they had families in locales where they had been taken and sought to remain. Men 16 and over could make the choice.

Menon and Bhasin's second chapter, "Honourably Dead: Permissible Violence Against Women," begins with testimonies of women defiled not only by those of the other faith, by abduction, rape, branding, being stripped and forced to parade naked, and disfigurement, but also by those of their own faith. The authors reported how some daughters were burned, poisoned, thrown into wells, and/or buried alive. Some women and girls immolated themselves, to save their honor with internalized shame, say the authors, yet others refused, even as they were made to "feel ashamed" at "cowardice" in embracing death. People left land and valuable possessions, with "souls bruised" and the "shock of horror." The authors' words even bruise the readers' souls.

Mob violence took hold, but gendered violence in most world regions is not only found during war and civil conflict but also in everyday life. Menon and Bhasin offered contrasts between the mundane violence of women's everyday life and these dramatic episodes that "during communal riots bring to the surface savagely and explicitly, familiar forms of sexual violence—now charged with a symbolic meaning that serves as an indicator of the place that women's sexuality occupies in an all-male, patriarchal arrangement of gender relations between and within religious or ethnic communities."[17] In their research, Menon and Bhasin said medical doctors reported that the amputation of breasts was one of the chief injuries inflicted on the female wounded.

In the second of her trilogy of films, *Earth*, Deepa Mehta focuses on a group of friends from the perspective of a young Parsee girl (a community that sought to remain neutral, also spelled Parsi) in Lahore. A turning point, midway through the film, occurs when one of the friends meets a death train that contained huge "sacks of breasts," cut off many women including his two sisters. At that unforgettable moment, relationships among friends changed for the worst. Films like this have a way of humanizing and personalizing events and their meanings for everyday life that one cannot always find in books and numerical reports.

To put their work in feminist perspective, Menon and Bhasin analyze "women's bodies as territory to be conquered, claimed or marked by the assailant, with stripping," and "culminate in raping, branding or tattooing" in public market places, temples, and *gurudwaras* (gateways to worship), "the latter two signifying the sacred space."[18] For women who survived, the branded tattoos became permanent reminders of violation. In this and other conflicts, "sexual mutilation" incorporated the wish to eliminate or befoul the perceived enemy's means of reproduction, their offspring, and the nurturing process, also found in the 1990s with the mass rapes of Bosnian women. The mutilation of men, via castration, is also a gendered reality in war and conflict.

In my search for films and documentaries for this book, I found many about Partition on YouTube produced in India and the United Kingdom. Under the videos, the comment sections often contain insights. Viewers posted long lists of revealing comments underneath many varied films about Partition. Without naming names or monikers, and continuing still in the 21st century, commenters posted hateful and ugly remarks against one or the other religious group about who started the violence, the horrendous acts committed, and so on (for example, "you ignorant [fill in the religion]"; "the [fill in the blanks] burnt women and children"). Like violence in other parts of the world, people often ask "but who started it?" A better question involves how to stop it. Comments like these show the "Othering" that continues to occur within and across world regions including within the South Asia diaspora. It was refreshing to see a comment noting "(Our) country and our people have not yet changed and they never will . . . The evidence lies in the comments on this video where our typical Indian brothers are commenting foolishly against each other." No wonder tension continues within and across borders.

India's Contemporary Bengal Borderlands: The Northeast

India is a hypersecurity conscious state, a mentality born not only with Partition but also over conflicts with Pakistan, the attempted Chinese invasion in 1962 over contested terrain in the northeastern borderlands, the Naxalite insurgency movements within India, and occasional terrorist incidents, such as those in Mumbai. As noted and picture-linked earlier in chapter 2, India's border fence with Pakistan, lit up at night with flood lights, is visible from outer space.

Several scholars have focused on the border and the fence on India's other side, through the Bengal heartland, which is the longest border to emerge during decolonization in the second half of the 20th century.[19] Here ethnicity and religion cut across identities. As Willem Van Schendel says, the border "separated tens of millions of Bengalis on one side from tens of millions of Bengalis on the other" as land allocations were treated like "spoils" or "awards" to each.[20] Border demarcations and length estimates are still in doubt. He says this is a 4,000-kilometer border for which imprecise lengths exist, from a low-end US Central Intelligence Agency (CIA) estimate of 4,095 to a high-end official Bangladesh estimate of 4,427 and an official India estimate of 4,246 kilometers.[21] Van Schendel called the demarcation process lengthy, complex, contested, and unfinished, relying in part on old *zamindar* (tax collector) records. In waterways, tiny islands emerge on one or the other side of the border in which people temporarily reside and make livelihoods, thus posing challenges for contemporary tax collectors.

Borderland scholars tend to focus on the ways border people survive, resist, and use multiple identities in their (newly) bordered world. What was once a borderland zone of markets, trading, and labor networks became a militarized one where increasing numbers of Border Security Force (BSF) agents regulate life. The BSF, created in 1965, is the largest border security force in the world with approximately a quarter-million agents, according to India's Ministry of Home Affairs website. Once a fluid, porous region of Bengali people, the state reclassified movement as legal or illegal, with risks for people maneuvering around boundaries, sometimes successfully and other times resulting in death. Figures are nearly nonexistent with regard to border activities in securitized areas of the northeast, bordering Myanmar (Burma), itself a postcolonial state and former military government which reported little information to international bodies. The lack of good governance there has been more problematic than in many other states.

In a poignant paragraph, Van Schendel outlines defiance and accommodation among border people with several aspects to consider.

> [T]he world as they had always imagined it was gone forever, their universe torn in two and half of it lost. They were subjected to the violent rescaling that results from state formation, and that rescaling took place in their backyard. Their geographical imagination abruptly violated, they needed to reinvent themselves as people with new identities: as borderlanders, as citizens of a new state and as inhabitants of a divided landscape. The strategies they employed were complex and variable, ranging from outright defiance to acceptance, accommodation and innovation.[22]

In many countries in the South, as well as South and Southeast Asia, more research is necessary about how borderlanders respond to their predicament and what this means for states' efforts to border and re-border their territorial lines, at what cost to people and government budgets.

At the 2015 border studies conference in Guwahati, from my field notes, I entered quotes of poignant comments that scholars expressed about their research albeit with resident scholars' cautionary remarks that "there are many Indias."[23] Thus, my observations and remarks here mainly focus on the border regions. Scholar after scholar discussed border barriers that aggravated people's lives and their livelihoods and undermined small-scale agricultural development and trade. Scholars spoke of the "illogical" ways officials drew borderlines and the "sheer madness" caused by borders: farmers accused of smuggling their own rice, needing permits to enter their fields, struggling to irrigate at night, and suffering injuries from land mines—all in the name of border security. Knowing the importance of trade, I was struck by how the state has redefined, stifled, and rechanneled the many formerly free cross-border traders in open-air markets into a selected few "border *haats*" that it rigidly controls with exact specifications about the amount of goods, their value, and the distance from territorial lines at which they may operate. When border scholars expressed the common view "Delhi doesn't understand us," it reminded me of the constant refrain one hears at the US-Mexico border about Washington, DC, and Mexico City.

In a southward field trip through the mountains of the State of Meghalaya into the valleys of Dawki and the border with Bangladesh, the winding roads contained few vehicles save those in which we drove and large Tata trucks decorated with multicolored pictures and words carrying boulders (one could see workers on the side of the road painstakingly break rocks into medium-sized pieces) to just across the border to be imported into Bangladesh. Larger-scale commerce seems to overcome hurdles more easily than small-scale traders and villagers. US President Obama had recently visited India, so I noted, then photographed a truck with a symbol of India and US flags joined in friendship (which, alas, was not sharp enough for inclusion in this book).

Northeastern India, one truck (among many) carrying rocks and boulders to the Bangladesh border.

Source: TRUCK STOP/Alamy Stock Photo.

India's Ministry of Development of North Eastern Region (MDONER), born as an agency in 2001, achieved an upgrade to ministerial status in 2004. Its vision: "To accelerate the pace of socioeconomic development of the Region so that it may enjoy growth parity with the rest of the country."[24] MDONER's website contains many goals and timetables, complete with a grievance officer and process and multiple stakeholders, including "civil society." MDONER acknowledges that most of the northeast's territorial borders sit side by side with other countries: Myanmar, with 15 proposed border *haats*, and Bangladesh, with 13 proposed border *haats*. The site notes overland trade agreements with Bangladesh, Bhutan, Myanmar, China (through Sikkim), and Nepal at land customs stations, along with the various goods exempted from duty with certain countries, but charging 5 percent on other items. The list of commodities traded is quite lengthy from citrus fruits, forest produce, industrial output like bicycle parts and brooms, and boulder stone, to raw hides, vegetables, woven fabrics, and spices (including the mild narcotic betel nut and leaves) among many other items. Here too one can find rigid rules for border *haats*, including when they can operate (that is, 7:30 a.m. to 3:30 p.m., Monday through Thursday) with fees charged for vehicles. With so many rules and regulations, discretion and lack of oversight, extortion opportunities emerge for border bureaucrats.

The study of border *haats*, the ability of people to trade outside the regulatory nets, and the extent to which the ministry and its officials stifle or enhance trade offer excellent opportunities for future research. Using Van Schendel's categories, one wonders how people accommodate or resist these various rules that no doubt stifle trade in legal and licit goods but provide revenue generation for the state, with administrative costs. In a later study of the Bengal borderlands (hypothetically named Prantapur which means border-place), Sahana Ghosh examines the continuing porosity though increasingly controlled borderlands and BSF occasionally complicit with illegal traders.[25] Relatively new postcolonial states often lack the ability and data to implement these precise details consistently.

The fact that bureaucratic machinery exists for the border region is noteworthy—a more elaborate apparatus with promised citizen input than what the governments serving the US-Mexico border offer their border residents, though India's trade-oriented bureaucratic machinery no doubt is well short of the funding coupled with institutional machinery that Euroregions have to offer (developed in the next chapter). Yet illicit trade also operates, with troubling consequences for ordinary people.

Paula Banerjee provides historical perspective on how the notion of borders has become "a marker of security," especially against undocumented migrants, but that increasing recent violence at borders is particularly burdensome for women.[26] Human trafficking has skyrocketed amid the structural violence of extreme poverty, as many scholars note. Although the recent film *Siddharth* does not take place in these borderlands, it shows the pain of child trafficking and the efforts of NGOs, albeit with meager resources, to recover those children.

Just as true historically, women's bodies become symbolic territory over which people struggle and challenge impunity. Gendered bodies offer potent symbols in the political process.

Gendered Bodies at Contemporary Borders

As symbolic of the violence in bordering processes, let us examine a recent case of murder and its adjudication. Bangladeshi teen Felani Khatun, 15 years old, worked illegally in India for which her employers bore no responsibility. Lacking documents, she sought to return to Bangladesh for marriage, but could not cross the border to her country legally, so she got caught on the barbed wire trying to cross the border fence. BSF *jawans* (constable) Amiya Ghosh shot her and confessed; in India's judicial system and its appearance of rule by law, he was tried not once but twice only to be acquitted, sending an impunity message to the BSF. Scholar Malini Sur analyzes the incident along with the cyber war and wiki sites that emerged around the "Killing of Felani," including horrendous pictures that show two guards carrying the murder victim upside down, hands and legs tied to a pole like what might be used for a dead animal. The article compares a Bangladeshi man also killed in a river, run over by border guards in a speed boat, but his death got less attention in the international global shaming media.[27] In the global world of international human rights activism, women killing (or what in Mexico and many Latin American states is called *feminicidio*) and abuse seem to rouse attention more than homicide (of men) in this region and others.

Ethnicity and "Scheduled Tribes": Affirmative Action and Defiance

The stance of postcolonial India—whether in its postindependence state-led developmental state ideology or its contemporary neoliberal ideology under current Indian Prime Minister Modi—is part militarization of contested terrain and part patronage as analyzed by Sanjib Baruah in his book *Durable Disorder*,[28] a compilation of academic articles. He offers the most insightful analyses of the ambivalence in northeastern Indian regarding alignment and nonalignment with the state over contested borders. Baruah outlines a complex coexistence of what some call insurgencies and counterinsurgency operations in border spaces that occur simultaneously with the trappings of democracy (elections, public investment, free speech and press). Multiple militias exist in India's northeast, he argues, in a politically engineered "cosmetic federal regional order" of states that cut across peoples of many ethnic identities and mobilize along those lines, for benefits from the state or against the state and other ethnic groups encroaching on their spaces.[29] Statist discourse frequently uses, or overuses, the word "terrorism" for such groups. In a global world of politically charged "border security" and "terrorist threats," the South Asia Terrorism Portal[30] at New Delhi's Institute of Conflict Management tracks these various movements. Google searches for Zomia bring up reports on this site in ways that contrast with the academic literature cited earlier in this chapter. Political opposition and resistance are not the same as terrorism.

Besides ethnic identities and language groups, the region also contains a state-imposed and individual- and group-claimed status of "Scheduled Tribes." India grants positive, affirmative benefits to people of such status in the form of public employment, business opportunities, reserved seats in elected offices, and educational opportunities. As Baruah further details, people promote this status to leverage benefits for their group in competition with other groups in this "two-tiered citizenship."[31] He and others note the interaction of established political party representatives and insurgents in the region, with some claiming fears about insurgency and the need for border security which in turn generates more resources from New Delhi.[32] So we can see simultaneous contradictory processes in this borderland and no doubt in others around the world.

Psychological Borders Yet Shared Space and Waters

Seventy years after Partition, readers may wonder, as I do, whether "Othering" and bordering will decline between formerly stateless, then colonized, and now partitioned and bordered states in the region. The simultaneous engagement and resistance among ethnic groups in India's northeast suggests a move toward accommodation and gradual normalization of the state and its boundaries.

Yet across the larger bordered region, the move has not yet arrived and "Othering" persists in school curricula of multiple countries. Environment security threats loom large, particularly with rising sea waters. Bangladesh's huge, densely settled population, coupled with environmental threats, will impel migrants to move northward for economic reasons and life itself. Global warming and rising sea waters, in addition to the regular flooding of lowlands in Bangladesh, threaten the security of the nation and its restrictive borders. One might ask the same about nearby countries, enticed into more Silk Road trade with China, their lumbering giant border neighbor.

Giant river basin systems begin in Tibet, now part of powerful China, with its largest population in the world, growing economy, and consequent water management needs that the government believes includes dams. China's relationship with its border neighbors downstream offers an uneasy future in a region of power asymmetries. (See chapter 7 on maritime borders.)

After several decades, one might think that citizens will accept the normalization of borders and assimilate, identifying increasingly with nationals inside state borders. India pursues social policies for access to health and human security, though past administrative complexity, identification of legitimate recipients, and poor governance result in gaps that do not get rations and food subsidies, estimated at 40 percent with many "ghost beneficiaries," to those who need them.[33] A new biometric identification system, Unique Identification Authority of India (UICAI, called Aadhaar) may correct such irregularities and thereby increase people's loyalty to the state. Yet the rights and protections of minorities, including undocumented people and economic migrants within states, are continuously threatened. Moreover, "Othering" processes have become routinized, including those in textbook constructions of the others and the ousted. Nationalism is an overarching umbrella in many texts here and elsewhere.

Dhananjay Tripathi compares psychological bordering in Indian and Pakistani middle-school textbooks.[34] He focuses on English-language texts, rather than those in Hindi, Urdu, and regional languages, and on nonreligious schools rather than the more than 40,000 *madrasas* in Pakistan which educate nearly two million boys. Tripathi finds that history and the complicated narratives of Partition are handled differently in both countries. Pakistan's texts detach its history from India and instead associate the nation with Arab and Central Asian places. Its birth-of-the-nation story narrates poor treatment of Muslims in India. Gandhi is criticized in colonial India as someone school children were "forced to adore" in pictures. As he analyzes, the textbook comparisons of children in India and Pakistan is telling, focusing on the homogeneity of Pakistani children but the differences between Muslim and Hindu children's clothing and food consumption (meat eaters versus those eating pulses and vegetables). In contrast, Indian textbooks celebrate India's diversity, but engage little with the Partition narratives. Right-wing political parties have sought not only to glorify the Hindu past and religion, but also to remove evidence that beef was once eaten in ancient India.[35] Such studies are important for understanding the construction of futures, but obviously far more research is necessary at all levels and types of education. In border studies, too few education studies exist.

In the meantime, on border security, India's Ministry of Home Affairs publishes on its home webpage that the fencing and floor lighting of borders continues toward completion. "In order to curb infiltration, smuggling and other antinational activities from across Indo-Pakistan and Indo-Bangladesh borders, the Government have [sic] undertaken the work of construction of fencing, flood lighting and roads along these borders."[36] At the Indo-Bangladesh Border (IBB), "marked by a high degree of porosity and checking illegal cross border activities," 2,654 of 3,345 kilometers of fencing have been completed, and three-fourths of intended roads. At the border with Pakistan, with "attempts at infiltration by terrorists and smuggling of arms, ammunition and contraband," at the most active "Line of Control," 1,915 of 2,043 kilometers have been fenced, so it is nearly complete. As is clear, official bureaucratic agencies have stakes a hard-bordered future for their mission, jurisdiction, and budgets.

Masculine Nationalism and the Transnational Diaspora

In many countries, borders no longer contain all the imagined nationals. The Philippines, as a subsequent chapter outlines, exports labor, complete with a government agency that facilitates recruitment, supply, and changes in demand. Mexico depends on remittances sent from workers in other countries. The global era also consists of extensive telecommunication. Ghosh reports that in Bengali borderland villages, even those without electricity, residents often own two mobile phones with both Indian and Bangladeshi SIM cards to facilitate communication.[37]

Given its population size, it is no wonder that India has produced a large diasporic community of 27 million people in almost all countries of the world, 190 of them, based on 2010 World Bank figures.[38] Most are located in the United States, the Persian Gulf, and Middle East. Madhavi

Mallapragada notes that they send home the largest amount of remittances of all countries in the world, $55 billion annually.[39] Her intriguing study of "homepage nationalisms" on websites analyzes imagined communities without territory, another take on border studies, and one that idealizes and celebrates the homeland. In her review of images online and in popular culture, she examines hypermasculinity in Indian American technological prowess: "if technology is a game, it is a blatantly phallic one."[40] Meanwhile, she discusses women married to men in the United States where professional Indian nationals are granted the largest number of H-1B skilled professional visas, yet wives are stuck in the H4 visa category forbidding paid work and generating total dependency on husbands. However, the global Internet culture also provides access to online activism about immigration and organizing for change. Mallapragada's sources draw on content from Facebook and online conversations, a creative source of analytic content. Whether these different categories of immigrants return or stay, they will no doubt be shaped by transnational experiences.

Concluding Reflections

In this chapter, we have examined borderlands in the postcolonial South, particularly the brutal nature of colonialism, the haphazard and absurd territorial Partition lines, and the violent aftermath that continues with collective memories. The entire South Asian region consists of relatively recent states (except for China) with their mixed successes and failures in democracy and good governance. The region is one of shared poverty amid asymmetrical power relationships with dominant giant China to the north and east.

India is a state that has militarized its borders with the largest-ever border police; many of these agents come from distant parts of India and are called *bideshis* (foreigners).[41] The chapter focuses primarily on the formerly stateless northeastern India and its ambiguous relations with a securitized state, huge Border Security Force, and hard, violent borders which undermine freedom and trade among Bengali people who transcend the borders into Bangladesh. As is the case elsewhere, however, border bureaucrats operate with considerable discretion and complicity for what the state in the last half-century defines as illegal.

India offers a troubling model that perpetuates border insecurity and poverty in the name of border security. What may appear to be an alienated or coexistent border is a characterization constructed by the state more than by border people. A militarized border, though becoming normalized over time, undermines the sort of regional interdependence that might lead to more border integration. Alas, in the postcolonial world, the highly controlled national security approach to borders may be the norm for newer states that have the resources and political will to harden borders. India's costly hard-border approach is undergoing consolidation. In so doing, it inefficiently uses precious resources to push for elusive national security that might have been invested in human development and antipoverty strategies instead.

Recommended Resources

Films

Earth
Inshallah, Kashmir
Siddharth

Maps

Historical South Asia: http://etc.usf.edu/maps/galleries/asia/regional/southasia.php
Zomia, from Geocurrents: http://www.geocurrents.info/cultural-geography/where-is-zomia

Notes

[1] *The Economist,* "The New Silk Road: Stretching the Threads," November 29, 2014, pp. 41–2. See the map in http://etc.usf.edu/maps/galleries/asia/regional/southasia.php.

[2] James W. Scott, *The Art of Not Being Governed* (New Haven, CT: Yale University Press, 2009).

[3] For example, see http://www.geocurrents.info/cultural-geography/where-is-zomia.

[4] Scott, *The Art of Not Being Governed.* Also see Willem Van Schendel and Erik de Maaker, eds., "Introduction to the Special Issue: Asian Borderlands: Introducing Their Permeability, Strategic Uses and Meanings," *Journal of Borderlands Studies* 29, 1, February 2014, pp. 3–10.

[5] Debojyoti Das, "Understanding Margins, State Power, Space and Territoriality in the Naga Hills," *Journal of Borderlands Studies* 29, 1, February 2014, pp. 81–94.

[6] Duncan McDuie-Ra, "Borders, Territory, and Ethnicity: Women and the Naga Peace Process," in Nancy A. Naples and Jennifer Bickham Mendez, eds., *Border Politics* (NY: New York University Press, 2014), pp. 95–119.

[7] Willem Van Schendel, *The Bengal Borderland* (London: Anthem, 2005), p. 16.

[8] Alex von Tunzelman, *Indian Summer: The Secret History of the End of an Empire* (NY: Henry Holt and Company, 2007), p. 14.

[9] Dr. Shashi Tharoor, "Britain Does Owe Reparations." The title can be found on You Tube. The site I accessed in July 2016 was https://www.youtube.com/watch?v=f7CW7S0zxv4.

[10] James Chiriyankandath, "Colonialism and Post-Colonial Development," in Peter Burnell, Lise Rakner, and Vicky Randall, *Politics in the Developing World* (NY: Oxford University Press, 2014), p. 35.

[11] Cited in Van Schendel, *The Bengal Borderland,* p. 24.

[12] Ritu Menon and Kamla Bhasin, *Borders & Boundaries: Women in India's Partition* (Delhi: Kali for Women, 1998), chapter 1 (pageless, on my Kindle).

[13] Multiple sources: Van Schendel, *The Bengal Borderland,* chapter 3; Von Tunzelman, *Indian Summer;* and William Dalrymple, "The Great Divide: The Violent Legacy of Indian Partition," *The New Yorker,* June 29, 2015, pp. 65–70 (a review of several books on the topic).

[14] See the BBC video, "Michael Palin at the India-Pakistan Border Ceremony" https://www.youtube.com/watch?v=n9y2qtaopbE.

[15] Deepti Misri, *Beyond Partition: Gender, Violence, and Representation in Postcolonial India.* (Champaign-Urbana: University of Illinois Press, 2014). Also see Urvashi Butalia, *The Other Side of Silence: Voices from the Partition of India* (Durham: Duke University Press, 2000).

[16] Menon and Bhasin, *Borders & Boundaries,* quotes from chapter 1, Kindle edition.

[17] Ibid., chapter 2.

[18] Ibid.

[19] Van Schendel, *The Bengal Borderland,* p. 53; Reece Jones, *Border Walls* (NY and London: Zed, 2012), and note 25 below.

20 Willem Van Schendel, "Spaces of Engagement: How Borderlands, Illicit Flows, and Territorial States Interlock," in Willem Van Schendel and Itty Abraham, eds., *Illicit Flows and Criminal Things: States, Borders, and the Other Side of Globalization* (Bloomington: Indiana University Press, 2005), pp. 47, 50.

21 Ibid., p. 53.

22 Van Schendel, *The Bengal Borderland*, p. 118.

23 The report, with names, can be found in Mirza Zulfiqur Rahman and Kathleen Staudt, "There Are Many Indias: A Call for Collaborations and Comparative Research," *La Frontera*, 35, 2 (a large-distribution newsletter of the Association of Borderlands Studies), Spring 2015, pp. 3–5. Rahman organized the March conference.

24 Ministry website, Government of India, http://mdoner.gov.in/content/citizens-charter.

25 Sahana Ghosh, "Cross-border Activities in Everyday Life: The Bengal Borderland," *Contemporary South Asia* 19, 1, 2011, pp. 49–60.

26 Paula Banerjee, "Bengal Border Revisited," *Journal of Borderlands Studies* 27, 1, April 2012, p. 31.

27 Syed Tashfin Chowdhury, "Acquittal of India Border Guard in Bangladeshi Girl's Killing Rekindles Human Rights Concerns," *Asia Times*, July 10, 2015. http://atimes.com/2015/07/acquittal-of-India-border-guard-in-bangladeshi-girls-killing-rekindles-human-rights-concerns/. Accessed 2/1/16.

Border policing has its dangers for guards as well. India's Ministry of Home Affairs lists agents who died in the line of duty, complete with pictures and details about their deaths.

28 Sanjib Baruah, *Durable Disorder: Understanding the Politics of Northeast India* (New Delhi: Oxford University Press, 2005).

29 Ibid., p. 5.

30 South Asia Terrorism Portal, http://www.satp.org.

31 Baruah, *Durable Disorder*, p. 10, chapter 9.

32 Ibid., p. 15.

33 *The Economist*, Special Report on India, "Modi's Many Tasks," May 23, 2015, p. 15.

34 Dhananjay Tripathi, "Creating Borders in Young Minds: A Case Study of Indian and Pakistani School Textbooks," *Regions & Cohesion* 6, 1, 2016, pp. 52–71.

35 The sacredness of cows has led some Indian state governments to apply harsh penalties to those who eat or kill cows.

36 Government of India, Ministry of Home Affairs, http://www.mha.nic.in. Accessed 5/1/15.

37 Ghosh, "Cross-border Activities in Everyday Life."

38 Madhavi Mallapragada, *Virtual Homelands: Indian Immigrants and Online Cultures in the United States* (Urbana: University of Illinois Press, 2014), p. 15. Remittances come from migrant workers in professional and humble occupations, often an exploited class in Persian Gulf states. On my trip to India, I changed planes in Doha, Qatar. As flight attendants passed on customs cards for arrival in Kolkata (Calcutta), I was asked to help a migrant complete his form. He could not read or write, and his village in India had no numeric street address as requested on the form.

39 Mallapragada, *Virtual Homelands*, p. 15.

40 Ibid., p. 34.

41 Ghosh says the mostly tall BSF men come mainly from north and western India, with a different stature than local Bengalis in the borderlands, so they are called foreigners.

Chapter 6

European Integration (Under Threat)

Mobility in a Superstructure

The world is filled with border conflicts over disputed claims about territory and waterways. Despite central involvement in two world wars, Europe has been spared some of the world's worst border conflicts in the last half-century, a major exception being the Balkans region, re-bordered from the amalgamation once called Yugoslavia. Metrocosm's map "A World of Disputed Territories," shows the minimal border conflict in Europe (in the map list at the end of the chapter).[1] Indeed, in Europe the word "regions" now complements or overwhelms the word "borders" (see box 6.1). Nevertheless, the European Union (EU)—with its huge common market and near half-billion population (to change, once Britain exits, given the Brexit vote in 2016), comparable to North America—still exhibits and reflects a tenuous compromise between European identity in its integrated institutions and territorially bounded states and their nationalist loyalties. Political and economic cooperation has been elevated to the highest levels in various institutions of the EU, with relatively open borders during the Schengen era (explained below), however challenged with the western Asia refugee migration in 2015 and thereafter. Is the region an institutional model for troubled and unequal borderlands elsewhere?

Historian Charles Tilly titled a famous article, "War Making and State Making as Organized Crime."[2] However intriguing the phrase, in this chapter, we need to look beyond war making to the kinds of institutions and sentiments that make integration and territorial cooperation among states possible and sustaining. We consider reasons that led to this relative peaceful border cooperation since the close of World War II (at least until the United Kingdom vote to leave in Brexit 2016): A reduction of border inequalities, including decent minimum wages? Institutional mechanisms to negotiate tension before conflicts become violent? Fatigue with wars? A spirit of compromise and tolerance for the supranational public good? Economic stakes in peaceful trade? A neoliberal ideological agenda and its political support base, with commitments to a minimum floor of human security through redistributive programs? The economic recession and subsequent austerity programs of recent years have put some of this reasoning to test. First, however, we address recent historical matters to frame and map the chapter, then we consider brief historical perspectives on the European Union (EU), and finally, we focus on the German-Polish border set at the Oder-Neisse line after World War II with the 1945 Potsdam Agreement. One of the most amazing features of the European Union—especially for North American readers with relatively hard borders between Mexico, the United States, and Canada—is the "Schengen Agreement" (actually two agreements, ratified in 1985 and 1990, respectively), permitting free and easy movement without border inspections, guards, and fees—that is, until the refugee crisis that began in 2014.

Box 6.1

States Covered as "European" in This Chapter

What countries do I include in the region called Europe? Alas, Europe is home to far too many countries to provide a chart on economic indicators as I included for the previous chapters. Imagining a map around the region (including most states in the middle), at its northward point we include the Baltic and Scandinavian countries, move southwestward to include the United Kingdom (to change after Brexit) and Ireland, and envelope Portugal and Spain to include Mediterranean countries (and island nations like Malta), then move northeastward to include Bulgaria, Romania, Moldova, Hungary, Slovakia, and Poland. (Switzerland is not a member of the European Union.) The Ukraine, amid a simmering civil war and divided into east and west, will be covered only tangentially as it is not part of the European Union, though serves as a buffer between post-Soviet Eastern Europe and Russia. I do not include Belarus, nor do I include candidates for EU membership such as Turkey and the Eurasian Heartland, released from the Soviet empire in the early 1990s, due to the Russian-US geopolitical tensions under which they struggle, their own democratization processes, and numerous border conflicts in the South Caucasus.*

Europe contains enclaves, most notably Kaliningrad, a Russian administrative unit in the Baltic region between Poland and Lithuania.[†] North Africa also contains geopolitical and bordered oddities like Spain's Melilla and Ceuta nestled in Morocco—once among the most unequal borderlands in the world, but now surpassed in inequality ratios (outliers in F, see chapter 3) by Israel and Palestine, near equivalent to Yemen and Oman. Cyprus, an EU member, has been separated by Partition for over 40 years from North Cyprus, the latter affiliated with Turkey which is the only country to recognize its sovereignty. States in the North Atlantic, such as Iceland, will not be covered in this chapter despite their partial incorporation into European integration efforts.

For a wider concept of Europe to include Russia and its Commonwealth of Independent States, see the website of OneEurope.[‡] (Note that this is not to be confused with global airlines' Oneworld Alliance!)

*See Tigran Torosyan and Arax Vardanyan, "The South Caucasus Conflicts in the Context of Struggle for the Eurasian Heartland," *Geopolitics* 20, 3, 2015, pp. 559–82; and Mark R. Beissinger and Crawford Young, eds., *Beyond State*

Crisis? Postcolonial and Post-Soviet Eurasia in Comparative Perspective (Washington, DC: Woodrow Wilson Center Press, 2002), pp. 19–50.

Several films often excellent insights about consequent tensions in the region including *Tangerines* (2015), a story about Estonian farmers who had long settled in the warring region of Abkhazia, with wounded Georgian and Chechen fighters in an uneasy truce under an Estonian roof.

[†]For a list of Europe's enclaves and exclaves, see Thomas Lundén, *On the Boundary: About Humans at the End of Territory* (Huddinge, Sweden: Södertörns högskola, 2004), p. 57.

[‡]http://www.one-europe.info.

Mapping Matters

Maps tell a visual story about states, potential national identities, and changes over time. As maps of Europe over the centuries show, however, the so-called territorial trap of states obscures the constantly changing boundary lines. The economies therein are still "trapped" in GDP per capita summary statistics of well-being, though binational *equalities* prevail, at least in the older members of the European Union. Perhaps that will spread to its newer members.

Mapping Historical Perspectives

In Europe, more national borderlines have been redrawn in the 20th century than elsewhere, a result of two world wars and the breakup of the authoritarian Yugoslavia and resultant Balkan crises of the 1990s.[3] A comparison of maps (see the list at the end of the chapter) from the Peace of Westphalia in 1648, to 1815, to 20th-century maps from 1900 and beyond displays a dizzying array of borders in prewar, interwar, and postwar years; consider, for example, the series of maps from 1900 to 1914, 1920, 1937, 1945, 1947, and 1970—with multiple redrawn boundaries in the 20th century alone. Germany and Poland expanded and contracted with frequency in size and shape, but the shape seems normalized in their current territorial spaces in the minds of many.

On the nationalistic and political use of maps noted in chapter 2, see the book, *The War in Maps*, edited by Giselher Wirsing in 1941, on an aggressive Germany in the 1939–1940 World War II era,[4] showing threats from countries encircling it, even as Germany invaded and occupied other countries. The captions alone are worth a look.

In the aftermath of two vicious 20th-century world wars in which scores of millions died through conflict and mass murder, Europe has recovered and more. US readers are constantly bombarded with visual images of European places through art, novels, medieval glory and horror, war films, glamorous but often obnoxious James Bond movies (24 and counting!), and World History courses in high school (that mainly focus on Europe as "Western heritage"). However, US readers may also recall once-stark images of an "Iron Curtain" running down the center, dividing "East" (and east-central states) from "West" in a Cold War that lasted through the 1989 fall of the Berlin Wall, the breakup of the Soviet Union and its satellite allies, and the warming of internal European relations. Yet in a world with growing numbers of fences and walls (see chapter 8 on security), although sparse in most of Europe, the current refugee crisis has spurred use of barbed-wire fences even in several European borderlands. A map of border barriers worldwide can be found in the list at the end of the chapter.

Citing figures from the Berlin Wall Association and Centre for Contemporary History Research, Matthew Carr says 125 people were killed crossing the wall. One person is too many, but far greater numbers die crossing the Mediterranean Sea and the US-Mexico border annually in the 21st century. Berlin Wall–era deaths and lack of freedom are remembered, captured in many films, and taught in world, international, and western history. Yet from 1988–2011, at least 15,551 migrants died crossing Europe's borders and thousands more thereafter.[5] Perhaps no one will ever count accurately the bodies in the Mediterranean Sea, or what is left of them. We could say the death rate is at least 100 times more than that during attempted escapes across the Berlin War.

From Historical Scars to Building Equality and Institutions

Territorial borderlines are the "scars of history."[6] European notions about states, from and since the Westphalian birthplace (located in modern Germany), spread institutionally around the world through colonialism's wide reach, as covered in chapter 2. The idea and structure of states became a solution to a 30-year religious war in 1648, but retained their essence over many re-bordered and new states through subsequent centuries as empires collapsed. Empires had been home to ethnic and linguistic enclaves including German communities in Central and Eastern Europe and Russia.

In the 20th century, German Nazi nationalists drew on long-held expansionist ideas to justify invasion and occupation across territorial boundaries to envelop and make space for a larger Germany. Nazis forced people to work and committed mass murders of ethnic, national, and religious groups, all of them "Others." The aftermath of war always includes the trauma of post-conflict economic recovery, refugees' out-migration, and ethnic, national, and religious cleansings as winners redraw national territorial boundaries. After World War II, with the changes in borders, governments forced the resettlement of millions of Poles, Ukrainians, and Germans among others, requiring them to start new lives and leave their homes and property amid treacherous circumstances. Historians analyze thousands of memoirs to reconstruct the trauma of individual and collective memory, as Beata Halicka has done with three national identity groups resettled into other territories, with a focus on the "wild west" of Poland.[7]

Many scholars say that Germany has a special place in European integration, especially in the suprainstitutional moves toward regional cooperation. It is centrally located, wealthy, and surrounded by nine countries and their borders. The first EUregions (also called EuroRegions and Euregios) occurred on Germany's western boundary.[8] A full outline of the evolution and dates of the treaties and agreements for European integration from six countries to more than quadruple that in size is beyond the scope of this book, and would require examination of such aspects as trade, defense/security, economic growth in freer trade, common currency, relatively free movement for citizens acceded in the Schengen Area, and collaboration. Core mover Germany continues in that role, despite the rotation of leadership and European Parliamentary elections. To skip ahead on institutional development, it suffices to say that a solidification of major European Union institutions occurred in 1995 and thereafter, with a process for identification, application, and candidacies for the expansion of membership. All of this unfolded in *stages*, as Michel Foucher has outlined, from division, conflict, and integration to Europe's development over time.[9]

Economic Equalities?

The European region, located in the North, has long been viewed as home to richer, more "developed" countries (using the parlance of international development over the last half of the 20th century). Under the European Union, people and goods can move more freely. Some open-border advocates view Europe as an alternative toward which other regions in the world might or should move, but it is relatively unique: industrialized, well-educated multilingual populations, and a social net that provides a floor of human security, welfare, and health care (with higher taxes compared to the United States and Mexico). Inequalities between countries have diminished, though the glossy picture contains subregional challenges, plus closed borders and inequalities at its external perimeter.

Using 2004 GDP per capita data, Spanish economist Iñigo Moré ranked per capita income data among binational pairs to show that seven of the ten *most equal* borders are found in Europe.[10] In this chapter, I chose not to include a figure for Europe, like in previous chapters 4 and 5, as noted in box 6.1. Why? The figure generated became an overwhelmingly complex, color-code of many countries—new and renamed, small and large, some of which entered the EU in different years, merged together. On that figure, I excluded one outlier country exception, the tiny state Luxembourg, center of finance and banks, with a GDP per capita and growth rate that moves it off the charts compared to the rest of Europe.

For the bulk of countries, however, I examined the binational pairs and found that they show steady economic growth and movement toward more equal ratios. Among the *early* Western European state members of the European Union in the 20th century, all binational pairs exhibit grades of A level equality ratios (see chapter 3 for explanations). Among state pairs with at least one or both later entrants from Eastern and Central Europe into the European Union (usually in 2004 and thereafter), one finds a mix of ratios among binational pairs, with the largest number at A levels, then several at both B and C levels, and fewer at D. So a question may be raised: Did EU common markets, currencies, and open movement facilitate more equality or simply consolidate connections between countries with a base of relative equality? The answer—not the main purpose of this book—is that probably both their baseline economies and the EU integration facilitated binational equalities, among those under the integrated umbrella for decades. Time will tell whether and how long more border equalities will prevail as those countries recover from centrally planned, low-growth economies prior to the 1990s and benefit from private and EU investment.

Inequalities within most of the European Union's member nations (as measured by GINI index showing internal inequalities) are low compared to many countries in the world due to wage and redistributive policies.[11] Legal minimum wages approximate half or more of GDP per capita incomes, a better proportion that in other world regions.[12] However, organized power dynamics have shifted over the decades, with a declining percentage of working people affiliated with labor unions (still very high in Scandinavian countries); moreover, business organizations comprise about two-thirds of interest groups formally recognized to lobby in the European Union.[13] A health and social welfare net, coupled with high taxes, cushions people who otherwise might live in desperate circumstances. Yet even in Europe, the GDP per capita figures could use some unpacking, given the relatively free movement for Europeans to study and work (albeit paying taxes too) among member countries, with wages and cost-of-living variations. One reason some British voters opted to vote for Brexit in 2016 was the presence of many Europeans, especially from Poland and other Eastern European countries. The influx amounted to more than the British outflux of workers and retirees elsewhere in Europe.

EU Institutional Webs

The European Union represents an uneasy compromise between the supranational, the national, and local cross-border regions. James Wesley Scott calls the European Union "ostensibly borderless," but in a region where "national borders are again seen as central to the organization of political community and the protection of group interests."[14] Nationalisms rear their heads periodically, such as in the refugee crisis (see chapter 9). When MP (Member of Parliament) Jo Cox was assassinated before the Brexit vote, her killer shouted "Britain First." At weekly, monthly, even daily bases, especially with the 2016 campaign over Britain's exit (Brexit) from the European Union, media headlines questioned whether its open, internal borders and common currencies would survive. So-called Euro-skepticism gets constant coverage, and the rise of a right-wing backlash in France leads some to wonder about a possible Frexit campaign. Yet a coexistent and integrative Europeanization process has a long history of accomplishments and has been underway for decades, complete with Eurostats, growing trust among nationals and binational pairs, and the generation of frequent opinion polls with the Eurobarometer.

National leaders debate cooperation or skepticism over mobility, economic gains and losses, and supranational influence over local accountability, pointing to European institutional structures. When the UK-France Channel Tunnel (also called the Chunnel) was built in 1994, after a 1986 agreement "aligned with the political and economic forces of free market expansionism" under Prime Minister Margaret Thatcher, "a new quasi terrestrial borderland (the Cross-Channel Region) became eligible for EU funding."[15] Thatcher-era support gave rise to criticism from those who worry about neoliberal elite collusion. Little did Europeans know that two decades later, Calais would be a major staging era for refugees from France, seeking to enter a destination like the United Kingdom perceived to offer better options.[16] Among the latest in violent-border genre television series, *The Tunnel* begins with a dead body in the Eurotunnel, draped across the territorial line, generating jurisdictional tensions among the police. *The Bridge*, actually two separate TV series with the same title, one set in Denmark-Sweden and the other in the US-Mexico borderlands, shares the same premise. Popular culture aggravates border fears of those glued to television series like these.

Those who dreamed of integration and a common market with standardized safety regulations in the 1950s sought the freer movement of people, goods, and services. While this chapter will not address the complex evolution of the European Union, including shifts to include both cross-border and "territorial cooperation" since 2007, Wassenberg and Reitel provide such a history with beautiful maps originally commissioned for their book.[17]

Beginning in 1985, with accords completed from 1990 onward over the so-called Schengen Area (named after a village in Luxembourg where negotiations occurred), 26 countries eliminated passport and immigration controls at their borders. Most belong to the European Union, but several do not (Iceland, Norway, Switzerland). A few EU members do not belong to the Schengen Area (United Kingdom and Ireland). Schengen Area people number 450 million in a space of over 1.6 million square miles, surrounded by a 26,515-mile land border and 5,484-mile coastline.[18] According to the Schengen Visa Information website, citizens "cherish the right to migrate" without limitations; free movement is "one of the basic human rights."[19] One can only imagine the different world in which we would live if such rights extended everywhere. Bridges and tunnels connect land spaces, for example, between Denmark and Sweden and France and the United Kingdom, the latter noted earlier. In other parts of the world, such as North America, free and unregulated movements into the United States would be viewed as security threats from terrorists, unauthorized migrants, or drugs to enter the country. The 9/11 attacks strengthened the US hard-borders approach.

A veritable alphabet soup of EU acronyms and multiple umbrella institutions exist, from regional to national and local levels. The European Commission, representing EU interests as a whole, is the EU executive body of five-year term appointees from each of the 28 member states.[20] The European Parliament—in which sit 751 MEPs, that is Members of the European Parliament—selects the Commission president with a majority of its votes. At the highest-level sits the European Union Council, consisting of the heads of state and setting directions but making no laws. Revenue to support the EU institutions comes from a variety of sources including under 1 percent of gross national product and value-added taxes, import duties, and fines from regulatory noncompliance.[21]

The European experience, says Emmanuel Brunet-Jailly, is influenced by "its regional policy, with its tradition of local level and intergovernmental networks and policy-making practices . . . in a manner coherent with preexisting polices of partnership and cooperation."[22] In Europe, security is conceptualized more broadly, to include economic, environment, and human securities (see chapter 8). In Canada, too, Konrad and Nicol note the broader concern with emergency management in security compared to the United States,[23] though the United States remains a hegemon in the region, able to influence, even impose its approaches on neighbors to the north and south.

At its external borders, the European Commission established a security perimeter around most Schengen Area countries with an agency known as Frontex. Its border guard teams manage not only databases and surveillance systems, but also the considerable sea and land borders around EU territory (42,672 and 8,826 kilometers, respectively—most countries use the metric system (!); see previous pages for miles) at a fraction of the US Department of Homeland Security costs.[24] In the early 21st century era, with an ongoing humanitarian crisis of thousands of drowning deaths by maritime migrants crossing the Mediterranean Sea (see chapter 9 on migration), Frontex established Operation Triton to share costs and responsibility with sea-border countries in the Mediterranean area (see video and also migratory routes map with multicolored triangular areas, with the warnings that a big entry route is via airports with visa overstays—common in the United States as well).[25]

States and regions pursue both hard- and soft-power strategies (some would call for a "smart" power mix) to pursue their interests. While Frontex could be classified as mostly a hard-power approach, soft-power strategies are in place as well. With its Neighbourhood Policy, established in 2003, the EU partners with nonmember countries in the Mediterranean and (former Soviet-affiliated) Eurasian areas to provide assistance, particularly for cooperation in preventing migrants from entering the European Union by sea or over land. Sixteen countries participate in this Neighbourhood Policy ostensibly to spread "prosperity, stability and security" if opportunities comply with EU standards.[26] Neighborhood Barometer data is available by country, along with other Eurostats, complementing national with some supranational numeric indicators.

Scholars and human rights activists have criticized agreements with North African authoritarian regimes such as notorious former dictators like Libya's Gaddafi; new negotiations became necessary with some post–Arab Spring governments in 2010 and thereafter.[27] At the time of this writing, Libya has no national government among warring factions. Among significant EU standards for assistance, Pinos lists the following:[28]

- migration control instructions in transit or sending countries
- retention centers to hold migrants who await return
- legal return procedures for asylum seekers
- readmission agreements

The neighborhood strategies aim to *preempt* unauthorized workers and refugees, the latter suggesting questionable consistency with United Nations international laws on refugees. Henk van Houtum uses striking language in his title of an article that criticizes arrangements: "Human Blacklisting: The Global Apartheid of the EU's External Border Regime."[29] Carr uses the verb "trapping" to refer to the Neighbourhood Partnerships to exclude the unwanted travelers.[30]

Clearly, despite the warmth of linguistic derivatives from the word "neighbor," the European Union's neighborly missions and aims involve contradictory interpretations. No doubt Russia also perceives these geopolitical arrangements as threats to its sphere of influence.

Regional Institutions: Wherefore Everyday Life?

Given the many changes in 20th-century European borders, peacetime Europe exemplifies the freedoms to move from one state to another with ease along with the potential development of regional or European integrated identities. As developed in this section, EU investments in institution-building and infrastructure have resulted in the creation of subregional collaborations across borders, most often between officials and businesspeople yet also via cultural exchanges and cross-border shopping. These efforts have optimistically been called "laboratories" for integration.

Empirical studies, however, question the optimism or suggest that the development of regional identities may be premature. In the Galicia-North Portugal Euroregion, Juan-Manuel Trillo-Santamaria cites research showing that few residents in the Euroregion know the entity or how it works. His own survey research shows that less than half of inhabitants had even heard of the Euroregion. He concludes that the Euroregion concept "lacks passion" and that gaps exist "between the elite's project and people's knowledge of it."[31]

Other studies include pictures and descriptions of cross-border networks consisting of shoppers, including the invariable crossing for cheaper cigarettes, liquor, and gas—or even sex shops—on the "other" side of the border.[32] Civic life would consist of cross-border NGOs (nongovernmental organizations). But Peter Jurczek notes that prejudices break down as more and more people interact over time; EU support exists for people-to-people projects like pupil exchanges and sports events.[33]

In scores of border regions, cross-border labor networks operate regularly in which people who live on one side (often the side with lower costs or wages) cross to work. While free movement and open borders facilitate such exchange, border scholars also note obstacles: unfamiliarity and mental "Othering" between "us and them."[34] Perhaps more time and experience will breed more familiarity. Of course, many European workers and professionals cross multiple borders in search of higher wages, at two or three times what they might earn in their own countries.

Empirical research suggests that business, policy, and official networks become better developed with financial investment and profit incentives. Despite constraints in measuring network development and density, Olivier Walther and Bernard Reitel demonstrate the diminishing role of border barriers in decision making in the Swiss-French-German cross-border metro Basel Region as joint processes take hold.[35] Rolf Bergs published a methodical assessment of an interregional strand cross-border cooperation worth multiple billions of Euro interventions for balanced growth. He concludes that history matters most for integration impacts. Yet his conceptualization of other factors, however problematic in their operationalization, offer useful ways to think about "willingness to cooperate" and its multiple forms: jointly examined needs for programming, range of partner stakeholders, and the percentages of mutually approved partnerships and truly joint initiatives among all initiatives.[36] We are clearly only at the beginning stages of quantitative approaches to analyzing cross-border collaboration.

Many European border scholars note the limitations of expecting fuller integration via top-down EU institutions, whether from the central European Union or in cross-border official commissions. However, John Wesley Scott sounds a more positive note, deeming Euroregions as successes for channeling resources into borderlands. Officials submit proposals to various funding sources for twin-city partnerships and cross-border cooperation. Such projects were pioneered in the Dutch-German region around the early 1960s, but also more recently at external borders with European Neighbourhood Policy (ENP) and European Neighbourhood and Partnership Instruments (ENPI). As such, projects could do more than prevent unwanted migration but also provide incentives for job creation, greater income prosperity, and balance in borderlands. By its fourth programming of an interregional EU structural initiative 2007–2013, 10 billion euros had been disbursed.[37] Program achievements since the outset include job creation, technology infrastructure, and the reduction of border barriers through bridges and other transportation, though often perceptions exist (and reality confirms) that one side benefits more than the other.[38]

Turning now to the German-Polish border, we have learned thus far about historical successes in moving toward equality, but uneven commitments to and identifications with the borderlands projects and with Europe itself persist. Whether this continues under Poland's new government elected in 2015 is yet to be determined.

The Polish-German Borderlands

As with any borderlands or region, an historical perspective adds to knowledge about contemporary contexts. Polish-German re-bordering is one that is scarred, from war and forced resettlements. The memories, still fresh and alive, emerge in oral histories and archives.

Border Peoples

After World War II's victors settled on the Oder-Neisse as the new borderline between Poland and Germany, governments forced many people to move. Poland's borders moved westward, and millions of people resettled into the newly bordered "territorial traps" after the trauma and economic instability of the war years: Polish people, from east to west, Ukrainians to the east, and Germans farther west. The records of thousands of memoirs of those forcibly resettled make clear the challenges faced with Germans forced to move west of the Oder River and with Poles moved from eastern Poland, Western Lithuania, and Belarus to repopulate the area.[39] Initially, officials used border towns in campaigns to re-nationalize residents with concomitant war and other symbolic memorials.[40] Historian Beata Halicka calls this postwar western region of Poland the "wild west" in the titles of her two books, one in Polish and the other in German (and various English-language academic journal articles, as cited herein).

Halicka analyzes the enormous challenges settlers faced in three patterns: from starting their livelihoods anew as enthusiastic pioneers, to coping with (temporarily) resettled looters, and to recovering from surviving the exhaustion and tyranny of war. The new authoritarian Government of Poland even established a new institution, the Ministry for the Recovered Territories, headed by high-level Władysław Gomułka, Secretary General of the Workers Party and Deputy Prime Minister.[41] Halicka combed the archives of collected memories from individuals with different nationalities—each with their own vantage points—and in different eras, with perhaps greater honesty in documents after the mid-1950s Polish "thaw" in government. The acute plight of children is noteworthy, many "persecuted for the sins of their parents," including orphaned German children left behind if insufficiently Polonized in the restored territory of Poland. Schools only began to reopen around 1950, and teachers wrote of the difficulties not only teaching new languages but also covering subjects for students unschooled during war.[42] The consequences of war last well beyond signed treaties in peace talks.

Using contemporary in-depth interviews of people in German and Polish twin cities, Katarzyna Stokłosa cites the still-vivid memories of Polish residents forbidden to travel west or even stroll along the river without border patrol guards surveilling and interviewing them in border watchtowers.[43] Stokłosa also compares neighborhood relations on three Polish borders, past and present, including the lengthy external borders of Europe (Russia and Ukraine) and the coexistent Kaliningrad (the odd Russian enclave administrative unit nestled within northeastern Europe). She said the artificially and arbitrarily constructed political borders among supposed ideologically aligned states were closed and conflictual: "relations between communist 'brother states' were anything but fraternal."[44]

In the once-whole but "divided towns" along the new East German–Polish border, travel was initially forbidden—even for the expelled Germans to visit their homes—until 1971, only to be closed again after 1980 with the rise of the Polish Solidarity movement whose resistance to government authoritarianism generated fears among officials about its spread to East Germany. But upheavals in 1989 and early 1990 produced more dramatic change in cross-border cooperation, with the fall of the Berlin Wall, democratization processes in Poland, German unification and collapse of the USSR. Yet stereotypes remained: Germans had "negative images of Polish car thieves, high levels of criminality and the perception of 'Polish slackers,'" while Poles disparaged Germans as Nazis.[45]

No doubt Poland sees Ukraine as a buffer between its eastern frontier and Russia, especially after the "return" of Crimea in eastern Ukraine to Russia. In perusing several issues of *New Eastern Europe* from 2014 and 2015, I read essays in Polish academic publications seemingly preoccupied with Ukraine. Stokłosa, noting surveys that show Polish fears about Russia, paints a vivid portrait of border crossing to Kaliningrad as a challenge, with waiting times in the hours and bribes to be paid, even though price differentials make the small-scale "ant" trade in alcohol, cigarettes, gas, gold, electronics, clothes, and food profitable.[46] (See chapters 4 on the Americas and 10 on trade for the frequent metaphoric use of the word "ants" for cross-border traders.) But a new agreement authorized "small border traffic," allowing applicants to cross without a visa. One can find a song by the popular music group Parovoz, with a background reggae beat, on YouTube about visits to Polish grocery stores.[47]

In *Borders of Inequality*, Spanish scholar Iñigo Moré brings his analysis to closure with a chapter focus on three case studies, one of them an icon of economic *inequality* (Spain-Morocco), another with economic interdependence but limited equality and few binational institutions (US-Mexico), and still another with proactive binational and regional EU institutional support—a relative success story in his eyes. That story is found at the German-Polish border and its many "twin cities" (once called divided cities), high economic growth rate in Poland, and extensive German investment. Later I provide a special focus on Germany's Frankfurt (Oder) and Poland's Slubice (the latter once a suburb of the German city in an historic non-border area). Iñigo Moré says that since the reunification of Germany (and demise of East Germany) and Poland's accession into the European Union and Schengen Area, the ratio of inequality fell from 8 to 4 in 2004, or 2.3 with purchasing power parity statistics,[48] though one might challenge the problematic economic statistics in the early 1990s of eastern Germany and the move toward a market economy in Poland. In my Border Inequalities Database, the ratio was 3.51 (with purchasing power parity), putting it in the C–/D+ category.

With attention to geography, industrial development, demographics, and occupations, Z. Anthony Kruszewski provides yet more insight into factors behind diminishing Germany-Poland inequalities over time. He begins with the re-bordering of 1945 to include Poland's industrial zones in its northwest, its deep-sea ports, and the decline of the Polish farming population (in the east) as factors which reduced economic gaps between Germany and Poland.[49] While he acknowledges the hardships and traumas of forced resettlement, his statistics and census data reinforce the long-term strengthening of the Polish economic base and the occupational shifts of its population after World War II.

To this, we must add EU and private investment to infrastructure and other economic development. Through phases of regional programming, border twin towns can be now considered "laboratories of European integration" with more intensive cooperative processes than in other areas.[50] Below I focus on twin cities Frankfurt (Oder) and Slubice, with a combined total of around 100,000 people, to the southeast of Berlin and a further distance west of Warsaw.

Frankfurt (Oder) and Slubice: Twin Cities

The model of the German-Polish border might offer inspiration to other regions. Yet my examination of academic literature coupled with a visit in 2013 to the European University Viadrina/Collegium Polonicum, higher education partnerships, and friendships with academic colleagues from Poland suggest that the realities are more complex. Context matters in a space where the differences in languages (German and Polish) may be more pronounced than in other border regions. Far more Poles seem to speak German than vice versa, and people are relatively new in the area, going back just a generation or two.

As in Halick's previously cited work, Francisco Llero Pacheco and Angeles López-Nórez stress the current population's shallow "roots" in the region, based on their interviews with officials, a review of studies on the region, and a theoretical framework that highlights local attachment or lack thereof as central to cross-border collaboration.[51] Moreover, the legacies of former governments (centralized and federal) and economies (market versus planned) pose challenges to regional development. Cross-border contact was rare until after the fall of communism. Former authoritarian, centralized regimes in planned economies gave way to market-oriented capitalist economies on both sides of the border in the 1990s. However, without a local manufacturing base, and with a loss in population especially on the Frankfurt (Oder) side, the local economy has lacked dynamism. Despite its lower wages, Slubice's small size (<20,000 people) and distance from Warsaw make it less attractive for foreign direct investment.

Nevertheless, the European Union invested in many joint projects, such as transportation (see the town bridge pictured), the first cross-border tram line for cross-border commuters, infrastructure, and the European University Viadrina and Collegium Polonicum, the latter of which had a symbolic integration monument built in its plaza. The University once reserved 30 percent of admissions for Poles and offers courses in German, Polish, French, and English, but Polish students also have begun to attend other distinguished universities nearby in their own country.

Entry into the European Union, called "accession," involved easier challenges in Western than with Eastern and Central Europe, with their planned socialist economies through 1990 as well as weaker civil societies under previous authoritarian governments that generated distrust of government.[52] From business and economic perspectives, integration in the European Union should reduce the costs associated with administrative barriers and transportation, thereby fostering more foreign investment and cross-border trade. Yet looking east, Birgit Leick says that "history matters for the formation of economic and business linkages:" the former separation of socialist and capitalist states, neglect of private communication and associated "mental barriers," language differences, and risk aversion.[53] Moreover, administrative systems of neighboring countries do not mesh well; Peter Jurczek notes also the high turnover of administrators on the eastern sides.[54] Institutional differences matter as well. Germany is a less-centralized federal state with considerable power, resources and authority in subnational governments, whereas Poland is a more centralized unitary state (see a map link on such institutional differences).[55] Yet centralized unitary government is common for most members of the European Union, as the map shows. In this book's comparative approach, one could point out how the United States and Mexico share a federal structure, with the former more decentralized and the latter's approach more centralized. Historical mistrust

Border bridge between twin cities Frankfurt (Oder), Germany, and Slubice, Poland, with free movement for cars, pedestrians, and bikes (no border guards or barriers).

Source: Photographer Kathleen Staudt.

and enormous inequality gaps seem more relevant. Also in South Asia, only China emerges as the centralized structure on the map, but it delegates some authority to outlying provinces on economic issues. Mainly, it is distrusted as an extremely powerful state amid impoverished states.

A once-lively series of joint initiatives gave way to residents seeking to focus on "their own side" of the border, though shopping has shifted from sex, petrol, and cigarette tourism at Polish bazaars to shopping centers and services.[56] When I crossed the open border in 2013 walking on cobblestone streets, formerly German, I saw shop after shop with the same cigarette brands posted in their windows with the words on packages in Polish, later translated to me: Cigarettes Kill. In the 1990s, Slubice's bazaar attracted over 90 percent of its customers from the German side of the border, third highest among twin towns.[57] I visited the largest bazaar and saw lots of shops selling cigarettes and liquor. Llera Pacheco and López-Nórez, complementing their narrative with a picture of a Euroregion sign on the street for the Pro Europa Viadrina, note the planning processes reflected in the Common Local Action Plan 2020 and the Joint Commission.[58] But they conclude that bottom-up civic input from local residents is missing in what is essential a top-down integration project.

One such creative grassroots activity consists of "Slubfurt" artists, a creative grassroots network that joins the first four and last four letters of Slubice-Frankfurt (Oder). James W. Scott mentions that activists had stronger European orientations on the Polish side, yet the picture may be more nuanced. At the Slubfurt artists' website, its launcher uses culture and art to counter and question official narratives about cross-border cooperation. Creative efforts are under way, even involving linguistic "code-switching" (mixing two or more languages, also common in the US-Mexico borderlands).[59]

The German-Polish borderlands, into which the European Union and private contributors have made tremendous investments, offer a mixed story of some successes but also challenges. Border inequalities have been reduced, but not to the levels of other EU members. "Othering" continues, as do memories from the war and forced resettlement. The East-West divide continues as well, but is not as visible. The open borders constitute a major achievement. Overall, as an integration story, the Polish-German border shows us a mixed but perhaps realistic picture of the stages and length of time for greater integration to occur. States still have a way to go before a more genuine integration occurs, achievable perhaps over time and with great equality.

Concluding Reflections

History matters in the establishment and successes of European integration. Both economic growth and expanded cross-border economic opportunities—coupled also with EU institutional financial investments in poverty reduction and border infrastructure—have diminished inequalities. Yet cross-border and territorial integration beyond local governments and business stakeholders face other challenges, namely multiple languages, limited cross-border civic activism, and continuing memories, prejudices, and overall "Otherness" from language and nationality differences from a bottom-up or borderlands perspective.[60]

Europe offers an institutional model, if modified, to which many states and their borderlands could aspire. Of course, Europe took over a half-century to develop the model in a rich, industrialized, and postindustrial region in a much poorer world of majority postcolonial states. However, the model shows what investment in cross-border regions, inequality reduction, and regulated market economies might achieve with a social safety net and redistributive policies. Recent challenges, such as the refugee crisis, economic recession, and imposed austerity policies show the ongoing tensions between states, their nationalisms, democracy, and superstructure EU institutions that appear distant and bureaucratic.

Despite all the advances, challenges remain in the European de-bordering model and prospects for its replication elsewhere outside of the European Union, given tightly controlled external borders, sometimes referred to as "Fortress Europe." The EU's Neighbourhood Policy funds external neighbors in collaborative efforts to control unauthorized migration and foster economic development. The refugee crisis of 2015, peaking with over a million people from Western Asia moving northward and northwestward—from especially Syria, Iraq, and Afghanistan—put to test Europe's relatively open borders as nationals searched for or rejected fairer and more consistent immigration policies that would share the resettlement burden beyond Germany, Sweden, and several other countries, especially at the first point of entry, Greece. See chapter 9 on migration.

Drawing on this book's framework in chapter 3, this chapter offers the best-case scenario for showing how institution-building activities amid challenging circumstances are associated with reduced inequalities and more prosperity within borderlands regions and across borders. But the underbelly of these achievements also deserves analysis, not the least of which are the Euro-skeptics who criticize "Euro-sclerosis" and the British exit, though it was never as fully integrated as much as other states. Some European analysts use the phrase "mental obstacles," which is a collection of historical memories, prejudices, and identities that seem to slow the growth and strength of grassroots nongovernmental civil society activism. Euro-skeptics' cynicism casts a shadow over the EU's top-down bureaucratic initiatives. Perhaps one of the biggest obstacles Europe now faces comes from its external borders and the homegrown-alienated citizens who commit terrorist attacks, such as that in Paris, 2015, and the right-wing political backlash.

Recommended Resources

Films

No Man's Land
Tangerines

Maps

Contemporary border conflicts

http://metrocosm.com/disputed-territories-map.html

Historical maps

http://www.lib.utexas.edu/maps/historical/europe_1648_westphal_1884.jpg
http://www.lib.utexas.edu/maps/historical/europe1815_1905.jpg
http://users.erols.com/mwhite28/euro1935.htm

Border barriers with French text, but obvious universal-language visuals

http://www.geo.fr/photos/reportages-geo/video-videographie-data-frontieres-toujours-plus-de-murs-159213

Maps of EU member states and regions (in Wassenberg and Reitel 2015)

http://bookshop.europa.eu/en/territorial-cooperation-in-europe-pbKN0415502/

Centralized and federal political structures

http://www.lewishistoricalsociety.com/wiki/tiki-print_article.php?articleId=136

Notes

I thank Beata Halicka for her thorough reading of an earlier version of this chapter along with Karolina Zajakala for reading a later version.

[1] The site uses graphics to analyze life with statistics and data: http://metrocosm.com/disputed-territories-map.html.

[2] In *Bringing the State Back In*, by Peter Evans, et al. (Cambridge: Cambridge University Press, 1985), pp. 169–91.

[3] The film, *No Man's Land,* focuses on the enmity of two soldiers, one Serbian and the other Bosnian, stuck in a foxhole with an invisible borderline between them in a futile conflict, with impotent UN peacekeepers and international journalists who do little of value to intervene.

[4] http://www.lib.utexas.edu/maps/historical/war_in_maps/

[5] Matthew Carr, *Fortress Europe: Dispatches from a Gated Continent* (NY: The New Press, 2012), pp. 4–5. Maurizio Albahari, *Crimes of Peace: Mediterranean Migrations at the World's Deadliest Border* (Philadelphia: University of Pennsylvania Press, 2015), provides a much higher number from a methodical source, but covers a later time period. See chapter 9 on migration.

[6] This is a phrase coined by A. Mozer in 1973, cited in Birte Wassenberg and Bernard Reitel, *Territorial Cooperation in Europe: A Historical Perspective* (Luxembourg: Publications Office of the European Union, 2015), p. 12, just as Gloria Anzaldúa, *Borderlands/La Frontera* (San Francisco: Spinsters/Aunt Lute Press, 1987) used scar metaphors in her pioneering study of the US-Mexico cultural borderlands.

[7] Figures and analysis from Beata Halicka, "The Shifting of Borders in 1945 in Memory of Poles, Germans and Ukrainians," *Warsaw East European Review* (*WEEReview*) III (2013), pp. 29–30 (where she cites a Polish source, of 1.1 million Poles, 480,000 Ukrainians, and 3.2 million Germans) and the limbo of "mixed marriage" couples in eastern Poland. The quotes about children come from her "The Everyday Life of Children in Polish-German Borderland during the Early Post-War Period," in Machteld Venken, ed., *Borderland Studies Meets Child Studies* (Frankfurt am Main: Peter Lang, 2017). Also see Halicka's "The Oder-Neisse Line as a Place of Remembrance for Germans and Poles," *Journal of Contemporary History* 49, 1, 2013, pp. 75–91.

[8] Doris Wastl-Walter and Andrea Ch. Kofler, "European Integration and Border-Related Institutions: A Practical Guide," *Journal of Borderlands Studies* 15, 1, 2000, pp. 85–106.

[9] Foucher is discussed in Ibid.

[10] Iñigo Moré, *The Borders of Inequality* (Tucson: University of Arizona Press, 2011), p. 23.

[11] Anthony Atkinson, *Inequality: What Can Be Done?* (Cambridge: Harvard University Press 2015); also see chapter 3 in this book.

[12] Google searches produce a Wikipedia site on minimum wages as a percent of per capita GDP, but I generally do not cite a source without bylines, despite well-footnoted references. The

OECD (Organization for Economic Cooperation and Development), http://www.oecd.org, also has tables on the numbers, easily accessible through its search function.

13 Deborah Stone, *Policy Paradox* (NY: W. W. Norton, 2012, 3rd edition), p. 233 on business lobbyists. One can also find lengthy lists of registered lobbyists in the transparent EU website. Figures on trade union membership can be found on the OECD website. The United States has seen a drastic decline in union membership to approximately a tenth of the labor force.

14 James Wesley Scott, "European Politics of Borders, Border Symbolism and Cross-Border Cooperation," in Thomas M. Wilson and Hastings Donnan, eds., *A Companion to Border Studies* (Malden, MA: Blackwell, 2012), p. 84.

15 Matthew Sparke, "A Neoliberal Nexus: Economy, Security and the Biopolitics of Citizenship on the Border," *Political Geography* 25, 2006, p. 195.

16 Carr, *Fortress Europe*, but crises came to a head in 2016. See chapter 9 on migration.

17 Wassenberg and Reitel, *Territorial Cooperation in Europe*. For colorful maps of member countries, see http://bookshop.europa.eu/en/territorial-cooperation-in-europe-pbKN0415502/.

18 Carr, *Fortress Europe*, p. 26.

19 The Schengen site at http://www.schengenvisainfo.com/schengen-visa-countries-list/.

20 The European Commission site at http://www.ec.europa.eu.

21 http://europa.eu/about-eu/basic-information/money/revenue-income/index_en.htm/.

22 Emmanuel Brunet-Jailly, "Securing Borders in Europe and North America," in Thomas M. Wilson and Hastings Donnan, eds., *A Companion to Border Studies* (Malden, MA: Blackwell, 2012), p. 100.

23 Victor Konrad and Heather Nicol, *Beyond Walls: Re-inventing the Canada-United States Borderlands* (Hampshire, England; Burlington, VT: Ashgate, 2008).

24 Brunet-Jailly, "Securing Borders in Europe and North America," p. 105. According to the US Department of Homeland Security budget, the Total Budget Authority in 2016 is $66.2 billion (accessed 7/24/16): https://www.dhs.gov/sites/default/files/publications/FY2017_BIB-MASTER.pdf.

25 http://www.frontex.europa.eu.

26 Anna-Lena Hoh, "'*Voir l'Autre*'? Seeing the Other, the Developments of the Arab Spring and the European Neighborhood Policy toward Algeria and Tunisia," *Journal of Borderlands Studies* 29, 2, 2014, pp. 204–16.

27 Hoh, "'*Voir l'Autre*'?" pp. 203–16. Jaume Castan Pinos, "The Conflicting Aims of the European Neighborhood Policy and its Secondary Effects," *Journal of Borderlands Studies* 29, 2, 2014, pp. 33–46.

28 Castan Pinos, "The Conflicting Aims," p. 136.

29 Henk Van Houtum, "Human Blacklisting: The Global Apartheid of the EU's External Border Regime," *Environment and Planning D: Society and Space* 28, 2010, pp. 957–76.

30 Carr, *Fortress Europe*, p. 23.

31 Juan-Manuel Trillo-Santamaria, "Cross-Border Regions: The Gap between the Elite's Projects and People's Awareness: Reflections from the Galicia-North Portugal Euroregion," *Journal of Borderlands Studies* 29, 2, 2014, p. 267.

32 See Thomas Lundén, *On the Boundary: About Humans at the End of Territory* (Huddinge, Sweden: Södertörns högskola, 2004) and this book's chapter 12 section on NGOs.

33 Peter Jurczek, "Cross-border Cooperation in the German-Czech-Polish Border Region at the Turn of the Century," *Journal of Borderlands Studies* 17, 2, 2011, p. 100.

34 Ad Knotter, "Introduction to the Special Section: Perspectives on Cross-Border Labor in Europe: '(Un)familiarity' or 'Push-and-Pull'?" *Journal of Borderlands Studies* 29, 3, 2014, pp. 319–26; and Henk van Houtum and Martin van der Velde, "De-politicizing Labour Market Indifference and Immobility in the European Union," in Olivier Kramsch and Barbara Hooper, eds., *Cross-Border Governance in the European Union* (London and NY: Routledge 2004), pp. 41–55.

35 Olivier Walther and Bernard Reitel, "Cross-border Policy Networks in the Basel Region: The Effect of National Borders and Brokerage Roles," *Space and Polity* 17, 2, 2013, pp. 217–36.

36 Rolf Bergs, "Cross-Border Cooperation, Regional Disparities and Integration of Markets in the EU," *Journal of Borderlands Studies* 27, 3, 2012, pp. 345–63. His three quantitative assessments, built off an unspecified number of managing authorities, asked for *subjective* ratings on

three-to-five point scales and percentages. Stronger measures and transparency about size of samples would be important to know.

[37] James W. Scott, "European Politics of Borders," p. 91.

[38] Wastl-Walter and Kofler, "European Integration and Border-Related Institutions," p. 93.

[39] Halicka, "The Oder-Neisse Line."

[40] Jarosław Jańczak, "Revised Boundaries and Re-Frontierization: Border Twin Towns in Central Europe," *Revue d'études comparatives Est-Ouest* 44, 4, 2013, p. 55.

[41] Halicka, "The Shifting of Borders in 1945," p. 11.

[42] Halicka, "The Everyday Life of Children in Polish-German Borderland," forthcoming.

[43] Katarzyna Stokłosa, "The Border in the Narratives of the Inhabitants of the German-Polish Border Region," in Katarzyna Stokłosa and Gerhard Besier, eds., *European Border Regions in Comparison: Overcoming Nationalistic Aspects or Re-Nationalization?* (London and New York: Routledge, 2014), pp. 257–74.

[44] Katarzyna Stokłosa, "Neighborhood Relations on the Polish Borders: The Example of the Polish-German, Polish-Ukrainian and Polish-Russian Border Regions," *Journal of Borderlands Studies* 27, 3, 2012, p. 248.

[45] This paragraph is from Stokłosa, "Neighborhood Relations on the Polish Borders," quote on p. 246.

[46] Stokłosa, "Neighborhood Relations on the Polish Borders," pp. 250–1.

[47] I am grateful to Beata Halicka for pointing out the EUR-Lex law and the YouTube. I found it, but cannot understand the language, so I will not insert the link. See also http://www.economist.com/blogs/easternapproaches/2013/10/poland-and-kaliningrad.

[48] Iñigo, *The Borders of Inequality*, p. 111, with a table that actually begins in 1989 (ratio is 12) and 1990 (almost 16), but I doubt the reliability of these figures given the turmoil in the German Democratic Republic and its move toward German unification.

[49] Z. Anthony Kruszewski, *The Oder-Neisse Boundary and Poland's Modernization: The Socio-economic and Political Impact* (NY: Praeger, 1972).

[50] Jańczak, "Revised Boundaries," p. 56.

[51] Francisco Javier Llera Pacheco and Angeles López-Nórez, *Cross-Border Collaboration in Border Twin Cities: Lessons and Challenges for the Ciudad Juárez-El Paso and the Frankfurt (Oder)/Slubice* (Ciudad Juárez: Universidad Autónoma de Ciudad Juárez, 2012).

[52] Liam O'Dowd and Bohdana Dimitrovova, "Promoting Civil Society Across the Borders of the EU Neighbourhood: Debates, Constraints and Opportunities," *Geopolitics* 16, 1, 2011, pp. 176–92.

[53] Birgit Leick, "Business Networks in the Cross-border Regions of the Enlarged EU: What Do We Know in the Post-enlargement Era?" *Journal of Borderlands Studies* 27, 3, pp. 300, 302.

[54] Jurczek, "Cross-border Cooperation in the German-Czech-Polish Border," p. 101.

[55] Map on federalism-centralism at http://www.lewishistoricalsociety.com/wiki/tiki-print_article.php?articleId=136.

[56] Jańczak, "Revised Boundaries," p. 73.

[57] Anna Bachmann, "Polish-German Cross-border Cooperation from the Neofunctional Perspective," in Elżbieta Opiłowska and Jochen Roose, eds., *Microcosm of European Integration: The German-Polish Border Regions in Transformation* (Baden-Baden, Germany: Nomos Verlagsgesellschaft, 2015), p. 93.

[58] Llera Pacheco and López-Nórez, *Cross-Border Collaboration*, pp. 48–9.

[59] See a Slubfurt critique in VOX at http://www.voxeurop.eu/en/content/article/71141-slubfurt-un real-city-some; accessed 11/11/2015. James W. Scott, "European Politics of Borders," p. 92. See the linguistic code-switching Nowa Amerika (New America) site: https://www.worldtranslationcenter.com/blog-posts/nowa-amerika?sw=1440.

[60] On the many categories of bordering, such as discursive, practical, perceptual, and representational including media images, see Scott, "European Politics of Borders," p. 88; and Wassenberg and Reitel on normative, cultural, linguistic, political and natural frontiers, *Territorial Cooperation in Europe*, pp. 9–10.

Chapter 7

Maritime and River Borders

The earth is 70 percent water and 30 percent land mass. With a water world that large, in an era in which states and entrepreneurs look for new market niches and security threats, it is no wonder that maritime conflicts and tensions exist. Such tension is partly alleviated with cooperative agreements and institutional procedures to resolve conflict over sea borders. Powerful countries exercise "navigation rights" in many distant seas to ship heavy physical goods, containers, and oil. Before the relatively recent United Nations Convention on the Law of the Sea (UNCLOS) (begun in 1967 through 1982, and enforced since 1994 with 166 countries and those of the European Union as signatories) established standards and dispute mechanisms, a type of anarchism prevailed, with freedom for powerful countries using sea space according to ancient "might makes right" principles as well as their technological capabilities to navigate at a distance from their own territorial lands. One might conclude that such a characterization still prevails in the South China Sea with superpower states' ships testing one another. Historically, naval superiority enabled early European colonial powers to grab lands far and wide.

Besides trade and transport routes, what other conflicts exist? As noted above, states view sea borders with a security lens. States admit or reject goods and people through official ports of authority, though smuggling is rampant and often occurs in cooperation with border bureaucrats, perhaps better called seacoast bureaucrats in this chapter, and with the prohibitive costs of examining each and every container that comes to shore. Like borderlands, customs uses canine patrols and technology to monitor samples of most and/or all incoming goods.

Besides security, states view their powerful economic interests and potential dams on river systems with an economic and energy lens. Seas contain valuable fish, vegetation, and minerals in the water, on the ocean floor, and in the subsoil. Alas, the sea is also home to much of the world's garbage and waste, reducing the capacity of fish and water to sustain themselves and aggravating climate change and ultimately affecting food supplies. Like forests, seas influence climate change: fuller forest cover and cooler seas absorb carbon, but deforestation and rising sea temperatures have reduced such capability. All states have stakes in oceanic and riverine sustainability, yet the dependency on measuring annual economic *growth* and GDP (gross domestic product) statistics does not *discount* standard economic figures with the numerically invisible environmental destruction that steadily threatens the planet. One wonders if the global community is damaging and destroying natural resources like sustainable water systems faster and more deeply than it is growing and spreading wealth as measured in common terms. In this chapter, we examine maritime border and transborder river issues in other world regions beyond those of chapters 4–6, with some coverage of south/southeast Asia, especially the dams for great river systems that originate in Tibet—itself a re-bordered area after the Chinese People's Liberation Army invaded in 1951 and annexed the territory as an autonomous region. I give special focus to Asia, the South China Sea, and migration both unauthorized to Australia and "labor exportation" officially managed by the Philippines—an odd supply system based on gendered demands for skills elsewhere in the world. I do not cover the Arctic with what has been called the "Scramble for the Arctic" (reminiscent of the "Scramble for Africa") given its importance in the world for global warming via ice thinning, melting, and what might be Russian claims, given its flag-planting at the bottom of the sea.[1] First, however, the chapter is framed, both with visual map concepts and the important UNCLOS, to address maritime border issues. I argue that water borders, the least studied, have the greatest capacity for generating environmental insecurity in our world today.

Water Cooperation

In 1968, Garrett Hardin wrote "The Tragedy of the Commons" which warned about how self-interested individuals might use, exploit, and deplete common resources without regard for the common good and sustainability. The famous Nobel Laureate in Economics, Elinor Ostrom, also wrote about the commons (that is, resources from which it would be costly to exclude users), but never addressed something I would call the "border commons."[2] Their ideas might be applied to the bordered seas and river systems as well. A look at the maritime map, discussed below and listed at the end of this chapter, illustrates such complexity; and the United Nations Convention on the Law of the Sea provides a rule-based institutional way to deal with conflict and avoid war. Whether it guards against depletion is another matter.

Maritime Maps: New Imaginaries

When viewed with maritime borders, map visuals alter our perceptions of states' shapes and sizes, close and distant "neighboring" states, and their allies. Tiny Pacific island states seem larger than what is seen on maps when their exclusive economic zones (EEZs) of 200 nautical miles are included. However, China and Japan remain the biggest state players in the Asia-Pacific region. Historic assertions and power asymmetries among state claimants of islands and rocks in the South China Sea make the area potentially volatile. Although China adheres to some agreements, it not only ignored a recent international court ruling in July 2016 about its claims to rocks situated close to the Philippines but responded with verbal belligerence and military showmanship. Moreover, when Japan discovers new islands, it makes territorial claims and extends its EEZ in ways that bump into equally powerful nearby neighbors such as Russia. Finally,

US activity in the region offers yet another bump into regional power pockets and conflicts, all of them posing potential sea-border security problems.

Superpower states navigate in the region, on other seas and oceans. US Navy ships patrol in or near "territorial waters," defined as 12 nautical miles from shores, exercising navigation rights. In a 2015 incident when a US ship entered Iran's territorial waters, the superpower and regional power-testing games seem a little like saber-rattling in the sea, evoking worries about a World War III without prudent and reasoned response. Quixotic leaders, like those in North Korea past and present, behave in unpredictable ways. In that partitioned peninsula scarred by a hard demilitarized border zone, north and south enjoy alliances, such as North Korea's (seemingly weakening) alliance with China. South Korea's alliance with the United States is solidified with defense commitments and multiple military bases. Taiwan's tenuous status vis-à-vis China poses a similar challenge.

Land-based territorial maps look very different from maps with maritime boundaries. For example, Japan, with four large main islands, agglomerates about 1,000 more islands as its territory. Rather than being shaped like a crescent moon, the territorial lines around Japan's maritime boundaries make it look more like a pear (my imagination!).[3] On an international maritime map, with many overlapping maritime boundaries, one can see that Japan's light shading around land borders overlaps with Russia and South Korea.[4]

UN Convention on the Law of the Sea (UNCLOS)

UNCLOS sets rules, standards, and foundations for maritime claims and dispute settlements. Its website is detailed, with a lengthy list of 320 articles, annexes and multiple articles in various annexes.[5] Many disputes can be found, probably more than land territorial conflictual claims, although mechanisms exist for claims and resolutions.

UNCLOS's usual standards allow for 12 nautical miles of territorial waters from shore of rocks (if not submerged during high tide) and 200 nautical miles of Exclusive Economic Zone (EEZ) territory for habitable natural islands. Because small-island and both small and large landed states' sea borders overlap jurisdictions, such standards cannot resolve potentially conflicting claims. For example, in the Gulf of Thailand, potentially rich with oil and gas, multiple claims come from multiple states: Thailand, Cambodia, Vietnam, and Malaysia.[6] Note that measures vary from land to sea. While land space and boundaries are measured in kilometers and miles, in sea measures, one nautical mile (n.m.) is equivalent to 1.1508 miles and to 1.852 kilometers. For most states, UNCLOS rules clarify whether contested sites consist of mere rocks or habitable islands with 12 n.m. and/or an EEZ continental shelf.

Conflicts in the South China Sea

The South China Sea is a huge shipping space. According to *The Economist* and its almost-always-clever titles, "Sunnylands and Cloudy Waters," 30 percent of the world's trade moves through these seas.[7] Among its many bases worldwide, the United States operates several in the region and asserts its freedom to navigate with warships.

For over a half-century, tiny uninhabited islands of reefs and rock formations have been claimed by and partially occupied by multiple countries, the most powerful among them, China. The other five state claimants include Brunei, Malaysia, the Philippines, Taiwan, and Vietnam, all with fishing industries and hopes for generating more economic development from oil and natural gas deposits. The Philippines calls the waters the Western Philippines Sea in the discourse wars, though most English-language maps call the waters the South China Sea. Some countries, like China, built artificial islands for airstrips and troop placements on those extensions of rocks.[8] Indonesia, seeking to protect its fishermen's interests, has destroyed ships from multiple states that poach in its territorial waters.

The reef and rock groups include the Spratly Islands of 750 reefs and islands (but 4 square kilometers of land),[9] occupying 38 percent of the space in the South China Sea,[10] the Paracel Islands (south of Nainan, China's southernmost sea island), and the Pratas Islands.[11] I use the names that English-language publications use rather than the Chinese, Vietnamese, and other language names, but readers should recognize the dizzying array of names for these places. The ASEAN (Association of Southeast Asian Nations), which neither China nor Australia joined, is a potential mechanism for institutional relief; China committed to exercise self-restraint over a decade ago, yet recent actions generate tension over China's ambitions in the region.[12] As the map embedded in the noted link shows, despite the name "China" found in the sea name, the island groups are far closer to the smaller, newer countries and would appear to fall within their EEZ. ASEAN established codes of conduct on the area, but powerful nonmembers may not abide by them.

China, however, is a signatory to the UNCLOS. Indeed, standards and international law do not always manage tensions in dealing with asymmetrical countries, some much more powerful than others. The Philippines filed a case in 2013 with the Permanent Court of Arbitration in the Hague over China's historic claim to the Scarborough Shoal, a reef far closer to the Philippines than to China. Finally in 2016, the court declared China's claims invalid, but to deaf ears in China. Moves like these create suspicion with regard to China's soft-power Silk Road land and sea efforts, as analyzed in chapter 5.

Several countries have made historic claims on the island groups, such as China and Vietnam, but the evidence is weak. For example, old Chinese coins and broken pottery pieces have been found in the South China Sea, though they could have fallen from ships. China's ancient history consists of border zones that have expanded and shrunk in size, as the *Pacific Century* PBS series shows. Given European and US colonial control over newer countries, their more recent independence and postcolonial status as states and the relatively new UNCLOS would forever doom claims such as this. Stakeholder states assign competing names to the island groups (that is, Nansha versus Spratly islands) and militarize threats with their naval boats, some of which have sunk other state ships or fishing boats. Chinese mapmakers, at work "imagining nations," have drawn U-shaped lines well below their EEZ, close to countries with seemingly legitimate claims under current UNCLOS and as far north as Japan.[13] The behavior appears to be a sea grab (like the land grabs by occupying countries in other borderlands).

Singapore, a city-state, has extended its land mass by over a fifth its size by importing sand and extending its shore.[14] Land reclamation, perhaps better called *land invention*, has implications for its territorial waters and EEZ. Neighboring states, with competing and overlapping claims for territorial waters and EEZ, challenge such practices by filing claims with the UNCLOS and refusing to export sand to support Singapore's ambitions.

As Alexander Diener and Joshua Hagen note about these emerging maritime borderlands, the demarcation of territory does not seem as fixed or stable as for the more than 300 land borders. While 160 sea borders are demarcated, 270 others remain in question, and the high seas "remain among the last frontiers in the modern world."[15] Are the islands an economic or security issue (or both)? The answer remains to be seen. Akihiro Iwashita calls the sea zones around Eurasia a "flashpoint for border issues."[16]

Prospects for trade, cooperation, and tourism also exist. Participants at the 2012 Border Regions in Transition (BRIT) conference crossed the maritime border by high-speed jetfoil in the southern part of the Sea of Japan on the way to Busan, South Korea, to spend a half-day in Tsushima, a beautiful rural island of mountainous forest and beaches which has become a tourist site for both Japanese and Korean visitors. Prior to departure from Fukuoka, we attended a dramatic play about the conflicts in centuries past in and over the island. After World War II, South Korea made claims on the island, but by the mid-1970s, both Japan and South Korea acknowledged Tsushima to be part of Kyushu Prefecture, Japan. Ultimately, interaction and trade took hold, cementing the relationship between both states. Naoki Arai analyzes how in 2009, both cities of Busan and Fukuoka agreed to establish an "ultra-wide cross-border economic zone and the launching of joint initiatives to promote a unified economic block."[17] His surveys of visitors show upward trends of numbers of visits, often on the way to the neighboring country, simplified admission procedures, and high school exchange programs.

Beyond this localized cross-border exchange, entrepreneurs, advocates, and governing body officials come together at periodic World Ocean Summits, the fourth in Bali, Indonesia, in February 2017 (the third was in 2015). The ocean economy is advertised on *The Economist*'s website as "at the start of a transition to a 'blue' sustainable economy," albeit with pressure from regulations and preferences for better stewardship. Its blue logo, with an artist's creative take on a decorative blue (gold)fish, speaks of investment opportunities amid intensive economic activity. The World Ocean Council (http://www.oceancouncil.org) calls itself "an international business alliance for corporate ocean responsibility"; its website contains conference reports, papers, and documents. At events like these, business NGOs and environmental NGOs network over the management of ocean resources. Vigilance is necessary to assure that management for oceanic sustainability retains priority over resource extraction.

Rivers Across Land Borders

Fresh water is an obvious necessity for life, for agricultural and livestock production, and for cleansing the body and surroundings. The desalinization of sea water is too costly to meet people's sustenance needs in this era. The same high costs could be claimed for reclaimed (from sewage) water, though such processes are in place in some desert regions for irrigation and even drinking water. While water comes from below in groundwater systems and from above via precipitation, surface water is a key common source for national, transnational, and border communities. Thus, a key challenge involves coordination among states to manage transnational river systems, equitably and for sustainability. The growth in world populations, the inequitable use of water, and widespread pollution and contamination have put people in danger.

Many river systems move over transnational borders, evoking potential conflict over use, particularly between upstream and downstream systems when dams get built that divert water for use that powers energy growth, potentially limits some people's livelihoods but enhances others, and causes pollution. A UN study found that most riparian states cooperate rather than conflict over water in the last half-century, signing water agreements.[18] Alexander Ovodenko analyzes agreements of 76 rivers, lakes, and seas, and identifies factors associated with success in incentivizing cooperation,[19] though in border studies, we focus more deeply on the context and regional histories. In the cases of South and Southeast Asia, we might ask: on whose terms and with what outcomes does cooperation occur? China is the regional powerhouse that shapes cooperation and conflict.

This section of the chapter compares the two most populous and powerful countries in the South Asia/Asia region: China and India and the respective great rivers shared with smaller countries downstream from origins in the much-contested Tibet Autonomous Region (part of China since the early 1950s), named the Mekong (but Lancang in China) and the Brahmaputra (Yarlung Zangbo in China) Rivers. Downstream countries include India, Bangladesh, Myanmar, Laos, Thailand, Cambodia, and Vietnam; for them, the Mekong River provides a living for 70 million people from fishing and irrigated rice production and the Brahmaputra River, for 80 million people along with hydropower potential.[20]

As an upstream locale and as the country with the largest number of dams in the world,[21] China is a power player in an obviously asymmetrical region of states. With 20 percent of the world's population, China controls less than 7 percent of the world's freshwater resources.[22] China also has the financial resources for transnational investments that carry great weight in the surrounding region. China's dam expansion is expected to export hydroelectric power to downstream countries, but "at what costs to people's very survival?" *The Economist* asks in the subtitle of a lengthy insert on the Mekong, "Requiem for a River: Can One of the World's Great Waterways Survive Its Development?"[23] The word "development," used uncritically in the 1970s, is now often placed in parentheses given the many losers, besides some winners it generates in an uneven process. China and India cooperate less with one another, for many reasons, especially past tension and disputes over territorial lines, Tibet's spiritual leader Dalai Lama's flight to India, the Sino-Indian border war of 1962, competition between them as the world's largest countries, and a militarized border along the contested kilometer Line of Actual Control with China (and a longer stretch with Tibet). Southeast Asian states seek to "socialize and engage China in multilateral forums," while South Asia does not. China gets regional leverage from water diversion away from India, improperly managed flood control, and adverse impacts on the livelihoods of downstream peoples. While China is not a full member of the Mekong River Commission and thus not subject to its provisions on environmental and dam-building restrictions, it participates in other Southeast Asia forums.[24] Even when powerful states join and sign treaties, one cannot assume they will abide by its provisions.

As the major power player in the region, China has been expanding trade and investment in the region, though tensions remain especially with binational military build-up at borders as well. India has pursued a strategy of "extended neighborhood' to include soft-power tools.[25] As Mirza Zulfiqur Rahman analyzes, India has been building up its infrastructure and road-building projects in Arunachal Pradesh, a contested border state, for military preparedness and dam construction by private contractors that carry heavy machinery. India thus stakes "its riparian rights over transboundary river waters with China," but misses the opportunity for comprehensive development of northeastern states: India's "Look East Policy" goes through Kolkata, not the northeast.[26] Recall from earlier chapters that this region might be called "Zomia," with its resistance, insurgency, and cross-border trade ("smuggling") outside the regulated economy.

Offshore Migration: Sea Crossers

Migrants cross maritime borders, just like borderlands. They cross legally and illegally in a complex myriad of national laws matching them with labor needs, assigning them points, or not, for their skills, and respecting, or not, international standards associated with refugees. In the previous chapter on Europe and in an upcoming chapter on migration, we analyze the serious dangers that refugees face in the high seas, put on overcrowded boats by unscrupulous traffickers. (The Italian film, *Terraferma,* also analyzes the ethical dilemmas that fishermen and residents face after migrants arrive.) Refugees may be placed in public and NGO facilities, to be monitored with relatives until their hearings, or even detained in private, for-profit detention facilities. After all, the neoliberal impulse to privatize seeks to facilitate market niches in many sectors of the economy.

Deterring Maritime Migrants

Some states package their people like export products, promoting temporary migration, such as the island states of the Philippines and Indonesia, gladly welcoming remittances from workers. Other states disown ethnic and religious groups living in their territory, such as the Rohingya people in Myanmar. Still other states, such as the focus of this section, Australia—once a settler colony and home to many European migrants—seek to prevent migrants from entering their territorial waters in the first place. Under international law, refugees and asylum-seeks who gain entry with "credible fears" about survival if they return should be sheltered and undergo processing in countries themselves, like Australia. In a famous case of boat people in 2001, a Norwegian ship rescued some 400 mostly Afghan refugees, sought to take them to Australia's Christmas Island, as initially authorized, but were then turned away and finally told to deposit them in Nauru with which Australia contracts detention facilities.[27]

Currently, Australia's maritime borders implement one of the world's harshest policies against unauthorized immigrants. According to Gabriel Popescu, Australia's policy is to intercept crossers at sea and divert them to the Australian territories of Cocos and Christmas Islands, far from public scrutiny and the media.[28] He goes on to say that Australia also pays other sovereign states, such as Nauru, Papua New Guinea, and Indonesia to accept refugees. In a more unusual move, Australia has excluded, even retroactively after potential refugees landed, "several thousand islands from the Australian territory for immigration purposes" so they cannot file asylum claims.[29] These are truly borders in motion, he says, "bending and stretching around the bodies of the immigrants without ever touching them." Under a new government in 2008, these practices ended except in Christmas Island. The Border Deaths Database at Monash University recorded 1,977 people from 2000–2016 by name, if known, nationality, and circumstances of their drowning.[30]

Potential refugees languish at remote detention facilities, with little or no voice. In the concluding chapter of her book, Kim Rygiel analyzes resistance as acts of citizenship. At Australia's Woomera Detention Center (in the middle of the central Australian desert), detainees conducted hunger strikes to protest horrific conditions. Some sewed their mouths closed, "meant to draw attention to their isolation, lack of rights, and inability to be heard."[31]

Australia pursues a relatively harsh policy to preempt and deter future refugees and immigrants: Operation Sovereign Borders. Its Department of Immigration and Border Protection uses naval technology and media campaigns and posters to send clear messages that unauthorized migrants are not welcome. On its website, one can see the frightening poster of treacherous waters with its startling message:

NO WAY
You will not make Australia home.[32]

Seas are indeed dangerous, so potential unauthorized crossers are deterred from crossing, thus saving their potential loss of lives at sea. However, deterrence may force people to return to equally problematic conditions or to live in terror with lack of opportunity in their home states. Migrants who cross land and seas for work to countries that lack labor laws or rule of law sometimes find themselves in slave or near-slave labor conditions. The 2016 Pulitzer Prize for Public Service was awarded to Associated Press investigative journalists who uncovered Burmese laborers enslaved for as long as 20 years on Thai fishing boats catching fish for US markets.[33]

Exporting Labor

Other states manage their excess labor supply somewhat like export commodities, complete with a dedicated government department, such as the Philippine

Overseas Employment Administration (POEA),[34] probably the most elaborate transnational temporary placement service in the world run by a government. The Philippines, once colonized by Spain and then the United States, became independent on July 4, 1946, with continuing US ties including large army and naval bases until the 1980s.

Robyn Malagit Rodriguez analyzes the POEA as neoliberal labor brokerage, comparing strategies under Presidents Marcos and Aquino. The state analyzes work force needs in various countries, recruits and trains workers to fill those needs, and authorizes "socially guaranteed identities," skilled temporary work sojourners who are not supposed to apply for citizenship in placement countries.[35] During a time of high foreign debt, former president then dictator Ferdinand Marcos mandated that remittances be sent through the Philippine banking system, based on percentages according to occupation remuneration; if export workers did not comply, they would no longer be eligible as an Overseas Filipino Worker (OFW).[36] Under subsequent governments, president Corazon "Cory" Aquino and officials monitored and lavished symbolic praise on the so-called OFWs. In both presidential eras and continuing to this day, relatively well-educated, English-speaking Filipinos and Filipinas face unemployment, underemployment, and low wages at home.

Later, under President Corazon Aquino, overseas workers were honored as patriotic "new heroes." Remittances became a responsibility of migrants, but if none are sent, "family members can enlist welfare services to demand payments" from errant workers.[37] Rodriguez also discussed the POEA's programs to encourage OFWs to invest back home in the Philippines for education, health, welfare, infrastructure, and disaster relief.

Almost a million Overseas Filipino Workers (OFWs) work in the Middle East, United States, and Asia, with the blessings and training of the POEA, "official recruiter and matchmaker." Workers pay for their training, document fees, and travel, and the state serves as a liaison and mediator to prevent unauthorized immigration. Overseas Filipino Workers are nearly gender balanced, but women are typically recruited as household service and caregivers and men, as plumbers and electricians.[38]

In her fifth chapter, Rodriguez genders the analysis with her focus on "The Philippine Domestic." Others have written about Filipina mothers who work overseas to raise a US family's children in order to send money home to their own children, but are unable to care for their own children and develop close relationships with them.[39] Films and television shows feature these dynamics as well. On the Philippines, Rodriguez frames her chapter in terms of state reification and regulation of patriarchal understandings of gender roles. The POEA issues periodic surveys, called Social Weather Stations, in which it poses questions that are designed to reinforce traditional gender roles: Do women workers bring shame to the nation? Do they care for their own children?[40] The shame question relates to what Rodriguez calls anxieties about "entertainment" work in Japan. She cited the case of Maricris Sioson, returned dead from Japan to the Philippines. The Japanese hospital claimed hepatitis as the cause of death, but an autopsy in the Philippines from the National Bureau of Investigation (NBI) said Sioson "died from traumatic head injuries. In addition, the NBI found stab wounds and cuts in Sioson's vagina."[41] Although the state claims to protect OFWs and exercises paternalistic oversight, Rodriguez says the POEA is powerless, citing examples in her chapter 6 such as Brunei striking factory workers who were ultimately repatriated and elsewhere, such as Flor Contemplacion, executed by hanging for murder in 1995 by the Singaporean government. In 1995, a film was made about the case: *The Flor Contemplacion Story.*

The Philippines lost many of its people, and the state's promotion and recruitment of labor for exportation continues. Nongovernmental organizations, such as Migrante International, call attention to numerous problems in the program: for examples, stranded workers in Saudi Arabia, as that country's economy downsizes; the reintegration of workers upon arrival back home, where minuscule stipends offer hardly enough once workers have paid their airfare (long having been the workers' responsibility). The most important issue is the lack of good jobs and pay in the Philippines that prohibits parents from living with their own children for years on end. The POEA is also criticized for its various fees and revenue generators, such as the Overseas Worker Certificate, called *kotong* which is the Tagalog (Pilipino national language) word for extortion. Border bureaucrats, or in this chapter sea-border bureaucrats, exhibit similarities around the world, though fees may be packaged in sophisticated form. See a large NGO, Migrante International, which organizes to support labor and human rights for overseas workers and for bringing many back home for decent jobs in their own country: http://migranteinternational.org/

Philippines NGO protest against labor export, calling for job creation at home.

Source: PACIFIC PRESS/Alamy Stock Photo.

Concluding Reflections

In this chapter we have looked at maritime borders in multiple ways, focusing especially on Southeast Asia and Australia. States guard their territorial waters and economic zones carefully for various reasons: resources in the water like fish and on ocean floors, navigation rights and access, and security including the militarization of rocks in the South China Sea. However, these sea borders overlap, creating conflict among states. The UN Convention on the Law of the Sea established rules that most states respect; however, more powerful countries like China and the United States do not necessarily comply with them. The chapter also examined multistate management of river systems, lifeblood of many people for agriculture or fishing along with the source for states to meet energy needs. Finally, we looked at migration, both across seas to encounter Australia's harsh policies and state neoliberal strategies to export their own people in matchmaking for temporary employment, with a focus on the Philippines. Despite invisible-to-many boundaries located in precious water, the barriers, rules, and regulations offer insight for part III of the book and its policies of security, migration, and trade.

Recommended Resources

Films

Babel
The Flor Contemplacion Story
Terraferma
Pacific Century

Maps

Maritime borders (overlapping)

  http://www.internationalmapping.com/international-maritime-boundaries-poster

Notes

[1] NPR covered subsequent activity in 2011, after the flag plant northeast of Finland, including interviews with Sami indigenous people who raised concerns about reindeer and the environment at http://www.npr.org/2011/08/16/139577789/russia-pushes-to-claim-arctic-as-its-own. (Accessed 7/1/16). The British *Daily Mirror* shows a photograph of the submarine flag plant at https://www.bing.com/images/search?q=russian+plant+-flag+on+arctic+floor&view=detailv2&&id=373E53D65762270C2B9CE1C8873BEA124A2B-769F&selectedIndex=0&ccid=nw5AkWyS&simid=608006321814045612&thid=OIP. M9f0e40916c92322b21591e62bcbf2cefo0&ajaxhist=0. See also Klaus Dodds, "Squaring the Circle: The Arctic States, 'Law of the Sea,' and the Arctic Ocean," *Eurasia Border Review* 5, 1, 2014, pp. 113–24.

[2] Garrett Hardin, "The Tragedy of the Commons," *Science* 162, 3859, 1968, pp. 1243–48. The late Elinor Ostrom, first woman named Nobel Laureate in Economics, wrote many articles and

books, among them *Governing the Commons: The Evolution of Institutions for Collective Action* (Cambridge: Cambridge University Press, 1990; 2015 reissue), although she never focused on borderlands. However, she examined potential environmental problems, including those related to water such as competitive pumping and fisheries.

[3] See the map (p. 298) in Koji Furukawa, "Bordering Japan: Towards a Comprehensive Perspective," *Journal of Borderlands Studies* 26, 3, 2011, pp. 297–314.

[4] http://www.internationalmapping.com/international-maritime-boundaries-poster. Accessed 12/1/2015.

[5] UNCLOS, accessed multiple times including 12/1/15 at http://www.un.org/depts/los/convention_agreements/texts/unclos/UNCLOS-TOC.htm.

[6] Daniel J. Dzurek, "Maritime Agreements and Oil Exploration in the Gulf of Thailand," in Paul Ganster and David Lorey, eds., *Borders and Border Politics in a Globalizing World* (Lanham, MD: Rowman & Littlefield, 2004), pp. 301–16.

[7] *The Economist*, "Sunnylands and Cloudy Waters," February 20, 2016, p. 10.

[8] Koichi Sato, "China's 'Frontiers': Issues Concerning Territorial Claims at Sea—Security Implications in the East China Sea and the South China Sea," *Eurasia Border Review* 3, 2, 2012, pp. 71–90.

[9] *The Economist,* "China v. the Rest," March 26, 2016, p. 47–9.

[10] Sato, "China's 'Frontiers,'" p. 172.

[11] Brittany Cheng, "The Philippines & Spratly Islands: A Losing Battle," *Scientific American*, June 4, 2013.

[12] Patrick Barta, "Sea Dispute Upends Asian Summit," *Wall Street Journal*, July 17, 2012. Accessed 8/1/16 at http://www.wsj.com/articles/SB10001424052702303919504577524133983292716.

[13] Sato, "China's 'Frontiers'"; the map is on p. 74.

[14] *The Economist*, "Banyon: Such Quantities of Sand," February 28, 2015, p. 36.

[15] Alexander Diener and Joshua Hagen, *Borders: A Very Short Introduction* (NY: Oxford University Press, 2012), p. 76.

[16] Akihiro Iwashita, "An Invitation to Japan's Borderlands: At the Geopolitical Edge of the Eurasian Continent," *Journal of Borderlands Studies* 26, 3, December 2011, p. 279.

[17] Naoki Arai, "Cross-strait Tourism in the Japan-Korean Border Region: Fukuoka, Busan, and Tsushima," *Journal of Borderlands Studies* 26, 3, 2011, pp. 315–25. Thanks to Iwashita Akihiro for organizing the event and BRIT, a paradigm-altering experience for many border scholars. See pictures and a map of the island: http://tsushima.weebly.com/.

[18] The *Atlas of International Freshwater Agreements* is cited in Selina Ho, "River Politics: China's Policies in the Mekong and the Brahmaputra in Comparative Perspective," *Journal of Contemporary China* 23, 85, 2013, p. 5.

[19] Alexander Ovodenko, "Regional Water Cooperation: Creating Incentives for Integrated Management," *Journal of Conflict Management*, published online October 16, 2014.

[20] Sebastian Biba, "Desecuritization in China's Behavior towards Its Transboundary Rivers: The Mekong River, the Brahmaputra River, and the Irtysh and Ili Rivers," *Journal of Contemporary China* 23, 85, 2013, p. 34, 37.

[21] Ho, "River Politics," p. 3. More than half of the world's 48,000 are in China.

[22] Biba, "Desecuritization in China's Behavior," p. 30.

[23] *The Economist,* "Requiem for a River: Can One of the World's Great Waterways Survive its Development?" February 13, 2016.

[24] Ho, "River Politics," pp. 1–2, 8, 12, 13.

[25] Biba, "Desecuritization in China's Behavior," p. 32.

[26] Mirza Zulfiqur Rahman, "Territory, Roads and Trans-boundary Rivers: An Analysis of Indian Infrastructure Building along the Sino-Indian Border in Arunachal Pradesh," *Eurasia Border Review* 5, 1 (2014), pp. 60–1.

[27] Jessica Tauman, "Rescued at Sea, but Nowhere to Go: The Cloudy Legal Waters of the Tampa Crisis," *Pacific Rim Law and Policy Journal Association*, http://digital.law.washington.edu/dspace-law/bitstream/handle/1773.1/761/11PacRimLPolyJ461.pdf?sequence=1. Accessed 7/24/16.

28 Gabriel Popescu, *Bordering and Ordering in the Twenty-first Century: Understanding Borders* (Lanham, MD: Rowman & Littlefield, 2012), p. 104.

29 Ibid., p. 104. A 2016 Papua New Guinea court case declared this involvement unconstitutional.

30 http://artsonline.monash.edu.au/thebordercrossingobservatory/publications/australian-border-deaths-database/

31 Kim Rygiel, *Globalizing Citizenship* (Vancouver and Toronto: University of British Columbia Press, 2010), p. 198.

32 The image is found on this website: https://www.border.gov.au/australian-border-force-abf/protecting/maritime. I requested permission to reprint the image from the Government of Australia, but they responded that they could not grant permission for copyright reasons. Also see Peter Chambers, "The Embrace of Border Security: Maritime Jurisdiction, National Sovereignty, and the Geopolitics of Operation Sovereign Borders," *Geopolitics* 20, 2, 2015, pp. 404–37.

33 See a series of their articles linked on the website, inspiring their emancipation and instigating reforms: http://www.pulitzer.org/winners/associated-press.

34 The agency website: http://www.poea.gov.ph/.

35 Robyn Malagit Rodriguez, *Migrants for Export: How the Philippine State Brokers Labor to the World* (Minneapolis: University of Minnesota Press, 2010), p. 22, 29.

36 Ibid., pp. 13, 81–3.

37 Ibid., pp. 86, 89.

38 Ibid., pp. 20, 35, 58.

39 See the lengthy article by Rachel Aviv, "The Cost of Caring: The Lives of the Immigrant Women Who Tend to the Needs of Others," *The New Yorker*, April 11, 2016, http://www.newyorker.com/magazine/2016/04/11/the-sacrifices-of-an-immigrant-caregiver. Accessed 4/15/16. Although I did not list the film *Babel* (2006) in chapter 11, one of its multiple stories deals with a Mexican woman who cares for the children of a San Diego couple visiting Morocco, crosses with them into Mexico to attend a wedding, and encounters life-threatening complications upon her attempt to cross the border to return with them.

40 Rodriguez, *Migrants for Export*, pp. 97, 100.

41 Rodriguez, *Migrants for Export*, p. 98.

PART III

Public Policy Issues

Part II, read together, reveals the diversity of world regions, with territorial lines drawn in contrasting eras, contexts, and states. Less visible "lines" in the sea, set by international UN standards, are fraught with tension; lines overlap and provoke conflict with material interests at stake. Yet some similarities across the regions and seas emerge, with borderlands and their people lacking voice or visibility in state-centric security policies. Europe and its supra-state institutional union is the exception. Powerful states pursue top-down security agendas that run contrary to efficient trade flows in this global era. The "Others" who seek to work or claim refuge in peaceful places encounter enormous bureaucratic and physical barriers, with the exception of the few with money to invest in fast-track entries to willingly accepting countries.

In part III, we compare major policy issues that have been introduced in the regional chapters. The chapter on security covers more than the current, knee-jerk reaction that this word evokes, such as an imperfect solution like border fence and wall construction in response to terrorism. While security from terror is addressed, the chapter also covers environmental, public, and human security as equally important for all peoples in the world and their futures. Given extensive police impunity, including at borders, in many countries people may need protection not only from violent "Others" but also from their security forces.

As for migration, the chapter compares the different approaches states have taken in the regions of part II. The historical and contemporary periods vary, so caveats must be made about tentative generalizations. Many governments that now pursue strictly controlled, even harsh immigration policies once had open-door policies and offered generous welcomes to economic, political, and postwar refugees, especially during eras with strong needs for labor. In the contemporary 21st-century era, comparing the regions, Europe once offered the most orderly, lawful refugee processing in accordance with international law and EU procedures, but these procedures broke down as individual nations felt threatened with overwhelming numbers of migrants. In the name of safety (given deaths on the open seas, including the Mediterranean Sea) and protection from traffickers, Europe, Australia, and the United States aim to deter refugees, preempt migration, and/or place migrants in detention facilities. Carved apart by Partition, Bengali people move into parts of India for work, however low the pay and vulnerable their status if from Bangladesh or elsewhere. Employers face no sanctions. The challenges to good governance in the postcolonial world, including costly and accurate censuses, mean that the extent of the "problem" (or opportunity, through the eyes of refugees) remains fully unknown. Meanwhile India's Border Security Force is particularly brutal and unaccountable, responsible for more deaths than in other world regions. The situation was and is similar to that in the United States with largely Spanish-speaking people of Mexican heritage in southwestern states, although in 1986 new laws imposed both amnesty and employer sanctions. Since then, draconian enforcement procedures and laws have been put into place, especially after the 9/11 attacks in New York and Washington, DC. The United States enlisted Mexico's aid in its efforts to deter migration from Central America, ravaged by war and impoverishment, just as the European Union does through its nicely named Neighbourhood Policies.

Trade is an important glue that produces cross-border interaction. It occurs in multiple dimensions: legal, illegal, licit, and illicit, usually under regulatory institutional umbrellas with multiple agendas. Rarely do these agendas include fair trade or wage standards that would reduce extreme border inequalities such as at the US-Mexico border. In the name of free, or best-called "freer" trade, national, regional, and international bodies foster tremendous growth in volume and rates of legal formal trade in the global economy. The freer umbrellas also gave rise to illegal trade, though perhaps illegal in some states but not others. Those who research the everyday practices of informal economies across borders call attention to trade in goods without harmful consequences (except for the loss of tax or license fees to governments, many of which are corrupt or unaccountable to their citizens). In most of the postcolonial world, border people make livelihoods for themselves or stretch their incomes in the opportunities that borderlands offer. Illicit trade, such as human trafficking, and near-slave wages ought to be the targets of institutional action.

Chapter 8

Securities
Environmental, Safety, and Survival

Hardly a year goes by when those of us who watch international politics do not worry that World War III will break out. At common core, states are expected to defend, secure, and protect citizens with their territorial boundaries along with citizens traveling outside those borders. Some states take this responsibility beyond those basic tasks to defend allies under treaty or to defend their actual or future economic interests. The task of policing the entire globe is not only costly in terms of lives and budgets, but also bound to generate backlash because the interests of all of the near-200 states rarely coincide. For reasons like this, the United Nations operates uneasily in a system of sovereign states. Borderlands are close to home, where joint and mutual action may be necessary.

As analyzed in the historical chapter 2, the former Cold War tensions between the United States and former Soviet Union, with associated hot proxy wars in developing countries, have given way to fears associated with Al Qaeda and the so-called, self-proclaimed Islamic State (better described as rebel group Daesh; various acronyms include ISIS, IS, ISIL) warriors and to new tension between the United States and Russia in their once-conflicting strategies around Syria: to undermine dictator Bashar al-Assad (US) or to strengthen him (Russia). Russia has an interest in producing more refugees who flee to an already-strained Europe and their economic sanctions due to Russia's claims on the eastern Ukraine (and Crimea annexation). As this security example shows, border conflicts constantly emerge and retreat in an interconnected global economy. Turkey's borders sit uneasily between the major tensions of 21st-century geopolitics. The military coup attempt in July 2016 shocked many, and its aftermath is pushing Turkey's politics in an even more authoritarian direction.

In late 2015, Turkey, a member of the Western alliance, the North Atlantic Treaty Organization (NATO), deployed "hard power" when it shot down two Russian warplanes for entering its air space and killing Turkmen people who live in Syria. The invisible air space—territorial borders in the sky—is precisely measured with radar. Why do Turkmen people live across the border in Syria? As we remember the century anniversary of the Sykes-Picot Treaty of 1916 and subsequent treaties through 1923, World War I victors drew territorial borderlines after the fall of the Ottoman Empire with their own interests in mind. Lingering conflicts continue to exist a century later.

Besides geopolitical tensions, Turkey faced terrorist attacks against civilians in 2015 and 2016, whether from the militant wing of its Kurdish minority and/or ISIS. Meanwhile, ISIS cross-border territorial occupation persists as US presidential candidates in 2016 threatened "targeted" bombing or "carpet bombing" seemingly unaware of huge numbers of people who could be killed or the even greater number of war refugees that would inevitably be created. Terrorists recruit impoverished, alienated, and naïve youth with social media videos; and cross-border trade strategists try to formulate policies that would diminish the trafficking, oil, and antiquities smuggling that maintains ISIS's economic base.

Security is the overwhelming issue connected with border discourse in 21st-century public affairs. This chapter analyzes the multiple meanings of the word "security" in and with a borderlands angle in the ever-increasing securitization of society. With a critical perspective, I argue that one must examine not only security by the state, but security from state overreach, state corruption, and at the very worst, state terrorism.

Multiple Security Agendas

Traditional state-centric and international relations studies typically conceive of national security in military and diplomatic terms, from capital-city rather than borderlands lenses. For a comprehensive treatment of security, other perspectives on security necessarily include the United Nations *human* security paradigm of survival needs and *environmental* security which, with unabated damage, could threaten the entire planet and its inhabitants.

Human security—living freely with food, under shelter, and in safety—is often neglected compared with national security approaches—despite decades of imprimatur by the United Nations Development Programme (UNDP) and its annual *Human Development Reports*. A human security approach also impels us to address gendered security and insecurity, that is, basic safety not only in streets, but also in families, often hidden in poverty or made less visible. Intimate partners might live in daily terror with threats of partners' acid attacks aimed at faces or of murder via extreme domestic violence, both of which evoke little attention from local police.

Warlike aims to occupy and control territory—border conflict—generally produce refugees fleeing from violence, and political and economic instability. From 2010 onward, the Arab Spring movements of North Africa—Tunisia, Libya, Syria, and Egypt—and their backlash drove maritime migrant refugees fleeing across the Mediterranean Sea and across land borders to neighborhood countries of Lebanon, Turkey, and Jordan, toward Europe (see chapter 9). The exit was reminiscent of the sea flight of stateless Jewish people in Holocaust-era Europe on boats like one named Exodus, with its biblical connotation.

Terrorism targets innocent people—often in public places—to generate fear and affirm power for those who promulgate such offenses. Each terrorist act prompts states and their people to prioritize national and regional security regimes until, for some states, *permanent* securitization is in place. After all the sine qua non of states involves defense of their territory and peoples. At or near the borders focused upon in this book, tragic terrorist events—in which hundreds or thousands were killed and injured—have radically changed policies, increasing surveillance and police presences: September 11, 2011 (9/11) on US eastern targets; 26 November 2008 (26/11, where month and date are re-ordered) in Mumbai; November 13, 2015, in Paris; and 7 July 2005 (7/7) in London. Terrorist incidents continued in 2016 in Belgium, Turkey, France, Iraq, Pakistan, and Afghanistan.

Although media attention in the North focuses on attacks, threats, and fears in the North, the website Statista shows more attacks and threats in the South, in numbers killed, since 1970.[1] Gun and weapons manufacturers and sellers have spread their goods widely. The 2016 terrorist incident in Nice, France, shows how an angry aggressor can use a 19-ton truck as a lethal weapon. The pool of angry people is so huge—domestic violence abusers, petty criminals, racist supremacists, religious fanatics—that surveillance would have to expand widely enough to break government budgets and reduce freedom for the nonaggressive to target the actual perpetrators of foul deeds.

And US mass murder continues unabated with trigger-happy citizens, or so-called lone wolf murderers, who can easily purchase assault weapons, altogether killing in total numbers that exceed deaths from external enemies. We must exercise caution with the "T" word, "terrorism," sometimes overused for political gain at budget-making time in political processes that pursue fear-mongering discourse. Furthermore, as a line of research highlights, including a journal *Surveillance Studies*, in a surveillance or national security state, everyone is suspect—the "Other." Tightening up all loopholes might be possible, but at the cost of establishing a police state with security bureaucracies accountable to no one, even in countries that claim rule of law.[2]

Security and insecurity are widely used rationales for criticizing existing policy or advocating alternative policies. In this chapter, we consider those words or phrases with a border dimension: terrorists crossing borders, violent thieves eluding capture to escape across a border, toxic pollution blowing across a border as relatively powerless states pursue their "comparative advantage" (lax or no law enforcement). Air quality knows no borders, nor do mosquitoes as the now-famous Zika mosquito reminds us in public health warnings beginning in 2016 and beyond as pests breed, multiply in warmer climates, spread north with global warming, and potentially infect larger numbers of pregnant women and those yet to be born, just as malarial mosquitoes have done great damage in tropical areas. *Contagion* (2011) is a poignant film about the spread of an unknown virus through transnational global travel; its devastatingly quick destruction, in uncommonly understated fashion, evokes homeland security measures, lawlessness, and panic.

Comparative advantage development strategies are linked with border inequalities at extreme levels; near-slave wages and poverty spur migration, for examples beyond lax environmental laws. Securitization strategies expand (that is, the increasing tendency to use security terms to pose threats in fear-laden societies) for building political constituencies and quickly passing bills and budgets into laws. Politicians use blunt policy "tools" to solve security problems (walls, fences, militarization), but such tools produce unintended consequences, not the least of which is an increased perception of insecurity. Interestingly, Human Security Reports, based on the Uppsala Conflict Data Program, document a decline in violence.[3] Yet fear surrounds us, for the attacks and destruction images get instant attention and shock via global media.

So the vicious circle continues. In popular culture, all-too-many blockbuster Hollywood films and television series, viewed by millions, augment fears and potentially distort problems and their solutions. Among many examples, in a planet facing severe climate change, glacier melts and consequent rising sea levels, one of many in the disaster film genre posed a day's notice to another ice age,[4] a totally inaccurate picture of global warming. Other documentaries, such as from PBS on *Global Warming: The Signs and the Science* (2012) offer credible information and warnings. The TV series *Homeland* aggravates paranoia about everything: terrorists, surveillance, and untrustworthy security personnel in governments.

Some Conceptual Issues

In her widely read book, *Policy Paradox: The Arts of Political Decision-Making*, (now in its third edition, 2012), Deborah Stone contrasts models based on the market and on the polis, to restore emphasis on the latter.[5] She analyzes five principles both to critique existing policy and to justify policy reform and to explore tensions among and between them. In a whole chapter, Stone uses "security" as one key rationale to criticize and to advocate past and future policies, respectively. Using a border lens, it is clear that the two words "border security" frequently come together as politicians and officials evoke fear and propose increased staffing and spending to control land and sea borders with technology, walls, and fuller biometric identity documents which, at some point, clash with liberty and freedom.

We must unpack the discourse of security into multiple dimensions, while at the same time being conscious of the securitization of everything. The fear evoked over security threats elevates security-oriented policy proposals to the top of priority actions. Even during heightened ideological polarization, it is easier to generate political support—at least enough to win election or re-election—with assertions of short-term threats, such as terrorism and crime, than with long-term threats, such as climate change, about which people disagree on consequences, their timing, and/or hopes for market innovation to overcome these threats.

Stone begins her discussion of the word "insecurity" in the context of worries about catastrophes (the "space between a bad thing and the fear of it"), although the definition of perfect security—the ideal of perfect safety as something that governments can provide with good risk-avoidance policies that "can be analyzed, strategized, and prevented . . . or . . . planned for—may not exist now or in the future."[6] Nationalism and budgetary scarcity often mean that commitments to human rights, liberty, and security *stop* at territorial borders and airports with their entry, exit, and inspection regimes.

In 2009, I compared national and human security paradigms in US border policy with Mexico and the implications for policy strategies in the introductory chapter of a volume on *Human Rights along the U.S.-Mexico Border*. The *national* approach emphasizes control over borders, with budgetary commitments to staff, barriers, and technological surveillance at borderlines. The *human* security approach, noted earlier as invented by the UNDP in the early 1990s, emphasizes people's welfare: food, safety, and shelter.[7] In a world with fewer border inequalities and civil peace, an increase in people's social and economic security would go a long way toward slowing migration and the bloated machinery of border controls.

Stone reminds us that people experience terror in everyday life, not simply during wars. She outlines five types of security: *economic* security (a reliable source of income); *food* security (enough safe, nutritious food to sustain life); *cyber* security (protection of personal identities and information thereabout); *personal* security (safety from crime and domestic abuse); and *environmental* security (reduced human threats to natural resources and ecosystems.[8] To this I would add unreasonable searches at the borders of territory and airports where "border exceptions" to constitutional legal principles prevail. Despite the US Constitution 4th Amendment prohibition of unreasonable search and seizure, several women underwent invasive body cavity searches of their vaginas and anuses in the ever-elusive search for drugs, though no drugs were found, and then sent bills for the procedures if they would not "consent." In one case the hospital asked to conduct the search paid a $1.1 million settlement in response to a lawsuit, and US Customs and Border Protection (CBP) settled for $475,000.[9] It is impossible to know how many of these abuses occur if time-consuming, expensive lawsuits are not filed. In cases like this, personal security, freedom, and privacy are sacrificed for national security assaults, all based on "canine hits" (that is, alerts from a trained dog).

While I cannot focus on all types of security in Stone's list, I will focus on short- and long-term security threats: (1) border people's personal security and (2) environmental threats around and across territorial borderlines from climate change and toxic substances in the air and water. Such long-term threats seem diffuse and distant, especially to the relatively invisible politically marginal people who undergo threat. Whole countries are under threat: the very existence of some low-lying island states and coastal cities could be over, once inundated under water or rendered uninhabitable. Planning for the inevitable is already underway in states like the Maldives, Kiribati, and Tuvalu. With its 150 million people, Bangladesh will face even greater threats with annual flooding. If and when this happens, one might ask where will consequent environmental refugees be resettled and at whose expense?

After analyzing environmental security, I consider the construction of politically popular border walls and fences as a security strategy. While acknowledging global threats, I also offer a counternarrative about the threats that security states pose to freedom, movement, and public budgets in a racially hierarchical and unequal world.

Environmental Security

Why begin the substantive security issue in this chapter with environmental security at borderlands and maritime borders around the world? Rising sea levels, deforestation, polluted water and air, among other dangers, pose the greatest long-term risks to human beings, their health, and their lives. As noted, low-lying island states may disappear with rising sea levels that result from climate warming and the fast-paced melting of glaciers and ice in the Arctic and Antarctic regions. Low-lying deltas in places like Bangladesh, already subject to regular flooding, will—with higher sea levels—make land uninhabitable and drive many environmental refugees across borders to neighboring countries. No doubt, with India's fence and militarist Border Security Forces, some refugees will be assumed to be terrorists and thus killed, jailed, or returned. All people face risk with environmental disaster whether on the richer, more powerful side of the borderline or the poorer, less powerful side in the power and economic asymmetries of the bordered world. The political costs of coping with these problems to countries in both the North and South may surpass all other policy resources, leaving little money left to support human life and economic development.

Environmental problems have developed over the long term with industrialization, waste, global population growth to over seven billion inhabitants (predicted to be over nine billion by 2050), and from all these factors, the release of toxic substances into the air and water. In everyday life, people hardly notice overall subtle temperature changes, caused by trapped greenhouse gases, and warming each year (higher changes at the north and south poles). Thus, it is mainly experts who monitor trends over the decades to document the change. Environmental issues have entered polarized politics, especially in the United States, with some politicians challenging science and others of a more scientific bent expressing uncertainty about policy solutions that interfere with economic growth that is prioritized in the global neoliberal economy. The political constituencies to mobilize political action still seem too narrow to impel political will for policy change beyond future commitments from the 2015 international climate change conference in Paris.

As border studies scholars have been writing about transnational water supply and air quality since the inception of the field forty years ago: "_____ [fill in the blank] knows no border." Disease and pollution flow across borders without regard for walls, fences, and border guards. Mosquitoes and rabid animals find ways to cross, from flying in swarms to digging tunnels under fences. Officials and border people have obvious stakes in addressing these issues, but the existence of two or more sovereign states side by side complicates policy and institutional solutions. In the chapter on water and maritime borders (chapter 7) and on institutional and policy solutions (chapter 12), I highlight several regional success-story models, but many more shared environmental resources and threats await leadership, political mobilization, and individual and policy actions.

Threats come from large and small-scale activities, formal and informal businesses and trade. Perhaps neoliberal freedom for global capital, even following rules of law but without regulation for people's safety and the earth's sustainability, poses the greater threat. Here, energy industries come to mind, frantically increasing their supplies of fossil fuels with potentially dangerous methods, even as prices and demand drop. However, even small-scale informal traders also do damage, with help from corrupt officials and the lack of good governance. In rural Ghana, Chinese illegal gold operators gouge the earth, undermine farmers' livelihoods, and pay off politicians and bureaucrats to look the other way.[10]

Environmental Health

Several studies in the US-Mexico central borderlands demonstrate risks associated with dangerous industries and individual practices, producing burdens (known as externalities) which fall heavily on border people (such as probable shorter life spans), not on the polluters. In the United States, this sort of research is framed with the concepts environmental racism and environmental justice, but the concepts could just as readily cross intellectual borders and go global.

Among the approximately 300 export-processing factories (maquiladoras) in Ciudad Juárez, a border city of 1.5 million, a Belgian-owned chemical plant sits in a residential neighborhood as the city population grows in size.[11] The production process creates health ailments for both residents and workers, but the looming threat is a possible gas explosion. The worst industrial accident in the world occurred in Bhopal, India, in 1984 when the Union Carbide pesticide plant released 30 tons of toxic gas in a city with hundreds of thousands of people. In a follow-up article with 28 photographs, Alan Taylor documents lingering consequences 30 years later beyond the official estimate of 15,000 killed over the years.[12] While Mexico has fine environmental laws in print, enforcement is problematic. The capability of the city's emergency and firefighter systems is limited, and US jurisdictional and insurance issues deter routine assistance from firefighters in El Paso. An explosion of magnitude cannot be contained on one side of a border in a large metropolitan region transcending the territorial line.

In one of my studies with an approximate 400-person sample, a near-half-century-old border steel plant, the first global owners of which were from the United States, then Mexico, and finally India (but in 2016, back to US owners), nearby *colonia* residents experienced heavy soot on their cars and homes, videotaped probable air pollution with high-visibility billowing smoke at night, and heard constant noise from the 24/7 three-shift production process. The residents in this impoverished, unplanned settlement worried about plant-related cancer clusters and respiratory illnesses. Moreover, the *colonia* sat just across from the interstate highway, also a source of pollution from once-leaded gasoline and idling trucks at truck stops which emit fine particulates into the air that settle into people's lungs.[13] While researchers found statistically significant replacements connecting some independent variables with negative health outcomes like cancer—namely the length of time living in the *colonia*—the clearest finding associated respondents' concerns about the pollution with mental illnesses: medically diagnosed depression and anxiety.

Environment health threats are not new to borderland people. The well-documented historic case in box 8.1 presents dilemmas hardly known to mainstream readers or policymakers.

Box 8.1

Unknown Health Consequences of Border Fumigation

In historian David Romo's carefully documented history of the El Paso–Juárez borderlands, he analyzed a change for the frequent, freely crossing northbound Mexican residents from 1917 onwards that lasted for decades. The so-called second-class crossers (illustrating the intersection of class and nationality) became subject to official fumigation processes for themselves and their clothing with a pesticide (Zyklon B) under a public health rationale.* After building a disinfection plant, US Public Health officials required these second-class Mexicans to strip, fumigated their clothing, and (for those with lice) bathed them in a kerosene and vinegar solution. The practices continued for 40 years. Others were sprayed. As *bracero* worker Raúl Delgado stated in 1958

> An immigration agent with a fumigation pump would spray our whole body with insecticide, especially our rear and our *partes nobles*. Some of us ran away from the spray and began to cough. Some even vomited from the stench of those chemical pesticides. . . . the agent would laugh at the grimacing faces we would make. He had a gas mask on, but we

didn't. Supposedly it was to disinfect us, but I think more than anything they damaged our health.[†]

In the name of health, bordering practices no doubt created health problems, the consequences for which will likely never be known. When I teach border politics classes, I expose students to the readings, the horrifying pictures of naked people humiliated and desperately trying to cover themselves, the telegram and media reprints in the book, and the video "Indignity on the Border"[‡] asking them to talk with aged relatives and then discuss materials. According to some of my students, grandparents were ashamed and did not want to speak about it; others relayed possible health consequences that would be difficult to trace over a lifetime. One said that she was told her great uncle died of breathing problems two weeks after crossing the border for work. We will never know how many people died early deaths due to this border policy.

*David Romo, *Ringside Seat to a Revolution* (El Paso: Cinco Puntos Press, 2005), pp. 223–40.
[†]Ibid., pp. 237–8.
[‡]"Indignity on the Border" on YouTube (https://www.youtube.com/watch?v=3Nz-253RaQo).

Global Challenges in a Bordered Policy World

In a world of power asymmetries and sovereign states, global solutions present difficult challenges. Large industrialized countries, such as the United States with only 4 percent of the global population, produce disproportional carbon emissions that generate greenhouse gases and global warming, estimated for the United States at a fifth to a quarter of total emissions. Other states are catching up on toxic emissions. Looked at another way, in a world of over seven billion people, with the populations of China and India each over one billion people, the economic growth and the expansion of their consumer middle classes will likely have huge impacts on environmental stress, pollution, and waste as well. Impoverished people in places like India and many countries of the South use polluting fuels, such as charcoal, dung, wood, and coal for lack of economical alternatives.

For its lack of political regulatory will, India has become home to 13 cities that exceed its own standards of dangerous particulates that lodge in people's lungs; in rural areas, impoverished people cook and farm with polluting substances; *The Economist* estimates that 600,000 people die early deaths from these factors.[14] In many parts of the world, women cook in what Kirk Smith calls "deadly kitchens" in his analysis of the gendered health effect of poverty. When women cook family meals with biomass and coal fuels in poorly ventilated spaces, women's third highest risk in loss of healthy life years (according to WHO/World Health Organization data) comes from indoor smoke, after malnourishment and unsafe water/sanitation.[15]

In many countries, tension exists between officials and businesses that seek to develop economic growth but also reduce death, illness, and the costs associated with treatment and productivity loss. Poor air and water quality transcends borders, but with little more than voluntary agreements negotiated in regional institutions and global meetings, the interests and committed budgetary resources of powerful nations and their businesses prevail. Perhaps after the latest Climate Change Conference in Paris (2015) participants reached a tipping point in popular and official attitudes, with a majority of big and small countries signing off on the agreement on Earth Day (April 22), 2016, although it only begins to be legally binding in 2020. No doubt some will continue to pollute as long as possible or delay reforms until new officials are elected into office.

The United Nations has long sponsored environmental meetings, from Stockholm and Rio de Janeiro Earth Summits, Kyoto Accord of 1997 (the US signed but did not legally bind itself with ratification; Canada withdrew in 2015, then rejoined under Trudeau's government), and more recently Copenhagen, Durban, and the Paris meeting. The Kyoto Protocol, an international treaty, extended the 1992 United Nations Framework Convention on Climate Change. At the Paris meeting, most observers agreed that national delegates achieved a framework with important goals aimed at reducing the global temperature increases over the next decade to under 2 degrees Celsius from preindustrial levels. Rich countries in the North also made commitments to transfer resources to the South to help realize these goals. However, the political will for national officials to tackle powerful interests in their own countries to achieve these goals is formidable. And the challenge for civil society oversight is enormous, whether at global, national, or border levels. The United Nations Environment Programme (UNEP), created in 1972 and labeled an "anchor organization" amid many international institutions, faces many challenges in its responsibility for key functions: monitoring, assessing, early warning without comparable data from all states; agenda-setting, catalyzing, and coordinating change in a fragmented system; and developing capacity—all with one of the lowest budgets ($215 million) in the UN system.[16] With many world conferences, many sovereign states, and limited political and economic capital to achieve lofty goals, it is difficult to be optimistic about environmental sustainability.

In the United States, the 1970s has been called its environmental decade, with seven key laws passed about water, air, and toxic emissions and wastes among other issues.[17] However, in almost dialectical fashion, strong laws passed, backlash set in, and officials reduced implementation budgets and committed leaders. It seems to take crises, like the oil tank spills in the Arctic (the Exxon Valdez tanker, 1989) or the British Petroleum oil spill in the Gulf of Mexico in 2010, along with their sensational crisis figures, to develop workable solutions.

Striking warning headline subtitles emerge, even in business-friendly news magazines like *The Economist:* "Air Pollution Kills 400,000 Europeans a Year." The problem is attributed in part to the accession of Eastern European countries to the European Union, which are still dependent on coal and exceeding EU limits, according to the European Environment Agency.[18] Authoritarian governments like China's have begun to respond to dense smog, citizens' complaints, and health problems in cities like Beijing. This is indeed the "Tragedy of the Commons," as Garrett Hardin wrote about decades ago in *Science:*[19] the tendency for self-interest to prevail amid shared resources in individual and national perspectives. Borderlands fall squarely in between national self-interest agendas. Wherefore tragedies in the many "Borderlands Commons"?

Green political parties have emerged in many countries around the world, but they rarely gain anything even close to a majority in legislative bodies. In Mexico, the Partido Verde regularly aligns with more powerful parties and dilutes its supposed environmental sustainability mission. Elsewhere, especially in Europe, Green Party presence in coalitions can strengthen the resolve of mainstream parties. Environmental NGOs, as we cover in chapter 12, also exert expertise and power in democracies.

Markets and Altered Awareness

Solutions for climate change, air and water pollution are not simply national or global; they require cross-border solutions. Once actions go *under, across,* or *above* land borders, like burning tropical forests, dumping chemicals into waterways, emitting pollution, and spraying crops with chemical pesticides that surely do more than kill insects in our global economy, natural processes can spread or dissipate the damage. Reforestation and carbon emission reductions require cross-border, regional, and global solutions. However, most states and their regional trading organizations adhere to neoliberal, low regulation regimes. Thus, market-type solutions have been proposed to deter environmental damage. Perhaps the work of public opinion and of governments, then, is to incentivize such solutions.

The strongest of market-like policy tools is a carbon tax which would levy fees on polluters and presumably incentivize them to reduce their emissions or move toward cleaner technologies. *The Economist* uses a more politically palatable language called *carbon pricing.* Dependent on the "price," the consequences of such penalties could range from easy absorption into the costs of doing business, passage of costs onto consumers, or a nudge toward greener practices.[20] However, such policies could be rendered impotent at borders or in global trade if poor countries, lacking much "comparative advantage" to attract foreign investment, set no tax/price or sell their emission rights to corporations. Perhaps in powerful countries, a "price" could be set on businesses that produce across borders for comparative advantages but pollute on both sides of the border. In the neoliberal economy emphasizing free trade, anything looking like a tariff would be a hard sell, possibly prohibited with existing trade agreements, and lobbied against in national politics where business interests speak with loud and powerful voices.

Visuals in pictures, maps, and popular culture in the form of films, novels, and documentaries can inform people and change their awareness and lead to reflection and different individual choices and reduce behaviors that aggravate a waste-producing, consumer-driven growth economy that practices little regard for environmental sustainability. Documentaries about global warming from a decade ago sound some of the same warnings as those today, for example, *Global Warming 101* (2007) to National Geographic's *Earth Under Water* (2013), or the fine PBS documentary noted earlier *Global Warming: the Signs and the Science* (2012). In a world of multiple nationalisms, the language of "global" public interest may not resonate, but regional neighbors that share a "Border Commons" have more obvious mutual concerns, such as water and air quality.

Serious films are interspersed among sensationalist films, like science fiction and dystopian genres such as the Mad Max series, which induce skepticism about future problems and solutions for popular audiences. Viewers may find it a challenge to absorb less-shocking, even boring environmental documentaries. Yet the environmental wastelands in Canadian author Margaret Atwood's near-future novels seem prescient. For nongovernmental organizations (NGOs) seeking to call attention to problems, strategic considerations must be made about where to draw the line between what might be viewed, then dismissed as tedious, versus albeit alarmist and colorful versions of environmental destruction.

The science of future risk prediction and costs is far from perfect and generates no consensus,[21] based as it is on numeric assumptions (remember numeric metaphors!) about population and economic growth, mixed with miscellaneous regulatory interventions in the global community of approximately 200 states, with only a loose overarching strategy from global governance, as policy analysts warn. Affiliated United Nations agencies such as UNEP (http://www.unep.org) and FAO (Food and Agriculture Organization at http://www.fao.org) produce many scientific studies which politicians might read, or more likely *avoid* reading, given the lack of time and of scientific bent among some. The *accelerated* scientific warnings launched in 2016, originally published in academic outlets, sometimes get translated for public consumption into credible media with startling pictures, such as from the *New York Times* and *Washington Post*, complete with pictures.[22] Spatial maps can personalize the threats to readers, as in the US map visual "How much warmer was your city?"[23]

We return to more security risks, including from the state, and the increasing use of border barriers such as walls, fences, and intimidation.

Security from Terror and State Terrorism

At the beginning of this chapter, I discussed terrorism definitions and incidents, to which we turn briefly, warning about state failures or terrorism, and state use of questionably effective walls and fences. Terror comes in different forms, perceived differently in various parts of the world. At the US-Mexico border, many people trace the hardening of the border to September 11, 2001, a tragedy that occurred *far* from the borderlands. On 9/11 as it is called, terrorists killed 3,000 people instantly.

In many places around the world, especially in the South, excessive equivalents or multipliers of the number of 9/11 deaths have occurred, centering residents' perspectives of the world based on those vantage points and the previously cited Statista numbers from the beginning of this chapter. Yet the North has led the way in defining strategies to address border security, involving arms sales, intelligence, surveillance, and militarism. In the United States, the Departments of Homeland Security and of Defense have awarded grants to many universities to develop national intelligence and security studies programs.

Terrors exist in ongoing, perpetual ways in other parts of the world. In states without the rule of law, people live in fear and terror not only of organized criminals and gangs, but also of the police who align with violent forces, tempted with bribes or threatened by intimidation, such as in Central America and parts of Mexico. The failure of states, or lack of good governance in states like these, calls into question Weberian notions that define states according to their legitimate use of force; transnational criminals may be stronger and better armed than the police and military. Crossing borders into and/or escaping from hardly lawful systems can be life-threatening, as studies of migrants show (see selections in chapter 9).[24] In occupied or rebel-controlled countries in civil war, like Afghanistan, Iraq, and elsewhere, people live in terror and insecurity not only from combatants in the civil war but also from foreign troops that may mistake residents for the enemy. Countless mass murders occurred in the Holocaust and elsewhere with genocides in various places from Rwanda and Lebanon to Cambodia and before those, Armenia, when and where the word was invented. To this we must add the terror of everyday life when people have insufficient food, shelter, and safety.

Gendering Sexualized Insecurity

In the 1990s and 2000s, the central US-Mexico borderlands region was plagued with sexualized killings and disappearances of girls and women. According to Amnesty International's 2003 report, 370 females had been killed in brutal ways over a 10-year period in what local human rights activists and mothers called *feminicidio*. Nevertheless, state and municipal police brought few perpetrators to justice. Few domestic violence victim-survivors trusted the police enough to report crimes; approximately three-fourths in a sample of 404 women aged

15–39 said they would not call the police to report domestic violence or attempted domestic-violence murder.[25] Inspired by the mothers, feminist and human rights activists painted pink and black crosses of quasi-religious symbolism around the city to generate awareness of disappeared and murdered women. From 2008–2011, the killings of men, or *homicidio* (a word often used, like homicide, for generic murder), emerged in far greater numbers, diluting attention to women's murders. While local and cross-border activists continuously called national and international attention to *feminicidio*, with little response from the police, only after lawyers took cases to the Inter-American Court of Human Rights, which ultimately held the Mexican state responsible, did government partially respond.[26] No binational border institutions operate to protect human rights; instead the US government prioritizes its war on drugs and close alliance with Mexico in the Mérida Initiative which is supposed to strengthen Mexican law enforcement which in turn operates the Mexican Frontera Sur program's efforts to preempt Central American migrants from reaching the United States.

Yet the disappearances and murders of girls and women continue, as this 2016 picture shows. I took the picture just before the visit of Pope Francis in February 2016. City officials painted over, or "cleansed," many of the public crosses and pictures for his visit to improve the city's image, but activists painted over the official cleansings.

In analyzing the security strategies of conflict or post-conflict societies, we must think beyond the US lens. With the decline of a "bipolar" world, mentality changed and the Cold War thawed, but the hot proxy wars that killed scores of thousands in many places, like Vietnam, and ensuing economic instability and environmental destruction set many states back, especially in the South. If 9/11 and the murders of 3,000 people was the defining moment in moves of the United States toward elaborate security strategies that hardened borders, we must acknowledge the multiple 9/11-type defining moments in many countries, with different dates and in some, extended civil war and foreign occupation over years.

The national security state uses several tools to strengthen security: thicker borders, strict scrutiny of documents that authorize movement across ports of entry, extensive surveillance in between official entry points and even in mainstream locations, and walls or fences to create barriers to outsiders. "Othering" discourses flood films and the media about those outside the territorial border. Tradeoffs occur between security strategies and other important principles, including human security or humanitarianism, freedom, and efficient costs to taxpayers. A novel which captures these mentalities is titled *Waiting for the Barbarians*, by South African Nobel Laureate J. M. Coetzee from South Africa. He writes from the perspective of a probable Apartheid-like civil servant called the Magistrate in the frontier (borderlands), participating in and observing brutal security law enforcement, then begins to look inward to ask: who is the barbarian?

In the name of security, some states use tactics that resemble the torture and terrorism of their enemies. A vicious cycle may be created. One common strategy to which states resort is the construction of walls or fences (terminology that varies depending on the perspectives of user).

Typical poster in Ciudad Juárez of girl who disappeared, with iconic cross at the top symbolizing violence against women and *feminicidio*.

Source: Photographer Kathleen Staudt.

Border Walls and Fences in Unequal Borderlands

When the Berlin Wall came down in 1989, freer trade regimes emerged and temporary openings seemed to occur on global bases along with celebratory media about global connectedness and economic exchange. Yet in our world today, numerous walls, fences, and checkpoints exist. The roots of those bordering processes go deeper as covered in earlier chapters of this book.

In border scholars' search for mid-level theorizing beyond the context-rich case study, Canadian scholars Élisabeth Vallet and Charles-Philippe David call for a comparative approach in the study of border walls.[27] Noting the 45 border walls in 2010, graphed to show an increase of twenty-fold since 1945, they list the many walls and barriers—totaling more than 29,000 miles, in multiple places, including the dismantled and the built. Among the *dismantled*, they include the famous Berlin Wall, the (former) Czechoslovakia-Germany (in Bavaria) border, around the US enclave in Panama and Gibraltar, and the two Vietnams among others. Walls that survived the post–Cold War world include those between South Africa and neighbors, Israel and neighbors, India and Pakistan, Morocco and the Western Sahara, and the demilitarized zone between the Koreas among others. Additional walls went up in post-Soviet republics, the Spanish enclaves of Ceuta and Melilla in Morocco, and more. Vallet and David say "9/11 marked a watershed in international relations," resulting in 28 border fortifications constructed and plans to include many in the South, from Eurasian to Western, South, and Southeast Asian countries.[28]

We must recognize that people tunnel under walls, jump over walls, and/ or shoot rockets above them. Walls also carry symbolic import, of inclusion and exclusion; they create spill-over effects in surrounding lands. As Vallet and David note, the wall is more than a fixed barrier on masonry foundation: "They are flanked by boundary roads, topped by barbed wire, laden with sensors, dotted with guard posts, infrared cameras and spotlights, and accompanied by an arsenal of laws and regulations (right of asylum, right of residence, visas) in a broader sense."[29] What do such security measures mean for borderlands and border people, once accustomed to a greater flow of people and goods? The negatives offer central dilemmas focused upon in this book.

We turn to geographer Reece Jones's book *Border Walls: Security and the War on Terror in the United States, India, and Israel.* Note that Jones's book title names the builders of walls in his title—all of which share the democracy mantle and the proclamation of "exceptionalism"—in these asymmetrical borderlands, not those people or states the walls are meant to exclude (Pakistanis and Bangladeshis; Mexicans or OTMs—in the US Department of Homeland Security's parlance, meaning "Other Than Mexicans"; and Palestinians). Although contexts differed, the three wall-building states used similar justifications for the construction associated with the global war on terror and the fears generated. The justification narratives focused on external factors rather than "underlying causes. . . . internal to each state."[30] In his chapter 1, Jones lists 25 barriers initiated or fortified since 2000, finding that they separate rich from poor: the average GDP per capita (US$) of the "countries that have built barriers since the fall of the Berlin Wall is $14,067; the average for the countries on the other side of these barriers is $2,801."[31] Thus we see how border economic inequalities lie at the root of security-evoking barriers.

Fences and walls send a negative sign to the "Other," including major trading partners. My picture for the cover of this book, evoking the Berlin War and calls to resist barriers, confronts travelers to and from the United States and Mexico in its central borderlands. Besides modest fencing, the US moved into serious fence and wall-building since Congress passed the Secure Fence Act of 2006 to now total approximately 800 miles on land (over 1,000 of the 2,000 mile boundary is river). This expensive project, coupled with technology and surveillance, requires costly maintenance. Striking photographs, both stills and aerial shots in the video "As the Coyote Flies,"[32] show the stark barriers in the US-Mexico landscape. What goes unseen is the tragedy of separated families, occasionally photographed over the years in the so-called Friendship Park of San Diego, from a kiss through the small openings in the fence to touching fingers, as the fence is reinforced leaving only tiny slits. At the once-chain-linked fence between Anapra, Chihuahua, and Sunland Park, New Mexico, Catholic mass and communion from multiple faith denominations were once served through the openings on occasional days. Now an 18-foot rust-colored steel wall, plus a 5-foot wall underground, is being constructed at the cost of $11 million by a private contractor.

Whose Homelands?

Because I cover the partly fenced US-Mexico and India borderlands in chapters 4 and 5, here we briefly examine the borderlands of Israel and the Occupied Palestinian Territories, a relatively small place but one with many walls, fences, military outposts, and checkpoints. Palestinians lived in the land now called Israel, but after two world wars that included the fall of the Ottoman Empire and the horrendous Holocaust in Europe, Palestine was governed as a British mandate. After World War II, the UN-proposed partition divided more than half the land to give to the Jewish population, about a third of the total population, and the rest to Palestinians. However after the 1948 Israeli war and independence, Israel claimed more than two-thirds of the land, then occupied most of the rest in 1967,[33] expelling many Palestinians and leading others to flee—some of them living long-term in refugee camps or in diaspora elsewhere in the world. Palestinians call this the *nakba* ("the catastrophe of defeat and exile").[34] Moreover, many Jewish people from other countries continue to settle in Israel, welcomed with generous resettlement resources, given demographic projections in Israel. Will the place eventually have a one-state or two-state solution?

Although international law (Geneva Convention, Article 49) is violated by Israeli civilian settlement beyond the 1967 boundaries into occupied Palestinian territory in the West Bank, officials authorized master plans that permitted many such settlements in the mountain summits and hilltops, to a total of over a half-million people. For Palestinians, the legacies of Israeli settlers involve land confiscation, bulldozed homes, orchards, and farms. And more settlements require more "security," to include bulldozed fields, fruit groves, and vineyards.[35] Architects Segal and Weizman view the spatial manipulation of planning and architecture as weapons or "tools in Israel's state strategy . . . to serve political agendas";[36] their maps and striking photographs show the extent of settlement in Occupied Palestinian Territories. Nongovernmental organizations like Peace Now and B'Tselem also provide aerial photographs in http://www.peacenow.org.il and http://www.btselem.org, the latter of which documents abuses in the OPT. Weizman titles his book the "architecture of occupation" with an "elastic frontier"; his analysis of a "new way of imagining space"[37] involves complex road construction, walls around roads, tunnels and elevated highways, suggesting an economic boom for construction industries.

Besides the visual images imagined or consulted from these websites, various films call attention to the injustices and struggles of re-bordering in the name of security and new market niches. Among them, I include films directed by both Palestinians and Israelis analyzed in chapter 11: *Lemon Tree* and *5 Broken Cameras*, among others. The landscape and generations of trees almost seem like characters in the films.

Palestinian resistance emerged sporadically, in the form of the Palestine Liberation Army, and later in phases, named *intifada* for struggle, in 2000 and thereafter with attacks against civilians. By 2010, Israeli had built over 100 settlements for thousands of their settlers on Palestinian lands, restricted highways, and established 99 military-style checkpoints inside the West Bank between Palestinian cities and towns.[38] The Arab-Israeli population (Palestinians) in Israel number almost a fifth of the population with several representatives in the Knesset (parliament), operating under diminishing rights and restrictions.[39] Some Palestinians seek a two-state solution, as idealized in the more tranquil 1990s, while others want a one-state solution, given the shrinking Palestinian enclaves in the West Bank and the battered Hamas-governed Gaza Strip at the coast, leaving little land, water and resources for viable governance.

Border barriers emerge as key for Israeli notions of security. The discourse about them varies depending on vantage points. Israelis use terms like fence (separation fence or anti-terrorist fence), suggesting a minimalist scale and benign character, while "Israeli and Palestinian opposition prefer the term 'Wall' . . . equating it in the Western imagination with the Berlin Wall" (see box 8.2).[40]

After a near half-century of unresolved tensions over displaced people, lands, and homes, without political or diplomatic solution even after the optimism associated with the Oslo Accords of the 1990s, Palestinian resistance activities emerged in phases, named *intifada*. Both communities evoke the

Box 8.2

Concrete Walls around Bethlehem

When I visited what I called (in titled presentations) "The Holy Land" in May 2009, I saw many watchtowers and a bewildering array of roads and color-coded license plates on taxis exhibiting religious and ethnic affiliations. Around Bethlehem, the land of perpetual Christmas with bells strung across streets, the ugly concrete walls reaching 25 feet high were covered with political graffiti and cartoons. Visitors from all over the world left messages in many languages. Some US visitors, apparently wary of Israel as their country's largest foreign aid recipient of $3 billion annually, wrote "I want my $ back!" Others wrote slogans: "To exist is to resist" and "*Viva Palestina libre! Abajo el muro fascista!*" (Long live free Palestine! Down with the fascist wall!). Among the many political cartoons, I photographed a peace dove with a target at its heart and Santa behind the wheel of a bulldozer. For people of faith, the biblical passage offered in the following photograph no doubt evoked reaction.

Israeli-constructed concrete wall surrounding Bethlehem, in the Occupied Palestinian Territories, with graffiti: "Jesus Wept" (New Testament of the Bible, John 11:35).

Source: Photographer Kathleen Staudt.

discourse of terrorism against the "Other," for civilians are killed, fears are generated, and space is increasingly militarized. Terrorism and official counter-terrorism strategies produced bitter populations on both Israeli and Palestinian sides in an increasingly nonsecular Jewish state for whom residents, including Arab-Israelis or Palestinians, must be loyal to "the state of the Jewish people."[41] The words of Israel's national anthem, Hatikva, leave no room for non-Jewishness. In 2014, Hamas-fired rockets were met with Israeli heavy military responses and a disproportionate number of deaths of Palestinians. The

United Nations Commission on Human Rights Report of 2014 concluded that both sides shared responsibilities, but that Palestinians experienced far more death and destruction.[42] With long-term occupation, will Palestinians succumb to assimilation and loyalty, reversing their long-claimed (and UN principle) "right of return" or will the system collapse, as with South African apartheid?

In this section, we have looked at border walls and fences with physical and symbolic meanings and barriers. Rather than declining since the Berlin Wall came down and the Cold War ended, the numbers of border walls and fences have increased dramatically in the last half-century. A striking map, while in French, shows the barriers and makes the meaning obvious.[43]

Concluding Reflections

This chapter examined multiple kinds of security, from the national model that controls borders to protect residents, to human security amid poverty, to environmental security and sustainability of the planet—probably the greatest security threat to people living in any border region, but one that does not gain the political traction associated with anti-terrorism and border barriers, even as homegrown aggressors engage in brutal and violent mass murders. In some countries, people need protection from the state itself, the impunity of its agents, and the routine abuse of human rights and liberty. Plenty of international conferences have addressed environmental issues over decades, but constant and additional vigilance and pressure will be necessary to press states to action, for the common state and global neoliberal economic agenda is inconsistent with the sorts of regulations and incentives needed for environmental sustainability. Borderlands would be a good place to start the mammoth move necessary to act on a global scale.

The global arms traders, sometimes called "merchants of death," deserve attention in a security chapter. With episodic terrorist acts in Western Europe, a year-long investigation uncovered how central, southeastern, and Balkan states sold over £1 billion worth of weapons and ammunition to Western Asian buyers and conduits.[44]

Poverty and climate change produce refugees, as do wars. Yet as we see in the next chapter, the world and its states are ill-equipped to welcome and integrate refugees in accordance with international standards, resolutions, and laws.

Recommended Resources

Films

5 Broken Cameras
Contagion
Earth under Water
Global Warming 101
Global Warming: The Signs and the Science
Lemon Tree

Novelists

Margaret Atwood, Canadian novelist
J. M. Coetzee, South African novelist
Kwei Quartey, Ghanaian American novelist

Notes

[1] https://www.statista.com/ and http://www.statista.com/chart/4093/people-killed-by-terrorist-attacks-in-western-europe-since-1970/.

[2] Mark Binelli, "10 Shots Across the Border: The Killing of a Mexican 16-year-old Raises Troubling Questions about the United States Border Patrol," *The New York Times Magazine*, March 3, 2016, https://www.bloglikes.com/blogs/2016-03-06/10-shots-across-the-border-the-killing-of-a-mexican-16-year-old-raises-troubling-questions-about-the-united-states-border-patrol, accessed 4/19/16, focuses on the fragmented US border security system which often fails in its attempts to hold Border Patrol officers accountable for killing Mexicans, even on Mexican soil. Despite scores of deaths, civilians' recourse is to file lawsuits, with attendant costs and delays in the legal process.

[3] Human Security Report, http://www.hsrgroup.org/human-security-reports/human-security-report.aspx. I am referring to HSR 2013. Accessed 3/23/2016.

[4] *The Day After Tomorrow* (2004), a film I do not recommend.

[5] Deborah Stone, *Policy Paradox: The Art of the Political Decision-Making* (NY: W. W. Norton, 2012, 3rd edition). Besides security, Stone also focuses on other principled rationales: liberty, welfare, equity, and efficiency.

[6] Stone, *Policy Paradox*, pp. 130–1.

[7] Kathleen Staudt, "Violence at the Border: Broadening the Discourse to Include Feminism, Human Security, and Deeper Democracy," in Kathleen Staudt, Tony Payan, and Z. Anthony Kruszewski, eds., *Human Rights along the U.S.-Mexico Border* (Tucson: University of Arizona Press, 2009), pp. 1–27.

[8] Stone, *Policy Paradox*, pp. 120, 129.

[9] Kathleen Staudt and Irasema Coronado, "Gendering Border Studies: Biopolitics in the Elusive US Wars on Drugs and Immigration," forthcoming *Eurasian Border Review*.

[10] Afua Hirsch, "The Price of Gold: Chinese Mining in Ghana Documentary," *The Guardian*, April 23, 2013, https://www.youtube.com/watch?v=ohrrE1rjzLo. (Also posted on Kwei Quartey's website; he is the author of a favorite place-based mystery based on this theme, *Gold of the Fathers* (2016), http://www.kweiquartey.com/ghana-gold/.)

[11] Oscar Morales, Sara E. Grineski, and Timothy W. Collins, "Structural Violence and Environmental Injustice: The Case of a US-Mexico Border Chemical Plant," *Local Environment* 17, 1, 2012, pp. 1–21.

[12] http://www.theatlantic.com/photo/2014/12/bhopal-the-worlds-worst-industrial-disaster-30-years-later. Accessed 4/1/16.

[13] Kathleen Staudt, Mosi Dane'el, and Guadalupe Márquez Velarde, "In the Shadow of a Steel Recycling Plant in These Global Neoliberal Times: The Political Economy of Health Disparities among Hispanics in a Border *Colonia*," *Local Environment* 21, 5, 2016, March, pp. 636–52.

[14] *The Economist*, "Particular about Particulates," January 16, 2016, pp. 43–4.

[15] Kirk Smith, "Women's Work: The Kitchen Kills More Than the Sword," in Jane S. Jaquette and Gale Summerfield, eds., *Women and Gender Equity in Development Theory and Practice: Institutions, Resources, and Mobilization* (Durham, NC: Duke University Press, 2006), p. 208.

[16] Maria Ivanova, "UNEP as an Anchor Organization for the Global Environment," in Frank Biermann, Bernd Siebenhüner, and Anna Schreyögg, eds., *International Organizations in Global Environmental Governance* (London and NY: Routledge 2009), pp. 151–73.

[17] Michael Kraft and Scott Furlong, *Public Policy: Politics, Analysis, and Alternatives* (Los Angeles: Sage 2013, 4th edition), chapter 11.

[18] "Choking on It: Air Pollution," *The Economist,* December 5, 2015.

[19] Garrett Hardin, "The Tragedy of the Commons," *Science* 162, 3859, 1968.

[20] See *The Economist,* "Climate Change: Hot and Bothered," Special Report, November 28, 2015.

[21] Stone, *Policy Paradox*, pp. 145, 150.

[22] http://www.nytimes.com/2016/03/23/science/global-warming-sea-level-carbon-dioxide-emissions.html?_r=1; https://www.washingtonpost.com/news/energy-environment/wp/2015/07/20/the-worlds-most-famous-climate-scientist-just-outlined-an-alarming-scenario-for-our-planets-future/?tid=a_inl

[23] http://www.nytimes.com/interactive/2016/02/19/us/2015-year-in-weather-temperature-precipitation.html#el-paso_tx

[24] See various chapters in Kathleen Staudt, Tony Payan, and Z. Anthony Kruszewski, eds., *Human Rights along the U.S.-Mexico Border* (Tucson: University of Arizona Press, 2009).

[25] Kathleen Staudt, *Violence and Activism at the Border: Gender, Fear and Everyday Life in Ciudad Juárez* (Austin: University of Texas Press, 2008), chapter 3.

[26] Kathleen Staudt and Zulma Méndez, *Courage, Resistance, and Women in Ciudad Juárez: Challenges to Militarization* (Austin: University of Texas Press, 2015). Also see selections in William Simmons and Carol Mueller, eds., *Binational Human Rights: The U.S.-Mexico Experience* (Philadelphia: University of Pennsylvania Press, 2014).

[27] Élisabeth Vallet and Charles-Philippe David, "Introduction: The (Re)Building of the Wall in International Relations," *Journal of Borderlands Studies* 27, 2 (2012), pp. 111–20.

[28] Ibid., p. 113.

[29] Ibid., p. 112.

[30] Reece Jones, *Border Walls* (London and New York: Zed, 2012), p. 3, chapter 1.

[31] Ibid.

[32] "As the Coyote Flies" at http://vimeo.com/92254329.

[33] Jones, *Border Walls*, p. 19.

[34] David Remnick, "Letter from Jerusalem. Seeds of Peace: Ayman Odeh's Unlikely Crusade," *The New Yorker*, January 25, 2016, p. 24.

[35] On recent numbers, see http://www.nytimes.com/2014/02/11/world/middleeast/palestinians-work-in-west-bank-for-israeli-industry-they-oppose.html?_r=0.

[36] Rafi Segal and Eyal Weizman, *A Civilian Occupation: The Politics of Israeli Architecture* (Tel Aviv: Babel Publishing, 2003), pp. 19, 24.

[37] Eyal Weizman, *Hollow Land: Israel's Architecture of Occupation* (London and NY: Verso 2007), p. 182.

[38] Jones, *Border Walls*, chapter 4; see also his maps on pp. 82, 84.

[39] Remnick, "Letter from Jerusalem," provides an excellent article on an Arab-Israeli Knesset member.

[40] Weizman, *Hollow Land*, p. 293.

[41] Remnick, "Letter from Jerusalem," p. 28.

[42] United Nations report: http://www.ohchr.org/EN/HRBodies/HRC/CoIGazaConflict/Pages/ReportCoIGaza.aspx.

[43] http://www.geo.fr/photos/reportages-geo/video-videographie-data-frontieres-toujours-plus-de-murs-159213.

[44] Ivan Angelovski, "Revealed: the £1bn of Weapons Flowing from Europe to Middle East," *The Guardian*, July 27, 2016. Accessed 7/28/16 at http://click.mail.theguardian.com/?qs=ba853a8d2c092555e03a4f5ab67b5591e8f93398e0250dff6b0ed9d5ea35bacf.

Chapter 9

Citizenship, Migration, and the Movement of People Across Borders

For decades "free" trade has been a rallying cry for many governments and corporations in this neoliberal era. However, the cry has rarely been accompanied by calls for freer movement of people, with the exception of the European Schengen Area countries (see chapter 6). As analyzed in previous chapters with the refugee crisis of 2015–2016, however, even what some Europeans call "the human right to move" within the Schengen Area is threatened with the internal checkpoints, fences, and the (perhaps temporary) use of some border controls. And reluctance to accept outsiders can provoke polarized politics, as the Brexit vote of June 2016 showed. This chapter is framed conceptually on attention to citizenship and biopolitics, a term with many meanings but defined and grounded at territorial borders in analysis below. People with privilege can negotiate many obstacles to movement, while those fleeing the inevitable drive to migrate from war, poverty, and inequality cannot. For example, since 1990 in the United States, the EB-5 Visa opens doors to outside investors of $500,000 who create businesses with 10 or more jobs in high unemployment or rural areas.

After the conceptual opening, the chapter begins by addressing historical and bureaucratic matters. Only a century ago or less, states established controls around movement across territorial boundaries. The state controls the authority to grant identification and documentation of personhood, citizenship, movement, and the rights and obligations thereof, but the controls change dependent upon economic needs for labor. In the late 19th and early 20th centuries, industrializing economies like the United States needed labor, and so in the 1840–1914 period, as many as 50 million people fled economic hardship and authoritarian governments from Europe, moving horizontally across the Atlantic in the North, with relative ease.[1] After that first section, the chapter examines migrations worldwide South-to-South and South-to-North, the economic and violent strife that prompts such movement, struggles during the journeys including their gendered nature, and the challenges faced in transit or receiving countries. International laws and rules supposedly govern the movement of refugees and asylum seekers, but national and supranational policies thwart those principles, depending upon political contexts and people's access to legal tools and potentially costly experts.

Throughout the chapter, I thread together contentious issues surrounding immigration policy debates and the government agencies that enforce those policies. The names of these agencies range from comforting images and words to ominous ones in contemporary and historical times. We discussed the European Union's Frontex in a previous chapter. The US Department of Homeland Security (DHS), a complicated attempt to coordinate 22 sometimes overlapping agencies under one bureaucratic roof after 9/11 and officially launched in 2003, uses the word "homeland"—which sounds sinister to some, due to its Germanic roots (*heimat* meaning homeland) and its use in 1930s German security enforcement with its Holocaust heritage.[2] India's Border Security Force, birthed in 1965 after conflicts with Pakistan, is located within its Ministry of Home Affairs and proclaims to employ the largest group numerically in the world (240,000), assigned to the prevention of transnational crime, counterterrorism, infiltration, and communal violence. While the "Borderlands in Films" chapter contains an entire genre of films about the dangerous migration journey, potential empathy for migrants is countered by multiple television series aligned more with the security apparatus of states, keeping out the "Others," and feeding suspicions about terrorists. Among them, though not analyzed like films in this book, we find *Border Security: Australia's Frontlines* (filmed in Vancouver, Canada) and the similarly titled *Border Security: Canada's Frontlines*, plus many in the United States.

Citizenship and Biopolitics

At its base, biopolitics focuses on physical bodies in motion across borderlines, as shaped by public policies, with rationales for inspection and action based on good, bad, and ugly behaviors. Liberty and privacy may be lost in the perennial tension between security and freedom. In border studies, a key issue would be the biological identifiers that essentialize and verify connections of named identities to body parts, often used in border inspections at international territorial lines and airports, such as fingerprints, and body, iris, and facial scans. Another issue relates to government surveillance and control over people's bodies—external and internal—and people's thoughts through communication (emails, social media, telephones). The physical examples of such surveillance include quick physical eyeballing by border guards to categorize border crossers as possible risks or not, to include racial profiling for law enforcement personnel who typically view "Others" as risky whether due to their skin color, dress, and/or language. Still another focus in biopolitics addresses gender: policies and laws that differentiate people based on gender and reproduction, with consequences for their freedom and livelihoods.

In her 2010 book *Globalizing Citizenship*, Kim Rygiel provides clear analysis of the meanings of biopolitics in citizenship. Rygiel draws on three major philosophers, two of whom offer insights for this chapter: Hannah Arendt's 1968 book on *The Origins of Totalitarianism* and Michel Foucault's essays and books over decades. I synthesize Rygiel's analysis here in her treatment of bio-politics, citizenship, and governmentality.

For Arendt, biopolitics (though not part of her philosophical discourse at the time) "governs over the very 'right to have rights,' that is the basic right to exist as a political subject."[3] Unlike those who see human rights as inalienable, "human rights are only meaningful and attainable within the context of polit-ical community and citizenship rights."[4] Arendt uses the extended example of Nazis who stripped Jews of legal rights and citizenship, essentially rendering them stateless. Thus, Arendt's politics of life and death involved Nazis' ability to encamp, then exterminate millions of people in various religious, national, and ethnic groups.

Rygiel's next philosopher is Foucault (and his selected works from 1978 and 1994) who writes about the reason of state shifting from control over terri-tory to control over population in recent centuries and the consequent disciplin-ing, regulation, and calibrating of people's bodies and lives. The state enhances individuals' lives in a particular population, but also degrades and segregates lives which, using a racialized discourse, threaten and endanger its population as a biological threat.[5] Thus, states protect the nation as a metaphorical body and prohibit intrusion.

Although left unsaid, the biopolitics of real body invasions deserve analysis. Mass rapes in the Balkan region, finally declared to be a war crime under United Nations auspices, can be understood as a way to degrade women and thereby a whole people for their symbolic representation of a community deemed to be lacking in value. Mass killings in genocidal regimes result in deaths of women and men, though the process by which women are butchered is often connected with reproductive body parts with symbolic interpretation: breasts cut off after Partition in India, knife-blows into pregnant women, for examples.

Surprisingly, neither philosopher discussed the biopolitics of individual body invasion. Elsewhere I discuss several lawsuits in the United States involv-ing warrantless body cavity searches by border patrol agents and their hospital contractors in the everlasting search for drugs. For several women named in lawsuits, not carrying drugs outside or inside their bodies as the dog-sniffing canine "hits" seemed to predict, anal and vaginal searches were conducted over hours. In one case, the middle-aged US citizen "Jane Doe" (so named for pri-vacy) won $1.1 million in damages from the public hospital (actually paid by local taxpayers) and nearly a half-million from the US Customs and Border Protection. In cases like these, biopolitics may be critiqued and alternatively conceived as the need for protection from the state and its border security agents to authorize internal and invasive body searches. The US Constitution 4th Amendment's supposed protection from "unreasonable searches and sei-zures" offers questionable security from the state.[6]

Of the regions covered in this book, Bangladeshi people may have the most to fear from India's Border Security Forces that kill at least 500 annu-ally and injure many more.[7] People die when traffickers book unsafe journeys across arid deserts or over volatile seas. From 2000–2014, methodical count-ers claimed 25,500 lives lost in the Mediterranean Sea ("mass graves at the bottom of the seas"), though maritime rescue operations saved 142,000 lives.[8] US border police also report annual death and rescue figures (numbering 307 and 1,457, respectively, for 2014),[9] though the next steps after rescue in the US involve detention and/or deportation. Philosophical assertions about biopolitics merit connections with actual loss of life, or death, at borders.

Let us now move to analyze the historical and pragmatic application of these conceptual ideas in history, kinship rules, and the state bureaucratic apparatus along with its "street-level bureaucrats," called border bureaucrats herein, who operate with considerable discretion, either by respecting human rights and the law or by abuse thereof, in migration control and policy.

History and Rules: Kinship and Bureaucracy

Human movement, which formed our world into what it is today, spread without territorial borderlines until one or two centuries ago. Some famous exceptions to this rule exist: the Great Wall of China and Hadrian's Wall (neither of which prevented movement or invasion). As covered in chapters 2 and 5, people who lived at or moved frequently at the edges, fringes, or frontiers of empires could have been called "stateless." In Europe, Roma people (pejoratively known as "Gypsies") do not enjoy the same national rights as citizens in all member states. In Myanmar, the Muslim Rohingya people lack citizenship rights and hostile nationals from various states label them Bengali as if they are undocumented migrants from their cross-border neighbor Bangladesh. Noted earlier, James C. Scott compares mountain and valley peoples—with the former seeking protection from tax, extortion, and exploitation—in an area referred to even to this day as Zomia, a symbolic shroud over peoples residing in multiple states that seek to control movement (see chapter 5). So-called modern state officials can be viewed as predators too.

Kinship rules may be as important as state rules for shaping people's lives. In many parts of the more recent postcolonial world, kinship and cultural rules coexist uneasily with those from government. Such rules often bear heavily on women.

In the last century or two, many factors prompted people to leave their homes: political repression, marriage, lack of economic opportunity, agricultural mechanization that displaced paid labor, poverty, domestic violence, and civil and interstate wars. Some states, as covered in other chapters, such as the Philippines and Indonesia, encourage migration with official incentives and training to export labor and thereby gain investment capital via associated remittances, while many other states like Mexico remain neutral but still benefit from remittances as a major foreign exchange earner. Such contemporary practices have a history shaped by social rules and public policies.

Gendered Kinship Rules

Through gendering border studies, we can understand the different rationales and consequences of migration within and across national boundaries. While both men and women migrate for labor, the rationale for women's migration differs as a result of marriage rules, modern citizenship rules which lodge authority with husbands in a sizable number of states, and the global trafficking in wives. Rajni Palriwala and Patricia Uberoi analyze marriage rules in Asia and its diasporic populations, in order to "stretch kinship studies in productive and new directions." The social rules of patrilocality and territorial exogamy meant and mean women leave natal homes at marriage to reside with husbands and their kin (technically called patrivirilocality).[10] When women marry outside their own groups, migration for marriage turns new wives into permanent outsiders in their new lands and they experience a period of isolation and dependency that lengthens the process of acceptance and assimilation in new locations. Kinship rules determine whether women may take children upon marital dissolution, or require children to stay with a father and his kin.

Many parts of Asia and Africa contain societies of these types in countries with multiple "rules of law," that is, both traditional and/or religious and secular laws. Where I lived in Kakamega District of Western Kenya for my dissertation research[11] among people with exogamous kinship rules, most Luhya women married in from other Luhya clans, also in the district, but fathers controlled the children. One Kikuyu woman married in from Central Kenya, an ethnic group with rules permitting women's control over children. She was viewed with suspicion, and few would assist her "escape" from an abusive marriage lest she "steal" their Luhya children. The state generally takes no interest in these matters, leaving them up to local elders.

Palriwala and Uberoi also analyze commercially negotiated marriage in which intermediaries (media ads, matchmaking, and tour services) facilitate the process. In Taiwan, for example, 27 percent of unions are "cross-border marriages," with men marrying women from mainland China and Southeast Asia.[12] In another kinship rule, bridewealth exchange—where the practices of husbands' kin providing compensation to wives' kin is viewed as value placed on women's reproductive and productive labor—operates in many African societies (such as in Kenya). However, Palriwala and Uberoi analyze how bridweath blurs as a sale when long distances are involved, the "right of return" may be limited, and/or sex traders are involved.[13] As for diasporic marriages where women seek to "marry up" in status or income terms, immigration rules (such as in the United States) may grant "dependent visas" that prohibit work, isolate the dependent (most often a woman), and perpetuate potential abusive relationships.[14]

Modern Bureaucracies

With the rise of state institutions comes bureaucratic procedures to control movement in and out of countries at their territorial boundaries, whether on land, in airports, or at coasts. To control those boundaries is both expensive and difficult. Relatively weak states with lengthy boundaries can hardly manage the tasks given the personnel, tax revenue, and technology required. Creative people sometimes find loopholes before government officials have caught up.

Imagine the challenge of controlling lengthy borders and fragmented territories, enclaves, and islands. The Canada-US boundary is the longest land border in the Americas, combining the 49th Parallel mainland plus the Alaska-Canada lengths. For island states, too, consider the impossible challenges of controlling archipelagos such as Indonesia and the Philippines, with 18,000 and 7,000 islands, respectively (though the largest numbers of island archipelagos, however populated at low numbers, are found in Finland, Sweden, and Canada near and in the Arctic). When boundaries are porous or leaky, opportunities exist for determined people to get around or past them and with assistance from what is euphemistically called officials' rent-seeking government behaviors to extort money in their discretionary spaces, problematic in states lacking good governance and relative freedom from corruption.

Where Kinship, Cultural, and State Rules Clash: South Asia

In the Bengali borderlands of South Asia, prospective workers often travel without identity papers. Here, Willem Van Schendel's research is insightful. How do border guards distinguish who is who? After all, people speak the same language and "might dress in Indian-made clothes smuggled into Bangladesh" to blend in, reminiscent of the "dress codes" that US-Mexico border NGOs advised undocumented people to use.[15] Local Indians sometimes protect Bangladeshis, and postcolonial records may not be thorough. According to Van Schendel, the birth and death registration system is imperfect: only 30 to 40 percent of births in India are registered, with a smaller percentage (12 percent) in Bangladesh.[16] In other words, despite all the laws and rules about legal identity documents in the imaginations that Anderson analyzes for nation-builders (recall chapter 2), many postcolonial societies do not have the data foundation to enforce laws accurately. Chalk up one more caveat for GDP per capita numeric metaphors with mere estimates of population numbers from which to calculate figures.

When Border Security Force agents capture unauthorized Bangladeshis looking for or finding work, they deport them with various rationales used in many parts of the world. Van Schendel says officials accuse people of filthiness; crossers undergo scapegoating as health hazards or law-and-order problems, again reminiscent of rationales in the United States (see chapter 8 on security). Although the India-Bangladesh border is not as violent a border as that of India and Pakistan, Van Schendel uses strong language to call it a "landscape of fear. . . . where both civilians and state personnel fall victim to violence almost on a daily basis."[17] In a chapter title with the words "Rifle Raj" and the Killer Border, he provides figures from 1998–2002 on the number of persons that border guards killed, wounded, and abducted: 2002 saw the highest number of killings at 533, a rate that surpasses US Border Patrol killings.[18] Indian border guards, he says, come from faraway places, *not* the Bengal region,[19] but the United States vigorously recruits from the Spanish-speaking students and residents of the Southwest.

In the Bengali borderlands, Border Security Force agents engage in proactive checks, for example squads that check neighborhoods, says Van Schendel. The guards themselves commit crimes, with impunity, reportedly raping women. Bangladesh sometimes refuses to accept deportees, rendering some people stateless with both countries potentially violating international laws and standards.[20] The urge to move across borders in an overpopulated Bangladesh beset by periodic floods and rising sea levels will likely increase, as the security chapter on environmental refugees makes clear. No matter the international laws about refugees and the rights of return, practical realities prevail on the ground, without lawyers, documents, and time to sort out violations of national and international laws.

Mexican police and border agents engage in unlawful practices,[21] robbing and assaulting adults, teens, and children. Coupled with bandits and other predators, journeys are fraught with danger, whether on foot, on tops of trains, or in buses. The problems have been aggravated with refugees who flee violence in the Central America triangle (Guatemala, El Salvador, Honduras) moving north, often stopped in Mexico's south.

Films offer startling images of these journeys, from the documentary *Dying to Live*, produced by the University of Notre Dame, to others such as *Sin Nombre*, *The Golden Dream*, and *7 Soles*. The parallels with those who move north from Mali and Niger through hostile, racist territory of North Africa and treacherous boat rides across the sea offer parallels to North America, such as shown in the Spain-produced film, *14 Kilómetros*. It is primarily faith-based organizations that offer humane but modest shelter, while sometimes women known as Las Patronas throw bags of food to riders on the tops of trains in Mexico (as shown in films and honored in Mexico and border faith-based efforts, such as Annunciation House).

Migration journeys have a history, but their dangers may be more recent than people imagine. For the US-Mexico border case, one border scholar historicizes those stages, as covered below.

The US-Mexico Historical Case

Recall from earlier chapters that half of Mexico's territory was ceded to the United States in 1848 and 1853 as a result of the Mexican-American War, negotiated claim withdrawals, and the payment of nominal sums to the fledgling new nation-state, independent from Spanish colonialism only since 1821. Of course, much of this land was occupied by indigenous peoples before the Spanish colonials, Mexico, and the United States set their eyes on occupation and land. This mostly arid and semi-desert region—in the slightly shorter western half of the border and the river boundary in the eastern half—could be called an iconic porous boundary for at least a half-century and more, depending on labor demand.

Border scholar Tony Payan historicizes the US-Mexico borderlands into four stages.[22]

- *Frontier Era*, 1848–1910, when the United States was preoccupied with European immigration.
- *Customs Era*, 1910–1970s, when Customs Agents enforced the 1882 Chinese Exclusion Act extension, the 1910 Mexican Revolution and the head tax system for entry that burdened Mexicans, the Prohibition (of Alcohol) Era beginning in 1920, and the Congressional requirement that Mexicans

have a visa in 1929. Most migration, driven by economic rationale, was welcomed in both countries.

- *Law Enforcement Era*, 1970s–2001, beginning with the Nixon era with concerns about drugs and immigration.
- *National Security Border*, 2001+, ushered in with the September 11 tragedy in the eastern United States, the newer anxieties about terrorism, and continuing anxieties about drugs and immigration.

From these four stages, we see that the Law Enforcement Era is relative recent. It has been strengthened with staff, technology, and fences/walls. No doubt many other borderlands around the world could be historicized as well, but the US-Mexico borders happens to be more thoroughly studied.

In most of the late 19th and early 20th century, the near 2,000-mile border between Mexico and the United States was porous, with people crossing back and forth dependent on labor demand. And some Mexican American descendants joke about their ancestors' nationality: they didn't change, the border changed! In this historic and inequitable context, regular citizenship rights in practice have been relegated to a second-class citizenship associated with poverty and racism, including linguistic racism against Spanish speakers.

The US Border Patrol was only established in the mid-1920s; before that, customs officers sought to control the underground railroad of Chinese immigrants who crossed sea borders in travels to Mexico, sometimes acquired Spanish language skills and surnames, and then moved northward after the passage of the 1882 first US racial exclusion act against the Chinese. Only after the early 1990s "prevention through deterrence" policies, triggered with official border blockades and their quasi-militarist labels (San Diego's "Operation Gatekeeper"; El Paso's "Hold the Line") did border patrol budgets increase, then quadruple after 9/11.[23]

Contemporary Bureaucratic Rules

States do more than monopolize the legitimate use of force within their territory, as the father of sociology Max Weber so famously analyzed. States use routine bureaucratic procedures to control the entry and exit of citizens and "Others" into "their" sovereign space. Lacking paper documents to establish citizenship and identity, whether seeking asylum or attempting to escape from terror, refugees and stateless people may lack rights hardly enforceable rights under UN principles. Children present a particularly vulnerable group.

With the growing sophistication of technology and data sharing across government agencies within states and across different states, a veritable lockdown can occur over records on paper, in virtual spaces, and on bodies in the form of biometric checks of fingerprints, iris and facial scans, and scans of other unique body parts. In accordance with International Civil Aviation Organization (ICAO) rules, states issue machine-readable passports for airline travel checks. The US government has taken space in major Canadian airports to preclear US arrivals through customs, as I learned waiting an hour from 5–6 a.m. in Montreal, 2016. US preclearance for travelers also exists in other borderlands—Tijuana, for example, to reduce congestion in the San Diego airport.

Exit and entry requirements have tragic histories. About the expulsion of Jewish people from Europe and the ultimate murders of millions, scholars write about potential receiving countries—unenthusiastic about accepting large numbers of Jews, trapped in 1939 and thereafter—whose leaders "never imagine[d]. . . . that they would be murdered in history's greatest genocide"; Nazis identified religious affiliation on passports.[24] Even in the United States, the language "Hebrew" as a symbolic code word for religious affiliation was mistakenly entered on my devoutly Catholic grandmother's entry document! (Documents are available on the Ellis Island website, the point through which many European immigrants arrived in the United States.)

Documents in Everyday Borderlanders' Lives

To cross national geopolitical boundaries, people cannot enter or depart without permissions and/or documents in the form of passports and visas of many types, specifying categories of whether they are traveling for tourism, business, or resettlement. These permissions may be granted in person, by mail, in embassy and consular offices—even "remotely controlled" as John Torpey says of offices outside the potential receiving country,[25] subcontractors that handle the processing to make sure all the documents, pictures, and payments are there. Failure to follow the ever-changing rules can result in long-term consequences that prohibit entry and movement.

Even inside US space, the border patrol sets up checkpoints in and near borderlands. According to an ACLU (American Civil Liberties Union) report on research, six checkpoints exist in southern New Mexico within 100 miles of the Mexico border. Although the border towns of Palomas, Chihuahua, and Deming, New Mexico, have long operated with the understanding that serious medical cases would be treated in the Deming hospital's emergency room, border patrol agents make life-and-death decisions at the port of entry. In one case, the refusal to allow a man in near-diabetic coma to go to the hospital ER room resulted in his death. Racial profiling is grimly part of everyday life in the stops for Latino/Hispanic residents, 26 times more likely to be stopped than Anglo/White residents.[26]

Local and state police may be enlisted, required, and/or incentivized to enforce federal border policies through programs like Secure Communities. In the US federal system during a three-month period in 2008, sheriff deputies set up checkpoints outside the City of El Paso (where a community-based policing system existed) in the *county* of El Paso to monitor internal space for unauthorized immigrants who commit other state-level civil, traffic, or criminal offenses. At the height of US border security rhetoric, the late Sheriff Samaniego authorized checkpoints, not for crimes, licenses, or car insurance verification, but for citizenship documentation—a federal legal responsibility. In community-based policing strategies, law enforcement hopes to encourage people to report crimes or serve as witnesses in trials—whatever their citizenship status. When drivers could not produce their citizenship documents, county sheriff deputies called border patrol which deported 800 people in that three-month period until NGOs held community events to protest the seeming overreach. The NGOs exercised political muscle in faith-based and human rights groups to counter heavy immigration enforcement, even in the federal governance system.[27]

In Phoenix, Sheriff Arpaio has gained fame in rounding up undocumented people, putting them in tent camps, and even parading men in pink underwear through streets as a particularly masculinist form of shame. As one can find in YouTube videos, in his reelection campaigns, Arpaio brags about the pink underwear saying that the federal government ought to be grateful. He gained support from at least a majority of the electorate and some state legislators who successfully got laws passed that would authorize more state and local enforcement against immigrants. Through lawsuits, unconstitutional portions of those laws and the sheriff's activities have been reduced or eliminated.

At the US-Mexico border, Mexican citizens at the northern border once acquired Border Crossing Cards with relative ease if they had formal employment. The once-called local passports permitted people to shop and visit up to 72 hours, but not to work. Among the many provisions of an ever-tightening immigration reform of 1996 and especially after 9/11, border people experienced increased security concerns, scrutinized procedures, and technologically monitored, limited term documents. From 2008 onward, rules require US citizens to show passports on returning from their shopping visits, work, and other trips in northern Mexico.

Traveling Across Borders

Travel between the United States and most European countries occurs with ease, especially for those with EU passports. Much money is spent during travel, and officials and businesses eagerly seek economic exchange, even though carbon footprints sink ever-more deeply with airline travel. Traveling ease is threatened in a world with terrorist incidents. In the United States, more scrutiny is underway to trace the previous travels of visa-seekers who have been to countries where training may have occurred. In a world of instant social media communication and recruitment videos, such policies may be blunt instruments for complex issues, homegrown terrorists, and a heavily armed citizenry. The US government is in the process of eliminating holes in other lax processes. The so-called fiancé(e) visas now require more scrutiny after the 2015 San Bernardino terrorist attack which permitted easy entry for a fiancée (his wife, co-shooter). Officials tighten rules after people learn to navigate around the soft spots, whether for jobs or criminal acts. New Mexico continues to be one of few states that issues picture-identification drivers' licenses to noncitizen unauthorized immigrants. A federal identification law allows states (until 2018) to change issuances without consequences for their travelers, thereby putting pressure on state legislatures to change laws. Under strict rules and electronic verify (e-verify) laws in some states, unauthorized workers have been unable to get jobs in the formal economic sector, partly explaining the *net* loss of Mexicans in recent years (that is, more returns than arrivals).

Box 9.1

Crossing Borders: Visa Application Forms

For analysts with an interest in government enforcement, forms offer some potentially illuminating insights. Some visa application forms are elaborate, complicated, and threatening. In preparing for 2014 travels to the ABS/World Borderlands conference, I found the visa application for Russia to be costly and complicated, requiring lengthy lead time, such as securing documentation from the exact hotel in which I would be staying in order to complete official forms. Questions seemed intrusive, even paranoid, with queries about relatives and their political orientations. Crossing the land border between Finland and Russia was quicker and more efficient than crossing the US-Mexico border (and the US-Canada airport border, given the preclearance waits).

My visa for another borderlands conference in northeastern India was intrusive in other ways, asking for religious affiliation, but seemingly progressive in the option to check one of three categories for gender identity (even though India's laws are based on heteronormative principles rather than fuller civil rights protection for all).

Work permits, immigration procedures, and naturalization processes have become extraordinarily complex. In an experience in Mexico, I needed guidance every step of the way, at every office where a seemingly rules-based and procedure-laden system still left it up to the discretion of a clerk to demand another form or fee. A colleague called this *tramitología* ("procedure-ology" or "red tape"). Of course, the United States is equally demanding in its procedures, requiring completed forms from both its State Department and university campuses in order to secure a semester-length visa for a visiting professor. Salary and insurance requirements can be daunting as well (especially when US insurance costs are 10 times the rates of those in Europe!), and criminal background checks and official translations of a candidate's transcripts are also mandatory.

One can make inferences about the sorts of priorities and obsessions in individual states, based on the banal or misleading questions in official forms. Visitors delayed at the border, sometimes for no apparent reason, sign "voluntary" departure forms, in English, perhaps without understanding or knowledge about what it means for future travel, criminal categorization, or possible citizenship applications. Perhaps forms reflect relics of past obsessions and the daunting challenges of revising forms. Cold War–era questions about affiliation with communist organizations can still be found on US citizenship application documents. A health professor colleague was surprised to see a question on US forms asking whether she had been a prostitute, although the last revision on the form indicated a relatively recent 2003.

To sum up this section, we have considered biopolitics and citizenship documents required for identity and crossing borders. We have also analyzed kinship and bureaucratic rules, including occasions upon which they clash.

We now turn to other clashes between international laws, rules, and national policies and practices relating to refugees, the more than 60 million displaced by war and conflict according to the United Nations High Commissioner for Refugees.[28]

Clashing Laws: Refugees and Resettlement

Historic and contemporary ethnic cleansings and genocidal practices culled populations long ago and in the not-too-distant past, particularly during and after wars (and civil wars), almost too many to name with victim numbers too large to fathom. Historic international organizations, like the League of Nations, sought to create documents which allowed refugees to resettle elsewhere in willing countries. Such was the case for Russian refugees from the USSR who settled in France.[29] By late 2012, the United Nations High Commissioner for Refugees (UNHCR) counted 15.4 million *registered* refugees,[30] but estimated many more to total over 60 million.

In these times, war in Syria created the largest group of displaced people and refugees, numbering over 4 million, but the biggest population movements occurred in Europe after World War II (15 million), then in India and Pakistan at Partition (14 million) to which 10 million must be added after the birth of Bangladesh.[31] To solve these problems of displaced people, UNHCR seeks voluntary repatriation, integration in the country where asylum is granted, or resettlement. International laws, agencies, and national laws and procedures, and border practices do not mesh well.

When the United Nations was founded in 1945, it facilitated the establishment of widely respected principles and mechanisms for human rights, reacting to the massive abuses and murders during World War II. The 1948 Universal Declaration of Human Rights states that "Everyone has the right to leave any country, including his own, and to return to his country." The document specifies many rights (alas, almost unenforceable), from civil to economic/social, with a Cold War cast to their emphases and state priorities. Western countries (once called first world) give priority to individual and civil rights, while many other states (once called second- and third-world) place a higher value on social and economic rights, especially the former Soviet Union, its allies, and many parts of the nonaligned world.

Gendered Rights

Historically, rights put men at the center. Only with subsequent advocacy, leadership, and international agreements and interpretations did women's rights come to be included as universal human rights, however much of a promise this may still be. Gendered double standards continue to exist. Even though almost all states have signed the 1979 Convention on the Elimination of All Forms of Discrimination Against Women (CEDAW), except for the United States and Somalia, many states practice double standards and discriminatory laws. According to Catherine Harrington of the Institute on Statelessness and Inclusion:[32]

Gender discrimination in nationality laws is one of the primary causes of state-lessness. Twenty-seven countries deny women equal rights to confer nationality to their own children. Over fifty countries have some form of gender discrimination in their nationality laws, such as permitting men to confer nationality to spouses, but not women; stripping the citizenship of women, but not men, who marry a foreign spouse; and denying unmarried men the same rights to pass nationality to their children. When children and spouses are denied access to a citizen's nationality due to her/his gender, they are at an increased risk of being stateless.

In the European refugee crisis, statelessness problems have emerged for children as well.[33]

Refugees: Practices and Promises

The United Nations highlighted refugees in the 1951 Geneva Convention on Refugees and the 1967 Protocol Relating to the Status of Refugees. The language adopted is an obligation by all signatory states to abide by the policy. It is language familiar to human rights advocates and lawyers in the United States, with its past practices of selective welcome but a relatively low rate of offering protection to asylum-seekers and refugees except those coming from nonideologically aligned countries like Russia/USSR, China, and Cuba, and from places in which it has fought wars, such as Vietnam. A half-century old special law for Cubans, the Cuban Adjustment Act of 1966, provided a fast-track to entry and potential citizenship in the United States. Now that the US has begun regularizing relations with Cuba, many refugees are entering the US southern border, in hopes of beating a possible repeal of the law. *Unlike* other refugees, Cuban refugees may immediately apply to receive Medicaid, "food stamps" (now SNAP, Supplemental Nutrition Assistance Program), and other welfare, as many NGOs at the border have processed in 2016. (Special benefits ended in 2017.)

In the language of international law, protection is to be provided to refugees "owing to a well-founded fear of being persecuted for reasons of race, religion, nationality, membership of a particular social group of political opinion."[34] In other words, migration for economic reasons is not covered, though many refugees from former "second-world" countries (such as China and the former USSR) probably acquired asylum and eventual citizenship in the United States as economic migrants, as noted above. Complicated procedures at ports of entry have been established around US borders (including airports and seaports) for those seeking asylum to make their "credible-fear" claims. As covered in chapter 4 on the Americas, asylum-seekers' claims from Mexico and Central America—whose governments are aligned with the United States and its Mérida Initiative—experience poor prospects for success. See figure 9.1 with its tangled flowchart of obstacles and limited success prospects for the United States and Texas. Applicant numbers begin big, but shrink at every level and milestone.

Mexico now runs a Frontera Sur program to prevent migrants' entrance from the violent triangle of Guatemala, El Salvador, and Honduras.[35] The

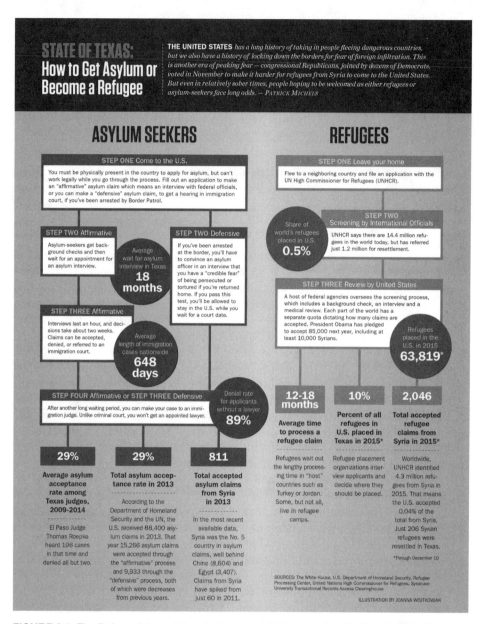

STATE OF TEXAS:
How to Get Asylum or Become a Refugee

THE UNITED STATES *has a long history of taking in people fleeing dangerous countries, but we also have a history of locking down the borders for fear of foreign infiltration. This is another era of peaking fear — congressional Republicans, joined by dozens of Democrats, voted in November to make it harder for refugees from Syria to come to the United States. But even in relatively sober times, people hoping to be welcomed as either refugees or asylum-seekers face long odds. —* PATRICK MICHELS

ASYLUM SEEKERS

STEP ONE Come to the U.S.

You must be physically present in the country to apply for asylum, but can't work legally while you go through the process. Fill out an application to make an "affirmative" asylum claim which means an interview with federal officials, or you can make a "defensive" asylum claim, to get a hearing in immigration court, if you've been arrested by Border Patrol.

STEP TWO Affirmative

Asylum-seekers get background checks and then wait for an appointment for an asylum interview.

Average wait for asylum interview in Texas
18 months

STEP TWO Defensive

If you've been arrested at the border, you'll have to convince an asylum officer in an interview that you have a "credible fear" of being persecuted or tortured if you're returned home. If you pass this test, you'll be allowed to stay in the U.S. while you wait for a court date.

STEP THREE Affirmative

Interviews last an hour, and decisions take about two weeks. Claims can be accepted, denied, or referred to an immigration court.

Average length of immigration cases nationwide
648 days

STEP FOUR Affirmative or **STEP THREE** Defensive

After another long waiting period, you can make your case to an immigration judge. Unlike criminal court, you won't get an appointed lawyer.

Denial rate for applicants without a lawyer
89%

29%

Average asylum acceptance rate among Texas judges, 2009-2014

El Paso Judge Thomas Roepke heard 196 cases in that time and denied all but two.

29%

Total asylum acceptance rate in 2013

According to the Department of Homeland Security and the UN, the U.S. received 88,400 asylum claims in 2013. That year 15,266 asylum claims were accepted through the "affirmative" process, and 9,933 through the "defensive" process, both of which were decreases from previous years.

811

Total accepted asylum claims from Syria in 2013

In the most recent available data, Syria was the No. 5 country in asylum claims, well behind Chine (8,604) and Egypt (3,407). Claims from Syria have spiked from just 60 in 2011.

REFUGEES

STEP ONE Leave your home

Flee to a neighboring country and file an application with the UN High Commissioner for Refugees (UNHCR).

Share of world's refugees placed in U.S.
0.5%

STEP TWO Screening by International Officials

UNHCR says there are 14.4 million refugees in the world today, but has referred just 1.2 million for resettlement.

STEP THREE Review by United States

A host of federal agencies oversees the screening process, which includes a background check, an interview and a medical review. Each part of the world has a separate quota dictating how many claims are accepted. President Obama has pledged to accept 85,000 next year, including at least 10,000 Syrians.

Refugees placed in the U.S. in 2015
63,819*

12-18 months

Average time to process a refugee claim

Refugees wait out the lengthy processing time in "host" countries such as Turkey or Jordan. Some, but not all, live in refugee camps.

10%

Percent of all refugees in U.S. placed in Texas in 2015*

Refugee placement organizations interview applicants and decide where they should be placed.

2,046

Total accepted refugee claims from Syria in 2015*

Worldwide, UNHCR identified 4.3 million refugees from Syria in 2015. That means the U.S. accepted 0.04% of the total from Syria. Just 206 Syrian refugees were resettled in Texas.

*Through December 10

SOURCES: The White House, U.S. Department of Homeland Security, Refugee Processing Center, United Nations High Commissioner for Refugees, Syracuse University Transactional Records Access Clearinghouse

ILLUSTRATION BY JOANNA WOJTKOWIAK

FIGURE 9.1 The Refugee Maze. A flowchart showing the decreasing likelihood of obtaining asylum in the United States, focused on Texas but with national data from multiple sources.

Source: Courtesy of the *Texas Observer*, used with permission.

program seems similar to the harsher side of European and EU Neighbourhood Policies with states at and near its external land and sea borders (see chapter 6). Perhaps nothing seems harsher than India or, in maritime borders, Australia's preemption in the high seas, saving lives that could perish in overcrowded boats at sea, but detaining people in off-shore facilities (see chapter 7).

South-to-South Movement: Camps or Resettlement?

In the 21st century, one can only wonder what history will tell about the reluctance to accept refugees from various parts of Western Asia, especially Syria, but also Iraq, Afghanistan, and other countries in perpetual war. Most of those who fled sought refuge in neighboring countries like Jordan, Turkey, Pakistan, and Lebanon—among the top four places of refugee camps, with almost 4 million people—far more than in Europe. But countries lack resources, some of them postcolonial, housing refugees in difficult circumstances, modest, semi-permanent places lacking hope with limited support from the UNHCR as it experiences "donor fatigue."

Maps and sites for refugee camps show the South-to-South migration, voluntary and involuntary, in the last half century. See a map link of the 50 largest camps, administered by the United Nations High Commissioner for Refugees, and home to approximately two million people. The largest, quasi-permanent refugee shelters can be found in countries like Kenya, home to multiple generations of Somalis.[36] Another key area of Western Asia on the map shows Israel's nearby neighbor countries, like Lebanon, which sheltered Palestinian refugees who fled in 1948 (temporarily Palestinians thought). In such circumstances, displaced people in camps become like stateless people, living in places reluctant to grant work permits yet sharing responsibility for food, utilities (or lack of them), and quasi-shelters made of tents and other temporary materials. A poignant film, *When I Saw You* (2012) begins in a refugee camp in 1967 where Palestinians await their right of return. A boy leaves to find his father, lands in a camp with Fedayeen (Arab militants), and is soon followed by his mother also anxious to find her husband, fortunate to have left because the Israelis bomb the refugee camp.

The book *City of Thorns* narrates the stories of camp survivors in northern Kenya who have built an informal city, markets, and mosques.[37] One can learn how people built an informal economy and spaces of worship, with residents acquiring a modicum of economic self-sufficiency given national prohibitions against their formal employment. However, some countries, like Turkey, permit refugees the option of formal employment and small business operations, thus benefiting both refugees and Turkey with more consumers and economic growth.[38]

Considering those many governments with laws that protect paid work for natives, citizens, or persons with legal status, such as in the United States, various levels of government have enacted laws to require employers to share responsibility for checking authorization to work, known as "e-verify." However, the electronic systems contain mistakes, just as do seemingly technologically advanced systems like the US "no-fly" list of presumable terrorists. With multiple identical names, famous mistakes are made, such as the late US senator Ted Kennedy's name appearing on the infamous list in 2004 until corrected.[39] The word "security" and its frequent, narrow use as rationale for policy critique and policy change have resulted in overreach "securitization" processes that envelop and blanket whole nations and their residents' communication under surveillance (see chapter 8).

Border security rhetoric has become part of the political discourse in the United States, especially around election times and the budget-making process. Yet US big cities in the Southwest with Mexico land borders, such as San Diego and El Paso, rise to the top 10 list of "safest cities," based on FBI statistics of felony crimes. Land border closures, with walls, fences, and border security guards, offer blunt but inaccurate tools to deal comprehensively with unauthorized migration. Government studies show that 40 percent of unauthorized people in the United States have overstayed their visas, which initially allowed entry. The terrorist perpetrators of 9/11 entered legally via airports but overstayed their visas.[40] Technology had not caught up with the loophole.

A Geopolitical Nightmare in Western Asia: Wherefore Refugees in the European Union?

Migrants fleeing civil wars and their disrupted economies exercise agency and all the cultural and financial capital they can muster from friends and relatives to escape their settings. Some bring their own documents; others purchase false documents; still others lose documents on the perilous journeys. In 2015–2016, the world was watching, reading, and listening to horrendous and courageous stories of people fleeing Syria, a former French colony once joined with Lebanon, and now turned into a geopolitical nightmare of transgressed borders through militarism and force. Wide coverage in special and popular magazines called attention to dangerous journeys with cover pictures and titles using words of biblical proportions: "EXODUS" (magazine cover word and pictures for both *The Economist* September 12–18, 2015, and *Time,* October 19, 2015), with subtitles, respectively "Refugees, Compassion and Democracy" and "The Epic Migration to Europe & What Lies Ahead." Discourse like this frames how people think about these issues, whether they are avid readers or scanners in grocery-store lines. Sympathetic discourse turned negative within a year, as overwhelmed European governments sought to prevent migrant arrivals, resettle them in Turkey and elsewhere, and stigmatize the traffickers who earned large sums ferrying migrants across the Mediterranean and other seas.

Wars create their refugees, with historic border problems often one of the root causes. Most media coverage aims to make sense of the geopolitical dynamics in sending countries. Syria, long under politically repressive authoritarian rule, faced and faces rebels against whom sophisticated weaponry, even chemical weapons, have been applied to large swaths of space and people. Inducing tension over and in this country and others, one can identify the Shiite-Sunni differences in Islam among those who seek sacred governance. Neighboring Iraq, with its poor governance during and after US occupation, and economic problems, has been perceived to favor particular regions and religious affiliations in a zero-sum governance game. Dare both countries be called, to employ a much overused phrase "failed states"? The answer is probably no, compared with worst-case state scenarios such as Somalia, Eritrea, the Central African Republic, and North Korea. *Foreign Policy* magazine produces an annual list in which it indexes failed states.

Meanwhile, other rebels known as the self-proclaimed Islamic State of Iraq and Greater Syria (ISIS, ISIL, IS, and Daesh) have used force to claim major swaths of land that cross borders and call into question territorial control over the former (colonial) borders. Hardly a "state" in the classic notions—for no other states recognize it—ISIS captures and traffics people, exports oil, sells precious antiquities through illicit underground channels, and levies heavy taxes and fees on residents to finance its military operations. Its institutionalized misogyny draws on medieval practices that authorize rape of captives, but allow modern birth control to avoid intercourse with pregnant slaves, information disseminated by media worldwide, including the *New York Times*.[41] In between and beyond lies Kurdistan, long struggling for territorial control over its own people, language, and culture, but with residents divided into four countries by fiat in the borders that colonial officials and war victors drew in 1919. Iraq underwent British rule until independence (under a new monarch) in 1932. Before, after, and in between wars, people wondered whether partition was a solution for Iraq or simply another example of neocolonial divide-and-rule policies.

Yet other forces hover over the entire region. One of those forces is the United States, willing to use "hard power" to militarize conflicts, perhaps aggravating them, or to join forces with its European or Gulf area allies to create no-fly zones (such as in Libya, rid of dictator Gaddafi but left without stable government). The other force is Russia, aligned with Syria's leader Bashar al-Assad to strengthen his government, while the United States does not, for it prioritizes the demise of ISIS. Turkey, a member of the western NATO alliance and candidate for EU accession, claimed that Russian planes, striking against Turkmen people rebelling against al-Assad, crossed into its air space and shot down the planes in late 2015. The Turkish government represses Kurdish people in its own southeast, while US policies praise and support Kurds in Iraq. Other border neighbors, and neighbors of neighbors, are implicated in these conflicts, but it is beyond the scope of this chapter to do more than discuss Syrian exiles caught in this mire.

Analysts point fingers about whom and what processes are responsible for the geopolitical nightmare: colonialism? authoritarian rule? the gun trade? rich-country meddling over oil and other resources or through occupation? The answers are complicated, and historical mistakes cannot be undone (though hopefully not repeated). The world still has scores of millions of migrants on the move, statelessness, people dying and/or sexually assaulted on the journey, human talent wasted, older populations in the North that need replenishment and consumers, and other crises. Yet many people in rich countries show little willingness to redistribute their wealth even slightly or to invite insecurity within their borders. What is to be done? The solutions thus far have involved offering refuge to some migrants, then sheltering them, or preventing their movement in the first place (see chapters on Europe and maritime borders).

And the larger question about Syrians and others in the South toward which we move in the conclusion involves the alternatives to rigid immigration controls amid the migrants' search for economic stability and prosperity. As we will see in the conclusion, this takes us back to global and border inequalities. People's movement is virtually inevitable amid the glaring inequalities that exist.

Perilous Journeys; Ambiguous Arrivals

Staggering numbers of migrants have moved sideways, northward, from the African continent and western Asia to Europe, from Mexico, the Caribbean and Central America to the United States, and from Southeast Asia to Australia (see chapter 7 on maritime borders). As stated, the United Nations High Commissioner for Refugees estimates 60 million people on the move, and the International Organization for Migration said it was the biggest movement since World War II (15 million) and certainly more than the 1.2 million refugees of the Balkan wars.[42]

Heartbreaking stories make it clear that the suffering might be comparable to 20th-century world wars and their aftermaths or genocides. Who was not emotionally moved with the picture of three-year old Aylan, a Syrian child drowned and washed up on a beach? Refugees move away from inequality, strife, and lack of opportunity toward hoped-for prosperity and the opportunity for economic gain. But how much movement can occur without generating backlash and the rise of antiforeign sentiments?

Little Aylan Kurdi was not the only one to die crossing treacherous seas. From the *Economist* we learn that in 2014, a likely 100,000 arrived in Italy, surpassing the previous record of 60,000 when people arrived after the Arab Spring and its aftermath in several North African countries and Eritrea[43] with its infamous human-rights abuses. In routes that depart from there, hundreds sometimes drown near the Italian island of Lampedusa. The Italian-made film *Terraferma* offers insight in this regard. The Dublin Regulation requires migrants' fingerprints to be stored in the first EU state where asylum claims are made (to avoid multiple asylum claims). Italy has received the most, followed by Germany, Sweden, France, and Britain. Frontex, underfunded and based in Warsaw, Poland, is hardly able to assist with the process, though efforts in 2015 and 2016 will strengthen support for "frontline" countries. The Dublin regulation, in practice and perhaps in future policy, will likely undergo changes.

Refugees have been crossing the Adriatic and Mediterranean Seas for decades. Although the unwritten "law of the sea" requires rescue, and many fishermen and governmental vehicles have valiantly obliged, it is impossible to know how many look the other way to avoid the complications therefrom. In his part-empirical, part-moral recount of the region in *Crimes of Peace,* Maurizio Albahari discusses corpses routinely found in the sea, then tossed back into this huge graveyard. His participant observation in so-called reception centers defies the meaning of the word "reception" with its confusion, border bureaucrats, and understandable self-mutilation among desperate refugees.[44]

In 2015, when over a million refugees reached Europe, Germany became the most celebrated state to accept refugees and supply them with start-up support until political backlash set in. Some media called the acts "redemption" after World War II, but others pointed to Germany's aging population, low birth rate, and need for skilled workers of all types. Germany received the largest number of asylum applications in 2014 (100,000) (more in subsequent years) and accepted them at the highest rate (40 percent), compared to other European countries. Sweden got the second-highest number (40,000), accepted approximately three-fourths, and Eurostat figures show the highest number of refugees (12.1) per 1,000 in the population.[45]

Numbers alone can numb us in a world of everyday crises and shocking headlines that compete for our sympathy. Like the rich-country malady called donor fatigue, refugee numbers and tragedies may be difficult for people to fathom and absorb, leading to refugee fatigue. (Remember dictator Stalin's quote about massive numeric statistics in chapter 3.) Personal testimonies can be evocative and detailed, so much more so than numbers. One such example is of a Syrian refugee named Ghaith, a young law student who crossed 10 borders to leave the violent chaos that Damascus had become. Ultimately, he succeeded in reaching Sweden, wherein he was fortunate to register (under the Dublin Regulation). In a lengthy, in-depth investigative *New Yorker* article, from which this paragraph's quotes come,[46] Ghaith's harrowing, dangerously violent, expensive, and risky yet courageous journey is narrated in great depth. He encountered many brokers, from honest to corrupt, that guided him across sea and land borders. His use of social media, like Facebook and WhatsApp, provided instant communication with relatives, extended family members who wired money, and contact with people like guide Abu Amar with "his own channel on Zello, a walkie-talkie app, becoming a real-time Harriet Tubman." Complete with a map of the journey, we learn not only the nationality of police and border guards who beat crossers or looked the other way, but also of human rights activists who provide direct assistance in the form of food, water, and dry clothing. Cross-border movements are never so neat and orderly as UN conventions and resolutions make them seem.

Some countries refuse to admit migrants and their families, even when one family member holds a British passport. In Calais, France, a hoped-for launching area to Britain, migrants lived in tent shanty spaces over a dump site in inhumane conditions. Periodically, officials threaten to or actually bulldoze the often muddy and garbage-strewn area they call a "jungle," due to conditions which causes some to scatter elsewhere, perhaps in less visible places, and still others are moved to contained spaces for processing and fingerprinting.[47] Meanwhile, Conservative and Labor Party officials interact in the typically rowdy atmosphere in the British Parliament over the fate of prospective migrants, given cost and employment problems in the United Kingdom,[48] leading eventually to the highly contentious Brexit vote in June 2016.

Gendered Journeys and Arrivals

Understanding migrant journeys requires a gender lens. While the refugees who settle in neighboring countries like Lebanon, Turkey, and Jordan are a relatively gender-balanced group, balance is less true of refugees who travel further into

Europe, estimated to be approximately two-thirds or more men perhaps hoping to root themselves before sponsoring families. National laws vary as to whether and when family members can join them. Women on long-distance trips encounter gendered risks in the journey, sexual violence, and abuse during travels and in shelters. These include examples like paying down one's own or a husband's debt with sex to smugglers, sleeping and bathing in unlocked shelter rooms where two-thirds of residents are male, and family violence or husbands' prohibitions against movement outside of the shelter.[49]

In the Americas, too, women migrants face perilous journeys from guides called *coyotes*, bandits, and law enforcement. In her comparison of both the Guatemala-Mexico and US-Mexico borders, social anthropologist Olivia Ruiz analyzes patriarchal norms that exoticize and sexualize women "from the south" and journeys wherein women take birth control before embarking on the trip, given anticipated sexual assaults along the way.[50] Anna Ochoa O'Leary interviewed 100 women in shelters on the Sonora, Mexico, side of the border, three of whom she analyzes in depth.[51] They fled for different reasons, domestic and organized crime, but encountered life-threatening incidents along the way. Several quality films depict these gendered dangerous journeys: *7 Soles,* a Mexican-produced film of travelers across the hot, dry desert encountering death from the journey, the elements, and rape with fellow travelers reluctant to intervene when they heard screams. The other is the Spanish film noted earlier, *14 Kilómetros,* about three travelers from central Africa crossing the Sahel. Memorable moments emerge in the desert outposts of North African state border guards, predators themselves and evincing a sexualized racism against people from the south.

Settlement and Assimilation?

The granting of asylum applications and the provision of temporary shelters are only the first steps to a long and complicated process of acceptance, language skills, and jobs. Obvious costs are associated with asylum acceptance, economically and politically. By 2015, Germany offered the most generous benefits (374 euros per adult, per month), followed by Australia (which accepts only minuscule numbers mainly from China, India, and Pakistan, at the equivalent of 275 euros) and then Sweden (226 euros monthly per adult).[52] The costs and challenges of assimilation have already begun to generate backlash against foreigners of different color, religions, and languages. Some of the backlash is tinged with racism and resentment about the expenses of refugee allowances as people settle in, hardly self-supporting upon arrival. In several countries, like Denmark, authorities confiscate economic and jewelry resources above a certain amount to share the costs of resettlement. Politically, many European states have seen immigration anxieties documented on surveys and in the rise of right-wing party strength during elections. The United States detains in public, NGO, and private for-profit centers—a country always open to market niches.

In media coverage, we see the challenges that both migration and gender politics pose to mainstream, established institutions like the European Union.

England's Brexit vote was in part an anti-migrant vote, including those from Europe authorized to work and study (Scottish voters sought to "Remain"). The refugee crisis, its size, and the lopsided, imbalanced gender demographics coupled with mismatched norms offer a case in point.

Germany, strongest nation economically within the European Union and one with an aging population, made the magnanimous gesture of accepting over one million migrants in 2015, at some political cost to Chancellor Angela Merkel. This has been called the *willkomenkultur* or the welcoming culture. Other EU member states did not do likewise, particularly the later EU additions in Eastern Europe with their weaker economies, lower per capita incomes, and nationalist-revivalist politicians. Who can forget the video of a Hungarian camerawoman deliberating tripping a migrant father carrying his child?[53]

The more cautious among Europeans wondered about the consequences of large numbers of newcomers in short periods of time. All answers to questions can be found in policy decisions. Refugees arrive with varying assets, such as skills, education, and language abilities. First, there is the financial issue of shelter and eventual housing and job accommodations. Second, short- and long-term assimilation involves careful analysis: how will people learn the lingua franca? How long before people acquire jobs and become self-supporting or able to support families? When will refugees be allowed to work—immediately, in three months, or in nine months? To what extent is assimilation even a goal if it means that people shed treasured cultural and linguistic backgrounds?

Questions like these have long been part of US policy thinking for more than a century in its former relatively open-door immigration policies for newcomers, albeit funded in large part through their own family members, social networks, and easy absorption into low-paying jobs. By the next or second generation, youth question assimilation, countering the narrative that pushes them to erase their heritage and language. Faith-based shelter staff try to treat migrants with respect and dignity, "seeing the face of Jesus" in the migrant as Father/Professor Daniel Groody of Notre Dame University says in his short film, *Dying to Live*. Occasional tender treatment of migrants can also be observed as one Mexican shelter staff worker demonstrates with treatment for damaged feet from the journey.[54]

Anxieties about migrants peaked in Cologne, Germany, at and after public 2015 New Year's Eve celebrations. At the core was gender politics and/or gender politics used by the right-wing to undermine welcoming policies. In most European countries, women have long crossed the metaphorical border from private to public spaces. Yet in Europe and elsewhere, women may be subject to sexual harassment and sexual assaults; nowhere has rape disappeared, including in Europe by Europeans. But the assaults of more than 600 women who reported incidents by men who "looked like" foreigners from North Africa and Western Asia produced a political uproar and protests by women who claimed their right to safe presence in public streets. The types of assaults resembled those that women reported in Cairo's Tahrir Square during the Arab Spring protests of Egypt. And the right-wing, anti-foreigner political forces used these incidents to protest the presence of refugees in large numbers. Subsequently, immigrants have faced mob violence and been assaulted. In the course of one evening, the volatile combination of gender and immigration politics produced a political crisis for German officials including chancellor Angela Merkel.

The years 2015 and 2016 will surely go down in history, marking as the humanitarian crises of the era: refugees and asylum seekers. We learn through the numbers of those who died crossing: at least 12,000 and perhaps as many as 25,000 crossing the Mediterranean since 2000, noted earlier, and 300–400 bodies found annually of those who died attempting to cross the US-Mexico border, yet just 125 who died trying to cross the Berlin Wall.[55] One death is one too many, but the contrast in figures is startling coupled with the seriousness with which some view past and present problems.

Concluding Reflections

In this chapter, we have examined people on the move across borders, the many kinship and bureaucratic rules associated with that movement, and the ways that international law and precedent do not necessarily mesh with such rules. We have considered biopolitical theorists who speak to such issues, and we note how gender shapes experiences, drives migration for different reasons, and undermines supposedly equitable international and national laws. The chapter also illustrates how wars create refugees both historically and in contemporary times, creating internal displacement and south-to-south movement and resettlement rather than a rush northward as has often been perceived. In the mid-20th century, states in various world regions coped with the millions of those who moved from the conflict settings. The dangers of lives lost and lives in limbo persist after conflict and war.

Border police, named differently in different states, operate as a line of control against state-defined illegal actions. The border line itself and the myriad rules and regulations inhibit people's crossings to escape poverty for work and potential refugees' exodus to escape violence. In crossing, migrants face threats not only from dangers in their journeys but also from the border police such as India's Border Security Force. Each year, surprisingly large numbers of people die on the journey for both those reasons. Some countries like the United States count "rescues" as well as "apprehensions," but the rescue there is ambivalent for it frequently leads to detention and deportation. Moreover, on occasion, border police subject citizens and visitors to racial profiling and violence with impunity. States' claims of these agents as the "first line of defense against terrorism" provide them with extraordinary and almost absolute power which, as the ancient aphorism goes, can corrupt absolutely. Thus, with the danger people face from state "security," rather than the protection that the word implies, states have a special responsibility to exercise oversight and control over police forces operating in borderlands, far from their capital cities.

What is to be done about people on the move? Thus far, we have covered harsh to welcoming policies and/or policies that selectively admit people based on money, relatives, talents, and/or credible fears about returning to their homes. In the ideal world, people could remain in their homes safely, with economic opportunities for themselves and their children.

Recommended Resources

Films

7 Soles
14 Kilómetros
Dying to Live
The Golden Dream
Sin Nombre
When I Saw You

Notes

[1] Matthew Carr, *Fortress Europe: Dispatches from a Gated Continent* (NY: The New Press, 2012), p. 16.
[2] Elizabeth Becker, "Washington Talk: Prickly Roots of 'Homeland Security,'" August 31, 2002, http://www.nytimes.com/2002/08/31/us/washington-talk-prickly-roots-of-homeland-security.html), Accessed 2/1/16.
[3] Kim Rygiel, *Globalizing Citizenship* (Vancouver and Toronto: University of British Columbia Press, 2010), p. 93.
[4] Ibid., p. 94.
[5] Ibid., pp. 99–104. Foucault means many things to many different people. One is the metaphorical treatment of the nation as body into which outsiders should not intrude.
[6] Kathleen Staudt and Irasema Coronado, "Gendering Border Studies: Biopolitics in the Elusive US Wars on Drugs and Immigrants," *Eurasia Border Review*, forthcoming.
[7] Odhikar is a Bangladesh human rights organization: http://odhikar.org/report-on-human-rights-violations-in-the-india-bangladesh-border/. Accessed 7/4/16.
[8] Maurizio Albahari, *Crimes of Peace: Mediterranean Migrations at the World's Deadliest Border* (Philadelphia: University of Pennsylvania Press, 2015), pp. 33, 105.
[9] US Customs and Border Protection, US Department of Homeland Security. https://www.cbp.gov/sites/default/files/documents/USBP%20Stats%20FY2014%20sector%20profile.pdf. Accessed 7/4/16.
[10] Rajni Palriwala and Patricia Uberoi, "Marriage and Migration in Asia: Gender Issues," *Indian Journal of Gender Studies* 12, 2 & 3, 2005, p. vi.
[11] Kathleen Staudt, *Agricultural Policy, Political Power, and Women Farmers in Western Kenya* (Madison: University of Wisconsin, PhD Dissertation, 1976).
[12] Palriwala and Uberoi, "Marriage and Migration in Asia," p. xv.
[13] Ibid., p. xvi.
[14] Ibid., p. xxiii.
[15] Willem Van Schendel, *The Bengal Borderland: Beyond State and Nation in South Asia* (London: Anthem Press, 2005), p. 2005. At the US-Mexico border, Debbie Nathan wrote about similar phenomena in "The Eyes of Texas Are Upon You," in *Women and Other Aliens: Essays from the U.S.-Mexico Border* (El Paso: Cinco Puntos Press, 1987).
[16] Van Schendel, *The Bengal Borderland*, p. 220.
[17] Ibid., p. 298.
[18] Ibid., 2005, p. 302. See Mark Binelli, "10 Shot Across the Border: The Killing of a Mexican 16-year-old Raises Troubling Questions about the United States Border Patrol," *The New York Times Magazine,* March 3, 2016. At the time of writing, the count over 15 years was estimated to be around 50 killings, both citizens and noncitizens. No agents had been prosecuted.
[19] Van Schendel, *The Bengal Borderland*, p. 346.

20 Ibid. Recall US border police techno-sexual assaults discussed earlier and occasionally reported or made public with lawsuits and media coverage in the United States (note 6).

21 See various chapter selections in Kathleen Staudt, Tony Payan, and Z. Anthony Kruszewski, eds., *Human Rights along the US-Mexico Border* (Tucson: University of Arizona Press, 2009). Many Amnesty International reports document police impunity in Mexico; see for example, the 2016 report on women raped in custody.

22 Tony Payan, *The Three US-Mexico Border Wars: Drugs, Immigration, and Homeland Security* (Westport, CT: Praeger Security International, 2006; second edition, 2016), pp. 6–13.

23 Water Ewing, " 'Enemy Territory': Immigration Enforcement in the US-Mexico Borderlands," *Journal on Migration and Human Security* 2, 3 (2014), pp. 198–222; Anastasia Brown and Todd Scribner, "Unfulfilled Promises, Future Possibilities: The Refugee Resettlement System in the United States," *Journal on Migration and Human Security* 2, 2, 2014, pp. 101–20; also see Timothy Dunn, *Blockading the Border and Human Rights: The El Paso Operation that Remade Immigration Enforcement* (Austin: University of Texas Press, 2009). See chapter 8.

24 John Torpey, "States and the Regulation of Migration in the Twentieth-Century North Atlantic World," in Peter Andreas and Timothy Snyder, eds., *The Wall Around the West* (Lanham, MD: Rowman & Littlefield, 2000), cites Aristide Zolberg, p. 39. Carr on Nazi identification of religious affiliation on passports, *Fortress Europe*, p. 20.

25 Torpey, "States and the Regulation of Migration," p. 38. See also the International Civil Aviation Organization, http://www.icao.int.

26 American Civil Liberties Union Regional Center for Border Rights, *Guilty until Proven Innocent: Living in New Mexico's 100-Mile Zone* (Las Cruces, NM: ACLU, 2014). Also see Todd Miller, *Border Patrol Nation: Dispatches from the Front Lines of Homeland Security* (San Francisco: City Lights Books, 2014).

27 See ethnographic and participant observer detail in Kathleen Staudt, "Bordering the Other in the US Southwest: El Pasoans Confront the Local Sheriff on Immigration Enforcement," in Phillip Kretsedemas and David Brotherton, eds., *Keeping out the Other: Immigration Enforcement Today* (NY: Columbia University Press, 2008), pp. 291–313.

28 United Nations High Commissioner for Human Rights, http://www.unhcr.org.

29 Carr, *Fortress Europe*, pp. 19–20.

30 Cited in Anastasia Brown and Todd Scribner, "Unfulfilled Promises, Future Possibilities: The Refugee Resettlement System in the United States," *Journal on Migration and Human Security* 2, 2, 2014, p. 102.

31 *The Economist*, "Looking for a Home," Special Report on Migration, May 28, 2016.

32 Institute on Statelessness and Inclusion, accessed 3/1/16 at http://www.institutesi.org.

33 Louise Osborne and Ruby Russell, "Refugee Crisis Creates 'Stateless Generation' of Children in Limbo," *The Guardian*, December 27, 2015, accessed 12/28/16 at http://www.theguardian.com/world/2015/dec/27/refugee-crisis-creating-stateless-generation-children-experts-warn?utm_source=esp&utm_medium=Email&utm_campaign=GU+Today+USA+-+Version+A&utm_term=146405&subid=16547393&CMP=ema_565a.

34 Cited in Carr, *Fortress Europe*, p. 20.

35 Nina Lakhani, "Human Rights Groups Sue US Over Immigration Payments to Mexico," *The Guardian*, February 12, 2016. http://www.theguardian.com/us-news/2016/feb/12/human-rights-group-sue-immigration-mexico?CMP=share_btn_fb. Accessed 2/16/16.

36 http://storymaps.esri.com/stories/2013/refugee-camps/.

37 Ben Rawlence, *City of Thorns* (NY: Picador/Macmillan, 2015).

38 Omer Karasapan, "The Impact of Syrian Businesses in Turkey," *Brookings*, March 16, 2016, accessed 3/17/16 at http://www.brookings.edu/blogs/future-development/posts/2016/03/16-syrian-business-turkey-karasapan. The attempted military coup in Turkey in July 2016, subsequent purges, and authoritarian tendencies have strained relations with Europe.

39 Benjamin Muller, *Security, Risk, and the Biometric State* (NY and London: Routledge, 2010), p. 8.

40 Alan Gomez, "Study: Nearly 500K Overstayed Visas," *El Paso Times* from *USA Today*, January 21, 2016, p. 3A. An inability to find work is a major deterrent to unauthorized migration.

41 Rukmini Callimachi, "To Maintain Supply of Sex Slaves, ISIS Pushes Birth Control," *New York Times,* March 13, 2016, accessed 3/13/16. http://www.nytimes.com/2016/03/13/world/middleeast/to-maintain-supply-of-sex-slaves-isis-pushes-birth-control.html?_r=0).

42 *The Economist,* "Exodus," September 12, 2015, p. 13.

43 *The Economist,* "A Surge from the Sea," August 16, 2014, pp. 41–2; *The Economist,* "Europe's Boat People: For Those in Peril," Briefing, April 25, 2015, pp. 21–3.

44 Maurizio Albahari, *Crimes of Peace,* see especially chapters 4–5 on his ethnographic research. Also see Carr, *Fortress Europe,* on reception in Greece, perhaps the most dismal of his comparative European country chapters.

45 *The Economist,* "Europe's Boat People."

46 Nicholas Schmidle, "Ten Borders: One Refugee's Epic Escape from Syria," *The New Yorker,* October 26, 2015, pp. 42–53.

47 http://www.theguardian.com/world/2016/feb/12/half-jungle-camp-calais-bulldozed-migrants-moved.

48 http://www.theguardian.com/politics/video/2016/jan/27/cameron-makes-calais-jungle-bunch-of-migrants-jibe-video

49 http://www.nytimes.com/2016/01/03/world/europe/on-perilous-migrant-trail-women-often-become-prey-to-sexual-abuse.html.

50 Olivia Ruiz Marrujo, "Women, Migration, and Sexual Violence: Lessons from Mexico's Borders," in Kathleen Staudt, Tony Payan, and Z. Anthony Kruszewski, eds., *Human Rights along the U.S.-Mexico Border* (Tucson: University of Arizona Press, 2009), pp. 31–47.

51 Anna Ochoa O'Leary, "In the Footsteps of Spirits: Migrant Women's Testimonies in a Time of Heightened Border Enforcement," in Kathleen Staudt, Tony Payan, and Z. Anthony Kruszewski, eds., *Human Rights along the U.S.-Mexico Border* (Tucson: University of Arizona Press, 2009), pp. 85–104.

52 *The Economist,* "Looking for a Home," August 29, 2015, pp. 41–4.

53 http://www.cnn.com/videos/world/2015/09/09/hungarian-camerawoman-trips-kicks-migrants-stelter-dnt-ac.cnn.

54 http://latinousa.org/2014/06/13/foot-massager-border/.

55 Iñigo Moré, *The Borders of Inequality* (Tucson: University of Arizona Press, 2011), from COLEF studies); Carr, *Fortress Europe,* on the Berlin Wall figures.

Chapter 10

Freer and Fairer Trade in Borderlands

Trade and cross-border business processes bind people together in borderlands, for good, bad, and ugly reasons, whether the goods and services traded are large- to small-scale or whether they are legal, licit, or illegal and illicit—distinctions discussed below. Producers, consumers, and extended family, among the first to interact in borderlands or to sustain interaction, generate jobs, income, profits, and trust (or lack thereof). Economic inequalities and rigid border controls at territorial borders can enhance opportunity for some but aggravate exploitation for others. Most assuredly, global, binational inequalities, conflict, and poverty stimulate migration: from rural to urban areas inside countries, from poorer countries to richer countries, and to escape from war. Nation-state containers (the "territorial traps" noted in chapter 1) make and enforce varying laws, protections, and wage structures that operate like an apartheid system for working people, constrained from moving across borders without skills, advantages, and documents in most world regions except for inside the European Union. Thus, this chapter focuses mainly on the South Asian and the US-Mexico borderlands where national security agendas, broadly defined, overwhelm other issues.

A central dilemma in developing countries with low incomes, and poorly funded health care and education (ranked low on the UNDP's Human Development Index, introduced in chapter 3) involves how to generate external capital to facilitate job creation, decent pay, and infrastructure investments, yet maintain enough internal voice or and leverage to benefit wider numbers of people. Foreign direct investment (FDI), according to rationales related to "comparative advantage" (that is, low labor costs, lax environmental laws, plentiful natural resources) may run contrary to people's interests in mainstream and borderlands economies. Under conditions of inequality and conflict in borderlands, the sad fact is that the more powerful interests and states not only grab land and property but also extract excessive value from labor. The less powerful are forced to make do with what remains.

A key question in this chapter asks how trade operates in the borderlands covered in this book. We look at formal and informal trade, maquiladoras/export-processing factories, and business development strategies in the historic and contemporary neoliberal global economy, including the controversial "war on drugs." In the name of liberty or freedom rationales, neoliberal ideology seeks to limit government regulation and maximize capitalist marketplace activities, including the privatization of functions formerly performed by government. However, the logic rarely applies to what I have called the "quintessential free traders,"[1] that is, those informal workers and microentrepreneurs who generate income from licit (that is, commonly accepted as legitimate) activity with its only harm being a loss of official control and revenue therefrom.

In the borderlands of part II's regional chapters, we see different approaches to trade in the contemporary global economy and the maintenance of security, the latter usually defined in national rather than human or environmental security terms. I argue in this chapter that two of the regional borderlands' approaches to trade have been ineffective from a variety of perspectives. The US-Mexican borderlands pursues classic neoliberalism, albeit under a heavily regulated security apparatus complete with border fences/walls that contribute to deaths as undocumented people try to cross borders in arid regions away from official ports of entry. This "globally competitive" borderlands (as business boosters call the place) perpetuates low wages for workers, before and after the NAFTA trade agreement. The India-Bangladesh borderlands follows stiflingly regulated yet ineffective trade practices, with the rationale of security, but has militarized the border to the extent of inducing insecurity for borderlanders. People manage to slip through or around and outside rules, albeit it at risk but in unknown numbers given the spotty collection of records of births, deaths, and other data in postcolonial, impoverished states. The European Union, while opening borders to facilitate regional trade, operates in a regulated neoliberal context to facilitate greater human and environmental security. But its long-term impact, to the extent that neoliberal ideology reigns supreme and supranational institutions become less accountable, could dampen wages. Border people and their voices have not been prominent in trade and security debates. This chapter and those chapters in part IV grapple with questions about ways to assure that border people benefit from trade and trade opportunities that flow through their borderlands.

Unregulated and Regulated Cross-Border Trade

Historically, most people traded locally, including at the porous places of the outer fringes of empires. Those empires began to break apart in a lengthy, century-or-more-old colonial era with the subsequent emergence of almost 200 states with territorial boundaries over the last two centuries. Governments sought to insert themselves in trade, and in so doing, created official positions in regulating border processes and revenue generation. Dutch anthropologist Willem Van Schendel notes that states seek an unfulfilled aim to control awe-inspiring numbers of territorial borders in the world—226,000 kilometers (140,130 miles)—an aim that generates government anxieties about control and policy agendas that regulate borderlands.[2] Yet both informal and formal networks of trade occur in such regions, long understudied. Recall from Benedict Anderson cited in an earlier chapter that states use tools such as censuses, maps, and museums to "imagine the nation." As part of their counts and measurements, states also try to count or estimate cross-border mobilities in trade and people. Informal movement and trade across borders cannot be easily captured in formal statistical models that focus on official ports of entry alone.

As long ago as 200 BCE, traders also moved great distances such as along the Silk Road. Nowadays, business and government boosters evoke such routes as exotic journeys with the new initiatives like the contemporary Silk Road, Southern Silk Road involving the so-called BCIM (Bangladesh-China-India-Myanmar countries), and Maritime Silk Road economic corridors.[3] News junkies may also recall the now-defunct illegal drug website of the same name! Let us now examine some conceptual issues in trade.

Legal-Illegal and Licit-Illicit Trade

With regulatory tools, officials work at borders to inhibit what was once called and continues to be called "smuggling"—a pejorative term—or transport of illegal goods (such as controlled drugs) or unauthorized crossers. Peter Andreas writes about the "border games" played by both officials and "smugglers" in dramatic rituals and reports of success in countering crime.[4] Others analyze informal workers who generate income outside of the regulated economy, usually sidestepping officials.[5]

Informal trade has long been global, celebrated and/or denigrated in multiple words and languages. In Spanish-speaking parts of the world, informal trade is referred to as the *hormiga* (ant) trade for its near-invisible but hardworking character. A local NGO in the US-Mexican borderlands is called Las Hormigas for its persistence. One town in Colombia near the Ecuador border is named La Hormiga. A reputed ant trade operates at the enclave of the Kaliningrad (Russia)-Poland border where small-scale shoppers buy to stretch incomes or to resell, and in the bazaar, open-air markets of central Poland, the cross-border so-called suitcase traders have been called ants.[6]

More recently, analysts have differentiated goods in a constructive framework: a fourfold typology of legal and illegal, licit and illicit. Taking as their point of departure the discourse surrounding international and transnational crime, Itty Abraham and Willem van Schendel analyze "the making of illicitness." They conceptualize distinctions between "what states consider to be legitimate ("legal") and what people involved in transnational networks consider to be legitimate ("licit").[7] Plenty of horrifying illicit and illegal trade occurs, but one might ask whether legal trade with near-slave wages could be called illicit.

The legal-illegal dimension is a function of state laws, so the definition of what is "criminal" becomes a social construct as well. For gendered examples, prostitution is regulated and legal in Northern Mexico, but illegal in the southwestern United States (except for Nevada); while it is practiced, first-trimester abortion is technically illegal in Mexico, but not in the United States.[8] Drug possession, in small amounts, is subject to a myriad of fragmented laws and their interpretations, both in Mexico and the United States, and *within* the United States among states that regulate marijuana through decriminalization or that legalize it for leisure and medical use *versus* those states that criminalize marijuana. Meanwhile in the United States, legal pharmaceutical prescriptions of pain-killing drugs have led to addictions, followed by use and addiction to cheaper heroin. These addictions are now one of the most serious drug problems in the United States, as the National Institute on Drug Abuse reports.[9]

Once established, states invented and required official documents to move people and goods across borders. Historically, laws forbid certain trade or set tariffs on legal and licit trade to protect national producers, making goods more expensive. Of course, despicable illicit trade also exists: sex- or slave-trafficked people and endangered animals; infectious pests, animals, and plants; murderers and currency leakage, among others. Notice that I did not mention drugs here; the prohibition and interdiction system falls under the category of illegal, not necessarily illicit trade, and the underground nature of the market often increases traffickers' profits in a brutal trade. The US Customs and Border Protection (CBP) reports drug seizures, including hard addictive drugs like methamphetamine and heroin, though marijuana constitutes more than 97 percent of the pounds confiscated.[10] Alcohol prohibition also has its historic parallels.

The Illegal Alcohol and Drug Trade

At various points in history, governments sought and seek to make alcohol and drugs illegal, though definitions of legality vary from one country to another. Narcotics might be prohibited (illegal) in one country and not the other country. Vivid examples emerge with the seeming neverending US "war on drugs" that began in 1969—"a war that can't be won," to quote the title of an edited volume.[11] Nation-states have begun changing policies to counter, perhaps to tax, drugs as legal trade in order to generate revenue and to reduce the costly control efforts at national, state, and local levels to prohibit drugs through interdiction at borders, to pay for both steep sentences and mass incarceration—all effects of which bear heavily on men of color in the United States. Formerly illegal drugs are legally regulated in various countries from Uruguay to Portugal and the Netherlands, among many others. With those transitions, government budget priorities shifted from supply-side interdiction approaches to demand reduction in prevention and treatment for addiction.

Even within the United States, tension emerges at internal state borderlands around the movement of substances which the public may view as licit or illicit. Around half of US states have regulated the sale of the so-called soft drug, marijuana, either for recreational and/or medical use. Consider Colorado, where marijuana is regulated and taxed (and therefore legal, generating profitable taxes for government rather than ruthless transnational crime organizations and shippers), and Nebraska, where the substance is illegal: Does surveillance occur in the Colorado-Nebraska borderlands? Should it? Similar tensions emerged during the US Prohibition era of 1920–1933 with liquor and beer, consumption of which increased with assistance from organized crime and corrupt police. The Canada-US and US-Mexico borderlands became prime spaces in which alcohol was temporarily illegal. With hindsight, most surely would not label beer as illicit! The US Department of Homeland Security outlines the history of the US Border Patrol, with pictures, of customs officers dedicated to stopping

the alcohol trade.[12] In the US federal system, decision-makers have the authority to determine whether to decriminalize and regulate marijuana within state
borders. In Washington and Colorado, authorities developed different strategies to roll out legalization and taxation of marijuana for leisure use. At both
a Drug Policy Alliance biennial conference and a Harm Reduction Conference,
I met advocates from the Hungarian Civil Liberties Union where rigid prohibition policies sometimes result in death when those who overdose drugs fear
the criminal consequences of accessing hospitals for medicine that would allow
them to stay alive. The group produced some of the most illuminating videos on
drug policy, including an eight-minute piece on implementation in Colorado.[13]
Colorado's delayed and careful implementation contrasted with the State of
Washington's immediate implementation. Both states took strict steps to label
products and license shops to restrict product use to adults. The marijuana regulation issue is an admittedly controversial issue, but one that needs serious and
rational evaluation of options.

Border Bureaucrats

In the South Asia region analyzed below, border walls and fences make life difficult not only for traders near borders but also for ordinary people to acquire
goods for which they once legally traded and shopped. Besides the fourfold typology above, perhaps best treated as continuums regarding the degrees of licit
and degrees of legal trade, states must also be analyzed for whether they consistently uphold the "law."[14] Border police and patrol officers may be tempted by
greed or threatened by organized criminals to look the other way when laws are
breached. High-level officials may charge the ever-euphemistically named "rent"
to look the other way and allow illegal goods to pass or to grant cross-border
business licenses.

At the very least, we must acknowledge imperfect state regulations and
dishonest practices. States come in all shapes, sizes, and with varying ethical
standards; Transparency International attempts to measure perceptions of these
on an annual basis.[15] Some comparative politics scholars have used strong terminology like "predator state" to analyze routine corruption and wage theft
practices therein. It is important to acknowledge that the opportunities for corruption run rampant in borderlands where the definitions of crime and corruption vary and where multiple legal systems operate, some of which hardly
operate according to the "rule of law."[16]

Besides the protection of national industries, albeit weakened after decades
of colonialism, customs enforcement generates revenue for governments in spatially focused formal trade—administratively perhaps less complex than collect-
ing taxes from informal and formal workers and especially from the wealthy
with political clout. In that process, people have relied on governments to protect national economies, industries, jobs, and the health and safety of workers
and consumers as well. However, freer trade reduces such protection; various
regional or global trade organizations such as NAFTA may trump national
laws or they may generate fears associated with polarizing debates about the
Trans-Pacific Partnership (TPP) or the Transatlantic Trade and Investment

Partnership (TTIP) between the United States and Europe. The 2016 US presidential elections, along with 2016 Brexit campaigns in the United Kingdom, reflect these tensions.

In states lacking transparency and good governance, regulations also offer opportunities for bureaucrats at the border to extort money for themselves or to generate funding for the government agencies that employ them with user fees. Border people bear the burdens of trade flows, official collections, and the infrastructure associated therewith, but little to no money may be left behind for trade that flows through but is not invested in the borderlands. Nevertheless, for the last quarter of the 20th century and beyond, nation-states have adopted free(r) trade policies and joined regional trading pacts to enhance trade, even though political constituencies within countries lobby to perpetuate protections and subsidies for their production (such as sugar, tobacco in the United States) that undermine free-trade principles. Few talk about fair trade (except occasional NGOs), or even *fairer* trade.

From Statelessness to a Quagmire in South Asian Borderlands

In many countries of the South, as discussed above, people generate income outside the regulated economy in what is called the informal economy. Perceptions of licit and illicit range from cross-border buying and reselling of consumer goods that hurt no one (for the price differential and profit therefrom), to cross-border "drug prescription" tourism for the huge price savings, to illicit sex- and slave-trafficking. Thus, it is important to understand that legal trade across borders may be only part of the picture.

In earlier chapters of this book, James C. Scott was cited, cautioning readers against "seeing like a state" but instead recognizing large swathes of "stateless" people living in valleys and mountainous borderless places (recall chapter 5) until the close of the 1940s, with the growth of a national road and technology network.[17] Before state control set in, people crossed spaces (later imagined as borderlands after colonialism) and traded in licit, illicit, legal, and illegal ways. In less-populated borderlands regions worldwide, officials in weak states are hardly aware of crossing. Case studies in Africa underline this reality (see chapter 2). Indeed, the costs of policing the border may be higher than the likely revenue generated or harms prevented from establishing border controls, staffed with officials, or even walls and fences under which tunnels can be built or over which rockets can be launched.

Willem Van Schendel produced the most detailed studies of the Bengali borderlands, a once more-homogenous area of "tens of millions" of people who shared language and ties but that was divided in two by Partition, the Radcliffe Line in 1947. Van Schendel identified how, for centuries, traders linked their goods—such as silk, cotton, indigo, opium, rice, sugar, and jute—to global commercial networks. In strong language, he said that the 1947 India-Pakistan (recall that Bangladesh emerged from East Pakistan in 1971) Partition, "precipitated what can perhaps best be described as the political assassination of this regional economy."[18] India's initial developmental state, with its proactive state-led economic protectionist (import-substitution) strategy, has been called the Development Raj, succeeding the British Raj and its predecessors. In South Asia, this meant that newly identified "transnational" trade flows required control and regulation, for "yesterday's trade might be criminalized today."[19] One can imagine the labor-intensive, rent-seeking behaviors and fearfulness created in the initial railway checks after independence periods in multiple countries.

At the 2015 Association for Borderlands Studies (ABS) conference, we visited open-air markets (*haats*) and heard about the tightly controlled border *haats*, with rigid regulations about space, distance, type of commodity, and so on. Van Schendel writes about *haats* too, but notes that unsanctioned goods were defined as "illegal, illicit, black, underground, contraband, clandestine, smuggling" through both India and (initially West and East) Pakistan in but a handful of designated posts on a 4,000 km border.[20] What was once normal in *haats* became illegal, but enforcement was selective and sporadic.

Although Peter Andreas coined the term "border games" in 2000, as noted earlier, such games exist everywhere as anthropologists have long noted about peasants and villagers who are wary of outsiders including government officials. Van Schendel continues with a description of seemingly parochial "sleepy border villages" where villages put on a show for outsiders. Villagers' economy involves nonofficial currency changes, for example, exchanging gold for perfume or a Swatch watch for ammunition.

Villagers facilitate mobilities as well. In Van Schendel's chapter 8, his picture contains a sign in India: "Bona fide Citizens should not shelter Foreigners." He goes on to identify multiple narratives that borderlanders use to describe the movement of people independent of the nationalist identities imposed upon them: (1) they are coming home, (2) they are infiltrating (especially in Assam and Tripura, northeastern states), and (3) they are taking over. Yet once they cross borders, the government treats them as international migrants if caught[21] with all the implications for documents, criminalization, and border games but with potentially deadly consequences, given the militarized Border Security Force.

In the ABS conference visit in 2015, we talked to villagers who described people who surreptitiously crossed the border to harvest wood at night, yet we saw a busy daytime border crossing that authorized India truck traffic to the Bangladesh border (in Dawki and Tamabil) which dumped boulders (that laborers had painstakingly pounded into smaller pieces) for Bangladeshi contractors who subsequently transport them, we were told, for building projects. Recall chapter 5's picture of one of the many trucks.

Everyday life in borderlands is complex, but understudied. The borderlines that divided once-whole villages acquire different names on each side, but life goes on as people continue to interact in marriage and burial ceremonies.[22] At the Punjab border in eastern India, Van Schendel describes formidable obstacles: barbed wire and concertina wire that the border police call "cobras: five electricity wires fixed at different heights from the ground." At night he said cobras come alive, with vapor lamps to illuminate fencing, but itinerant workers are sometimes electrocuted with attempts to crawl across.[23] Trade can hardly occur in circumstances like these.

Once again, to return to the licit-illicit distinctions in trade, questions may be raised about trafficking: Do aspiring workers self-smuggle? Commute? Consent? Or are they tricked or compelled by force?[24] Gender enters trafficking narratives, whether as victims or perpetrators. Van Schendel says that sometimes well-dressed women recruit women for seemingly legitimate work, but only later do those who are trafficked realize that they have been tricked. He continues on about children who are forced into labor (the film *Siddharth* covers this painfully, though inside of India), sold into bondage, or kidnapped: boys to become jockeys in camel races of the Gulf States; girls as domestics and sex workers. Young girls "were said to command a high price as they are likely to be free from HIV/AIDS."[25]

Reading Van Schendel's lengthy book, I could only conclude that states would make better use of regulatory staff and budgets by tackling slave-importation schemes or applying employer sanctions rather than harassing petty traders. The volume of trade and migration is enormous, but limited resources, low levels of government transparency, and lack of data from countries like Myanmar (for example, in my Border Inequalities Database) make accurate counts impossible. Van Schendel estimates the reserve pool of Bangladeshi laborers in India at perhaps 12 to 20 million, with "Indians keen to employ them."[26] Bangladeshi workers contribute to both India's and Bangladesh's economies, the latter by sending remittances to their relatives left behind. And he says the Bangladesh state has failed many of its people who cannot find decent work and wages. Alas, this is the plight driving migrants to move across borders in so many parts of the world.

Summing Up Informal Trade

In many world regions, people living in the borderlands may engage in income-stretching activities ("shopping"), working, or buying and re-selling goods on one to the other side of the border. Usually those on the wealthier side of the border are best positioned to take advantage of price differentials, but on the other side, border people turn this sales opportunity into income generation. Informal, small-scale entrepreneurs make their livelihoods in these ways without depending on state social safety nets, the latter of which frequently do not exist in weak states and economies lacking good governance. So-called vice taxes, often easy to impose, may be lost when people cross to purchase untaxed products, such as cigarettes or alcohol. Checkpoints and enforcement may cost more than the revenue gained therefrom, but the practice continues. Cigarettes become the frequently traded "'illegal" good, unhealthy to smoke to be sure, but hardly illicit in the minds of many whether in Slubice, Poland, where I saw many shops, or in the Kahnawake (Mohawk) Reserve in Canada where I saw numerous street-corner signs advertising cigarettes for sale, including one that caught my eye: "best butts." Alas, cigarette trade is one of the few border-related economic development strategies to generate external capital. Cleary, trade like this alone will never produce greater prosperity for larger numbers of people.

Questions may be raised about informal trade: Should it be freed up? Should it be formalized, registered, and regulated? Or could a microenterprise be scaled up to generate more employment? Border people, if living beyond survival levels, should be able to use the opportunity of borderlands to trade and cross for short-term employment.

In this section, I make several major points with policy implications. First, distinctions must be made about social constructions associated with trade and crime. Informal work and trade often involves *licit* exchange that governments ought not inhibit. Besides, administrative costs alone may not be worth the revenue generated. Second, the continuum of legality to illegality deserves to be unpacked in order to discover new options that might be developed over border controls. The case of marijuana in the failed "war on drugs" at the US-Mexico border is a good example in this era of contradictory and changing laws in fragmented federal systems of government. Finally, South Asia's Zomia example illustrates the tragedy of near-statelessness that morphed into a hypersecurity-oriented postcolonial state. While state resources enforce labor-migration laws with a vengeance, horrific illicit slave and other trafficking continues, thanks to misdirected, off-target policies and bureaucratic practices.

The move toward formal trade in the form of export-processing manufacturing and job creation therefrom often occurs in borderlands where the "comparative advantage" of lower-cost labor can be realized. Whether this temporary strategy becomes permanent is a question addressed below, focusing on the highly formalized model at the US-Mexico border of export-processing industrialization; the maquiladora model works for investors and business, but remains stuck at extremely low wage levels for most workers, often placing nearby residents in danger from industrialization's environmental hazards. In everyday life, Mexican workers cross borders to purchase goods on the US side, but their limited income from extremely low wages limits the health of retail businesses on both sides of the borderlands while profits go to foreign managers' salaries, distant corporate headquarters, and stockholders.

US-Mexico Borderlands: The Maquiladora Model . . . Still

With or without territorial borderlines, traders have moved legal and illegal goods to markets during historical decades of porous borders. The US Border Patrol, established in 1924, can hardly monitor all movement in the combined borders that total over 7,000 miles (including Alaska-Canada). For decades, borderlands remained relatively porous, as did historic openness to immigration. Over time, growing trade and investment in borderlands has led to remarkably high levels of foreign trade, formally counted. However, historians and anthropologists also document contraband and informal cross-border income-generating activities, unevenly counted if at all. While the border economy is relatively vibrant, costly securitization stifles some exchange but privileges those who can afford to negotiate and pay around procedures. As North American governments and businesses readied their preparations for freer trade from the 1960s onward, they reduced tariff barriers and used their comparative advantages in time, labor, and transportation to take advantage of the long-peaceful cooperation between countries. Both US and Mexican governments developed policies to facilitate export-processing manufacturing on the Mexico side of the border, drawing on US capital and management, and strengthening the political-economic and professional class in Mexico.

Most Canadians live within a hundred miles of border in an advanced economy, but historically, Mexico's population and industrialization centered in its central core of Mexico City and surrounding areas. With low labor costs as comparative advantage, it was in Mexico's interest to encourage industrialization in its north, at the borderlands, with the consequent rise of manufacturing plants in Tijuana, Reynosa, Matamoros, Nuevo Laredo, and Ciudad Juárez, the last of which has now become the "maquiladora capital" of the Western Hemisphere.[27]

Once Mexico established its Border Industrialization Program in 1965, foreign investors worked with real estate and building contractors to establish plants in industrial enclaves along the border. Workers in maquiladoras, also called maquilas, process goods for export in assembly-line production, primarily in electronics, garments, and automobile harnesses (internal electrical systems). With Mexico's entry into the General Agreement on Tariffs and Trade (GATT) in 1988 and later into the 1994 NAFTA, the number of plants in Ciudad Juárez alone grew to 300 with a workforce of more than 250,000 workers and more than two million nationwide. Manufacturing output, trucked north of the border, creates extreme congestion at border official ports of entry. The Interstate-35 corridor in Laredo–Nuevo Laredo is the busiest, with the Pacific (Tijuana–San Diego, El Paso–Juárez) following. Mexico thereby generates job creation for its underemployed workforce at low-wage levels, and the US generates jobs for security and customs professionals, at middle-class wage levels.

Mixed Blessings: Benefits and Costs to Whom?

Maquiladoras appear to be a bustling, healthy trade operating out of modern-looking plants. US firms and consumers clearly benefit from this trade, and *all* US states have stakes in the *volume of trade*, most especially Texas (US$86 billion!), California, Michigan, Illinois, and New York as the table in the appendix illustrates. The trade *creates thousands of jobs* in most of the United States as well, also covered in the appendix table. Border congressman from the Texas 16th District Beto O'Rourke educates colleagues and posts data on his website that comes from the Mexico Institute of the Woodrow Wilson International Center. Border businesspeople speak with pride at annual border summits about the integrated manufacturing processes, supply-chain coordination, and just-in-time scheduling. Yet in the wider mainstream politics, the vitriolic security fears and language about Mexico and Mexicans continues, hardly abated.

Although US Customs and Border Protection agents work for the *federal* government, several US border local governments applied for pilot programs to pay up to $1.5 million for additional CBP agents and overtime pay. El Paso was one of those to succeed in their application, although that success burdens local taxpayers with costs for goods that flow across the border through their city to other mainstream locales. All of this trade moves *legally* across borders, but accounts for the long wait times at ports of entry, sometimes lasting hours for mile-long waits. The CBP "wait time" data seem to underestimate actual waits, so people listen to Mexican radio stations for more accurate numbers, based on drivers who call in. See the picture below from the vantage point of Mexico with separate lines for cars and trucks, far from the actual ports.

Most US political and journalistic narratives about Mexico focus on drugs, violence, and border security. To continue caveats about numerical metaphors, Anderson and Gerber note that such formal, regulated trade figures may overlap or be double-counted, such as what happens when the US exports components for export-processing industries in Mexico, then recounts the imports of more fully processed products from Mexico.[28]

Foreign-owned export-processing plants near the border offer mixed blessings to Mexico and borderlands residents, benefiting some groups but hurting others. The plants increase foreign direct investment, and create well-paying positions for professionals and land developers. The plants generate much-needed job growth in Mexico where approximately half of the

Congestion at the Córdova Port of Entry, El Paso, with long lines of trucks and cars, and likely hours of waiting. Taken from Ciudad Juárez.

Source: Mike Booth/Alamy Stock Photo.

population subsists below its poverty line, but plant wages in real terms have held steady over 50 years, even as the cost of living has risen.[29] *Peso* fluctuations and devaluations benefit employers, not employees. Maquiladoras obtain most of their source material from other countries, undermining linkage to job creation in other parts of Mexico's economy, and nearly half of Mexico's exports to the United States come from maquiladoras.[30]

Export-processing factories also generate considerable everyday pollution, as the security chapter analyzed, in environmental health costs that affect residents on both sides of the border. Truck traffic in highly congested corridors, the ports of entry, emits fine particulates into the air in neighborhoods near busy bridges across the Rio Grande, like in south-central El Paso's busy Córdova Port of Entry. Pollution goes virtually unchecked in both Texas and Mexico, with pro-business state regulatory agencies' policies offering little but symbolic demonstrations of their claims to protect residents. Should disaster occur, the impacts would fall on *all* border people.

Low Wages, Precarious Living Conditions

Low wages for assembly-line workers, approximately a quarter-million in the central borderlands alone, constitute the largest burden for borderlands. Workers take home the equivalent of one-to-two legal minimum wages, plus bonuses for good discipline, amounting to approximately US$30–40 *weekly*. About 8 in 10 employees work in low-paid positions at just above the legal minimum wage of 73 *pesos* daily (2016 figures): equivalent to US$4–5 per day (but less with the *peso* devaluation in 2017 of 21:US$1), plus bonuses for perfect attendance and punctuality. In 2015–2017, Mexico's currency lost considerable value to the dollar, from 12 to 21 *pesos* (US$6 to US$4 per day), creating even more severe hardship for workers but a boon to foreign investors. Wages in US dollars, or pegged to constant dollar rates, or better yet, based on a bottom-line decency level, would offer a minimalist approach to predictable living wages and disposable income for workers.

Calculated in legal minimum-wage terms, maquila workers earn *less than a 10th* of the wages of US workers only miles north, across the border in El Paso, Texas ($7.25/hour or approximately $60/day). While the cost of living is less in Ciudad Juárez, it is far more than a 10th of costs in the United States. If US minimum wages rise to $15 per hour, the wider gap would mean Mexican workers earn less than a 20th of US workers, just a few miles to the north. Such wage levels reduce the standard of living for families, forcing them to live in extremely modest houses with two to three rooms, sometimes shacks, at the periphery of big cities like Ciudad Juárez. As femicide analyst Alicia Gaspar de Alba so eloquently said regarding the many women murdered near Juárez, "We did not know anything about these [women] . . . when they were alive, did not even realize they *were* alive or that they were living in such squalid and inhumane conditions just a stone's throw from El Paso, working at their mind-numbing, carpal tunnel-warping factory jobs."[31] Gay Young's pictures illustrate "workers in postindustrial factories going home to preindustrial conditions."[32] Contrasting living conditions like these do not exist in Europe.

Mexico's low legal minimum wages provide a strong incentive for US, European, and Asian corporations to go "offshore" (a strange metaphor for US businesses in Mexico's northern desert) to establish export-processing manufacturing plants. The demise of Michigan's manufacturing base occurred side by side with the rise of export-processing plants in the central US-Mexico borderlands.[33] Mexico's official poverty level is approximately "three minimum wages," which provide the equivalent of a food basket for two household members, but insufficient income. Even the business-oriented magazine *The Economist* takes Mexico to task both for its slow-to-no growth in workers' wages, compared with China and Turkey over a decade, and for its legal minimum set, ironically, by a political appointee in Mexico City earning a US$ six-digit salary.[34] Global neoliberalism is closely related to the devalued feminization of labor-intensive manufacturing work.[35]

Gendering Work in the Maquiladoras

When maquiladoras began their operations in the late 1960s and 1970s, women comprised 80 percent of assembly-line workers. Various studies documented the low wages and gender dynamics on assembly lines.[36] A 1986 documentary by Lorraine Gray, *The Global Assembly Line*, compared the similarities between export-processing zones in the Philippines and Northern Mexico. By the mid-to-late 1980s, plants recruited a more gender-balanced, but still female majority, underpaid workforce. According to Young, the gender wage gap has "converged (with men's wages moving downward towards women's wages)."[37]

Many scholars documented working conditions over the years, focusing initially on the mostly female labor force and the gendered dynamics of male control. The latest and most thorough of these studies comes from Young. In a complex comparison of two matched samples, maquila and service workers totaling 1,254 respondents, she complemented analyses with rich qualitative material of women's survival strategies in male-controlled work and family settings. In contrast with a neoliberal model that assumes wage labor empowers workers in the labor force and household, she found a persistence of gender hierarchy using multiple indicators of empowerment, especially among the maquila workers who experience what she calls a *wage penalty* in their choice of work. For sector-to-sector job change examples, in their *first* jobs, maquila workers' average *monthly* pay was equivalent to US$39 versus US$57 for service workers. "Women who have done no other work but export production experience a penalty of about $65 in their *monthly* pay, compared to women whose work has been solely in the service sector."[38] Foreign companies clearly enjoy a comparative advantage in the undervaluation of labor in a sector long feminized.

Border Inequalities: Little Budge in the Binational Gap

Mexico, Canada, and the United States, chief trading partners with one another, display strong economic interdependence, solidified after the North American Free Trade Agreement (NAFTA) that went into effect in 1994. While the interdependence operates on relatively equal terms between Canada and the United

States, with A-level equality in my Border Inequality Database (recall chapter 3), highly inequitable gaps continue between Mexico and the United States in 2014, with a ratio of 5:1, using GDP per capita purchasing power parity figures.

The Border Inequalities Data Base allows comparisons to be made over time. One might expect that trading partners in an interdependent borderlands economy would gradually show comparative relative progress for the lower-income binational partner, Mexico. One might also expect that NAFTA would have benefited Mexico, putting it on more equal terms with the United States. Instead we see the persistence of inequalities at similar, even worsening levels. With a 1975 base, the US-to-Mexico ratios show the following: 4:1 (1975); 3.9:1 (1980); 5:1 (1990), 5:3 (2000), and 5.4:1. (Iñigo Moré reported 4:1 with GDP per capita purchasing power parity with 2004 figures.[39]) NAFTA benefited the United States more than Mexico. In relative terms, the trend augments the already powerful United States rather than fostering greater binational equality.

Everyday Life in the Borderlands in the Time of Security Controls

In the borderlands themselves, people often cross borders to shop for price advantages on the other side of the border. While low wages for the large labor force leave little disposable income, El Paso (and other Texas border cities) depend extensively on Mexican shoppers. Cross-border shopping alone helps make the case for policy changes that would induce mutual shared prosperity in the central borderlands. According to figures from the City of El Paso on total consumer spending, Juarenses spend $1.7 to 1.8 billion annually in the El Paso economy. Scores of thousands of jobs in El Paso depend on its sister city, and the same is true for the other 13 US cities and towns in the borderlands. Considering "the retail sector alone, the Federal Reserve Bank estimates that 10–15 percent of El Paso's retail activity can be attributed to Mexican shoppers, accounting for $950 million of El Paso gross sales supporting 13,600 jobs."[40] With figures like these, one might expect those in the US border business community to become stronger advocates of decent wages for the mass of export-processing workers in Ciudad Juárez to increase workers' disposable income.

In a 2014 study, " 'Getting It': Business NGOs and Political Actors Talk about the Central US-Mexico Borderlands," Pamela Cruz and I analyzed 43 stake-holder individuals in in-depth interviews and profiles from the central borderlands as part of a larger, eight-site study on cross-border institutions in North America and Europe.[41] Among many findings, we learned of businesspeople's frustration with the costly compliance required by the US government's security apparatus at the border, including complex clearance procedures and delays in crossing bridges. Yet most business and chamber professionals acclimate to the new procedures, pay the additional costs to comply, and pass the additional costs on to consumers. Despite frustrations, businesspeople celebrated the many opportunities in the borderlands and viewed themselves as binational people in solidarity with the people and the region, with hopes and visions for the future in which more capital-city decisionmakers would understand the trade opportunities in the region. None of the border or local government interviewees mentioned maquila workers' low wages.

The positive remarks resonate with a large 2016 survey of 1,427 borderlanders, approximately half from each country (Mexico and the United States). The majority of people on both sides favor immigration reform, easier crossing, and temporary work permits. They do not want a border wall.[42] I will revisit survey results in chapter 12, in terms of border people's voices in border institutions. Unlike the business stakeholders, it is not in the interests of a broad, representative sample of border people to maintain wage suppression.

The US security regime has complicated crossing both for business and everyday consumers. A turning point toward securitization occurred after the New York and Washington, DC, tragedies of 9/11. Also, the central borderlands of Mexico and the United States, once a major gateway for illegal drugs into the United States, saw extreme violence as transnational criminal organizations competed over control of the space, especially apparent from 2008–2011, but this activity has now moved to northeastern Mexico. During the violent period, figures from the US Department of Homeland Security showed reductions in northbound crossing. Although the city returned to its "normal" rates of violence, border bureaucrats tightened regulations, augmented their numbers, and used more advanced technology to prompt careful scrutiny, with the usual port of entry checks in place not only from south to north, but also exiting north going south. The result is extreme congestion and delays for trucks, pedestrians, and automobiles waiting to cross the border which sometimes takes hours (generating even more pollution from idling vehicles). More institutional cooperation is in place at the Canada-US border[43] compared to the Mexico-US border, though as noted above, costly preclearance procedures for individuals and trucks permit speedier movement for those businesses and professionals who can afford to pay.

For Mexico, the maquiladora model of development, a dependent model that offers little opportunity to strengthen Mexican-owned manufacturing industries, rises and falls with US recession and recovery. It perpetuates the comparative advantage of low wages and transport costs. Independent sources criticize the perpetually low legal wages and the lack of wage increases compared to those in other countries like China.[44]

After 50 years of export-processing manufacturing, Mexico is still heavily dependent on foreign direct investment using its low-wage workforce whose earnings hardly match with wages in *cities* elsewhere in its own nation. High-growth countries, like the so-called Asian Tigers of South Korea, Taiwan, Singapore, and Malaysia, have moved to diversify, strengthen their economic bases, and spread prosperity to higher proportions of their people, unlike Mexico. The usual rationales for lower minimum wages involve avoidance of inflation, productivity levels, entry-level qualifications of *secundaria* (secondary school, equivalent to US middle school), and worries that plants will move elsewhere if worker pay is increased.

Mexico's long-term transition to democracy is one that leaves low-income, working people with little political voice and clout, raising questions about the comprehensiveness of its so-called democracy (see box 10.1). Yet two of Mexico's wide range of political parties have lost some legitimacy, so much so that some voters have produced victories for "independent" ("party-less") candidates in state gubernatorial elections.

Box 10.1

Women Workers Struggle for Higher Wages and Respect

In late 2015, workers at several manufacturing plants sought to organize independent unions to represent their interests, a small wage increase of (in US$) 35 cents *daily*, and better treatment at their assembly-line jobs at several US firms and a Taiwanese-owned corporation. Established unions in Mexico, tied to government and the dominant political party and a declining percentage of the labor force (13 percent, a bit higher than the US, now only 10 percent,* similar to declines in other parts of the world), do not represent workers; the challenges to organizing independent unions are formidable, given government regulations and the practice of establishing paper unions that workers know little about. Some workers leave plants ("voting with their feet") for other options, if available, or migrate elsewhere, thus producing relatively rare labor shortages. Labor turnover is costly to employers. When labor shortages occur, plant recruiters go to Mexico's interior states where job prospects are dimmer, and where costs of living are less, to generate more supply.

To call attention to their situations, in late 2015 and early 2016, workers camped near plants, round the clock in shifts 24/7 (in *plantones*), but they were fired just before the deadline to receive annual *aguinaldos*, Christmas holiday payments required by law. They applied to a conciliation and negotiation council

(*junta*) for recognition of their union, but were denied in a problematic and complicated legal process that gives voice to and favors government-supported or already-established paper unions. By law, the names of those who petitioned for an independent union cannot be released to their employers, but the names were released anyway, no doubt through irregular methods, leading to terminations for workers. One maquila worker tried to run for *presidente municipal* (mayor equivalent), but she was unable to obtain the scores of thousands of signatures required, which usually necessitate solicitation of considerable donations. Workers continue their struggle, with the potential to transform labor movements and paltry wages in Mexico, but their numbers are a fraction of the huge, impoverished labor force. No strike funds are available as in labor unions in industrialized countries.†

*From OECD figures; http://www.oecd.org. Working people in northern European countries continue to exercise union power in large numbers, although all of Europe has seen declining trends.
†Alana Semuels, "Upheaval in the Factories of Juárez," *The Atlantic*, January 21, 2016, http://www.theatlantic.com/business/archive/2016/01/upheaval-in-the-factories-of-juarez/424893/. Accessed 1/22/16. I participated in and observed a Workers' Support Committee (Fall 2015) and served on a panel (January 2016) with Oscar Martínez and two Juarense activists involved in one of the plants.

To sum up this section, we have examined trade in the formal economies of the US-Mexico border. In coordination with the United States, Mexico fostered a maquiladora model of export-processing development in the mid-1960s which served the interests of foreign corporations in search of low-cost female labor, a receptive journey in the freer trade neoliberal economic era of recent decades and one that became a gender-balanced workforce of depressed wages.

The maquiladora model, after 50 years, has produced benefits for global consumers and investors, but little change for working people in Mexico or their wages. Occasionally strikes and work stoppages occur, to little avail. Corporations that operate in borderlands share little of the burdens associated with the cost of infrastructure—such as roads, electrical lines, and so on—in the places where they manufacture goods. The prospects of gaining employment in Mexico's export-processing plants (maquiladoras) have served as magnets for migrants from the interior whose settlement in the large cities of Ciudad Juárez, Reynosa, Matamoros, and Tijuana has created challenges for local and municipal governments with regard to housing, water, and the extension of other utilities to the periphery of cities.[45]

Concluding Reflections, with European Perspectives

We have analyzed informal and formal business in two borderlands covered in this book, South Asian and US-Mexican. Considerable obstacles exist to border people attempting to make better lives for themselves, given the way that some trade is constructed as illegal while other business may be considered illicit, depending on one's vantage point. More importantly, the shroud of the state security apparatus hangs heavily over borderlands.

Trade, cross-border business, and jobs are means by which interaction and cooperation across borders can be developed in private, nongovernmental sectors. In the two regions analyzed, few institutions exist to foster freer and fairer trade except for government security agencies and the Ministry of Development of North Eastern Region (MDONER, India) that seems more control-oriented in this admittedly challenging political atmosphere (see chapter 5). In regions like Europe, major stakeholders at the supranational to national and local levels provide voice, dialogue, and policies in a variety of institutions, including organized power in unions.

One must always ask: In institutions, who and which stakeholder sectors are accorded legitimate voices? In the former Bush-era North American Security and Prosperity Partnership (SPP) which ended in 2007, institutional designers granted authoritative voices to Canadian, US, and Mexican heads of state (and their executive branch leaders) and a business stakeholder advisory council, excluding other major stakeholders like unions, workers, consumers, and environmental health advocates. One cannot assume that business leaders will represent the interests of employers, taxpayers, and consumers.

Globalization, which fostered worldwide economic interaction, might be predicted to reduce the power of states and their international boundaries. Yet state territorial boundaries are central to low-cost manufacturing or "low-cost geographies," as referred to in discourse on corporate websites. In the 1990s, economists applauded the seeming move toward a borderless world (as chapter 1 outlined), but said nothing about if or where corporations would pay a share of taxes (along with residents and citizens) where they produced and sold their products or maintained their headquarters. A US loophole called tax inversions allows corporations headquartered in the United States to move transnationally across borders to tax havens for the purpose of lowering their tax burdens.

Trade and security agendas often sit side by side competing for priority access to resources. Militarized borders, not conducive to trade, are surely less desirable than cross-border business and trade, as long as national security concerns (see chapter 8 on security) are addressed, albeit with tension over who bears the costs of that security. However, without attention to reducing obscene wage inequalities and enhancing some degree of shared prosperity in borderlands, tensions may fester, then arise along with *inevitable* unauthorized migration. In advanced regional cooperation, such as the internal borderlands of the European Schengen Area, policymakers address issues like these, although tension and inequality remain at external borders. Security-trade tensions remain ongoing in the global economy.

Shared prosperity in trade gives rise to strong political constituencies, like business, which has a stake and interest in peaceful cooperation rather than conflict. However, one segment of business shares a stake in cross-border tension and militarization: the border-security-industrial complex.[46] In their short-term perspectives, many other businesses profit from their stakes in low-cost labor on one side of the border. With A or B level ratios, such as in Europe, a base of investment and long-term prosperity development may be established. At the US-Mexico border, the tenfold minimum-wage differential and fivefold inequality ratio, coupled with low-cost transportation to the close US markets and with wage stagnation for assembly-line workers, turned business opportunity into wage sclerosis.

If governmental policy enables cross-border labor movement and investments, such as in the European case, inequalities between countries might be reduced. Comparative price differences can foster cross-border shopping and facilitate border people's interaction on the ground. Yet in a world of fear, migration, and occasional terrorist incidents, governments set up obstacles requiring documentation and inspections that delay crossing and trade, with symbolic and real barriers such as fences and walls. Tension frequently exists between trade and security as we see in all three regions covered in this book and chapter.

Ultimately, a normative question emerges alongside that of free trade principles. Is the trade fair? Is it legal, but illicit? Is it illegal, but licit? In places with high levels of poverty and few living-wage jobs, can the quintessential free traders in the informal sector work without excessive control and extortion? And how would we measure standards of fairness in a world of many states and counting systems? For analysts wedded to state-centric thinking, little thought is given to borderlands, but in regional and global economies, fairness questions should matter and be given voice through institutions that reduce inequalities. Solutions lie in setting standards that move toward greater equality, reinforced with inclusive institutions.

Recommended Resources

Films

The Global Assembly Line
Siddharth

Notes

[1] Kathleen Staudt, *Free Trade? Informal Economies at the U.S.-Mexico Border* (Philadelphia: Temple University Press, 1998).

[2] Willem Van Schendel, *The Bengal Borderland* (London: Anthem, 2005), p. 46.

[3] Anwara Begum, *Sino-South Asian Relations: Missed Opportunities?* (Dhaka: AH Development Publishing House, 2015).

[4] Peter Andreas, *Border Games* (Ithaca, NY: Cornell University Press, 2000). Smuggling is a pejorative term for what might be state-defined illegality, but licit or illicit exchange.

[5] Staudt, *Free Trade?*; Melissa Gauthier, "*Fayuca Hormiga*: The Cross-border Trade of Used Clothing between the United States and Mexico," in Emmanuel Brunet-Jailly, ed., *Borderlands* (Ottawa: University of Ottawa Press, 2007), pp. 95–116; Van Schendel, *The Bengal Borderland*.

[6] Katarzyna Stokłosa, "Neighborhood Relations on the Polish Borders: The Example of the Polish-German, Polish-Ukrainian and Polish-Russian Border Regions," *Journal of Borderlands Studies* 27, 3, 2012, pp. 245–56; Martin Van der Velde and Szymon Marcińczak, "From Iron Curtain to Paper Wall: The Influence of Border Regimes on Local and Regional Economies—The Life, Death, and Resurrection of Bazaars in the Łódź Region," in Emmanuel Brunet-Jailly, ed., *Borderlands* (Ottawa: University of Ottawa Press, 2007), p. 173.

[7] Willem Van Schendel and Itty Abraham, *Illicit Flows and Criminal Things: States, Borders, and the Other Side of Globalization*, eds. Willem van Schendel and Itty Abraham (Bloomington: Indiana University Press, 2005), p. 4.

[8] Kathleen Staudt, "Violence at the Border: Broadening the Discourse to Include Feminism, Human Security, and Deeper Democracy," in Kathleen Staudt, Tony Payan, and Z. Anthony Kruszewski, eds., *Human Rights along the U.S.-Mexico Border* (Tucson: University of Arizona Press, 2009), pp. 1–27.

[9] National Institute on Drug Abuse: https://www.drugabuse.gov/about-nida/legislative-activities/testimony-to-congress/2016/americas-addiction-to-opioids-heroin-prescription-drug-abuse. Accessed 6/1/16.

[10] Kathleen Staudt and Beto O'Rourke, "Challenging Foreign Policy from the Border: The Forty-Year War on Drugs," in Tony Payan, Kathleen Staudt, and Z. Anthony Kruszewski, eds., *A War That Can't Be Won: Binational Perspectives on the War on Drugs* (Tucson: University of Arizona Press, 2013).

[11] Tony Payan, Kathleen Staudt, and Z. Anthony Kruszewski, eds., *A War That Can't Be Won* (Tucson: University of Arizona Press, 2013).

[12] US Customs and Border Protection, https://www.cbp.gov/border-security/along-us-borders/history). Also see George Díaz, "Twilight of the Tequileros: Prohibition-Era Smuggling in the South Texas Borderlands, 1919–1933," in Elaine Carey and Andrae Marak, eds., *Smugglers, Brothels, and Twine* (Tucson: University of Arizona Press, 2011), pp. 59–82.

13 Hungarian Civil Liberties Union, http://drogriporter.hu/en/milehighindenver. Accessed 8/1/15.

14 Josiah McC. Heyman and Alan Smart, "States and Illegal Practices: An Overview," in Josiah McC. Heyman, ed., *States and Illegal Practices* (NY and Oxford: Berg, 1999), pp. 1–24.

15 Transparency International (TI, with multiple measures, though ultimately flawed in this difficult-to-document arena). See the map and multiple indicators in http://www.transparency. org. On perceptions of corruption, the United States ranks 16 of 168 countries, Mexico 95 of 168, India 76 of 168, and Bangladesh 139 of 168.

16 See selections in Kathleen Staudt, "Violence at the Border," especially Olivia Ruiz.

17 James C. Scott, *The Art of Not Being Governed* (New Haven: Yale University Press, 2009) and *Seeing Like a State* (New Haven: Yale University Press 1998).

18 Van Schendel, *The Bengal Borderland*, both quotes p. 148.

19 Ibid., p. 149.

20 Ibid., pp. 159, 167.

21 Ibid., chapters 8 and 9 especially on the multiple narratives.

22 Van Schendel, *The Bengal Borderland*, p. 214. Also see Sahana Ghosh, "Cross-border Activities in Everyday Life: The Bengal Borderland," *Contemporary South Asia* 19, l, 2011, pp. 49–60, for a later iteration in a single borderlands locale.

23 Van Schendel, *The Bengal Borderland*, p. 218. Also see Reece Jones, *Border Walls* (London: Zed Press, 2012).

24 Van Schendel, *The Bengal Borderland*, p. 228.

25 Ibid., p. 229.

26 Ibid., p. 230.

27 See selections in Kathleen Staudt, César Fuentes, and Julia Monárrez Fragoso, eds., *Cities and Citizenship at the U.S.-Mexico Border* (NY: Palgrave USA, 2010).

28 Joan Anderson and James Gerber, *Fifty Years of Change on the US-Mexico Border* (Austin: University of Texas Press, 2008), p. 81, on intrafirm trade and chapter 4 generally. Gay Young, *Gendering Globalization on the Ground* (NY: Routledge, 2015) provides a history of Mexico's neoliberal economy, grounded in Ciudad Juárez, in her chapter 2.

29 Anderson and Gerber, *Fifty Years of Change*, p. 153, Oscar Martínez, *Mexico's Uneven Development: The Geographical and Historical Context of Inequality* (NY and London: Routledge, 2016). Gay Young, *Gendering Globalization on the Ground*, gives detailed information on Mexico's poverty line on p. 23, note 2.

30 Anderson and Gerber, *Fifty Years of Change*, pp. 100, 82, respectively.

31 Alicia Gaspar de Alba, pp. 4–5, quoted in Young, *Gendering Globalization*, p. 13. Food is the largest cost in household expenditures. Young cites work from the Coalition for Justice in the Maquiladoras (no longer in operation) before the mid-1990s *peso* devaluation in which the average maquila worker had to work seven hours to purchase five common items in a food basket: "forty-five minutes for a dozen eggs; eighty-seven minutes for a pound of chicken," p. 81.

32 Young, *Gendering Globalization*, p. 70. See chapter 2.

33 Alejandro Lugo, *Fragmented Lives, Assembled Parts: Culture, Capitalism, and Conquest at the U.S.-Mexico Border* (Austin: University of Texas Press, 2008).

34 *The Economist*, "Stingy by Any Measure: In the Name of Curbing Inflation, the Government Is Hurting Workers," August 16, 2014. http://www.economist.com/news/finance-and-eco nomics/21612255-name-curbing-inflation-government-hurting-workers-stingy-any. Accessed 7/1/15.

35 Young offers the clearest exposition, *Gendering Globalization*, chapter 1. Also see V. Spike Peterson, *A Critical Rewriting of Global Political Economy* (New York: Routledge, 2005).

36 One of the first came from María Patricia Fernández-Kelley, *For We are Sold, I and my People: Women and Industry in Mexico's Frontier* (Albany: SUNY Press, 1983); see also Lugo, *Fragmented Lives*; Susan Tiano, *Patriarchy on the Line: Labor, Gender, and Ideology in the Mexican Maquila Industry* (Philadelphia: Temple University Press, 1994); Melissa Wright, *Disposable Women and Other Myths of Global Capitalism* (NY: Routledge, 2006).

37 Young, *Gendering Globalization*, p. 21.

38 Ibid., figures on p. 172, quote on p. 173. The figures are from 1991. On p. 175, she discusses some of the in-kind benefits associated with some, not all maquilas, for example food coupons, access to secondary education programs at the plant, and for a third of workers, subsidized

transportation. Also, in the formal sector, maquila workers were eligible to participate in the health care system, although in 2008, Mexico's Seguro Popular covered all citizens.

[39] Iñigo Moré, *Borders of Inequality* (Tucson: University of Arizona Press, 2011), pp. 98–108. He also analyzes the export-processing model.

[40] Kathleen Staudt and Beto O'Rourke, "Challenging Foreign Policy from the Border," p. 223.

[41] Kathleen Staudt and Pamela Cruz, " 'Getting It': Business NGOs and Political Actors Talk about the Central U.S.-Mexico Borderlands." Paper presented at the Association of Borderlands Studies Conference, April 2014, Portland, Oregon.

[42] Molly Bilker, "Border Residents: Don't Build a Wall between Cities." Cronkite News, Arizona PBS, July 17, 2016. I have the full survey results, courtesy of Tony Payan, Rice University.

[43] See Donald K. Alper, "The Idea of Cascadia: Emergent Transborder Regionalisms in the Pacific Northwest-Western Canada," *Journal of Borderlands Studies* XI, 2, Fall, pp. 1–22.

[44] Besides *The Economist* (note 34), see also the Hunt Institute for Global Competitiveness, "Paso del Norte Economic Indicator Review," Spring 2015, http://huntinstitute.utep.edu/wp-content/uploads/2014/04/Paso-del-Norte-Economic-Indicator-Review-No-1-April-20151.pdf. Accessed 7/1/15.

[45] See GIS maps of the borderland in César Fuentes and Sergio Peña, "Globalization and its Effects on the Urban Socio-Spatial Structure of a Transfrontier Metropolis: El Paso, TX–Ciudad Juárez, Chih–Sunland Park, NM," in Kathleen Staudt, César Fuentes, and Julia Monárrez Fragoso, eds., *Cities and Citizenship at the U.S.-Mexico Border* (NY: Palgrave USA, 2010), pp. 93–118.

[46] Kathleen Staudt, Tony Payan, and Timothy Dunn, "Closing Reflections: Bordering Human Rights, Democracy, and Broad-based Security," in Kathleen Staudt, Tony Payan, and Z. Anthony Kruszewski, eds., *Human Rights along the U.S.-Mexico Border* (Tucson: University of Arizona Press, 2009), pp. 185–202.

PART IV

Bridging the Borderlands

We have covered considerable material in multiple world regions and maritime borders, in both historic and contemporary eras. Together with the regional focus, we have threaded major policy issues into the analysis, focusing on security in its multiple forms, migration, and trade, both formal and informal. In each and every chapter, we have examined inequalities, institutions, and states, including the length of time since their independence (or borderlessness), especially in the postcolonial world of the South.

With normative dimensions of the analysis in mind, part IV focuses on action and change. Chapters cover popular culture in films and documentaries as well as change that nongovernmental organizations, governments, and regional institutions might pursue. In the final chapter, which sums up the book, we answer questions posed in the beginning chapters, consider potential research issues on the frontier, and pose speculative questions about re-bordering and bordering in the future.

Chapter 11

Borderlands in Films

In this book, we have examined definitions, maps, historical perspectives, and theoretical constructions of borderlands and border people as dynamic, changing, socially constructed territorial lines. Although I place special focus on the land borders in the US-Mexico, South Asian, and European regions in chapters 4–6, I include in this chapter some film coverage of borderlands in Eurasia, maritime borders, and Africa, hoping to strengthen emphases on the border lens from the global South. Each of the preceding chapters contains a few words about high-quality films, suggested at the chapter's close, but this chapter offers more depth, with films organized and cross-listed by content genre and region. My aim is not to describe whole films or to provide synopses but to highlight the borderlands angle in the films, using concepts and regions mentioned in earlier chapters, and to tempt readers to watch the films or parts of them.

In my classes, I typically use supplemental visuals and narratives, such as novels, for those participants who seek to immerse themselves in material through multiple senses: reading, seeing, writing, listening, and feeling. Short of visits and lived experience in a region, the visuals of films and documentaries offer some substitutes, occasionally with emotive characters with which viewers might personally identify (for better or worse). Of course, the films must be viewed with a critical eye and are best unpacked through discussion: To what extent do the films reflect or represent realities? What intellectual and emotional agendas do filmmakers communicate to viewers? When does a film cross the line to become propaganda?

Popular culture and visual representations expose far greater numbers of people to the border issues covered in this chapter and book than do specialized articles in academic journals and books. Alas, I sometimes refer to specialized academic journals as potential burial grounds; they are not easily accessible to people outside of academia. Thus, films can become part of the learning process, whether more or less consciously approached as such. In more detailed treatment of contemporary borderland films, we can analyze and sense their impacts not only on border people but also on people in mainstream societies whose information about borderlands and border people might be limited.

Politicians in mainstream societies, importantly in capital cities away from borderlands, make decisions about border policy, security, and trade. Films about border violence no doubt influence those decisions, including the many on violent drug lords such as *Sicario*, *Cartel Land*, and others in that genre that I opted to exclude. I also do not cover TV series on homeland security, drug

Curiously, none of the borderlands films and documentaries discussed in this chapter contain keywords like "border" or "borderlands" in their titles.

Source: Photographer Kathleen Staudt.

traffickers such as *La Reina del Sur*, or *VICE* documentaries because of their sensationalism. (In a Netflix series, *Documentary Now!*, the tone of some of such productions has been ridiculed and captured well.) In not one, not two, but actually three televised series, a dead body is found on a borderline (*The Bridge,* Denmark and Sweden, and another with the same title, *The Bridge*, US and Mexico; *The Tunnel,* UK and France). Multiple shows like these seem like overkill, communicating a repetitive violent message about borderlands.

Published in 2014 and with a focus on the US-Mexico borderlands, I analyzed 25 Mexico City and Hollywood films in historic and contemporary times.[1] Almost uniformly, no matter the source of production and direction, the films portrayed the borderlands as chaotic, violent, lawless, and sexualized. I titled the article "The Border Performed in Films: Produced in Both Mexico and the US 'To Bring Out the Worst in a Country.'" The quote comes from *Touch of Evil* (1958), made by Mexican drug agent "Mike" Vargas (played by Charlton Heston) dealing with a villainous Texas border sheriff, played by Orson Welles who produced and starred in this border classic that reversed the usual stereotypes about lawlessness: the good guys (usually in the United States, but this time, from Mexico) and the bad guys, so to speak.

This chapter, with just a few overlapping exceptions, covers other films in a worldwide perspective, bringing the global to borderlands. My question still remains similar: do films bring out the worst in borderlands? If not, what are the patterns and themes in borderlands films? As in previous chapters, I seek a comparative perspective to borderlands to move beyond the US-Mexico region elsewhere to the other 95 percent of the world's population. In so doing, we may begin to illuminate what is exceptional or unexceptional about US borderlands.

The chapter covers 40 films, both commercial and documentary, of quality and accessibility, including those in English or with subtitles. In the interests of placing some "boundaries" around the scope of the chapter, I limit attention to those films with explicit focus on territorial borders and people crossing borders rather than films on identity borders or on wars, invasions, and occupations, categories too large to cover here. I do not necessarily agree with the points made in the films covered herein. Indeed, good films tend to be nuanced; they offer many insights at multiple levels and layers. In recent decades, it has become more common for cross-border/transnational collaborative film coproductions to emerge, given the uneven availability of capital to launch film projects that challenge the sometimes hackneyed, stereotyped, and patronizing features of films made in one place about the "Other." As such, film production and dissemination operate in global markets, in a global era, as highlighted in the title of this book. Once again, given that films provide visual and not simply narrative coverage as in books and articles, they may make a more lasting impression on readers and learners for the way they work on emotions as well as on the intellect in full color, with loud music, and on big screens in movie theaters.

Films allow us to consider the "Othering" processes that operate at levels beyond what chapter 2 covered, including the magazines, such as *National Geographic*, and the narratives that Edward Said and Frantz Fanon criticized. In the book, I share only cryptic comments here on the racism and stereotyped images found in many historic genres of the 1930s and thereafter: images of indigenous peoples (cowboys and "wild Indians") shown on cable channels like Encore Westerns and Turner Classic Movies along with Tarzan movies, for examples, or even movies that show White people as saviors (*Blood Diamonds*, set in west Africa). Many of the films I selected for this chapter counter some of those old "Othering" narratives. Due to nonaccessibility issues, I exclude the so-called Bollywood (after Bombay productions, but now named Mumbai) or Nollywood (Nigerian) productions. I had hoped to include the highly recommended film about Partition in Bengali India, *Subarnarekha*, but the only version I could find, on YouTube, is off an old video without complete subtitles. By accessible, I mean that people can easily rent, purchase, or watch DVDs and instant streaming (from, among many, Netflix, Amazon, Blockbuster), YouTube, and websites.

Film Impacts: Realities, Agendas, Propaganda

How can we understand possible film impacts? Short of experimental design studies, we can only estimate impact by size of audience and availability, sales and viewer numbers but it is difficult to find firm figures on how many people are exposed to films. The industry counts showgoers for major Hollywood films, but once issued on DVD (for rentals and sales) or posted on television channels or subscriber services like Netflix, Blockbuster, and Amazon, it is difficult to estimate viewings that could generate exponential expansions of the base numbers not only in the United States but also elsewhere in the world. Some of the films in this chapter have been nominated by their countries for film awards. Others, as independent issues, do not show large earnings or costs on various sites. A useful website is the Internet Movie Database (IMDb), http://www.imdb.com, for easy searches on details about production and importantly, for trailers to get a 2–3 minute sense of whether one wants to invest time in watching the film. I will not insert IMDb links in this chapter or a list of films in notes at its end.

To take a key example of opinion-forming films, consider the blockbuster *Exodus* (1960), with Paul Newman and Eva Marie Saint. The film covers the immediate post–World War II, post-Holocaust, and hateful anti-Semitic period when many Jewish refugees sought to resettle, but states would not accept them. It is historically accurate that Jewish refugee-laden ships wandered the seas seeking friendly ports, and in fact a ship called *Exodus* was among them. In 2016, it is insightful to watch this more-than-half-century-old film with the lens of Syrian refugees seeking resettlement and making dangerous crossings over the Mediterranean Sea to go to Europe.

In the film *Exodus*, based on a best-selling fiction novel by Leon Uris, Paul Newman finds a way to take Jewish refugees from British-controlled Cyprus to Palestine, then governed under British Mandate. The striking title of the book and film, named after the second chapter of the biblical Old Testament, Book of Exodus, symbolizes the journey toward freedom for people of two major world religions: Judaism and Christianity. Newman's victory—after making suicide bombing threats—and the victory of all those on the freighter, evokes an emotional response of deservedness and destiny. The film's musical score, with hit song by Andy Williams, is titled "This Land Is Mine," followed by the second line of the verse, "God gave this land to me." The song is easily found on YouTube with the search mechanism.

I would argue that this film shaped the minds and hearts of many viewers who, even today, continue to believe that the Deity inspired resettlement into an Israeli homeland and returnees fought for their right to occupy the land and displace others. Israel became independent in 1948 after a United Nations–brokered partition of Palestine on territory where the borders have continuously changed since then, leaving Palestinians who did not flee with shrinking or no land. While the film centered on the struggle of Jewish refugees, it gave little but stereotyped attention to Palestinian struggles. The film has gone global long ago. On YouTube, one can find Russian, German, and Portuguese translations of the film, though it has been translated into scores of other languages as well. Thus, exposure to the film has been huge compared to most films, even blockbuster movies of the last half-century, and certainly far more people have viewed it than the independent Israeli and Palestinian films and documentaries more recently produced, covered in several genres below.

I am not the only person to make that argument. In a 2012, article from the Jerusalem-based newspaper *Haaretz*, writer Bradley Burston argues that the work constitutes "American-flavored Zionism."[2] Former Israeli prime minister David Ben-Gurion is quoted as saying about the book *Exodus,* "As a literary work it isn't much . . . But as a piece of propaganda, it's the best thing ever written about Israel." Recall chapter 2's attention to Edward Said; he is also quoted in *Haaretz* as saying the film demonized Arabs.

This film example shows the power of a film narrative to shape people's knowledge and sentiments about a state, its borders, and solidarity with the primary protagonists. Subsequent films of the region, whether made in Israel, Jordan, or elsewhere and covered below, never acquired the epic, worldwide quality of this blockbuster film. Yet some of the finest contemporary films about Israel and Palestine come from Israeli filmmakers with funding from Israeli sources, among them Ari Forman's haunting animated documentary, *Waltz with Bashir* (2008), about memory, masculinity, and guilt of those in Israel's 1982 invasion of Beirut and its complicity in the right-wing Christian Phalangist massacre of Palestinians in the Sabra and Shatila refugee camps, who "only followed orders," the usual refrain heard in films and real life. The last minutes of the documentary show real footage of the survivors' cries after finding up to thousands of men's, women's, and children's dead bodies.

Several US television series shape public opinion to portray Central Intelligence Agencies operations as heroic, with help from the agency itself. With a former liaison to Hollywood and subsequent grants of special access to "Langley" (CIA Headquarters), officials have been quoted expressing appreciation for the way their agents are portrayed.[3] None of the films in the endnote analysis fit my focus on nonwar border and borderlands films, and the extensive analysis of *Homeland* is a cable-channel television series, out of bounds for this chapter.

Let us now move to analyze the borders in a variety of genres that dovetail with the previous chapters and regions of this book. I mix documentaries and commercial films in each section.

Genre #1: Historic Perspectives, Indigenous Peoples

Several documentary series offer substantive, high-quality coverage of world regions. While they may be considered dated, the documentaries include original film footage, cover history, and show maps with constantly changing borders: both PBS 10-part series, *The Pacific Century* (1992) examines Asia with a special focus on China's expanded and contracted territorial boundaries; and *The Americas* (1993) is a fine companion series to Peter Winn's book, now in its third edition, of the region.

The Motorcycle Diaries (2004), a 1950s-era road-trip film, is based on the South American journeys of Ernesto ("Che") Guevara and his friend Alberto Granado as they travel from Argentina northwestward. One cannot watch the film without questioning the impact of colonialism and territorial boundaries on the impoverishment of peoples, many of them once indigenous but over time, imagined or transformed into peoples with national identities. *Even the Rain* (2010) builds layers of understanding on historic and contemporary exploitation. A Mexican film crew seeks to recreate the Spaniards' devastating conquest of the "New World" as it set foot in Hispaniola, but for cost reasons produces their film in Bolivia where impoverished workers face mounting protests from the privatization of water and rising costs for this essential good. The story is built around the actual water protests in Cochabamba, 1999–2000.

Turning to another part of the world, *The Battle of Algiers* is a classic portrayal of the violence and counterviolence in French colonialism and Algerian resistance, with the feel of a black-and-white documentary. The film would offer a useful companion to Caribbean-based writer Frantz Fanon and his famous book *The Wretched of the Earth*, on a dying colonial era and the birth of postcolonial societies and governments that perpetuate the elitism and hierarchy that made the construction of good governance and democracy so problematic for decades, even generations thereafter.

Several films cover the dying Ottoman Empire at the close of World War II, the violent birth of new solidarities and struggles among peoples of the desert, and the imagined nations now trapped in bordered places. The blockbuster epic film, *Lawrence of Arabia* (1962), focused on British agent T. E. Lawrence about whom much has been written, including his own autobiography. Although the Jordan-made recent film *Theeb* (2014) will never acquire the blockbuster status of *Lawrence of Arabia*, the era and the stark desert context emerge in both. In *Theeb,* the protagonist is a Bedouin boy who accompanies his brother to act as guides to two characters aiming to strike a final blow in the distant location of struggle and demise of empire in soon-to-be-drawn borderlands that will not likely make rational sense for those on the ground. Viewers can only imagine the folly of boundaries in such regions.

The descendants of the continent's original inhabitants in settler colonialism acquire voice in several Australian films. Viewers learn the destructiveness of forced assimilationist policies which separated families and sought to destroy both languages and indigenous cultures. *Rabbit-Proof Fence* (2002) focuses on three "Aboriginal" children kidnapped from parents by government agents during the 1930s to socialize them in schools and force them to learn the English language. In actuality, this policy persisted until 1970. The children escape several times, only to be recaptured, but follow markers in the desert for their sense of direction. Although I avoid retelling stories and their endings, it is worth noting that the real-life children, once grown into aged adulthood, appear at the end of the film—a remarkable story of persistence and survival. Another Australian film, *Charlie's Country* (2013), shows the complexity and confusion that beset a marginalized man, trapped in all sorts of rules, regulations, laws, and consequences of the Australian state.

(See also genre #4 below, on gendered experiences, regarding the film *Frozen River* about indigenous people in North America, specifically in the US-Canadian borderlands that divide the Land of the Mohawk, as signs proclaim in the territory dividing New York and its "reservation" and Quebec and its "reserve.")

Genre #2: Border Conflict and Border Security

Various films focus on stateless peoples and people recently bounded by territorial borders not of their own making. Borderlands people suffer burdens from the wars that others have made and funded.

Inshallah, Kashmir (2012) is a documentary from India focused on the heavily militarized area where partitioned Kashmiri people have lost sons and daughters, buried in unmarked graves. The filmmaker interviews people who offer testimonials about torture and loss. At protests, mothers held pictures of their disappeared children, reminiscent of the Mothers of the Plaza de Mayo in Buenos Aires, but especially of border mothers in Ciudad Juárez doing the same with their pictures of disappeared or murdered daughters.

Two other films focus on the birth of a re-bordered independent India. In her film trilogy, director Deepa Mehta's *Earth* (1998) begins with a group of Muslim and Hindu friends, accompanied by a Parsi (also called Parsee) girl, in Lahore before the Partition. Horrifying communal violence not only alienates friends but also leads to equally horrifying individual betrayal. Also directed by Mehta, *Midnight's Children* (2013) is based on Salman Rushdie's 1981 book of the same title. A familiar fantasy-like storyline in many parts of the world, two boys are switched at birth and their family's class positions put them on totally different life trajectories in a tumultuous period.

The Israeli film *Lemon Tree* builds the story around a Palestinian widow who owns a lemon tree orchard which has been part of her family for generations. To her misfortune, an Israeli defense minister occupies the house next door to the orchard and her home, so in the interests of security against possible terrorists hiding in the trees, a wall goes up and security forces destroy her trees. The film shows gender politics within Palestinian society and the futility of seeking justice under Israeli rule of law as she works with a lawyer to make court claims.

No Man's Land (2001) is a film about two enemies stuck in a literal borderland, a trench during the Balkans war. A Bosnian and a Serbian soldier each bring hateful "Othering" to their conflictual interaction. The film shows a relatively impotent United Nations operation to intervene.

Two films focus on former re-bordered Soviet republics in Western Asia. In the Estonian film *Tangerines* (2015), located in a beautiful area and climatic region near the Black Sea, a few remaining immigrant Estonian farmers make their living growing and selling tangerines during the early 1990s Georgia-Abkhazian conflict and separatist movements. Two injured soldiers appear, one of them a mercenary, both of different ethnic and religious backgrounds in post-empire republics. The film shows the sort of "Othering" that leads men to fight futile wars. The film's musical score and melodies are among the most haunting and memorable of many films I have seen.

Prisoner of the Mountains (1996) is a Russian film set in the Caucasus, with lingering tension between mountain people and those who seek to occupy or control the region. The storyline focuses on the mountain leader's captured son and two Russian soldiers who enter the village. In the film, a mountaineer sings longingly about the fiercely desired autonomy of these "children of the mountains."

> We're the children of the mountains.
> We have been here for years.
> The wind
> Frightens the heart
> Of any stranger here.
> Nobody understands us.
> The mountains will protect us.
> The wind frightens the heart
> Of any stranger here.

What struck me about the film was its basis from a Leo Tolstoy short story written in 1872 based on the actual events, "The Prisoner in the Caucasus," suggesting the age-old tension between relatively stateless mountain people and soldiers of empire.

Timbuktu (2014), set in the ancient city of learning and religious tolerance, focuses on the Islamic fundamentalists' invasion into Mali, crossing the border to occupy land and attempting to impose rigid, medieval, authoritarian, and arbitrary rules upon a tolerant people, their music, gender relations, and dress but facing courageous everyday resistance from residents.

Genre #3: Human Mobilities and Dangerous Journeys

The migration journey is fraught with danger and death, whether across land or maritime borders. Most migration films show not only the vulnerability of travelers, but also special gendered experiences. Women generally face sexual assault on their journeys. The genre of migration journeys often induces empathy and sympathy through personalizing the protagonists. As such, the narratives counter the emphasis of those with different agendas: numbers who perish among those attentive to human rights or the fear of "Others" in national border security narratives.

Several films focus on the journey north from Central America and Mexico to the United States. Two films begin in Guatemala at Mexico's southern border: *Sin Nombre* (2009) and *The Golden Dream* (2013) (*La Jaula de Oro*, which in Spanish translates as the Golden Cage, perhaps a word more apt, given the closing scene). *Sin Nombre*'s first half feels like a documentary, beginning in southern Mexico and the anarchic border location of Tapachula near Guatemala. A young man flees a cell of the vicious Mara Salvatrucha (MS-13) gang to ride the tops of trains (*la bestia*), only to encounter more thieves and criminals, some of them official police. *The Golden Dream* begins with three young teens, one of them a girl who dresses like a boy, hoping to avoid rape. One of the boys stays behind in Guatemala, but an indigenous boy joins the group only to face hostility and racism from the Spanish-speaking boy. They, too, ride "the beast," train tops, where gang members extort money at stops along the way. The only relief on this journey comes from faith-based shelters and Las Patronas, the women who bag food for migrants and throw the bags to them if and when the trains pass slowly. Two of the three teens do not make it—one kidnapped and the other shot by a US vigilante minuteman. The remaining character, once crossed and working in the United States, reveals the poignancy of arrival and work at the US destination. Notre Dame University produced a short documentary, *Dying to Live: A Migrant's Journey* (2005), with scenes of migrants on trains and a strong religious message of seeing the Deity in migrants (a common message, along with mandates to "welcome the stranger," in the Old and New Testaments of the Bible).

Closer to the United States, but set in the hot and arid Arizona-Sonora borderlands, two films stand out. One, Mexican-produced, is *7 Soles* (2008), focused on a guide who leads a group in a crossing meant to take only a day or two, but extended to several days to avoid nearby US Border Patrol agents. Travelers run out of water, and several are weakened or injured along the way. The guide takes a young mother off to bushes for rape as her children hear her screams. Another is a documentary, *389 Miles* (2008), with border filmmaker Luis Carlos Davis crisscrossing the borderlands from one end of the state to the other, a 389-mile trip. With both grim and comic narration and a wide, balanced set of border voices, viewers see the diversity of the borderlands.

Lost in Detention (2011), a fine PBS documentary, offers balanced coverage of a period in recent US history of peak detention rates, up to 400,000 annually, due to the Department of Homeland Security quotas set in Congress to maintain performance goals linked to budgets, as officials describe. The documentary is set in a time period when federally imposed secure communities arrangements with local police and sheriff departments require data-sharing information with Immigration and Customs Enforcement (ICE) of unauthorized people committing such minor offenses like changing car lines without a signal. Over time, the arrangement undermined community-based policing and public trust in the police to report serious crimes. The film also covers a for-profit, private, prison-like detention facility in South Texas, with former staff and detainees' testimonies about guards' abuse and impunity.

Similar dangers of the migration journey emerge in two more films about Africans trying to cross to Europe over land and sea boundaries. The Spanish production, *14 Kilómetros* (2007), begins with three young people fleeing Niger and Mali due to impoverishment, lack of opportunity, and in one case, forced marriage to an aged predator. One brother dies along the way, while the other two are nourished back to life by seemingly stateless Tuareg people of the desert. They continue northward through desert terrain, encountering borders invisible except for the racist predatory guards who man the crossing barrier on a rough unpaved desert road. Viewers may await with suspense to see whether they complete their journey across the sea from Morocco to Spain. In *Terraferma* (2011), an Italian film, viewers see the familiar images of the 2015–2016 exodus across the Mediterranean, but set in an earlier time period, for the crossing attempts have gone on for many years as noted in earlier chapters. Fishermen and island residents confront their familiar dilemma when overloaded boats capsize—whether to help or avoid the boat people who crossed borders from as far southeast as the Horn of Africa.

To conclude this grim section on migration journeys, albeit with occasional ethical human intervention, I include a somewhat lighthearted yet dark comedy set in the authoritarian and masculinist Franco era of fascist Spain, *Los Años Bárbaros* (1998). The border angle involves the possibility of crossing to freedom in France with border scenes near its end.

Genre #4: Gendered Experiences in Borderlands

Films can illuminate the consequences of border politics and policy for gender: violence, "citizenship" entitlements via birth and marriage, and masculinist/militarist security agencies among other issues. The nation-state has traditionally aimed to control reproduction, marriage, and sexuality, with different impacts on women, men, and transgender people in borderlands spaces. What happens in borderlands, with hybridized multiple rules of law?

Set in a bleak, cold winter of upstate New York near or in the Mohawk reservation, *Frozen River* (2008) depicts two impoverished women who live in trailers and struggle with racism and male privilege to support their children. One woman's baby was literally kidnapped from the hospital delivery room by her mother-in-law, but "Tribal Police" do not interfere with family matters in their jurisdiction. Desperate for cash, the women help migrants from China and Pakistan cross from Canada to the United States over the Saint Lawrence River. Isn't this illegal, asks one? "There is no border. This is trade between nations." As the ice thaws and thins, viewers see whether this declaration is real.

The documentary *Vessel* (2014) takes viewers from maritime borders within the 12-mile territorial limit to freer international waters. Women on Waves (WoW)—a Dutch reproductive justice nonprofit organization—connects women with NGOs in states where laws prohibit them from voluntarily deciding whether to pursue motherhood or carry their pregnancies to term. In many countries where abortion is illegal, scores of thousands of women annually resort to unsafe methods, such as poisons, sticks, or hangers, with the prospect of dangerous complications. The film begins in Ireland in 2001, then continues in 2004 when the boat docks in places with hostile political forces, depicting harrowing experiences in Poland; it tries to dock in Portugal in 2008 where military ships treat the boat (on which misoprostol can be administered) as a national security threat. The film portrays women's responses to citizens' pleas for help as well as various NGO campaigns, such as those distributing information via live televised broadcasts about how to use misoprostol, based on World Health Organization (WHO) protocols posted on the global Internet. The NGO's website, Women on Web, responds to women and NGOs in many countries, such as Ecuador, Spain, and Tanzania, by training medical personnel and women at risk in procedures they can control themselves.

(See also genre #2, *Lemon Tree*; genre #5, *The Global Assembly Line*; and genre #6, *Syrian Bride* and *Pray the Devil Back to Hell*)

Genre #5: Legal and Illegal Trade and Business

The global economy has captured filmmakers' attention in order to convey insights about both legal industrial production (but is it licit?) and the illegal drug trade across borders (is it illicit?). Recall the conceptual distinctions from chapter 10 on trade.

Two documentaries examine global export-processing manufacturing. One of them, *The Global Assembly Line* (1986), compares Ciudad Juárez in the US-Mexico borderlands with the Bataan Export-Processing Zone of former US colony, the Philippines. In the early 1980s, when the documentary was filmed, young women comprised the vast majority of assembly-line workers. Filmmaker Lorraine Gray's interviews with the businessman, their brokers, workers, and NGO leaders offer especially revealing insights about the role of borders in "Othering" processes. *Maquilopolis* (2006) is a later documentary set in Tijuana, another large Mexico border city in its northwest. It examines work and life experiences from the perspective of assembly-line *operadoras*.

The 2000 US blockbuster film, *Traffic* (2000), takes its storyline from the British six-part television series, *Traffik* (1989) (from which it bought the rights), which was set in different contexts, utilizing maritime borders. With multiple stories told, *Traffik* begins in Hamburg where two honest policemen find a big heroin shipment from a boat from Karachi, Pakistan. The story unfolded involves a British minister and chair of a parliamentary drug-abuse committee who is reviewing Pakistani government programs to divert poppy production to irrigated agricultural production. A German building contractor, married to a ruthless British woman (incorrectly dismissed as a "mere" *hausfrau*), and a Pakistani drug lord supply major parts of the German and British market for heroin, with help from corrupt Pakistani officials at all levels. Also threaded into the story is a former Peshawar Province poppy farmer and the British minister's teenage daughter, a heroin addict. When Pakistani control efforts tighten up somewhat, pertinent advice is articulated near the

Khyber Pass: "Go to where the authorities have no power . . . [long pause] . . . Afghanistan" where assault weapons from the Soviet occupation era and from the US-equipped *muhajadin* are traded for drugs. The advice seems prescient with regard to 21st-century wars in the region. A central dilemma is whether drug trafficking can be fought by interdiction of supply alone or with more attention to prevention and treatment for addiction.

These same themes emerge in the US-Mexico version, *Traffic*, with a US presidentially appointed drug czar, a Mexican military leader (who goes after one drug cartel because he works for another drug cartel), DEA and Mexican police, and a rich businessman in La Jolla married to a ruthless European woman. Most of the action takes place in the Tijuana–San Diego borderlands.

Grim stories of trafficking are set in other locales. Set primarily in Russia, the film *Transsiberian* (2008) focuses on two seemingly naïve US travelers on the railroad onto which drugs have been smuggled. Mishaps disrupt the usual trafficking relationships between Russian police authorities and the drug shippers. In the India-Canada coproduction *Siddharth* (2014), child labor trafficking is the theme along with the difficulties that impoverished parents face when trying to locate their children, despite assistance from NGOs that are struggling to feed orphaned or runaway children, and the half-hearted help from the police. One can feel the despair of a father and mother searching for their 12-year-old, with the support in everyday life from neighbors and friends; social capital is the only resource available. With a contact from his brother-in-law, the Delhi-based father (reliant only on informal labor to fix zippers) sends the son to work in a Ludhiana factory which uses child labor to supplement family income, but the child disappears after two weeks. Parents have no savings for the search—not even a picture of their son—and they are uncertain of his age. The structural violence of poverty undermines their search at most steps of the way.

Genre #6: People's Triumphs, People's Defeats

Around the world, border people use creative strategies to exercise their voices and visions for a more just future in NGOs, through social movements, and via all-around transnational civic society. Films from various borders illustrate their activist triumphs and defeats.

The documentary *5 Broken Cameras* shows documentary film footage over five years in the Palestinian village of Bil'in where Israeli soldiers further shrink the people's increasingly scarred land, uprooting and burning olive trees and bulldozing cultivated fields in order to make way for Israeli settlers whose high-rise housing on mountaintops is separated from Palestinians with a fenced barrier. Viewers see everyday life and the almost poetic narrative of the Palestinian filmmaker, his wife, and family of four children, as villagers persist with protests trying to reason face-to-face with the army, sophisticated military equipment and gas grenades—"following their orders." The film shows ways that villagers, joined by Israeli and human rights international activists, maintained hope amid despair about state terrorism and the near-absence of rule of law for Palestinians. Despite killings and injuries inflicted by soldiers, villagers gain a minor victory—the removal of the fence barrier (which took a year to implement)—only to have Israelis replace it with a concrete wall a short distance away.

Pray the Devil Back to Hell (2008) is a documentary about Leymah Gbowee's leadership and the solidarity of Liberian Muslim and Christian women to end a brutal civil war. Toward the end of the film, with peace talks going nowhere after warlords crossed borders into Ghana to negotiate, the women's group pushed toward post-conflict resolution with traditional shaming techniques.

A Russian-made film, *Leviathan* (2014), focuses on a maritime sea border, frontier town far from the rule of law, and the capital-city lawyers who try to use legal leverage to undermine a property grab by local politicians and the orthodox church. Besides the landowner's loss, the democratic deficit in vulnerable, distant borderlands is revealed as the larger tragedy.

As with a previous genre, I include a lighter film in this section. Although it begins as a grim documentary of the talented Detroit musician named Rodriguez whose music never succeeded in the United States, *Searching for Sugar Man* (2012) continues as an inspiring example of the power of transnational popular culture and music. Albeit unintentionally, his creativity transcended international boundaries and many of his songs became hits in South Africa, inspiring anti-apartheid activism with words that offer a critique of a dying racially segregated society.

An Israeli Film Fund production, *The Syrian Bride* (2004) focuses on a wedding, nearly six months in planning due to paperwork complications in the Golan Heights, Syrian territory occupied by the Israelis. In the documents of people who live there, the word "undefined" is used for nationality. A Druze woman is marrying a Syrian television actor, exiting the Golan Heights and migrating to Syria, and both of their extended families meet in the demilitarized zone on the day that al-Assad ascended to power. The film shows the everyday lives in all their diversity including political disagreements in the village: the bride's father, paroled from Israeli jail, is supported by Druze elders for his pro-Syrian stance but simultaneously criticized because one of his sons, a lawyer, has married a Russian. Gender relations also come into play as the bride's sister is unhappily married to a man who believes he must control her publicly to prove his manhood, denying her desires to attend the university.

The film shows the ludicrous border barriers imposed upon people who seek only to go on with their lives. United Nations officials stationed in the demilitarized zone try to negotiate. In the last 30 minutes, we learn that new Israeli regulations require the border bureaucrat to stamp "exit" in the bride's document, but the Syrian border bureaucrat cannot accept the stamp because it would legitimize Israeli occupation. More border bureaucratic games and delays ensue. A noteworthy quote in the film is "Once you cross the border there is no way back."

(See also films in genre #2, *Timbuktu*, and genre #4, *Vessel*. In chapter 4 on the Americas, see the documentary, *The Time Has Come*, about student activists allied with the Border Rights Coalition against border patrol harassment and abuse in neighborhoods around their campus. Also in chapter 12 to follow, there is a section on children and schools; see the documentary *Peeking Over the Wall* (2016) on YouTube (https://www.youtube.com/watch?v=d-L9RDsbla0), focused on growing separation between Palestinian and Israeli communities.

Concluding Reflections

Once one studies and crosses borders, there may be no way back to the old-style views of the world and its countries with their state-centric perspectives. Perhaps films will induce the same reflections. Films can become teaching and learning resources in courses on borders and comparative and international politics. Each of the previous ten chapters includes films, some of which are categorized by genre and examined at greater length here.

This chapter has examined six genres of films focused on and in borderlands. Interestingly, none of the films use the word "border" or its derivatives in their titles. Yet the films address very real issues we have examined: border regions in North America, South Asia, and Europe; security, migration, and trade; and people's everyday lives in borderlands that policies, politicians, and land grabbers elsewhere generally try to shape with varying degrees of success by incorporating "Othering" processes as well as conflicts only distantly related to, or perhaps even entirely contrary to, the ideals and concerns of the people who actually live in bordered space.

In response to the question posed earlier in this chapter's introduction—whether borderlands are portrayed elsewhere as they are in the US-Mexico borderlands—we do not see borderlands as violent, chaotic, and sexualized except at the edge of empire: the former USSR, the United States, and South Asia during Partition, Britain's once colonial "jewel in the crown." While my 2014 analysis of 25 films on the US-Mexico border represented the near universe of that regional genre, the 40 films in this chapter offer only partial coverage of the thousands of films about war, occupation, and post-conflict societies. Recall that I chose to include neither films that sensationalize nor the routinely macabre drug and murder films about Mexico. The old adage about media headlines (those that bleed, lead) is also the case with Hollywood and the appetites of viewers to which it often plays. Independent filmmakers produce for a different audience.

In the films I have chosen, selected from many in over two decades of viewing, we see common themes: the dangerous migrant journey and arrival; the senselessness of conflict based on the "Othering" and racism about similar peoples, such as soldiers who "follow orders from above"; the universal "land grabs" in which dominant entities exert authority in asymmetrical power contexts; and questionable "security" agents who induce insecurity. Yet for all the grim patterns and themes, we also see inspiring and courageous individuals and transnational activism. Each of the films exposes the artificiality of constructed bordering and re-bordering, and how it creates barriers to community and solidarity in borderlands.

Notes

1 Kathleen Staudt, "The Border Performed in Films: Produced in Both Mexico and the US 'To Bring Out the Worst in a Country,'" *Journal of Borderlands Studies* 14, 4, 2014, pp. 465–80.

2 Bradley Burston, "The 'Exodus' Effect: The Monumentally Fictional Israel That Remade American Jewry," *Haaretz*, November 2, 2012. www.haaretz.com/Israel-news/the-exodus-effect-the-nomonmentally-fictional-israel-that-remade-american-jewry-1.476411. Accessed 6/1/15.

3 http://www.theatlantic.com/entertainment/archive/2016/07/operation-tinseltown-how-the-cia-manipulates-hollywood/491138/?utm_source=nl-atlantic-daily-071416.

Chapter 12

Toward Solutions
NGOs and Policy Change, Global to Regional

In the last 10 chapters, we have examined borderlands in great breadth, their histories, inequalities, and the "Othering" that has persisted given the nationalist territorial traps of recent centuries. We have examined three specific regional borderlands in detail, focusing on how perceptions of the "Other" are shaped by language, education, migration, and institutions from the supranational to the local. In the preceding chapter specifically and in occasional references in others, organized thematically, the sweep of popular culture in films and documentaries reveals a mix of blunt "Othering" and propaganda as well as nuanced pictures of bordering in recent decades, with an emphasis on conflict, land grabs, and dangerous journeys albeit with occasional stories of triumph. Many things must change if borderlands and their people are to share greater prosperity through cooperation and exchange, not the least of which is to ensure that militarism and extreme inequalities no longer prevail or that they are at least significantly reduced.

If the global conditions discussed in this book are allowed to perpetuate without increased cooperation across borders, we will face more serious environmental problems, missed opportunities for prosperity, and individual human tragedies from engendered human *insecurity*. Cooperation can hardly occur without a reduction in the obscene inequalities that exist in borderlands, between states, or among the great geographic regional world divisions, North and South. Institutions, whether official or nongovernmental (NGOs), must connect, communicate, and coordinate border regions with deeper democracy. Shared poverty across borders is not an option if solution-makers are serious about addressing human security and welfare. Thus attention to reducing inequalities at multiple levels—global, regional, and borderlands—is in order. A sequential change is the more likely route in the I-2 model focused on inequalities and institutions: First, *inequalities* must be reduced, followed with the construction of democratic *institutions* in borderlands and in states. I thread these themes throughout the chapter.

This chapter offers the "big picture" perspective on ideas and strategies for change, focusing on global regimes, regional and cross-border institutions at governmental and nongovernment levels, and individuals. Solutions hinge on a big question: If a political-economic power elite shapes the world—a premise to which so many sociologists and political scientists have alluded—is it possible for nonelites to counter that power through accountable governance, social movements, and nongovernmental organizations (NGOs), altered popular culture, and changes in individual choices? Maybe. This chapter argues for multiple voices and actions, especially border voices in league with democratic governance. Individual choices deserve analysis as well; I include analysis of education, choices, and ethics, topics too often neglected in border studies.

Economic Health in the Global Era

In the interconnected global economy, with its neoliberal ideology of limited government regulation in an unfettered marketplace, almost-unrestrained inequalities pervade the world. Clearly, global trade achieves mixed blessings, benefiting those with or aligned with capital, but leaving others behind or stagnating in what I earlier referenced as low-cost geographies—often located in borderlands. Global trade requires focus on wages, their increase over time, and the reduction of inequities among them at borderlands, between states, and among people in all the intersecting categories of gender, class, ethnicity/race, and age.

The Three Borderlands (and Sea Border Tensions)

In the borderlands chapters, we covered very different models: unbridled neoliberalism in the US-Mexico and South Asian regions, with a lumbering powerful state and no attention to inequality reduction. Europe's project over decades shows neoliberalism tempered with investment in border regions, poverty reduction, and free markets, albeit with debt crises and the ensuing austerity budgets.

History and states matter in these three borderlands, each of them bordered or re-bordered in very different eras: 18th–19th-century independence and subsequent national loyalties (US-Mexico), mid-20th-century postcolonial Partition among relatively stateless peoples (South Asia), and mid-20th-century re-bordering of old states with national loyalties, recovered from war and conceding some sovereignty in exchange for freer common markets and movement under supranational European governance. Two regions contain trade linkages bodies, NAFTA (with periodic meetings of the so-called Three Amigos) and the European Union, while a relative vacuum exists in South Asia–China with powerful China dominating capital and Tibetan hydropower in the region and spreading into the South China Sea.

Securitization prevails in all regions—most extensively in the US-Mexico, then in South Asia, and finally in Europe, all with different budgets and administrative capabilities. While all of these regions operate in a neoliberal global economy, North America leans toward unchecked capitalism while the European Union tends toward a more regulated free enterprise structure. Sizable numbers of people in these two regions have lost economic leverage due to shifts in global manufacturing jobs, but often maintain that immigration is responsible, as witnessed in the Brexit vote in England and the US presidential election campaign outcome of 2016. While all regions favor "free trade," preferential treatment is afforded to formal business ventures rather than to the *licit* informal business (declared *illegal* in some regions) of quintessential free traders who cross borderlands outside the regulated economy, attempting to earn a living. States attempt to control migration, but the forces that impel people to move—like poverty and insecurity—are strong and drive mobility despite risks. Little provision exists for temporary work permits, even though people may long to return to their homes once they have accumulated money to sustain themselves in their own countries.

Investments in Borderlands

We need multiple ways to think about and act on political economy in order to integrate attention to wages in borderlands. And we need new ways to think about and act on governance in borderlands, from regional institutions to nongovernmental organizations (NGOs) and social movements that engage with governance. More government is not necessarily the answer, particularly if it privileges the business and security sectors only or over-bureaucratizes decision-making processes and renders them inefficient or susceptible to corruption. Throughout the book, I provide multiple examples of flaws in governance, in regulatory policies and their enforcement, and in accountability from top border bureaucrats to those at the bottom of the hierarchy. Genuine democracies exist in all-too-few states, particularly near or in their borderlands. Little freedom exists for temporary movements of informal traders, workers, taxpayers, and shoppers to cross borders, except in the European Union. We need new ways to call attention to and measure borderland inequalities and damages in the existing economic growth models as well as new methods to extract natural resources without negative externalities that affect people and impact environmental sustainability.

All too often, moneyed economic interests gain advantages in political processes where regulatory decisions are made, even in countries that claim the democratic mantle but where money talks and people pay to exercise influence, whether legally or illegally, ethically or not. Nevertheless, in states with strict and heavy border control enforcement, the near-inevitable discretion available to border bureaucrats can result in corruption, the abuse of human rights, and loss of liberty for "Others" who cross borders or even for their own citizens.

Economic Growth Discounted with Environmental Costs

For the last century, economists and Bretton Woods Institutions like the World Bank and IMF have used economic growth and gross domestic product (GDP) per capita figures to measure and compare the economic health and well-being of states. Economists developed more nuanced measures with the use of purchasing power parity (PPP) and constant-dollar comparisons, given fluctuations in the costs of living and currency volatility, respectively. Average figures offer only crude approximations, given the leakage of hidden wealth, mere estimates or miscounts of populations, informal income generation (that is, outside the regulated formal economy), and spatial, class, or gendered inequalities, including those in borderlands spaces (caveats discussed in chapter 3). We now have GINI indexes of inequality, the UNDP's Human Development Index (HDI) and its gendered variation.

The concepts of GDP per capita and economic growth rates do not calculate environmental damage that occurs with the extraction of fossil fuels, emissions of excessive pollutants to air and water, and the consequences for long-term climate change and rising sea levels. High economic growth often requires or leads to environmental destruction and externalities, such as in health consequences, which people pay for with future tax burdens, illness, and early death. We have no good measures that *discount* absolute growth or growth rates for their simultaneous environmental *damage*. Policymakers and number crunchers need to develop ways to assess well-being and prosperity, including *wages*, for the many without resorting to figures based on GDP, economic growth, trade, and exports alone.

Our world must be shaped in ways that promote environmental sustainability, reduce economic inequalities at many levels, and end the glorification of economic growth and large GDPs as the supreme measures of states' strength and well-being without regard for the people who produce the commodities and their living conditions. At the same time, solutions can be found in the marketplace and private sector. For example, global production adheres to changing standards connected with the International Organization of Standardization (ISO; http://www.iso.org) in various improved management and environmental practices. ISO standards can be developed to foster wiser use of natural resources for sustainability and decent wages for workers. Governments can incentivize innovation toward renewable energy. The list could go on.

International Laws and Their Precedents

Previous chapters of this book made multiple references to international laws and United Nations principles, presumably upon which all signatories have agreed. Many evoke noble ideas and they deserve a strong place in state policies and actions. NGOs cite them for leverage. Yet we see over and over that in a world of sovereign states and limited resources, international principles go only so far in addressing migration, trade, and security in a bordered world. A good place to enact and practice such principles begins in borderlands.

Institutions at Multiple Levels: Global, Borderlands, Official, and NGOs

Institutions operate in and outside of governments. They exhibit routines and patterns that embody collective behavior. Ideally in democracies, elected representatives respond to nongovernmental organizations (NGOs), social movements, and individuals who communicate issue and policy preferences. Representatives oversee government agencies, and through the rule of law, challenges and judgments are made to determine consistency with constitutional standards. Free speech and media should open decisions to transparency and scrutiny. These ideals part ways with reality in many places. We begin this section with voices outside government. From border theories discussed in chapter 3, we know the importance of cross-border clout, but beyond that, we need to know which among multiple sectors exercise clout and the extent of democratic *inclusiveness*.

Social Movements and NGOs

Social movements and nongovernmental organizations (NGOs) differ in their organizing styles, visions and goals, and duration of action. Movements tend to be shorter-term, articulating broader visions; they often use high-visibility, creative strategies designed to attract media attention and change awareness. NGOs tend to operate on a longer term, articulating achievable goals and developing relationships with decision-makers in positions to alter policies. NGOs, too, thrive on media attention, but for both movements and NGOs, media spaces are crowded with multiple, competing images and messages. A dilemma for both types of groups involves ways to occupy long-term space in media attention and follow-up. In a world of instant global communication, a "like" click on Facebook or a tweet may have a life span of just a few days.

Global transnational movements and NGOs have a broad reach, including those that advocate for human rights (like Amnesty International and Human Rights Watch), alternative economies like the World Social Forums and their regional offshoots, and environmental organizations. NGOs use the power of global communications and fund-raising through the Internet, websites, and social media. Transnational movements and NGOs, usually smaller in scale, operate across borders, sometimes in and from the borderlands. Grassroots efforts and their participants in unequal borderlands may suffer from a "digital divide," with potential participants unable to pay for access to the Internet and electronic mail. However, Internet cafes and cell phone usage have increasingly expanded and spread worldwide. Facebook, electronic mail, and smartphone software like "WhatsApp" make instant communication possible.

Grassroots borderland groups usually do not make their way into the NGO directories and yearbooks that populate library reference rooms, quantitative researchers' designs, or global directories without resources and skills to create and pay for domain websites and their maintenance. The seminal work on transnational advocacy networks, alas, limited their studies to such directories.[1] Similarly, to understand NGOs in the European Union, one cannot rely only the list of organizations registered to lobby in its institutions, overwhelmingly business groups, as mentioned in an earlier chapter. However, European social groups also operate under the Social Platform (http://www.socialplatform.org). Likewise, the United States requires lobbyists to register and nonprofit organizations to acquire tax-exempt status from the Internal Revenue Service, but many more groups operate outside official eyes at the interstices of government and society.

Cause for optimism exists in the expansion of NGOs. In their volume's introduction, coeditors Joe Bandy and Jackie Smith examined the *Yearbook of*

International Organizations and saw increasing growth trends in transnational organizations from 1973 to 2000: for examples, from 41 to 247 human rights organizations, 21 to 98 peace organizations, 16 to 94 women's rights organizations, and 7 to 109 multiple-issue global justice organizations, among others.[2] However, they and their chapter contributors address the challenges faced in coalition-building across borders, from transnational campaigns to end child labor in South Asia and the invisibility of gender in trade liberalization (that is, "free trade") efforts like NAFTA, to campaigns to monitor "multinational compliance with international codes of conduct" in the past apartheid-era South Africa. On the latter, Gay Seidman highlights the power asymmetry between global capital and states.[3] Voluntary codes offer no match to effective regulation in states that practice good governance. Seidman's work calls attention to the important reality that states are not the only institutions for which power asymmetries can be analyzed. Global capital overwhelms even large states.

Transnational nonprofit and charitable humanitarian action organizations have a long history. Groups like the Red Cross/Red Crescent began in 1864 at the first Geneva Convention, now operate in 189 countries as the world's largest humanitarian network, and use the sacred red-colored symbols on white backgrounds.[4] Other transnational medical organizations such as Médecins Sans Frontières/Doctors Without Borders operate at great risk; on occasion, they and their patients experience bomb attacks whether deliberate or accidental such as in Syria and Afghanistan. When crises occur, as Piers Robinson analyzes,[5] the transnational mobilization of support has become remarkable and easy (through smartphone contributions!), but relief agencies may foster sensationalist media frames and dependency narratives about disasters. And reactions to prolonged media attention can evoke the ugly, but real "donor fatigue." Johan von Schreeb warns about the good, bad, and reckless with regard to transnational medical NGOs; the "fundamental rule for a doctor is to do no harm!" yet after the Haiti earthquake generated visits from hundreds of NGOs, some of them performed poorly or simply contributed to "disaster medical tourism."[6]

So many groups operate with the words "without borders" in their organizational titles: Reporters Without Borders, Engineers Without Borders, Clowns Without Borders, Accountants Without Borders, Executives Without Borders, Academics Without Borders, and Professors Without Borders. People *in* borderlands could use access to these groups as well.

Bringing in Borderlands People and Groups

Social movements, nonprofits, and NGOs operate in the mainstream and borderlands, but few full inventories exist of cross-border institutions, governmental and nongovernmental. Recall that border theorists like those analyzed in chapter 3 posit the importance of cross-border "political clout" for integration, but if we hardly know about groups except the prominent and well-endowed business groups like chambers of commerce, how is analysis possible? One pioneering effort to develop an inventory exists at the Mexico Center of the Baker Institute at Rice University in the United States.[7]

Not all movements at borders, even women's movements, operate with a justice agenda or one that offers more inclusivity with "Others." Nancy Naples and Jennifer Bickham Mendez compiled a volume entitled *Border Politics: Social Movements, Collective Identities, and Globalization*[8] that brings conservative, ethnoreligious exclusivity and identity into analysis, among Hindu women for example, with case studies from around the world. Among many intriguing chapters, Renata Blumberg and Raphi Rechitsky analyze how even in the borderlands of a "No Border Camp" in the Transcarpathian borderlands of the Ukraine, considerable disagreements occurred over language (Russian and English languages dominated discussions), nationality, and region among the nationals from 15 countries. Called "Europe's Mexico," Ukraine counts nearly half their population below its poverty line; Ukrainian migrant workers and asylum seekers cross the borders of Fortress Europe with varying successes. The analysts focus on the No Border Network with its slogans "no one is illegal" and "no border, no nation, stop deportation" to show its challenge to the architecture of borders and state sovereignty.[9] Such slogans are commonly seen and heard in the US-Mexico borderlands. Cross-border cooperation and solidarity is a huge challenge, so the development of such clout vis-à-vis national governments will be no easy feat.

Dutch graffiti in Brussels, "No one is illegal."

Source: Lourens Smak/Alamy Stock Photo.

For me, Blumberg and Rechitsky's work on this "anti-authoritarian" movement reveals several additional insights: the difficulty of organizing without even minimal hierarchy, the nearby risks and dangers (with what were termed fascists of different nationalities), and the folly of organizing within borderlands without the voices and actions of local border people. Yvonne Braun and Michael Dreiling[10] made a similar point in analyzing "border distortions," between gigantic international NGOs like International Rivers which dwarfed local border environmental groups. Another organizing feat involves crossing from global to local levels. A decade ago, Sally Merry argued that transnational human rights organizing must be translated in terms with local meaning.[11] Border people often share expertise on brokering language, contacts, and power on both sides of their borderlands.

At the US-Mexico border, grassroots organizations flourish, albeit with limited resources and volunteer leaders.[12] In one of the pioneering studies comparing transnational groups in different sectors, Irasema Coronado and I observed three major types of NGOs that share common interests at the US-Mexico borderlands: feminist and human rights groups with high energy but extremely limited resources; environmental groups resourced and legitimized with Mexican and US environmental agencies and the fought-for side agreements of NAFTA; and both labor and business groups. Business groups enjoyed the greatest successes; besides high fees from their members, they were not only subsidized by governments on both sides of the border with expertise and loans, but also motivated by a keen sense of material interest and profit.[13] More recently, border environmental groups faced challenges both in dealing with the securitized post-9/11 "thickening" of the border, even in the Tijuana–San Diego's Pacific borderlands, and in generating grant funding.[14] Little connection exists with global environmental groups like those in Europe, such as 350.org, an international environmental organization which envisions a "global grassroots climate movement" that can reduce or end the use of fossil fuels in favor of renewable energy and hold leaders accountable to "the realities of science and principles of justice."[15] But chambers of commerce and binational business groups in unequal borderlands with long-standing power asymmetries continue to experience success as their influential members work closely with local governments, keen to seek economic growth and job creation without any corporate codes of conduct.[16]

NGO activities in the Arizona borderlands offer us insights as well. After federal agents established border blockades in major urban areas in the early 1990s, many migrants moved to unpopulated, remote areas to cross the border including the hot and extremely arid Sonoran Desert which counts migrant deaths in the hundreds each year. In a comparative study of active NGO discourses and strategies in the region, Cari Lee Skogberg Eastman focuses on high-visibility NGOs that frame their commitments differently in the borderlands: Humane Borders, No More Deaths, and the vigilante militia of the Minuteman Civil Defense Corps. The first two groups take risks to save lives by providing water for desert crossers while the last seeks to prevent crossings with volunteers who carry weapons, claiming that they do the job the government does not do well. Volunteers seeking to save lives have been charged with crimes, some with misdemeanors (littering the landscape with water containers) and others with felonies (aiding and abetting an "illegal presence" in the United States) in transporting dying, severely dehydrated migrants. Group actions generated both positive and negative supporters, whatever the ideological framing of the groups, plus national media attention over stalled immigration reform. I might turn the slogan of No More Deaths ("Humanitarian Aid is never a Crime") into a question: Is humanitarian aid ever a crime? Does the presence of water stations encourage migration, as some conservative groups ask?[17] Here we see the dilemmas of the legal-illegal, licit-illicit categories from chapter 10. Human rights activists, while pointing to principles in law and precedent, sometimes argue that harsh laws should be illegal, so to speak: they are illicit, immoral, and unethical in the minds of some, including some faith-based activists to whom we turn below.

Human rights and immigrant advocacy organizations supply multiple kinds of assistance in borderlands. They offer legal assistance for people seeking asylum, they document abuses by border police, and they file lawsuits for particularly egregious cases to obtain damages and/or change policies. Among the many possible to name, I include Las Americas Immigrant Advocacy Center, the Border Network for Human Rights, and the American Civil Liberties Union (ACLU). ACLU lawyers in border states file complaints regarding verbal and physical abuse, along with US Border Patrol killings.

Worldwide, many human rights groups exist. Many Europeans travel to locales to assist refugees who come to the shore after treacherous sea journeys. Some work with governments and international agencies; others raise funds on their own. All such organizations need resources for basic operations. NGOs may be able to build alliances across ethnicities, nationalities, and religious affiliations; Peace Now and B'Tselem offer good examples in Israel and Palestine as noted in chapter 8 on security. The International Organization for Migration works with governments. Like many US think tanks, IOM collects data and informs policymakers and action strategies.

Faith and Conscience Groups

My questions in the above paragraphs prompt consideration of faith-based nonprofits and churches themselves. The Catholic Church gives particular attention to the plight of migrants, and it partially funds many shelters not only in Mexico and the United States, but also in other countries as well. Bishops and priests evoke the multiple biblical messages in Old and New Testaments about "welcoming the stranger," as do mainstream Protestantism and Judaism, though no doubt the message does not ring true to a good portion of congregants, some of whom assert that people should follow the law as set down by government.

Humane Borders emerged out of faith- and conscience-based activism, including the Sanctuary Movement of the 1980s which welcomed Central American immigrants fleeing the violence of civil war and state-sponsored terrorism, supported by the United States, still operating in Cold War mode. In

El Paso, Annunciation House has welcomed migrants from the countries in the South for nearly 40 years, grown from the same roots.[18] The church and various NGOs use religious icons such as the white cross for migrant deaths as did the anti-femicide groups with the pink and black crosses in Ciudad Juárez. Professor and Father Dan Groody, at the University of Notre Dame which produced the documentary *Dying to Live*, "sees the face of Jesus" in the immigrant.

As chapter 9 indicated, clergy conduct mass and communion at the US-Mexico border fence, with bread and wine passed through the former chain-linked fences in Sunland Park–Anapra in the central borderlands. My recent excursion to the area in 2016 revealed large-scale construction: a no-man's land dry mote between two fences that will soon see a more-than-20-foot wall erected. Here and in other parts of the borderlands, walls and fences get thicker and taller, harsher and harder. In San Diego's Friendship Park, border barriers make it harder and harder for family members to touch one another.

People of faith bring a powerful moral message in their words. Pope Francis visited Mexico in mid-February 2016, including the border in Ciudad Juárez. At a Sunday mass in Ecatepec, he told approximately "300,000 attendees to make Mexico a land of fulfilled opportunities" (quoted in Council on Hemispheric Affairs, February 16, 2016):

> where migration is not necessary in order to dream, where one does not need to be exploited at work, where there is no need to make the despair and poverty of many the opportunism of a few. A land that does not have to mourn men and women, young people and children who end up destroyed at the hands of the traffickers of death.

In Mexico's large border city of Juárez, Pope Francis visited the prison to communicate hope and forgiveness and the business community to remind them of moral responsibilities to provide wages that no longer require employees to exploit themselves just to work. With symbolic and dramatic meaning, he spoke at a huge outdoor mass facing the border which many interpreted to mean with the eyes of migrants facing northward. Public schools closed and the UTEP Sun Bowl opened for scores of thousands to watch on big screens in the United States. The visit happened in cooperation and peace, as thousands waited and listened in the sun. Many US federal police employees, mobilized to work overtime, patrolled the border fence and streets on the US side, without incident.

Challenging and Resisting the State

In a world of hyper-politicized border security, states have been quick to stigmatize NGOs and social movements that protest abuses with the overreaching and overused "T" word, terrorism. In formerly stateless parts of northeastern India, many so-called tribal groups that distance themselves from state affirmative action and patronage can be located on terror watch networks. Room should exist for people to mobilize challenges without such stigma. Mexico's quasi-democracy and assassination risks for journalists and activists pose

Life-size cardboard signs throughout Ciudad Juárez in preparation for Pope Francis's visit.

Source: Photographer Kathleen Staudt.

threats to NGOs and social movements. Yet groups, often couching their names in cultural terms, occupied enough space to challenge the militaristic narrative of President Calderón and his war on drugs.[19]

Engagement with Decision-Makers

While businesses and organizations that promote economic growth get public subsidies, democracy, human rights, and civil society movements and NGOs rarely enjoy such benefits or appointments to public boards. Indeed, they even face risks from the state and militarized hate groups as the Arizona cases show. With this book focused on borders, readers might heed the call in the transformative volume of mid-1980s political science *Bringing the State Back In*[20] and bring borders into multiple parts of governance, comparative politics, and international studies. The state can and should offer space for multiple voices, not simply those from national security and business. To this topic we now turn.

Regional and Cross-Border Governance Institutions

Here we examine public institutions for their ability to open borders, reduce or further reduce inequalities, and create or deepen democracy, good governance, and accountability to border people in borderlands. Several continents have affiliations with long-standing regional organizations such as the African Union (once the Organisation of African Unity), which holds borders sacrosanct but promotes borderlands development, and MERCOSUR, which focuses mainly on South American trade. However, without civic oversight and grassroots voices from border people, official institutions are likely to become bodies of mostly men who promote business and security agendas. There is more to the quality of life than producers and profits; the voices of working people, consumers, and taxpayers also belong at the decision-making table. With the decline, distrust, and ambivalence about seemingly democratic institutions, as reflected in low voter turnout, institutional leaders and builders will face challenges in securing ways for all voices to be heard.

Public Institutions in the Three Regions

Trade is often the harbinger for interaction, exchange, and potentially, growing prosperity for border people on both sides of a territorial line. The global economy would seem to produce conditions for institutions to facilitate such exchange and move away from alienated borderlands of militarized national security models. Regional free-trade organizations can be the first step or stage in such movement, as was the case with the European Coal and Steel Community in 1951, less than a decade after the horrors of war, which grew into a region of 28 countries (soon minus the United Kingdom) in an economic block of a half-billion people where 60 percent of trade is internal.[21]

To its credit, the European Union moved well beyond the interests of business and trade. Its social policies, cross-border regions, and investments toward poverty reduction have transformed the entire region. The bureaucracy of institutional sclerosis, claim Euro-skeptic critics, can be stultifying. And the austerity policies imposed upon Greece gave many cause for concern about the ongoing tension between national and supranational decisions.

NAFTA is one example of a free-trade organization that has done little except ease the operation of formal businesses and contribute to infrastructure development in the borderlands. Had it not been for vigorous civil society activism by labor and environmental groups, no NAFTA side agreements would have emerged. The labor side agreement is virtually impotent, while the environmental side agreement created several institutions that deepened a border perspective and improved borderlands: the Border Environment Cooperation Commission (BECC), the North American Development Bank (NADBank), and the Commission for Environmental Cooperation (CEC) based in Montreal. Border people and business operations have strong stakes in better sanitation, infrastructure, and water management. Although the CEC has a strong participatory mandate, technocrats manage the other organizations,[22] though much depends on its CEO, a political appointee who rotates from each of the three countries for three-year terms. Binational contributions are equal, and no investment in poverty reduction exists. More is necessary to expand participation and reduce border inequalities. While laudable for long-term cooperation and narrow achievements, the narrow missions of counterpart organizations—the US International Boundary and Water Commission (IBWC) and the Mexican Comisión Internacional de Límites y Aguas (CILA)—cannot accommodate all the policies that need to be addressed in the US-Mexico borderlands.

During US President Bush's administration, the Security and Prosperity Partnership (SPP) was born, with heads of state meeting annually. (New heads of state met annually through 2016, under the name "Three Amigos," reminiscent of a 1986 film comedy.) Governments appoint advisory committee members, all from business and government security agencies. Internal trade within the North American region is strong, dynamic, and vital, serving another half-billion people, equivalent to the European Union through 2016. But the SPP mission was not enough to include the interests of consumers, taxpayers, and employees or their associations and unions. No labor standards were set that would improve the obscene inequalities of minimum-wage workers at the US-Mexico border, a 10:1 ratio or the 5:1 of GDP per capita. The wounds of 9/11, still strong in the United States, overwhelmed other agendas. While cross-border institutions might start with business and trade, the institutions can neither stop at that, nor limit cooperation to the security "wars" against drugs, immigrants, and terrorists. Rather than moving to raise wages on the Mexico side of the border, business interests have strong stakes in maintaining low wages.

Intervention Necessary, But from Where and Whom?

In the South Asia region, internal trade is limited. Pakistan and India interact with tension, having fought wars; there are also continuing conflicts over Kashmir, and both have experienced sporadic terrorist attacks. The state stifles licit informal border trade with inefficient overregulation, coupled with Border Security Force threats. But the region is experiencing spectacular economic growth rates, both in India and China, with likely increasing demand for infrastructure, consumer goods, and energy. Dhananjay Tripathi focuses on the potential for regional cooperation over energy, noting figures for electricity, oil, gas, and coal (though expanded coal use endangers the whole planet and region, not the least of which is India, home to many of the most polluted cities in the world, as the security chapter noted). He cites the 2004 South Asia Free Trade Agreement as once offering promise, but with still "abysmal" results.[23] The website of the eight South Asian Association for Regional Cooperation (SAARC) member countries, offers networking opportunities in 103 languages, many beyond the region and national languages, to include Kurdish, Zulu, and others—even Esperanto, the once-hoped-for global language of a century past.[24]

Cross-Border Regions: Analytic Perspectives

In chapter 3, I introduced Markus Perkmann and Ngai-Ling Sum who edited one of the first volumes to put cross-border regions on the analytic map. In that volume, Bob Jessop analyzes rescaling strategies in cross-border regions. He puts forth nine trajectories for the emergence and consolidation of cross-border regions[25] several of which apply to regional cases in this book as I note below.

One trajectory focuses on *obscure and liminal forms*, namely historical trade, even if "disapproved by their respective national states."[26] This is reminiscent of the illegal-legal trade dimension covered in chapter 10 and the India-Pakistani borderlands covered in chapter 5. In other world regions, lively trade moves across porous boundaries in Africa, from legal and licit to state-defined illegal and the horrifying illicit trafficking in persons and weapons. Take the case of dynamic, same-named border communities Busia, Uganda, and Busia, Kenya, where many residents benefit from the opportunities of the borderlands. Yes, truckers may underestimate the value of their loads, border guards may pocket money, and Ugandans gladly pay double the price of services and pharmaceuticals in Kenyan health clinics unavailable in their own country, but the business of border trade generates incomes for many.[27] Similarly, the dynamic informal economies at the US-Mexico border, referred to in earlier chapters, provided ways for small-scale entrepreneurs to generate incomes making use of price differentials and the greater availability of goods in the borderlands. To this day, the reasonable cost of birth control pills on the Mexico side of the border keeps US borderlanders crossing to pharmacies for these and other prescriptions, available at a fifth to a tenth of the cost. On a grander scale, medical tourism is alive and well in border communities and on a transnational scale.

In another of Jessop's trajectories, the focus is on *the resurgence of historic economic spaces*, such as what reemerged after the Cold War and in places with shared river-border resources. The Oder River which runs between twin cities on the German-Polish border, from chapter 6, fits in this category.

And still another of Jessop's trajectories calls attention to *supranational bodies to stimulate regional activity*, as has been obvious with the European Union, but stuck at a NAFTA trade level in North America. However, economic spaces have been created in the New Silk Road of South and South East Asia, albeit in asymmetrical relations with powerful China driving much of that movement.

At the US-Mexico border, yet another of Jessop's trajectories is relevant—wherein *uneven development is exploited*, all too common in the region. Exploitation may be most useful for understanding the so-called Fortress Europe and its surrounding neighbors. Jessop simply provides us with cross-border trajectories and strategies, emphasizing that they begin at different scales and levels, thereby complementing theorists outlined in chapter 3.

What we learn from the Perkmann and Sum volume suggests both that trade is the crucial catalyst, and that regional cross-border cooperation varies enormously, operating quite differently in diverse contexts. As such, no "one-best-way" solutions can be advocated for contexts with different histories. Jessop's final trajectories involve potential solutions. One involves states *empowering regional or local governments to pursue "foreign relations,"* potentially applicable to the US-Mexico border and already underway in Yunan Province of China for many years. Jessop also notes how local leaders use *institution-building initiatives to exploit national crises.* The crisis for the United States was and continues to be 9/11, but the federal government remains in charge and security trumps trade and democracy in that agenda. In the United States, under what geographers call the "New Localism," the neoliberal state and its manufactured crisis (through federal and corporate tax cuts) devolved responsibility to local levels. Alas, nowhere in the Perkmann and Sum volume do chapter authors insert "security" into their discussions, no doubt in press around the time of the US tragedy. In many states, the national security apparatus sets the stage that enables trade and institution-building to flourish or diminish in various degrees, both in the United States and India as the regional cases show.

Despite the glue that trade has to offer, a comparison of cross-border relations in Mexico-US and European borders shows limited development in the multiple locations of the lengthy Mexico-US borderlands. Despite the existence of huge foreign direct investment sums, over 3,500 export-oriented plants in Northern Mexican states (compared with its other states), and $84 billion of trade for Texas-Mexico alone a decade ago, Brunet-Jailly, Payan, and Sawchuk say that central governments define basic parameters of relationships, and "governmental cooperation has been fragmented and limited in scope" dependent on US policy toward border security.[28] In Europe, long-term development of Euroregions, in advanced iterations, reveals maps in which cooperation and coordination cluster around the borders of EU members; although not broken down for each border, they say "internal trade increased from 1,000 billion euros to about 1,800 billion euros in 2000, and trade has remained at that level."[29] While people speak 35 national languages in the European Union, and several in some countries, the EU official languages total 20 with the most common language as English.[30] In EU regional community initiatives, with ever-advancing iterations and funding, economic disparities served neither as an "impetus nor a barrier to intensity of project cooperation."[31]

Perhaps the disparities at the US-Mexico border are too wide, compared to Europe if measured in wage terms, as a result of limited standards for decent wages in North America. Once again, from chapter 4, the trends over time show that the free trade regime of NAFTA in 1994 and thereafter appear to have aggravated disparities (5:1), producing more benefits for US investors than for Mexico. To its limited credit, however, and only with political pressure, NAFTA helped generate the North American Development Bank (NADBank) to fund environmental projects that the Border Environment Cooperation

Commission (BECC) recommends with equal contributions from both Mexico and the United States. While top-down and technical in orientation, its infrastructure projects have been positive but environmental NGO access to decision-making is limited as noted earlier.[32]

State Policies: Toward Shared Prosperity in Friendly Borderlands

A border lens requires not only narrow conceptions of controlled border security, walls/fences, and militarized models. The broader border lens also focuses on human security, greater wage equality, and quality of life and the environment in borderlands. Good policies on borderlands emanate from border voices, not just lobbyists and economic interests in the national capital (remember the capital-city Homeland Security Council lacking border voices!).

Educational Curricula, Nationalist Rituals: Wherefore Bridging Borders?

Decades ago, civic education and political socialization generated much interest among political scientists. They studied the social studies content that governments or commercial publishers developed for children in textbooks, including what was emphasized along with the so-called hidden curriculum, such as obedience to authority. They studied the political attitudes and preferences of children who acquired, for example, political party preferences as early as in primary school. They studied the civic rituals, such pledging allegiance to flags and singing national anthems, along with the national identities, loyalties, and values that become part of classroom and campus practices. Postcolonial states put special emphasis on developing national loyalty among children in schools. In Kenya, I vividly remember how primary-school children learned about Kenyan Independence Day and national heroes like Jomo Kenyatta through songs and course content.

In one of the few border research studies of the interplay of agendas imposed by government structures and their mix with hybrid border cultures in the practices of students and teachers, a colleague and I conducted video observations of and interviews in everyday classroom dramas in multiple schools and classrooms on both sides of the central borderlands[33] from which we edited a film to share with teachers, administrators, and students on both sides of the border for their feedback and perceptions. US and Mexican policies imposed their own national rituals from casual everyday US pledges (combined with allegiance pledges to Texas) to the weekly, highly formal rituals on the Mexico side in school courtyards and periodic city-wide march competitions at different grade levels. The holidays and their meanings convey subtle and overt messages to children, such as the military holidays in the US to honor veterans and the Día de la Expropiación Petrolera (Oil Expropriation Day) in Mexico, declared in 1938 after President Cárdenas nationalized oil interests. (Now that Mexico has opened its energy sector to foreign interests again, the celebrations may take on new interpretations.)

School policy incentivizes certain economic behaviors through material rewards, such as free pizza or fast-food parties in classrooms that returned parent-signed report cards. After NAFTA opened wider doors for fast-food franchises in Ciudad Juárez, the students could be incentivized for such treats, but the cost of a children's Happy Meal amounted to a full-day's adult wage, given the artificially low legal minimum wages in Mexico. Thankfully, creative teachers did far more than instill a desire for fast-food culture in classrooms. Teachers used holidays and language from *both* sides of the border in classroom lessons: in Mexico, the calculation of percentages of students who like "hamburgers" and "pizza"; in the United States, the celebration of Día de los Muertos (Day of the Dead) to remember and honor ancestors and beloved leaders.

Mono- to Multilingualism

During the 1990s, border cities in Mexico began offering English as a Second Language (ESL) in order to prepare students for the economically interdependent border region, while in the same era, US and Texas policy offered bilingual education which gradually prepared students to learn and take standardized tests in English. Nowadays, more US school districts offer dual-language instruction in Spanish and English to prepare students for life and work in the whole of the Americas (save Portuguese and indigenous languages, the latter slowly dying out). Although formal relations between the decentralized school districts of the United States and Texas and the centralized system of Mexico do not exist, the informal relations among Mexicans and an 80-percent Mexican-heritage population in El Paso help to create a hybridized educational culture in both teaching and learning strategies. Yet many state standards imposed by the Texas Education Agency stress social studies geared toward Texas in the United States.

Even prior to borderland examples like the above and regional supra-state institutions like the European Union, some educational systems fostered multilingualism. In places like India with over 30 major linguistic groups in its one-billion-plus population, multilingual capability becomes a political-economic part of life, trade, and upward mobility. All too often postcolonial states assumed the language of the colonizer as the lingua franca, such as French or English. And monolingualism is the policy preference of some in places like the United States, without an official language (though there is often an additional language "requirement" in some secondary and post-secondary education). As former Texas state governor Ma Ferguson has been attributed as saying long ago about teaching in English in public schools in the interwar period, "If English was good enough for Jesus, it's good enough for me!"

European and National Values

When the supranational European Union consolidated itself and made potential new members eligible, Gordon Bell edited a volume, *Educating European Citizens,* with state-specific chapters about European "values" that educators might stress beyond "national values." In his introduction, Bell notes values such as tolerance, citizenship (i.e., civic) education, international understanding, and human rights. Bell lists barriers to intercultural education: deference to experts, resistance to practical and action-oriented studies, and grand theory among others.[34] In another chapter, Don Rowe notes that however valuable, patriotic education could detract from tolerance and intercultural understanding. If schools rely on religious education alone for civic virtues, he says, inequity will reign for secular, multicultural, and nonreligious communities and instead privilege the dominant group whose religious traditions may be infused with patriotism and nationalism.[35]

As I review research like this, with its cross-border and regional implications, Bell's volume seems somewhat quaint as the European Union faces 21st-century criticism, Brexit, and other potential leavers, and also copes with reemergent nationalisms in dealing with the refugee crisis. We lack studies about schooling in borderlands. We could use more attention to how border peoples and nationals view transformative events, such as World War II, for such understandings are relevant to borders. At the One Europe website, the Youth Association for a Greater Europe compares how World War II is taught in Austria, England, and France.[36] To synthesize their summary, Austria emphasizes its victimization by the Nazis, but also stresses war, peace, and the dangers of extremism, while England and France emphasize the Holocaust and lives lost. Until 1980, France emphasized resistance, but downplayed collaboration. Note that One World's summary is not an academic analysis, and that teachers and students interact with formal curricular materials in a multitude of ways. Into the minds of intellectually undeveloped and vulnerable children, nationalist or cultural propaganda can easily be slipped into texts, with a power that holds into adulthood. Recall the comparison of Pakistani and Indian texts cited in chapter 5.

Texas Educational Standards: Ignore Mexico and the Borders

In the United States, 50 states develop 50 sets of standards about what students should learn in multiple content areas, from social studies to math, at different grade levels. The large State of Texas, noted in chapter 2, sets a lengthy list of standards, to which teachers teach and about which students take standardized tests. They are called the TEKS, or Texas Essential Knowledge and Skills.[37] I thank the Ctrl+F function in Microsoft Word for enabling a count of keywords in massive pages of text to find items related to this book. In the 302 standards for social studies in middle school, the words border and borders *never* get mentioned, but the word boundaries is mentioned twice in connection with art and with innovations transcending boundaries. The word Mexico is mentioned twice, and Mexican eight times for the standards of required 7th grade Texas history courses, the Mexican stage of Texas (until 1836), and the US-Mexican War. Clearly, with a more-than 1,000-mile border between Texas and Mexico and $82 billion in trade (2013 figures), one might expect more coverage and content. Mexico's more centralized Secretariat of Public Education does not list standards and it categorizes content differently. Grades 1–6 consists of primary school, and three years comprise secondary education (what in the United States would be grades 7–9). *Secundaria* describes three parts of social studies: geography, history, and civic and ethical formation. Without the detail of TEKS, it is impossible to know the comparable content.

Educational Interventions

The meanings of citizenship and education for its practice undergo transformation in states that are affiliated with supranational bodies such as the European Union, to some a distant bureaucracy, but with its own flag, anthem, currency, and civil rights standards for minorities and immigrants in member states, such as Cyprus. Stavroula Philippou analyzed the complex layering in historical and contemporary curriculum of Greek-Cypriot students' sense of citizenship.[38] She devised a research design of students in experimental and control groups, with the former involved in curriculum and dialogue about immigrants. Some students shifted their narratives about citizenship, but value foundations are inculcated earlier, in both schools and families. More content like this *and* more research of this type would be useful for borderlands study.

In borderlands with great tension and conflict, films and other interventions could be a useful way to bridge communities. David Newman narrates an illuminating documentary, available on YouTube, entitled *Peeking Over the Wall* (2016). It consists of interviews with adults who reminisce about previous decades of greater interaction between communities. The documentary also shows interviews with children living under the reign of border barriers and walls. An unforgettable comment for me was when an Israeli settler child asserted that God gave them this land. Children learn quite early about stereotypes and "Othering" characteristics to apply to one another. These processes do not bode well for the future.

In yet another border-relevant education study of Australia,[39] where former white Anglo-Celtic settlers once identified with Great Britain before federation in 1901, a quarter of the population claimed birth overseas as White Australia accepted immigrants from South East Asia (fleeing the Vietnam war). Dispossessed of their lands, indigenous (Aboriginal) peoples who speak 170 different languages and finally acquired voting rights in 1962 and full citizenship rights in 1967 have now been reduced to just 2 percent of the population. Researcher Joan DeJaeghere examined the interpretive meanings of intercultural curricula which, like most, are never neutral, as she says, given their permeation with values and objectives, and ultimately they are not exchanged in critical ways.

Early education ought to extend beyond nationalist, historical constructions. Curriculum ought to include borders as constructions that can and should be bridged rather than mainly as barriers. All too often, history and knowledge are conveyed as nationalist projects. Even comparative education volumes on civic education and educational policy use state-centric "territorial traps" rather than approaches that transcend borders. States and their educational curricula ought to move away from monolingual languages into bi- or multicultural fluency, as has occurred in many European countries. To do this, it will likely take NGOs and INGOs (international nongovernmental organizations) to press for action at national, regional, and international bodies for incentivized policy change.

Beyond State Centrism

State-centric policies do not work well in the borderlands where issues, people, and communities transcend territorial lines. At long last, a survey of border people in twin cities on both sides of the Mexico-US line shows the discrepancy between mainstream and capital-city orientations and the realities of border people. The vast majority of border people do not support more walls and fences; their everyday lives depend on interaction across borders.[40] The spread of Zika virus cannot be stopped with a wall. River basins and bolsons must be managed cooperatively, with equity principles in mind.[41] Immigration reform is and must involve a binational or regional effort, not addressed by one state alone, especially when states sit side by side. And procedures meant to protect the environment will only backfire without including partners on both sides. US policymakers once thought that environmental impact statements would provide accurate assessments to improve policy and practice, but a comparison of two large water systems at both the Canada-US and Mexico-US boundaries reveals inattentiveness to the concerns of Canada and Mexico beyond "informing" them and, in the case of Canada, engaging in some "consultation" in the process.[42] Federalism works differently in North American countries, one with a parliamentary, two with presidential systems, and bureaucratic discretion often prevails. How, the authors ask, can policies and practices with transboundary implications be better harmonized? The answers go well beyond the provocative questions raised here and elsewhere in this book, awaiting future action from readers, researchers, and policymakers.

NGOs often instigate ideas for change, but even after that, social movements, education and greater awareness build the base for pushing change, actual reform, and persistent vigilance on implementation. Social media offers speedy transmission, but often shallow commitment and follow-up. Moreover, social media may be vulnerable to state actions that suspend or limit Internet or mobile communication. Many border disparities require changes in official policies and regional bodies, and critical masses of people—not only border people—need to communicate those issues with decision-makers.

Individual Choices, Individual Connections

People make choices. In everyday life, they can lean toward empathy and humanitarian actions or not. They can contribute to nonprofit organizations that assist border crossers with time and money. They can visit borderlands, meet and interact with border people face to face. They can push for economic, trade, tax, and wage reforms in global production, especially regarding their border neighbors. They can watch films that offer realistic portrayals of borderlands in multiple parts of the world. They can choose consumer products which depend less on fossil fuels, or use them ever more efficiently. They can avoid wasting water that evaporates quickly in the arid heat. They can invest or disinvest in corporations to support those that use comparative advantage principles in borderlands. Plenty of diverse opportunities for standards, investment in equity, and development of democratic institutions exist in borderlands, particularly those with uneven or unequal growth.

In their professions and businesses, people can raise questions or refuse to participate in unethical practices, expose malpractices, and/or join with others in solidarity and alliance. Courageous professionals like Eyal Weizman and Rafi Segal won an Israel Association of United Architects (IAUA) competition, then were chosen to prepare an exhibition and catalog at the International Union of Architects congress in Berlin about their profession's role in Middle East conflict. But an IAUA steering committee cancelled the exhibition and destroyed the 5,000 copies of the catalog. Instead, they prepared a second edition in 2002 and Weizman wrote a lengthy book in 2007.[43] Courage has consequences, but ethics and wider understanding may prevail.

Concluding Reflections

In this chapter, we examined multiple strategies toward solutions for the unequal borderlands worldwide and the lack of institutions, both NGO and official, that include voices and interests from borderlands people. The comparative models from three world regions, from earlier chapters and woven herein, show what is possible, what needs change, and realistic strategies to effect that change. Schools and educational curricula are good places to start and sustain new ways to think about and act on borderlands policy. Even in everyday lives, people can make choices that bring a border lens into decisions and communications.

Recommended Resources

Films

Dying to Live
Peeking over the Wall

Notes

[1] Margaret Keck and Kathryn Sikkink, *Activists Beyond Borders* (Ithaca, NY: Cornell University Press, 1998).

[2] Joe Bandy and Jackie Smith, eds., *Coalitions across Borders: Transnational Protest and the Neoliberal Order* (Lanham: Rowman & Littlefield, 2005), p. 6.

[3] Gay Seidman, "Monitoring Multinationals: Corporate Codes of Conduct," in Joe Bandy and Jackie Smith, eds., *Coalitions Beyond Borders* (Lanham, MD: Rowman & Littlefield, 2005).

[4] Mukesh Kapila, "The Red Cross and Red Crescent," in Roger MacGinty and Jenny H. Peterson, eds., *The Routledge Companion to Humanitarian Action* (London and NY: Routledge, 2015), p. 183.

5 Piers Robinson, "News Media and Communication Technology," in Roger MacGinty and Jenny H. Peterson, eds., *The Routledge Companion to Humanitarian Action* (London and NY: Routledge, 2015).

6 Johan von Schreeb, "Medical NGOs," in Roger MacGinty and Jenny H. Peterson, eds., *The Routledge Companion to Humanitarian Action* (London and NY: Routledge, 2015), p. 295.

7 The project is under Tony Payan's direction at the Mexico Center, Baker Institute, Rice University.

8 Nancy Naples and Jennifer Bickham Mendez, eds., *Border Politics* (NY: New York University Press, 2014).

9 Renata Blumberg and Raphi Rechitsky, in Nancy Naples and Jennifer Mendez, eds., *Border Politics* (NY: New York University Press, 2014), p. 302. Also see chapter 3 in Kathleen Staudt and Irasema Coronado, *Fronteras no Más* (NY: Palgrave USA, 2002) for factors that facilitate and block cross-border cooperation, chapter 3.

10 Yvonne Braun and Michael C. Dreiling, "Frames, Boomerangs, and Global Assemblages: Border Distortions in the Global Resistance to Dam Building in Lesotho," in Nancy Naples and Jennifer Mendez, eds., *Border Politics* (NY: New York University Press, 2014), pp. 261–91.

11 Sally Merry, *Human Rights & Gender Violence: Translating International Law into Local Justice* (Chicago: University of Chicago Press, 2006).

12 For an overview, see Carol Zabin, "Nongovernmental Organizations in Mexico's Northern Border," *Journal of Borderlands Studies* XII, 1–2, 1997, pp. 41–72.

13 Staudt and Coronado, *Fronteras no Más.*

14 Francisco Lara-Valencia, "The 'Thickening' of the US-Mexico Border: Prospects for Cross-Border Networking and Cooperation," *Journal of Borderlands Studies* 26, 3, 2011, pp. 251–64; Irasema Coronado, "Whither the Environmental Nongovernmental Organizations on Multiple Regions of the US-Mexico Border?" *Journal of Borderlands Studies* 29, 4, 2014, pp. 449–64.

15 http://www.350.org.

16 Kathleen Staudt and Pamela Cruz, " 'Getting It': Business NGOs and Political Actors Talk about the Central US-Mexico Borderlands," paper presented at the Association of Borderlands Studies Conference, April 2014, Portland, Oregon.

17 Cari Lee Skogberg Eastman, *Shaping the Immigration Debate: Contending Civil Societies on the US-Mexico Border* (Boulder: Lynn Rienner Publishers 2012), p. 98.

18 Kathleen Staudt and Zulma Méndez, *Courage, Resistance, and Women in Ciudad Juárez: Challenges to Militarization* (Austin: University of Texas Press, 2015), chapter 5.

19 Ibid.

20 Peter Evans, Dietrich Rueschemeyer, and Theda Skocpol, eds., *Bringing the State Back In* (Cambridge: Cambridge University Press, 1985).

21 Dhananjay Tripathi, "Energy Security: The Functional Area of Regional Cooperation for South Asia," *Eurasian Border Review* 3, 2, 2012, pp. 91–102.

22 Jo Marie Rios and Joseph Jozwiak, "NAFTA and the Border Environmental Cooperation Commission: Assessing Activism in the Environmental Infrastructure Project Certification Process," *Journal of Borderlands Studies* (1996–2004) 23, 2, 2008, pp. 59–81.

23 Tripathi, "Energy Security," p. 94.

24 http://www.saarctrade.info.

25 Bob Jessop, "The Political Economy of Scale," in Markus Perkmann and Ngai-Ling Sum, eds., *Globalization, Regionalization and Cross-Border Regions* (NY: Palgrave Macmillan, 2002), pp. 38–41.

26 Ibid., p. 38.

27 William Allen, " 'I Am from Busia!': Everyday Trading and Health Service Provision at the Kenya-Uganda Border as Place-Making Activities," *Journal of Borderlands Studies* 28, 3, 2013, pp. 291–306.

28 Emmanuel Brunet-Jailly, Tony Payan, and Gary Sawchuk, *The Emergence of Cross-Border Regions along the Mexican-US Border and in Europe*. Canada: Policy Research Initiative, February 2008, p. 26.

29 Ibid., pp. 36, 37.

[30] Ibid., p. 39.

[31] Ibid., p. 45.

[32] Rios and Joswiak, "NAFTA and the Border Environmental Cooperation Commission."

[33] Susan Rippberger and Kathleen Staudt, *Pledging Allegiance: Learning Nationalism in the El Paso-Juárez Border* (NY: Falmer/Routledge, 2003).

[34] Gordon H. Bell, ed., *Educating European Citizens: Citizenship Values and the European Dimension* (London: David Fulton Publishers, 1997), pp. 12–13.

[35] Dan Rowe, "Education for Citizenship in Europe," in Gordon H. Bell, ed., *Educating European Citizens: Citizenship Values and the European Dimension* (London: David Fulton Publishers, 1997), pp. 56–7.

[36] http://www.one-europe.info/how-wwii-is-taught-in-european-countries-part-1.

[37] http://www.tea.state.tx.us.

[38] Stavroula Philippou, "Curricular Intervention and Greek-Cypriot Pupils' Constructions of Citizenship: Can 'Europe' Include Immigrants?" in Doyle Stevick and Bradley A. Levinson, eds., *Reimagining Civic Education* (Lanham, MD: Rowman & Littlefield, 2007), pp. 91–115.

[39] Joan DeJaeghere, "Intercultural Meanings of Citizenship in the Australian Secondary Curriculum: Between Critical Contestations and Minimal Constructions," in Doyle Stevick and Bradley A. Levinson, eds., *Reimagining Civic Education* (Lanham, MD: Rowman & Littlefield, 2007), pp. 293–316.

[40] Alfredo Corchado, "Common Ground: Poll finds U.S.-Mexico border residents overwhelmingly value mobility, oppose wall," *Dallas Morning News*, July 18, 2016. http://interactives.dallasnews.com/2016/border-poll/. Accessed 7/19/2016. I have all the survey results, courtesy of Tony Payan.

[41] In her chapter on the equity principle, Deborah Stone (*Policy Paradox: The Art of Political Decision Making*, 2012) identifies eight ways to conceptualize equity in budgets and access to resources.

[42] Lilias Jones, Pamela Duncan, and Stephen Mumme, "Assessing Transboundary Environmental Impacts on the U.S.-Mexican and U.S.-Canadian Borders," *Journal of Borderlands Studies* 12, 1–2, 1997, pp. 73–96.

[43] See their work cited in chapter 8 on security.

Chapter 13

Conclusions and Reflections on Border Politics in a Global Era

The earth is tired from all the borders we have carved on her back.

Benjamin Alire Sáenz, novelist[1]

What a difference it does and could make to analyze the world with a border lens. In this book, we have compared and contrasted three borderlands, each of them offering models for replication or rejection, in part or in whole. In the maritime borders chapter, the prospect of serious conflict and loss of lives is coupled with the sea context of tiny microstates and gigantic powerful states like China. That chapter illustrates the problems associated with the limited institutional mechanisms available to deal with conflicting issues over precious resources.

This final chapter offers a succinct summary of the book, some answers to questions posed in chapter 1, comments on advancing border theories, and the future research frontier. I close with some prospects for our future in a world of more or less re-bordering.

A Succinct Summary

To get a handle on ways to compare borders, I review previous border categories and theories to emphasize key factors heretofore missing in analyses. The first focus is the so-called I-2: *inequalities* and inclusive border *institutions* (or their lack) and the voices to be heard within them. The second focus is on governance: *states* and the length of *time since independence*, with a special focus on the postcolonial South which has not yet been well-integrated into the field of border studies. I have repeatedly called attention to history, good governance or its lack, and the discretion available to *border bureaucrats* who do their work with some unpredictability: with justice, with impunity, and with corruption.

My normative intent is to move toward greater binational equalities in *interdependent* states with emphasis on *wages* and GDPs, but with the latter *discounted* for environmental damage, and the long-term security threat whether we live in borderlands or the mainstream. And my emphasis on trade and inclusive institutional political voices, so crucial in moving toward regional integration, unpacks and highlights several factors worthy of critical examination.

First, trade's illegal-legal, illicit-licit dimensions deserve review. Excessive illegality, primarily to generate revenue, hinders trade, interaction, and livelihoods, and simply costs too much administratively, inviting inefficiency and corruption in the process. Rather, particular attention should be given to reducing demand for illicit goods and practices, especially in mainstream places. Mainstream employers and consumers who hire people who are unauthorized to work, who enslave people, or who use illegal goods ought to be the focus.

Second, border people deserve voices and representation in institutions. It is incomplete to authorize only business and official security voices without regard for local border workers and taxpayers. The challenging work of building institutions for a border commons has only recently begun conceptually, but Europe's regional institutions provide us with two decades of practice, even without the sort of high-volume grassroots and NGO participation that would make a more complete whole. Eurostats are not enough to gauge voices, especially in closed-ended survey instruments in which people cannot explain their responses.

The cross-regional comparative analysis covered in chapters 4–6 highlights the key factors in divergent borderlands. Model 1, the US-Mexico borderlands involves old states, heavily securitized with unequal borderlands, albeit with extensive trade and under-resourced nongovernmental organizations. Model 2, the postcolonial, formerly stateless (called Zomia for lack of an alternative name) region of northeastern India, Bangladesh, Myanmar, Bhutan, and China (the powerful, noncolonized exception to this characterization) involves mostly new states, relatively equal but impoverished borderlands, with cross-border trade stifled and heavily securitized by India. Colonialism and Partition shaped India's current dispositions in warped ways that reduce informal trade and burden border people. Model 3 consists of Europe and specifically, the European Union of old states, equality among most, and relatively new borderlands called regions in which cooperation is facilitated with investment and institutional development. Models 1 and 2 reveal only limited institutional development, around water and river basins. The more powerful nations in both regions (China, the United States), which sporadically promote binational or tri-national cooperation, set agendas; their primary focus is trade and national self-interest. Business and security voices prevail in such efforts. Model 3 targets and diverts investment and resources *to* borderlands, easy enough, some might say, for rich countries, but possible for many countries if they realize the potential opportunities afforded with shared prosperity in borderlands. In this last sentence, we can see the importance of mainstream political forces viewing and articulating their borders as sites for opportunities, not as insecure wastelands.

In chapter 7 on the many maritime borders and the overlap and conflict among them, the sea scene is almost anarchic. The architecture for cooperation and conflict-resolution, the UN Convention on the Law of the Sea, is in place, but powerful states have shown a willingness to contravene the rules and the decisions of international courts (that lack enforcement capability).

Although the world regions differ enormously, some eerily similar patterns emerge across thousands of miles in between the regions. For example, capital-city decision-makers overwhelm border voices and border people tend to be politically marginalized. Over eight in ten US-Mexico border people do not want a wall built, but mainstream politicians and bureaucrats continue promising them or building them to appease those who, though many have never been to the border, have been whipped into a frenzy by fear-mongering about "Others." The United States claims to be a federal system of government, but local control does not operate in the "democratic deficit" at the border. Border people learn ways to get around rules and susceptible corrupt officials in order to build livelihoods. Many informal workers support themselves, in spite of officials. Ugly insults from the long-in-place "Othering" processes continue to be heard, attributing less-than-human qualities to individuals and especially to refugees and those seeking jobs who come from failed states that lack good governance and robust economies. Animal metaphors are used for women and men, with crude verbs and adjectives. I sometimes hope we can develop a "Humane Society" for people. A final example, among so many culled from analysis, is that the gender lens seems to offer special insights at borderlands. Hypermasculine securitization strategies spread and/or reemerge in aggressive, militarist institutions. Borders also appear to be a magnet for violence against women and the devaluation of their labor.

Answering Chapter 1's Questions

There *is* a common core in interdisciplinary border studies, but the empirical research is and must be attentive to history, context, and place. The common core consists of border concepts like de-bordering and re-bordering, of border categories, and of border theories about process and movement toward integration to include the I-2, attention to reducing border inequalities and building inclusive institutions in democratic states.

As this book shows, past border concepts and theories—developed in the North and especially Europe and North America—are not enough; research must include the South (and its former stateless regions), with scholars in and from the South, to add postcolonial states and governance issues in the relatively short time since independence. We need accessible measures of borderland inequalities, to include wages and earnings from licit informal trade. We need more studies *in* borderlands, drawing on the perceptions of border people and their experiences. That is not the same as state-centric analysis of discourses and policies.

Border people have long worked, engaged in trade, and socialized in borderlands. Many continue to do so, but they face challenges. One major challenge is the state itself, its border bureaucrats, and the security apparatus which sometimes generates insecurity given the force and impunity with which border guards operate. State policies, usually state-centric, are generally not made with the interests of border people in mind.

India's Border Security Force, largest in the world, is the best example of efforts to create hard, hypermasculine borders with walls and with extremely high rates of killing and injury by the security forces themselves, some of whom are compromised by the temptations of rent and extortion. Historically, the mountain peoples of places now known as northeastern India, Bangladesh, Myanmar, Bhutan, and China have tried to shield themselves from the demands of outsiders, deemed "foreigners." After Partition and the rise of the Indian Developmental Raj, these peoples simultaneously resist and negotiate with the state, creating a complex reality for all involved, especially if their resistance is deemed "terrorism," an overly applied term.

Since 9/11, the United States has also built a quasi-militarized, fenced, and high-technology border exhibiting hypermasculine characteristics, depending on the president in power and the political appointees heading the Department of Homeland Security. Impunity exists, with little action for accountability according to data analyzed in think tanks like the American Immigration Council.[2] The United States continues to fight wars against drugs, immigrants, and terrorists, but these wars produce mixed results, and even backfire. The US border with Mexico is highly unequal, measured in GDP and wage terms, with no changes in sight given the way the freer trade of NAFTA and other policies have benefited the already strong political constituencies of business and the privileged in Mexico without attending to workers' wages or the quintessential informal free traders. However, minimal advances have been made with environmental agreements and institutions related to river boundary, water, and environmental issues.

Under conditions like these, border people manage to maintain some of the fluid, interactive experiences with similar peoples, the vast majority of whom share Mexican heritage. The lines, scrutiny, and delays at the border continue to pose challenges to people, yet lively social movements and cross-border NGO solidarity organizations, including those from faith-based institutions, offer camaraderie to people with similar interests. Faith-based organizations reintroduce values into border activism, but one does not need Catholic affiliation or inspiration from Pope Francis to make good choices and behave in ethical ways. These civic relationships are unmatched in the official sector; businesses have material stakes in maintaining their global competitive edge by using comparative advantage realities to pay extremely low wages to hundreds of thousands of export-processing employees.

Europe is the exceptional case here, at least prior to the refugee crisis of 2015. Before that and continuing to a large extent, Europe opened borders and invested in cross-border regions, facilitating networks and building institutions.

Poverty makes for fertile ground of "comparative advantage" practices and policies that use low wages and environmental damage to compete in a global economy. One might wonder if neoliberal limited regulation is compatible with de-bordered, shared prosperity. Yet the European Union built a regulated common market, more equality, and propelled basic social principles—that is, regulated capitalism, in need of more democracy than bureaucracy.

In chapter 12, "Toward Solutions," I offer ways in which international, regional, national, and grassroots people might begin to address the problems and opportunities in borderlands. With far too many suggestions therein, I will not synthesize them all except to emphasize investment in borderlands equality and wage standards, in border people and their expert voices, and in inclusive institutions that offer democratic voices about the many issues that shape people's lives. Education can play a fuller role in broadening knowledge about borderlands and neighboring countries. Unlike most comparative politics and border studies research, I highlight education and popular culture in the form of films that may illuminate opportunities to build bridges across, and not more barriers to, the borders in our world. All too few academics cross the "border" of specialized journals, hardly accessible to those outside academia, to write and speak to the mainstream, larger society.

Advancing Border Theories

With more research on states in both the South and North, with the heavy legacy of colonialism in the former and the socialized national loyalties in the latter, border scholars should extend the current four categories used to classify borderlands—alienated, coexistent, interdependent, and integrated—to include the experiences of formerly borderless people in the South living with the legacies of recent colonialism. Moreover, we need to know from whose vantage points such categories are created: the states or border people? And we must raise the always-great phenomenological question: *how do we know?* Border theorists still wedded to state-centric analysis will examine state discourse and practices. Border theorists with an anthropological or sociological bent will ground analysis *in* borderlands. The field of border studies needs more of the latter.

Based on this book, a case can be made to add a category that addresses formerly stateless peoples in some of the postcolonial states of the South. There, states create the tensions and conflicts, even the dangers, from their security forces that deter interaction and trade and that foster alienation. No doubt, once more border studies emerge from the South, we will gain insights about yet more categories. But within that huge category, we must understand the variations among states—more or less democratic and well-governed, more or less securitized—and the numerous patterns likely to emerge.

This book also makes the case to unpack the *interdependence* category into multiple patterns: those with extensive inequalities, content to maintain them and focus on trade growth alone but not on wages or wage penalties from globalized work; and those with the sorts of interventions and inclusive institutions that move borderlands toward shared prosperity and perhaps integration. The sine qua non of integrated borderlands, I believe, is relative wage equality, at least at the A or B grade levels (recall chapter 3 and the Border Inequalities Database) and in legal minimum wages.

A Research Frontier

Clearly, this book emphasizes the need for more border studies in the South, ideally from scholars located in the South. And the book calls attention to filling other research gaps.

We need better measurements of *borderland* inequalities, including *gendered* inequalities, in order to find ways to reduce them. We need more inventories and analyses of border institutions, official and NGO: Who has voice, women and men? What issues are addressed? Do the institutions operate with resources and budgets (and from where)? And what authority do such institutions have to counter or add a borderlands nuance to state centrism? Under what contexts can securitization be demasculinized toward professionalism and comprehensive attention to multiple securities, or at least toward less hypermasculine swagger and aggressive organizational cultures and interactions with everyday people? How have those with cross-border clout been able to gain support and resources for genuine but complicated borderlands institutions that invariably challenge state sovereignty? Are those models transferable elsewhere, and by whom?

Political scientists and related disciplinarians should expand the scope of their analyses to include an examination of the ways in which education, curriculum, and socialization of national loyalties that normalize state-centric history, language, and identities in the minds of youth reinforce borders instead of building bridges. The subfields of comparative politics and international relations should also grapple with borderlands issues.

Researchers should also consider moving beyond the typical social science categories of nationality or citizenship to differentiate those they interview. In hybrid borderlands, people may be born on one side of a border and live on the other. They may attend school across the border from where they live. We need new categories for data collection besides, for example, "Mexican, US, or dual citizen" and "White or Hispanic" to include borderland people who fit "none of the above." Their vantage points and experiences deserve analysis.

More or Less Re-bordering in the Next Decade?

In book conclusions, as authors draw their analyses to a close, they sometimes take the luxury of raising big questions and offering predictions. Permit me to indulge in this process. To what extent will more re-bordering occur? Hardly major news items, adjustments are continuously being made.[3] Maps may be slow to portray this dynamism in re-bordering or perhaps preempt it and make political judgments.[4] A crucial take-away from this book is that borders are social *constructions* that can and do change.

I wonder whether borders will become more open or closed—for people and for trade—and under what conditions it will happen. Stunning pictures from Spanish photojournalist Javier Bauluz reveal human suffering during conflicts and migration journeys. His 2001 photo "Tarifa" of a couple enjoying themselves on a Mediterranean Sea beach in Southern Spain ignoring the dead body washed up on shore nearby illustrates the casual disregard among some for the humanitarian crises of our times.[5] The film *Sleep Dealer* (2008) evokes an ominous picture of the US-Mexico closed border future: the privatization of water sources that undermines small-scale Mexican farmers even more; mistaken security drone strikes that terrorize and kill; profiteering from private conversations; US exit procedures outsourced to South Asian contractors; and the US use of low-cost labor in Mexico through dangerous robotics plugged into body nodes—without presence on US soil. This is not a future in which I would wish to live.

The security rationale for totally closed borders strains compatibility with the global economy and a freer flow of migrant labor and talent. Surely terrorist incidents generate fears, but terror has occurred in earlier and contemporary decades as well from a variety of sources, including starvation, though often unseen and therefore ignored by many in the North. Many states have superlative abilities to surveil and control with technology and sharing among their agencies and states. To what extent will these abilities alone drive the atmospheres within states and their borderlands, and how much invasion of liberty and privacy will people tolerate or be willing to fund?

Will efforts remain that maintain regional integration, common markets, and regulation with some redistribution to share prosperity, such as in the European Union? The Brexit vote of 2016 surprised many, with Scotland (whose voters overwhelming sought to stay, not leave the EU) claiming the option to offer another vote for its independence from the United Kingdom. And what of the fate of Northern Ireland, where voters also sought to stay? Some think Northern Ireland should leave the United Kingdom and join the Republic of Ireland, while others imagine renewed border controls between both parts of Ireland. Past conflicts called the "Troubles" still linger in the minds of Irish people.

Questions might also be raised about the continuity and stability of approximately 200 states; for example, several island states are likely to "sink" into the sea due to rising water levels caused by climate change.[6] Will states join others in a consolidation of nations (hardly imaginable even in my local context with nine school districts in one county all protecting their "territorial turf")? Perhaps the regional economic bodies would reach a compromise, like ASEAN, MERCOSUR, NAFTA, and the European Union (or the three regions Orwell wrote about in *1984*).

Perhaps fragmentation and secession will emerge as a strategy to deal with people who never fit well into the territorial cages drawn around them. I cannot close this book and chapter without adding yet another map that shows the many peoples who might claim the right of statehood, listed at the end of this chapter. If we add or multiply more states into the complex terrain that currently exists, we could exponentially increase the number of borderlands, nonviable economies, and dependence on the global economy and its use of comparative advantage principles. Without attention to the people and the places in borderlands, our world would be the less for it.

We need to address the world's many borderlands and their people with the same vigor and attention we devote to mainstream people. Border people's experiences provide clues for dealing with major issues of the century: security, migration, and trade—freer trade for all, including informal workers, but also *fairer* trade, with basic decency standards for workers. In borderlands, the global meets the local; these places and their people are the entrée to understanding and acting on key issues for our times and for the future. Borderlands are the best places to begin complex tasks toward greater wage parity and shared prosperity.

Recommended Resources

Film
Sleep Dealer

Novelist
George Orwell, British novelist (again!)

Maps
"True World Map Does Not Look as Usually Portrayed." Accessed 5/1/16.

http://www.dailyplebiscite.com/en/2015/02/17/true-world-map-not-look-usually-portrayed/.

"Economic Impact of Climate Change in the World." Accessed 2/1/16.

http://www.voxeurop.eu/en/content/news-brief/5004193-map-showing-how-climate-change-will-affect-economy.

Notes

[1] Used with permission, February 2016.
[2] American Immigration Council, *No Action Taken: Lack of CBP Accountability in Responding to Complaints of Abuse*, 2016. Also see chapters on the Americas and migration.
[3] India and Bangladesh exchanged 162 enclaves ("sovereign" territory surrounded by another country), with 50,000 people perhaps best called borderline "stateless" without the access to schools, health clinics, and electricity that other nationals enjoyed in the Cooch Behar District, West Bengal, India. Residents can decide whether to remain or relocate based on their original citizenship (http://www.economist.com/blogs/economist-explains/2015/06/economist-explains-19). As Adam Taylor notes about this unique border, complete with maps in the article, the world will "lose the only third-order enclave" remaining, one "surrounded by an enclave surrounded by an enclave surrounded by another state" (https://www.washingtonpost.com/news/worldviews/wp/2015/08/01/say-goodbye-to-the-weirdest-border-dispute-in-the-world/).

   Other border changes have occurred as well, between Belgium and the Netherlands (http://www.theguardian.com/world/2015/dec/30/belgium-and-the-netherlands-exchange-land-because-it-makes-sense?CMP=fb_gu), Norway and Finland. At the US-Mexico border, through the famous Chamizal agreement, the United States returned approximately one square mile of land to Mexico in efforts to channel a meandering Rio Grande, as noted earlier. Territory was also ceded after war: Karelia in Finland to the USSR, as I learned at the ABS/World meetings and panels on memory and monuments.

   Witness also Google Maps' decision in 2015 to remove Palestine as a separate state from Israel, but rather inside a "divided line" in Israel, even though the United Nations granted Palestine observer-state status in 2012.
[4] Adam Taylor calls these "gray areas." Wherefore Crimea, the peninsula hanging by a tenuous land thread in the Black Sea? It was formerly part of the 20th-century Soviet Union, then

Ukraine, and then annexed by Russia after a vote in 2014 (and disputes over eastern Ukraine with Russian invasion/Russia-backed supporters). *National Geographic* places Crimea in part of Russia, while Google Maps does not. Can people have it both ways? Taylor continues with cartographic oddities in analyzing Arunachal Pradesh ("claimed by China but administered by India") differently to India-based and China-based viewers, depending on the website from which the maps are viewed! (https://www.washingtonpost.com/news/worldviews/wp/2014/04/01/the-simple-way-google-maps-could-side-step-its-crimea-controversy/).

[5] Javier Bauluz is Spain's first Pulitzer Prize winning photographer (accessed 11/15/15) http://galeon.com/javierbauluz/fotos2.html.

[6] See this map from VoxEurop about future environmental-economic changes if efforts to curb unbridled damage, gluttony, and waste are neglected: http://www.voxeurop.eu/en/content/news-brief/5004193-map-showing-how-climate-change-will-affect-economy.

Postscript

As I finished the book manuscript and assembled all the material for submission to the publisher, several learning opportunities emerged that I want to share with readers. The opportunities are reminders of both the horrifying and the hopeful issues associated with borderlands.

Australia's harsh refugee policies and practices have become clearer to many people around the world. Readers may recall from chapter 7 that Australia outsources detention to Nauru, a tiny island state for which the more-than-$1-billion contract is its major revenue generator. And the management of the facilities is contracted to a worldwide for-profit "correctional and detention" management corporation—a group based in Florida but with operations in the United States, United Kingdom, South Africa, and Australia—named with the first three letters of an historic discipline geography. The abuse of women, men, and children has been ongoing and publicized for more than 15 years. It has been written about in several venues, but the latest from *The Guardian* draws on data leaked from over 2,000 reports that cover guards' physical and sexual abuse as well as self-harm and suicide by refugees in detention to escape from what seems like and looks like a living hell.[1]

What will be done? Will people do more than wring their hands in distress and then move on to read more in the crowded mash of media stories? Or will they take the next steps in and with nongovernmental organizations (NGOs); engagement with officials at local, national, and international bodies; and/or individual choices about their investments or disinvestments, their travel plans, communication, and so on? The refugees should not be stuck in their living hell for another 15 years before action is taken.

Besides this horrifying news, I also got a shot of hope with regard to interaction in my central US-Mexico borderlands locale. Two NGOs, in an event called HUGS NOT WALLS, arranged for hundreds of families, separated by border control and immigration policies, to embrace one another on August 10 at the borderline of what is left of the concrete-walled, muddy Rio Grande/Río Bravo over which a tarp had been thrown. The secular Border Network for Human Rights (BNHR) and the sacred (Catholic) Hope Border Institute (HBI) arranged this complex, minutes-long reunion of small groups of family members totaling hundreds from each side of the border. Part of the complexity involved gaining permission from ICE, the chilling acronym for an enforcement agency of the Department of Homeland Security. I was there to witness the screams of joy, the crying, and the grandmas and grandpas, married couples, grandchildren, and other relatives hugging one another after long separations due to a US policy that keeps families apart and prohibits human contact: *Muy triste*, very sad, as many people said at the event. Even some of the journalists were tearing up at the emotionality of it all. The pictures tell the story well.

Although one might not see it well in one picture, the blue-shirted BNHR people from the US side, and the white-shirted people from the Mexico side saw

Border NGOs arrange for long-separated families in El Paso and Ciudad Juárez to embrace one another on Rio Grande/Río Bravo borderline at August 10, 2016, "Hugs not Walls" event.

Source: Photographs by Kathleen Staudt and Luis Pablo Hernández, used with permission.

a sign hung down over the concrete: HOPE. Hope is part of the NGO name for the white-shirted HBI families with their message on the T-shirt: MAKE IT YOUR/OUR BORDER. Whether border people are separated from family members or not, this phrase speaks to the sentiments of many border peoples here and elsewhere. The border is our space, and we deserve to have a voice in its everyday interactions and governance.

Note

[1] See Paul Farrell, et al., "The Nauru Files," accessed 8/11/16, https://www.theguardian.com/ australia-news/2016/aug/10/the-nauru-files-2000-leaked-reports-reveal-scale-of-abuse-of-childr en-in-australian-offshore-detention. The in-depth article provides pictures and videos. Major media outlets in the United States, like PBS and NPR, have covered the findings in their shocking details. And international NGOs like Amnesty International will now extend revelations about more seemingly civilized countries that routinely ignore human rights tragedies. Australia will "investigate," but amazingly, nothing had been investigated or done about the many reports over the years, perhaps buried in bureaucracies by border bureaucrats. Whether one agrees with Hannah Arendt's thesis about the "banality of evil" (paper pushers who follow orders), one must acknowledge that government officials often do nothing despite evidence of the harmful consequences of action. (And yes, there is a recent film on the topic: *Hannah Arendt*, 2013.) One heartening aspect of this process is that an individual had the courage to leak documents, reinforcing one avenue of moving "toward solutions" (chapter 12). Research and writing are also actions that may lead toward solutions. As far back as 2003, the late Charles Bowden exposed the horrors with field research in the article "Outback Nightmares & Refugee Dreams," in *Mother Jones* which mainly reaches left-of-center readers: http://www.mother jones.com/politics/2003/03/outback-nightmares-refugee-dreams.

Appendix

The Value of US Exports to Mexico and the Number of US Jobs That Rely on Trade with Mexico, 2012 (by State)

US State	Exports to Mexico (USD)	Number of Jobs
Alabama	**2.03 billion**	86,212
Alaska	9 million	14,835
Arizona	620 million	**111,216**
Arkansas	544 million	51,379
California	**26.32 billion**	**692,240**
Colorado	848 million	**105,776**
Connecticut	**1.1 billion**	74,841
Delaware	145 million	18,312
Florida	**2.24 billion**	**342,054**
Georgia	**2.32 billion**	**186,208**
Hawaii	2 million	29,442
Idaho	257 million	29,767
Illinois	**5.72 billion**	**252,931**
Indiana	**3.28 billion**	**120,763**
Iowa	**2.18 billion**	64,748
Kansas	**1.63 billion**	59,341
Kentucky	**1.72 billion**	78,588
Louisiana	**6.5 billion**	83,206
Maine	28 million	27,706
Maryland	332 million	**115,499**
Massachusetts	**1.6 billion**	42,557
Michigan	**8.96 billion**	**175,249**
Minnesota	**1.3 billion**	**117,395**
Mississippi	**1.15 billion**	50,023
Missouri	**1.44 billion**	**119,793**
Montana	53 million	20,594
Nebraska	**1.81 billion**	40,565
Nevada	330 million	53,593
New Hampshire	474 million	28,531
New Jersey	**2.1 billion**	74,481
New Mexico	618 million	36,200
New York	**2.6 billion**	**381,238**
North Carolina	**2.3 billion**	**187,337**

US State	Exports to Mexico (USD)	Number of Jobs
North Dakota	282 million	15,646
Ohio	**4.7 billion**	**224,337**
Oklahoma	627 million	68,498
Oregon	371 million	75,558
Pennsylvania	**2.84 billion**	**246,409**
Rhode Island	**1.43 billion**	**174,257**
South Carolina	**1.76 billion**	85,763
South Dakota	395 million	17,992
Tennessee	**3.81 billion**	**122,085**
Texas	**86.63 billion**	**463,132**
Utah	488 million	54,881
Vermont	130 million	14,372
Virginia	**1.058 billion**	**161,394**
Washington	**2.864 billion**	**128,277**
West Virginia	239 million	**161,394**
Wisconsin	**2.2 billion**	**117,665**
Wyoming	56 million	12,266

Source: Website of Congressman Beto O'Rourke, https://orourke.house.gov/ (accessed 2/7/14).

Note: States with exports worth billions of USD are in bold. States with over 100,000 jobs relying on trade with Mexico are also in bold.

Bibliography

Agathangelou, Anna, and L. H. M. Ling. 2004. "Power, Borders, Security, Wealth: Lessons of Violence and Desire from September 11." *International Studies Quarterly* 48, 3, September, pp. 517–38.

Agnew, John. 1994. "Still Trapped in Territory?" *Review of International Political Economy* 1, 1, pp. 53–80.

———. 2010. "The Territorial Trap Fifteen Years on." *Geopolitics* 15, 4, pp. 779–84.

Albahari, Maurizio. 2015. *Crimes of Peace: Mediterranean Migrations at the World's Deadliest Border*. Philadelphia: University of Pennsylvania Press.

Allen, William. 2013. "'I Am from Busia!': Everyday Trading and Health Service Provision at the Kenya-Uganda Border as Place-Making Activities." *Journal of Borderlands Studies* 28, 3, pp. 291–306.

Alper, Donald K. 1996. "The Idea of Cascadia: Emergent Transborder Regionalisms in the Pacific Northwest-Western Canada." *Journal of Borderlands Studies* XI, 2, Fall, pp. 1–22.

Alper, Donald, and Bryant Hammond. 2011. "Bordered Perspectives: Local Stakeholders' Views of Border Management in the Cascade Corridor Region." *Journal of Borderlands Studies* 26, 1, pp. 101–14.

American Civil Liberties Union (ACLU) Regional Center for Border Rights. 2014. *Guilty until Proven Innocent: Living in New Mexico's 100-Mile Zone*. Las Cruces, NM: ACLU.

American Immigration Council. 2016. *No Action Taken: Lack of CBP Accountability in Responding to Complaints of Abuse*. https://www.americanimmigrationcouncil.org/research/no-action-taken-lack-cbp-accountability-responding-complaints-abuse. Accessed 5/21/2016.

Anderson, Benedict. 1991. *Imagined Communities: Reflections on the Origin and Spread of Nationalism*. 2nd ed. NY: Verso.

Anderson, Joan, and James Gerber. 2008. *Fifty Years of Change on the US-Mexico Border: Growth, Development and Quality of Life*. Austin: University of Texas Press.

Anderson, Malcolm. 2000. "The Transformation of Border Controls: A European Precedent?" In Peter Andreas and Timothy Snyder, eds., *The Wall Around the West: State Borders and Immigration Controls in North America and Europe*. London: Rowman & Littlefield.

Andreas, Peter. 2000. *Border Games: Policing the US-Mexico Divide*. Ithaca, NY: Cornell University Press.

Andreas, Peter, and Timothy Snyder, eds. 2000. *The Wall Around the West: State Borders and Immigration Controls in North America and Europe*. Lanham, MD: Rowman & Littlefield.

Angelovski, Ivan. 2016. "Revealed: the £1bn of Weapons Flowing from Europe to Middle East," *The Guardian*, July 27. http://click.mail.theguardian.com/?qs=ba853a8d2c092555e03a4f5ab67b5591e8f93398e0250dff6b0ed9d5ea35bacf. Accessed 7/27/2016.

Anzaldúa, Gloria. 1987. *Borderlands/La Frontera: The New Mestiza*. San Francisco: Spinsters/Aunt Lute Press.

Arai, Naoki. 2011. "Cross-strait Tourism in the Japan-Korean Border Region: Fukuoka, Busan, and Tsushima." *Journal of Borderlands Studies* 26, 3, pp. 315–25.

Asiwaju, A. I. 1985. "The Conceptual Framework." In A. I. Asiwaju, ed., *Partitioned Africans: Ethnic Relations across Africa's International Boundaries, 1884–1984*. NY: St. Martin's Press, pp. 1–18.

———. 1985. "The Global Perspective and Border Management Policy Options." In A. I. Asiwaju, ed., *Partitioned Africans: Ethnic Relations across Africa's International Boundaries, 1884–1984*. NY: St. Martin's Press, pp. 233–51.

———. 1985. *Partitioned Africans: Ethnic Relations across Africa's International Boundaries, 1884–1984*. NY: St. Martin's Press.

Atkinson, Anthony B. 2015. *Inequality: What Can Be Done?* Cambridge: Harvard University Press.

Aviv, Rachel. 2016. "The Cost of Caring: The Lives of Immigrant Women Who Tend to the Needs of Others." *The New Yorker*, April 11. http://www.newyorker.com/magazine/2016/04/11/the-sacrifices-of-an-immigrant-caregiver. Accessed 4/15/16.

Bachmann, Anna. 2015. "Polish-German Cross-border Cooperation from the Neofunctional Perspective." In Elżbieta Opiłowska and Jochen Roose, eds. *Microcosm of European Integration: The German-Polish Border Regions in Transformation*. Baden-Baden, Germany: Nomos Verlagsgesellschaft.

Bachmann, Veit. 2013. "Political Geography's Blindspots: Introducing Joanna Sharp's 'Geopolitics at the Margins.'" *Political Geography* 37, pp. 18–19.

Bandy, Joe, and Jackie Smith. 2005. *Coalitions across Borders: Transnational Protest and the Neoliberal Order*. Lanham, MD: Rowman & Littlefield.

Banerjee, Paula. 2012. "Bengal Border Revisited." *Journal of Borderlands Studies* 27, 1, pp. 31–44.

Banerjee, Paula, and Anusua Basu Ray Choudhury, eds. 2012. "Introduction: Women in Indian Borderlands." *Journal of Borderlands Studies* 27, 1, pp. 27–9.

Barry, Ellen. 2016. "In India, a Small Band of Women Risk It All for a Chance to Work." *New York Times*, January 30. http://nyti.ms/1Q0Z2dE. Accessed 2/9/16.

Barta, Patrick. 2012. "Sea Dispute Upends Asian Summit." *Wall Street Journal*, July 17. http://www.wsj.com/articles/SB10001424052702303919504577524133983292716. Accessed 8/1/16.

Baruah, Sanjib. 2005. *Durable Disorder: Understanding the Politics of Northeast India*. New Delhi: Oxford University Press.

Baud, Michael, and Willem Van Schendel. 1997. "Toward a Comparative History of Borderlands." *Journal of World History* 8, 2, pp. 211–42.

Beckwith, Karen. 2010. "Introduction: Comparative Politics and the Logics of a Comparative Politics of Gender." *Perspectives on Politics* 8, 1, March, pp. 159–68.

Begum, Anwara. 2015. *Sino-South Asian Relations: Missed Opportunities?* Dhaka: AH Development Publishing House.

Beissinger, Mark R., and Crawford Young. 2002. "Convergence to Crisis: Pre-Independence State Legacies and Post-Independence State Breakdown in Africa and Eurasia." In Mark Beissinger and Crawford Young, eds., *Beyond State Crisis? Postcolonial and Post-Soviet Eurasia in Comparative Perspective*. Washington, DC: Woodrow Wilson Center Press, pp. 19–50.

Bennhold, Katrin. 2016. "On Perilous Migrant Trail, Women Often Become Prey to Sexual Abuse." *New York Times*, January 2. http://nyti.ms/1ZGurcg. Accessed 2/19/16.

Bergs, Rolf. 2012. "Cross-Border Cooperation, Regional Disparities and Integration of Markets in the EU." *Journal of Borderlands Studies* 27, 3, pp. 345–63.

Biba, Sebastian. 2014. "Desecuritization in China's Behavior towards Its Transboundary Rivers: The Mekong River, the Brahmaputra River, and the Irtysh and Ili Rivers." *Journal of Contemporary China* 23, 85, pp. 21–43.

Bilker, Molly. 2016. "Border Residents: Don't Build a Wall between Cities." *Cronkite News*, July 17. http://

cronkitenews.azpbs.org/2016/07/17/ border-poll-overview/. Accessed 7/18/16.

Binelli, Mark. 2016. "10 Shots Across the Border: The Killing of a Mexican 16-year-old Raises Troubling Questions about the United States Border Patrol." *The New York Times Magazine*, March 3. https://www.bloglikes.com/blogs/2016-03-06/10-shots-across-the-border-the-killing-of-a-mexican-16-year-old-raises-troubling-questions-about-the-united-states-border-patrol. Accessed 4/19/16.

Black, Jeremy. 1997. *Maps and Politics*. Chicago: University of Chicago Press.

Blatter, Joachim, and Norris Clement. 2000. "Cross-Border Cooperation in Europe: Historical Development, Institutionalization, and Contrasts with North America." *Journal of Borderlands Studies* 15, 1, pp. 15–54.

Blumberg, Renata, and Raphi Rechitsky. 2014. "Networks, Place, and Barriers to Cross-Border Organizing: 'No Border' Camping in Transcarpathia, Ukraine." In Nancy A. Naples and Jennifer Bickman Mendez, eds., *Border Politics*, NY: New York University Press, pp. 293–322.

Borton, James. 2015. *The South China Sea: Challenges and Promises*. Xlibris US (e-book, Kindle).

Braun, Yvonne A., and Michael C. Dreiling. 2014. "Frames, Boomerangs, and Global Assemblages: Border Distortions in the Global Resistance to Dam Building in Lesotho." In Nancy Naples and Jennifer Mendez, eds., *Border Politics*. NY: New York University Press, pp. 261–91.

Brown, Anastasia, and Todd Scribner. 2014. "Unfulfilled Promises, Future Possibilities: The Refugee Resettlement System in the United States." *Journal on Migration and Human Security* 2, 2, pp. 101–20.

Brunet-Jailly, Emmanuel. 2012. "Securing Borders in Europe and North America." In Thomas M. Wilson and Hastings Donnan, eds., *A Companion to Border Studies*. London: Blackwell, pp. 100–118.

———. 2004. "Toward a Model of Border Studies: What Do We Learn from the Study of the Canadian-American Border?" *Journal of Borderlands Studies* 19, 1, pp. 1–12.

———, ed. 2007. "Introduction: Borders, Borderlands, and Porosity." In Emmanuel Brunet-Jailly, *Borderlands: Comparing Border Security in North America and Europe*. Ottawa: University of Ottawa Press, 2007.

Brunet-Jailly, Emmanuel, Tony Payan, and Gary Sawchuk. 2008. *The Emergence of Cross-Border Regions along the Mexican-US Border and in Europe*. Canada: Policy Research Initiative, February.

Burnell, Peter, Lise Rakner, and Vicky Randall, eds. 2014. *Politics in the Developing World* (London and NY: Oxford University Press, 4th edition).

Burston, Bradley. 2012. "The 'Exodus' Effect: The Monumentally Fictional Israel That Remade American Jewry." *Haaretz*, November. www.haaretz.com/israel-news/the-exodus-effect-the-monumentally-fictional-israel-that-remade-american-jewry-/1.476411. Accessed 9/1/16.

Butalia, Urvashi. 2000. *The Other Side of Silence: Voices from the Partition of India*. Durham: Duke University Press.

Butler, Judith. 2004. *Undoing Gender*. NY: Routledge.

Carey, Elaine, and Andrae Marak, eds. 2011. *Smugglers, Brothels, and Twine: Historical Perspectives on Contraband and Vice in North America's Borderlands*. Tucson: University of Arizona Press.

Carr, Matthew. 2012. *Fortress Europe: Dispatches from a Gated Continent*. NY: The New Press.

Cashman, Timothy G. 2015. *Developing a Critical Border Dialogism: Learning from Fellow Educators in Malaysia, Mexico, Canada, and the United States*. Charlotte, NC: Information Age Publishing.

Castan Pinos, Jaume. 2014. "The Conflicting Aims of the European Neighborhood

Policy and its Secondary Effects." *Journal of Borderlands Studies* 29, 2, pp. 33–46.

Chambers, Peter. 2015. "The Embrace of Border Security: Maritime Jurisdiction, National Sovereignty, and the Geopolitics of Operation Sovereign Borders." *Geopolitics* 20, 2, pp. 404–37.

Chatterjee, Piya. "Ethnographic Acts: Writing Women and Other Political Fields." In Kriemild Saunders, ed., *Feminist Post-Development Thought*. London: Zed Press, pp. 243–62.

Cheng, Brittany. 2013. "The Philippines & Spratly Islands: A Losing Battle." *Scientific American*, June 4.

Chiriyankandath, James. 2014. "Colonialism and Post-Colonial Development." In Peter Burnell, Lise Rakner, and Vicky Randall, eds., *Politics in the Developing World*. NY: Oxford University Press, pp. 29–43.

Chowdhury, Syed Tashfin. 2015. "Acquittal of India Border Guard in Bangladeshi Girl's Killing Rekindles Human Rights Concerns." *Asia Times,* July 10. http://atimes.com/2015/07/acquittal-of-India-border-guard-in-banglades hi-girls-killing-rekindles-human-rights-concerns/. Accessed 2/1/16.

Corchado, Alfredo. 2016. "Common Ground: Poll Finds US-Mexico Border Residents Overwhelmingly Value Mobility, Oppose Wall." *Dallas Morning News*, July 18. http://interactives.dallasnews.com/2016/border-poll/. Accessed 7/19/2016.

Coronado, Irasema. 2014. "Whither the Environmental Nongovernmental Organizations on Multiple Regions of the US-Mexico Border?" *Journal of Borderlands Studies* 29, 4, pp. 449–64.

Correa-Cabrera, Guadalupe. 2013. "Drug Wars, Social Networks, and the Right to Information: Informal Media as Freedom of the Press in Northern Mexico." In Tony Payan, et al., eds., *A War That Can't Be Won*. Tucson: University of Arizona Press, 2013, pp. 95–118.

———. 2014. "Violence on the 'Forgotten' Border: Mexico's Drug War, the State, and the Paramilitarization of Organized Crime in Tamaulipas in a 'New Democratic Era.'" *Journal of Borderlands Studies* 29, 4, pp. 429–34.

Correa-Cabrera, Guadalupe, and Kathleen Staudt. 2014. "An Introduction to the Multiple US-Mexico Borders." *Journal of Borderlands Studies* 29, 4, pp. 385–90.

Dalrymple, William. 2015. "The East India Company: The Original Corporate Raiders." *The Guardian*, March 4. http://www.theguardian.com/world/2015/mar/04/east-india-company-original-corporate-raiders. Accessed 11/1/15.

———. 2015. "The Great Divide: The Violent Legacy of Indian Partition." *The New Yorker*, June 29, pp. 65–70.

Das, Debojyoti. 2014. "Understanding Margins, State Power, Space and Territoriality in the Naga Hills." *Journal of Borderlands Studies* 29, 1, February, pp. 81–94.

DeJaeghere, Joan G. 2007. "Intercultural Meanings of Citizenship in the Australian Secondary Curriculum: Between Critical Contestations and Minimal Constructions." In Doyle Stevick and Bradley A. Levinson, eds., *Reimagining Civic Education*. Lanham, MD: Rowman & Littlefield, pp. 293–316.

Díaz, George. 2011. "Twilight of the Tequileros: Prohibition-Era Smuggling in the South Texas Borderlands, 1919–1933." In Elaine Carey and Andrae Marak, eds., *Smugglers, Brothels, and Twine: Historical Perspectives on Contraband and Vice in North America's Borderlands*. Tucson: University of Arizona Press, pp. 59–82.

Diener, Alexander C., and Joshua Hagen. 2012. *Borders: A Very Short Introduction*. NY: Oxford University Press.

Dodds, Klaus. 2014. "Squaring the Circle: The Arctic States, 'Law of the Sea,' and the Arctic Ocean." *Eurasia Border Review* 5, 1, pp. 113–24.

Donnan, Hastings, and Thomas M. Wilson, eds. 1999. *Borders: Frontiers of Identity, Nation and State*. Oxford: Berg Publishers.

Dunn, Timothy. 2009. *Blockading the Border and Human Rights: The El Paso Operation That Remade Immigration Enforcement*. Austin: University of Texas Press.

Dzurek, Daniel J. 2004. "Maritime Agreements and Oil Exploration in the Gulf of Thailand." In Paul Ganster and David Lorey, eds., *Borders and Border Politics in a Globalizing World*. Lanham, MD: Rowman & Littlefield, pp. 301–16.

Eastman, Cari Lee Skogberg. 2012. *Shaping the Immigration Debate: Contending Civil Societies on the US-Mexico Border*. Boulder: Lynn Rienner Publishers.

The Economist. 2015. "Banyan: Such Quantities of Sand." February 28, p. 36.

———. 2016. "China v. the Rest." March 26, pp. 47–50.

———. 2015. "Choking on It: Air Pollution." December 5, p. 54.

———. 2015. "Climate Change: Hot and Bothered." Special Report, November 28, pp. 3–16.

———. 2015. "Europe's Boat People: For Those in Peril." Briefing, April 25, pp. 21–3.

———. 2015. "Exodus." September 12, p. 13.

———. 2015. "Free Exchange: The Best Is the Enemy of the Green." December 5, p. 75.

———. 2015. "Green Light." December 19, pp. 89–90.

———. 2015. "Migration in Europe: Looking for a Home." August 29, pp. 41–4.

———. 2016. "Looking for a Home." Special Report on Migration, May 28.

———. 2015. "Modi's Many Tasks." Special Report on India, May 23, pp. 1–15.

———. 2014. "The New Silk Road: Stretching the Threads." November 29, pp. 41–2.

———. 2016. "Particular about Particulates." January 16, pp. 43–4.

———. 2015. "Raise the Green Lanterns." December 5, pp. 43–4.

———. 2015. "A Real Border Guard at Last." December 19, pp. 76–77.

———. 2016. "Requiem for a River: Can One of the World's Great Waterways Survive Its Development?" February 13, pp. 43–8.

———. 2016. "Sighing for Paradise to Come." June 4, pp. 21–4.

———. 2014. "Stingy by Any Measure: In the Name of Curbing Inflation, the Government Is Hurting Workers." August 16. http://www.economist.com/news/finance-and-economics/21612255-name-curbing-inflation-government-hurting-workers-stingyany. Accessed 7/1/15.

———. 2016. "Sunnylands and Cloudy Waters." February 20, p. 10.

———. 2014. "A Surge from the Sea." August 16, pp. 41–2.

———. 2016. "The Trouble with GDP" and "How to Measure Prosperity." April 30, pp. 7, 21–4.

———. 2015. "Why India and Bangladesh Have the World's Craziest Border." June 24. http://www.economist.com/blogs/economist-explains/2015/06/economist-explains-19. Accessed 12/31/15.

———. 2015. "World Ocean Summit 2015." June 3–5. http://oceansummit.economist.com. Accessed 12/1/ 2015.

Enloe, Cynthia. 1980. *Bananas, Beaches, and Bases: Making Feminist Sense of International Politics*. Berkeley: University of California Press.

———. 2007. *Globalization and Militarism: Feminists Make the Link*. Lanham, MD: Rowman & Littlefield.

European Public Health Alliance. "European Year of Citizens: Are Roma People European Citizens Like Any Others?" European Roma Information Office Conference, Brussels, 22 October 2013. http://v2.epha.org/spip.php?article5680. Accessed 11/1/15.

Evans, Peter B., Dietrich Rueschemeyer, and Theda Skocpol, eds. 1985. *Bringing the State Back In*. Cambridge: Cambridge University Press.

Ewing, Walter. 2014. "'Enemy Territory': Immigration Enforcement in the US-Mexico Borderlands." *Journal on*

Migration and Human Security 2, 3, pp. 198–222.

Falke, Simon. 2012. "Peace on the Fence? Israel's Security Culture and the Separation Fence to the West Bank." *Journal of Borderlands Studies* 27, 2, pp. 229–37.

Fernández-Kelly, María Patricia. 1983. *For We Are Sold: I and My People: Women and Industry in Mexico's Frontier*. Albany: SUNY Press.

Filkins, Dexter. 2016. "The End of Ice: Exploring a Himalayan Glacier." *The New Yorker*, April 4.

Ford, Michele, and Lenore Lyons. 2012. "Labor Migration, Trafficking and Border Controls." In Thomas M. Wilson and Hastings Donnan, eds., *A Companion to Border Studies*. London: Blackwell.

Frayling, Christopher. 2014. *The Yellow Peril: Dr. Fu Manchu and the Rise of Chinaphobia* London: Thames and Hudson.

Fuentes, César, and Sergio Peña. 2010. "Globalization and Its Effects on the Urban Socio-Spatial Structure of a Transfrontier Metropolis: El Paso, TX–Ciudad Juárez, Chih–Sunland Park, NM." In Kathleen Staudt, César Fuentes, and Julia Monárrez Fragoso, eds., *Cities and Citizenship at the US-Mexico Border*. NY: Palgrave USA, pp. 93–118.

Furukawa, Koji. 2011. "Bordering Japan: Towards a Comprehensive Perspective." *Journal of Borderlands Studies* 26, 3, pp. 297–314.

Ganster, Paul, and David E. Lorey, eds. 2005. *Borders and Border Politics in a Globalizing World*. Lanham: SR Books.

García, Mario T. 1981. *Desert Immigrants: The Mexicans of El Paso, 1880–1920*. New Haven: Yale University Press.

Gaspar de Alba, Alicia. 2010. "Poor Brown Female: The Miller's Compensation for a 'Free Trade.'" In Alicia Gaspar de Alba, ed., *Making a Killing: Femicide, Free Trade, and La Frontera*. Austin: University of Texas Press.

Gauthier, Melissa. 2007. "*Fayuca Hormiga*: The Cross-border Trade of Used Clothing between the United States and Mexico." In Emmanuel Brunet-Jailly, ed., *Borderlands*. Ottawa: University of Ottawa Press, pp. 95–116.

Ghosh, Sahana. 2011. "Cross-border Activities in Everyday Life: The Bengal Borderland." *Contemporary South Asia* 19, l, pp. 49–60.

Gomez, Alan. 2016. "Study: Nearly 500K Foreigners Overstayed Visas in 2015." *El Paso Times* from *USA Today*, January 21, p. 3A.

Guardian. 2015. "Belgium and the Netherlands Swap Land—Because It 'Makes Sense.'" https://www.theguardian.com/world/2015/dec/30/belgium-and-the-netherlands-exchange-land-because-it-makes-sense. Accessed 12/31/2015.

Halicka, Beata. 2017. "The Everyday Life of Children in Polish-German Borderland during the Early Post-War Period." In Machteld Venken, ed., *Borderland Studies Meets Child Studies*. Frankfurt am Main: Peter Lang.

———. 2013. "The Oder-Neisse Line as a Place of Remembrance for Germans and Poles." *Journal of Contemporary History* 49, 1, pp. 75–91.

———. 2013. "The Shifting of Borders in 1945 in Memory of Poles, Germans and Ukrainians." *Warsaw East European Review* III, pp. 29–35.

Hardin, Garrett. 1968. "The Tragedy of the Commons." *Science* 162, 3859, pp. 123–48.

Heyman, Josiah McC., and Alan Smart. 1999. "States and Illegal Practices: An Overview." In Josiah McC. Heyman, ed., *States and Illegal Practices*. NY and Oxford: Berg, pp. 1–24.

Hirsch, Afua. 2013. "The Price of Gold: Chinese Mining in Ghana Documentary." *The Guardian*, April 23. Accessed 5/1/16 (also on the website of Ghanaian-American author http://www.kweiquartey.com, https://www.youtube.com/watch?v=ohrrE1rjzLo).

Ho, Selina. 2014. "River Politics: China's Policies in the Mekong and the Brahmaputra in Comparative Perspective." *Journal of Contemporary China* 23, 85, pp. 1–20.

Hoh, Anna-Lena. 2014. "'Voir l'Autre'? Seeing the Other, the Developments of the Arab Spring and the European Neighborhood Policy toward Algeria and Tunisia." *Journal of Borderlands Studies* 29, 2, pp. 204–16.

Hooks, Chris. 2016. "Closing Our Doors, Closing Our Minds (with accompanying Chart, "How to Get Asylum or Become a Refugee")." *The Texas Observer* 108, 1, January, pp. 6–7.

Hunt Institute for Global Competitiveness. 2015. "Paso del Norte Economic Indicator Review." Spring. http://huntinstitute. utep.edu/wp-content/uploads/2014/04/ Paso-del-Norte-Economic-Indicator-Review-No-1-April-20151.pdf. Accessed 7/1/15.

India, Government of. Ministry of Home Affairs. http://www.mha.nic.in/hiadi/ sites/uploadingfiles/inhahindi/files/pdf/ BM_Fenc%28E%29.pdf. Accessed 5/1/15.

Ivanova, Maria. 2009. "UNEP as an Anchor Organization for the Global Environment." In Frank Biermann, Bernd Siebenhüner, and Anna Schreyögg, eds., *International Organizations in Global Environmental Governance*. London and NY: Routledge, pp. 151–73.

Iwashita, Akihiro. 2011. "An Invitation to Japan's Borderlands: At the Geopolitical Edge of the Eurasian Continent." *Journal of Borderlands Studies* 26, 3, December, pp. 279–82.

Jacobs, Andrew. 2015. "China Fences In Its Nomads." *New York Times International Weekly*, July 20, p. 1.

Jańczak, Jarosław. 2013. "Revised Boundaries and Re-Frontierization: Border Twin Towns in Central Europe." *Revue d'études comparatives Est-Ouest* 44, 4, pp. 53–92.

Jessop, Bob. 2002. "The Political Economy of Scale." In Markus Perkmann and Ngai-Ling Sum, eds., *Globalization, Regionalization and Cross-Border Regions*. NY: Palgrave Macmillan, pp. 25–49.

Johnson, Corey, Reece Jones, Anssi Paasi, Louise Amoore, Alison Mountz, Mark Salter, and Chris Rumford. 2011. "Interventions on Rethinking 'the Border' in Border Studies." *Political Geography* 30, 2, pp. 61–69.

Jones, Lilias C., Pamela Duncan, and Stephen P. Mumme. 1997. "Assessing Transboundary Environmental Impacts on the US-Mexican and US-Canadian Borders." *Journal of Borderlands Studies* XII, 1–2, pp. 73–96.

Jones, Martin, Rhys Jones, Michael Woods, Mark Whitehead, Deborah Dixon, and Matthew Hannah. 2015. *An Introduction to Political Geography: Space, Place and Politics*. 2nd ed. London: Routledge.

Jones, Reece. 2012. *Border Walls: Security and the War on Terror in the United States, India, and Israel*. London and NY: Zed Press.

Judt, Tony. 1996 (original, reprint 2011). *A Grand Illusion? An Essay on Europe*. NY: New York University Press.

Jurczek, Peter. 2011. "Cross-border Cooperation in the German-Czech-Polish Border Region at the Turn of the Century." *Journal of Borderlands Studies* 17, 2, pp. 97–104.

Kapila, Mukesh. 2015. "The Red Cross and Red Crescent." In Roger MacGinty and Jenny H. Peterson, eds., *The Routledge Companion to Humanitarian Action*. London and NY: Routledge, pp. 179–90.

Karibo, Holly M. 2015. *Sin City North: Sex, Drugs, and Citizenship in the Detroit-Windsor Borderland*. Chapel Hill, NC: University of North Carolina Press.

Karasapan, Omer. 2016. "The Impact of Syrian Businesses in Turkey." *Brookings*, March 16. http://www.brookings. edu/blogs/future-development/posts/ 2016/03/16-syrian-businesses-turkey-karasapan. Accessed 3/17/16.

Keck, Margaret, and Kathryn Sikkink. 1998. *Activists Beyond Borders*. Ithaca, NY: Cornell University Press.

Knotter, Ad. 2014. "Introduction to the Special Section: Perspectives on Cross-Border Labor in Europe: '(Un)familiarity' or 'Push-and-Pull'?" *Journal of Borderlands Studies* 29, 3, pp. 319–26.

Konrad, Victor, and Heather N. Nicol. 2008. *Beyond Walls: Re-inventing the Canada-United States Borderlands*. Hampshire, England; Burlington, VT: Ashgate.

Kraft, Michael, and Scott Furlong. 2013. *Public Policy: Politics, Analysis, and Alternatives*. Los Angeles: Sage, 4th edition.

Krätke, Stefan. 2002. "Cross-Border Cooperation and Regional Development in the German-Polish Border Area." In Markus Perkmann and Ngai-Ling Sum, eds., *Globalization, Regionalization, and Cross-Border Regions*. NY: Palgrave Macmillan, pp. 103–24.

Kruszewski, Z. Anthony. 1972. *The Oder-Neisse Boundary and Poland's Modernization: The Socioeconomic and Political Impact*. NY: Praeger.

Lahiri, Jhumpa. 2013. *The Lowland*. NY: Vintage.

Laine, Jussi, and Andrej Demidov. 2013. "Civil Society Organizations as Drivers of Cross-border Interaction: On Whose Terms? For Which Purpose?" In Heikki Eskelinen, Ilkka Liikanen, and James W. Scott, eds., *The EU-Russia Borderland: New Contexts for Regional Cooperation*. London: Routledge, pp. 131–48.

Lakhani, Nina. 2016. "Human Rights Groups Sue US Over Immigration Payments to Mexico." *The Guardian*, February 12. http://www.theguardian.com/us-news/2016/feb/12/human-rights-group-sue-immigration-mexico?CMP=share_btn_fb. Accessed 2/16/16.

Lamb, Vanessa. 2014. "The Politics of Place Naming Reaches the Salween River" (3 videos also embedded in site, including "A River of Ethnic Minorities"). *Mekong Commons*. http://www.mekongcommons.org/politics-of-place-naming-salween-river/. Accessed 6/13/2016.

Lara-Valencia, Francisco. 2011. "The 'Thickening' of the US-Mexico Border: Prospects for Cross-Border Networking and Cooperation." *Journal of Borderlands Studies* 26, 3, pp. 251–64.

Leftwich, Adrian. 2014. "Theorizing the State." In Peter Burnell, Lise Rakner, and Vicky Randall, eds., *Politics in the Developing World*. NY: Oxford University Press, pp. 179–95.

Leick, Birgit. 2012. "Business Networks in the Cross-border Regions of the Enlarged EU: What Do We Know in the Post-enlargement Era?" *Journal of Borderlands Studies* 27, 3, pp. 299–314.

Lipsky, Michael. 1980. *Street-Level Bureaucracy: Dilemmas of the Individual in Public Services*. NY: Russell Sage Foundation.

Llera Pacheco, Francisco Javier, and Angeles López-Nórez. 2012. *Cross-Border Collaboration in Border Twin Cities: Lessons and Challenges for the Ciudad Juárez-El Paso and the Frankfurt (Oder)/Slubice*. Ciudad Juárez: Universidad Autónoma de Ciudad Juárez.

Lorentzen, Lois Ann, ed. 2014. *Hidden Lives and Human Rights in the United States: Understanding the Controversies and Tragedies of Undocumented Immigration*. Santa Barbara, CA: Praeger.

Lovenduski, Joni. 1998. "Gendering Research in Political Science." *Annual Review of Political Science*, pp. 333–56.

Lugo, Alejandro. 2008. *Fragmented Lives, Assembled Parts: Culture, Capitalism, and Conquest at the US-Mexico Border*. Austin: University of Texas Press.

Lundén, Thomas. 2004. *On the Boundary: About Humans at the End of Territory*. Huddinge, Sweden: Södertörns högskola.

Lutz, Catherine A., and Jane L. Collins. 1993. *Reading National Geographic.* Chicago: University of Chicago Press.

Lyon, Beth. 2014. "International Law and Undocumented Migration." In Lorentzen, *Hidden Lives and Human Rights in the United States.* Santa Barbara, CA: Praeger, vol. I, pp. 123–56.

MacGinty, Roger, and Jenny H. Peterson, eds. 2015. *The Routledge Companion to Humanitarian Action.* London and New York: Routledge.

Maddison, Sarah. 2014. "Indigenous Peoples and Colonial Borders." In N. A. Naples and J. Bickham Mendez, eds., *Border Politics.* NY: New York University Press, pp. 153–76.

Mallapragada, Madhavi. 2014. *Virtual Homelands: Indian Immigrants and Online Cultures in the United States.* Urbana: University of Illinois Press.

Mandela, Nelson. 1995. *Long Walk to Freedom.* Boston: Back Bay Books (Little Brown and Company).

Marak, Andrae, and Laura Tuennerman. 2011. "Official Government Discourses about Vice and Deviance: The Early Twentieth-Century Tohono O'odham." In Elaine Carey and Andrae M. Marak, eds., *Smugglers, Brothels, and Twine: Historical Perspectives on Contraband and Vice in North America's Borderlands.* Tucson: University of Arizona Press, pp. 101–21.

Martínez, Oscar J. 1978. *Border Boom Town: Ciudad Juárez since 1848.* Austin: University of Texas Press.

———. 1994. *Border People: Life and Society in the US-Mexico Borderlands.* Tucson: University of Arizona Press.

———. 2016. *Mexico's Uneven Development: The Geographical and Historical Context of Inequality.* NY and London: Routledge.

Massey, Douglas S. 2014. "Why Migrate? Theorizing Undocumented Migration." In Lois A. Lorentzen, ed., *Hidden Lives and Human Rights in the United States.* Santa Barbara, CA: Praeger, vol. I, pp. 71–106.

McClintock, Anne. 1995. *Imperial Leather: Race, Gender, and Sexuality in the Colonial Contest.* London/NY: Routledge.

McDougall, Allan K., and Lisa Philips Valentine. 2004. "Sovereign Survival: Borders as Issues." *Journal of Borderlands Studies* 19, 1, pp. 23–36.

McDuie-Ra, Duncan. 2014. "Borders, Territory, and Ethnicity: Women and the Naga Peace Process." In Naples and Mendez, eds., *Border Politics.* NY: New York University Press, pp. 95–119.

Menon, Ritu, and Kamla Bhasin. 1998. *Borders & Boundaries: Women in India's Partition.* Delhi: Kali for Women (and e-book on Kindle).

Merry, Sally Engle. 2006. *Human Rights & Gender Violence: Translating International Law into Local Justice.* Chicago: University of Chicago Press.

Miles, William F. S. 1994. *Hausaland Divided: Colonialism and Independence in Nigeria and Niger.* Ithaca; London: Cornell University Press.

———. 2014. *Scars of Partition: Postcolonial Legacies in French and British Borderlands.* Lincoln: University of Nebraska Press.

Miller, Todd. 2014. *Border Patrol Nation: Dispatches from the Front Lines of Homeland Security.* San Francisco: City Lights Books.

Misri, Deepti. 2014. *Beyond Partition: Gender, Violence, and Representation in Postcolonial India.* Champaign-Urbana: University of Illinois Press.

Morales, Oscar, Sara E. Grineski, and Timothy W. Collins. 2012. "Structural Violence and Environmental Injustice: The Case of a US-Mexico Border Chemical Plant." *Local Environment* 17, 1, pp. 1–21.

Moré, Iñigo. 2011. *The Borders of Inequality: Where Wealth and Power Collide.* Tucson: University of Arizona Press.

Mukherjee, Neel. 2014. *The Lives of Others.* NY: W. W. Norton.

Muller, Benjamin J. 2010. *Security, Risk, and the Biometric State: Governing Borders and Bodies.* London and NY: Routledge.

Mumme, Stephen, and Kimberly Collins. 2014. "The La Paz Agreement 30 Years On." *The Journal of Environment & Development* 23, 2, pp. 1–28.

Naples, Nancy A., and Jennifer Bickham Mendez, eds. 2014. *Border Politics: Social Movements, Collective Identities, and Globalization.* NY: New York University Press.

Nathan, Debbie. 1991. "The Eyes of Texas Are Upon You." In Debbie Nathan, ed. *Women and Other Aliens: Essays from the US-Mexico Border.* El Paso: Cinco Puntos Press. Reprinted from the *Village Voice* 9/9/86.

Nevins, Joseph. 2008. *Dying to Live: A Story of US Immigration in an Age of Global Apartheid.* San Francisco: City Lights Open Media.

Newman, David. 2006. "The Lines That Continue to Separate Us: Borders in our 'Borderless' World." *Progress in Human Geography* 30, 2, pp. 143–61.

Ngai, Mae M. 2004. *Impossible Subjects: Illegal Aliens and the Making of Modern America.* Princeton: Princeton University Press.

———. 2014. "Undocumented Migration to the United States: A History." In Lois Lorentzen, ed., *Hidden Lives and Human Rights in the United States.* Santa Barbara, CA: Praeger, vol. I, pp. 1–24.

Nugent, Paul. 1996. "Arbitrary Lines and the People's Minds: A Dissenting View on Colonial Boundaries in West Africa." In Paul Nugent and A. I. Asiwaju, eds., *African Boundaries: Barriers, Conduits and Opportunities.* London: Pinter, pp. 35–67.

Nugent, Paul, and A. I. Asiwaju, eds. 1996. *African Boundaries: Barriers, Conduits and Opportunities.* London: Pinter.

Ochoa O'Leary, Anna. 2009. "In the Footsteps of Spirits: Migrant Women's Testimonios in a Time of Heightened Border Enforcement." In Kathleen Staudt, Tony Payan, and Z. Anthony Kruszewski, eds., *Human Rights along the US-Mexico Border.* Tucson: University of Arizona Press, pp. 85–104.

O'Dowd, Liam, and Bohdana Dimitrovova. 2011. "Promoting Civil Society across the Borders of the EU Neighbourhood: Debates, Constraints and Opportunities." *Geopolitics* 16, 1, pp. 176–92.

Ohmae, Kenichi. 1987. *Beyond National Borders.* NY: Richard D. Irwin.

———. 1995. *The End of the Nation State: The Rise of Regional Economies.* NY: Free Press.

Olick, Jeffrey K., Vered Vinitzky-Seroussi, and Daniel Levy, eds. 2011. *The Collective Memory Reader.* NY: Oxford University Press.

Osborne, Louise, and Ruby Russell. 2015. "Refugee Crisis Creates 'Stateless Generation' of Children in Limbo." *The Guardian,* December 27. http://www.theguardian.com/world/2015/dec/27/refugee-crisis-creating-stateless-generation-children-experts-warn?utm_source=esp&utm_medium=Email&utm_campaign=GU+Today+USA+-+Version+A&utm_term=146405&subid=16547393&CMP=ema_565a. Accessed 12/28/16.

Ostrom, Elinor. 1990 (reissue 2015). *Governing the Commons: The Evolution of Institutions for Collective Action.* Cambridge: Cambridge University Press.

Ovodenko, Alexander. 2014. "Regional Water Cooperation: Creating Incentives for Integrated Management." *Journal of Conflict Resolution* 60, 6, pp. 1071–98.

Paasi, Anssi. 2011. "A 'Border Theory': An Unattainable Dream or a Realistic Aim for Border Scholars?" In D. Wastl-Walter, ed., *The Ashgate Companion to Border Studies.* Farnham, UK: Ashgate, pp. 11–32.

Palriwala, Rajni, and Patricia Uberoi. 2005. "Marriage and Migration in Asia: Gender Issues." *Indian Journal of Gender Studies* 12, 2 & 3, pp. v–xxix.

Payan, Tony. 2010. "Crossborder Governance in a Tristate, Binational Region."

In Kathleen Staudt, César Fuentes, and Julia Monárrez, eds., *Cities and Citizenship at the US-Mexico Border*. NY: Palgrave USA, pp. 217–44.

———. 2006. *The Three US-Mexico Border Wars: Drugs, Immigration, and Homeland Security*. Westport, CT: Praeger Security International, 2006; 2nd edition, 2016.

Payan, Tony, Kathleen Staudt, and Z. Anthony Kruszewski, eds. 2013. *A War That Can't Be Won: US-Mexico Perspectives on the War on Drugs*. Tucson: University of Arizona Press.

Perkmann, Markus, and Ngai-Ling Sum. 2002. *Globalization, Regionalization and Cross-Border Regions*. NY: Palgrave Macmillan.

Peterson, V. Spike. 2005. *A Critical Rewriting of Global Political Economy*. New York: Routledge.

Philippou, Stavroula. 2007. "Curricular Intervention and Greek-Cypriot Pupils' Constructions of Citizenship: Can 'Europe' Include Immigrants?" In Doyle Stevick and Bradley A. Levinson, eds., *Reimagining Civic Education*. Lanham, MD: Rowman & Littlefield, pp. 91–115.

Popescu, Gabriel. 2012. *Bordering and Ordering in the Twenty-first Century: Understanding Borders*. Lanham, MD: Rowman & Littlefield.

Pratt, Mary Louise. 1992. *Imperial Eyes: Travel Writing the Transculturation*. NY: Routledge.

Ragazzi, Francesco. 2014. "A Comparative Analysis of Diaspora Policies." *Political Geography* 42, July, pp. 74–89.

Rahman, Mirza Zulfiqur. 2014. "Territory, Roads and Trans-boundary Rivers: An Analysis of Indian Infrastructure Building along the Sino-Indian Border in Arunachal Pradesh." *Eurasia Border Review* 5, 1, pp. 59–75.

Rahman, Mirza Zulfiqur, and Kathleen Staudt. 2015. "There Are Many Indias: A Call for Collaboration and Comparative Research." *La Frontera* 35, 2, Spring, pp. 3–5.

Rakner, Lise. 2014. "Governance." In Peter Burnell, Vicky Randall, and Lise Rakner, eds., *Politics in the Developing World*, pp. 225–40.

Rawlence, Ben. 2015. *City of Thorns*. NY: Picador Macmillan.

Reid-Henry, Simon. 2013. "An Incorporating Geopolitics: Frontex and the Geopolitical Rationalities of the European Border." *Geopolitics* 18, 1, pp. 198–224.

Remnick, David. 2016. "Letter from Jerusalem. Seeds of Peace: Ayman Odeh's Unlikely Crusade." *The New Yorker*, January 25, pp. 24–30.

Rensink, Brenden. 2011. "Cree Contraband or Contraband Crees? Early Montanan Experiences with Transnational Natives and the Formation of Lasting Prejudice, 1880–1885." In Elaine Carey and Andrae Marak, eds., *Smugglers, Brothels, and Twine: Historical Perspectives on Contraband and Vice in North America's Borderlands*. Tucson: University of Arizona Press, pp. 24–43.

Rios, Jo Marie, and Joseph Jozwiak. 2008. "NAFTA and the Border Environmental Cooperation Commission: Assessing Activism in the Environmental Infrastructure Project Certification Process." *Journal of Borderlands Studies* 23, 2, pp. 59–81.

Rippberger, Susan, and Kathleen Staudt. 2003. *Pledging Allegiance: Learning Nationalism in El Paso–Juárez*. NY: Falmer/Routledge.

Robinson, Piers. 2015. "News Media and Communication Technology." In Roger MacGinty and Jenny H. Peterson, eds., *The Routledge Companion to Humanitarian Action*. NY and London: Routledge, pp. 254–66.

Rodriguez, Robyn Magalit. 2010. *Migrants for Export: How the Philippine State Brokers Labor to the World*. Minneapolis: University of Minnesota Press.

Romo, David Dorado. 2005. *Ringside Seat to a Revolution: An Underground Cultural History of El Paso and Juárez: 1893–1923*. El Paso: Cinco Puntos Press.

Ross, Janell. 2016. "3 Charts That Challenge the Conventional Wisdom of 2015." *The Washington Post*, January 2. https://www.washingtonpost.com/news/the-fix/wp/2016/01/02/3-charts-that-challenge-the-political-conventional-wisdom-of-2015/. Accessed 1/4/16.

Rothenberg, Tamar Y. 2007. *Presenting America's World: Strategies of Innocence in National Geographic Magazine, 1888–1945*. Hampshire, England: Ashgate Publishing.

Rowe, Don. 1997. "Education for Citizenship in Europe." In Gordon H. Bell, ed., *Educating European Citizens: Citizenship Values and the European Dimension*. London: David Fulton Publishers, pp. 46–55.

Ruiz Marrujo, Olivia. 2009. "Women, Migration, and Sexual Violence: Lessons from Mexico's Borders." In Kathleen Staudt, Tony Payan, and Z. Anthony Kruszewski, eds., *Human Rights along the US-Mexico Border*. Tucson: University of Arizona Press, pp. 31–47.

Rygiel, Kim. 2010. *Globalizing Citizenship*. Vancouver and Toronto: University of British Columbia Press.

Sáenz, Benjamin. 1992. "The Exile." In Benjamin Sáenz, ed., *Flowers for the Broken*. Seattle: Broken Moon Press.

Said, Edward. 1978. *Orientalism*. NY: Pantheon.

Sahlins, Peter. 1989. *Boundaries: The Making of France and Spain in the Pyrenees*. Berkeley: University of California Press.

Salter, Mark. 2008. "The Global Airport: Managing Space, Speed, and Security." In Mark Salter, ed., *Politics at the Airport*. Minneapolis: University of Minnesota Press, pp. 1–28.

Sambanis, Nicholas. 2000. "Partition as a Solution to Ethnic War: An Empirical Critique of the Theoretical Literature." *World Politics* 52, 4 July, pp. 437–83.

Sassen, Saskia. 2007. *A Sociology of Globalization*. NY: W. W. Norton.

Sato, Koichi. 2012. "China's 'Frontiers': Issues Concerning Territorial Claims at Sea—Security Implications in the East China Sea and the South China Sea." *Eurasia Border Review* 3, 2, pp. 71–90.

Sato, Yuki. 2011. "Exploring 'Borderlity' on the Ogasawara Islands." *Journal of Borderlands Studies* 26, 3, pp. 327–44.

Saunders, Kriemild, ed. 2002. *Feminist Post-Development Thought: Rethinking Modernity, Post-Colonialism and Representation*. London and NY: Zed Books.

Schladen, Marty. 2015. "Large Sheen Concerning: Source of Oil Spill Off Corpus Christi Unknown So Far & State Environment Agency Tight-lipped on Oil Spill Records." *El Paso Times*, June 19, 1B, 5–6B.

Schmidle, Nicholas. 2015. "Ten Borders: One Refugee's Epic Escape from Syria." *The New Yorker*, October 26, pp. 42–53.

Schou, Nicholas. 2016. "How the CIA Hoodwinked Hollywood." *The Atlantic*, July 14. http://www.theatlantic.com/entertainment/archive/2016/07/operation-tinseltown-how-the-cia-manipulates-hollywood/491138/?utm_source=nl-atlantic-daily-071416. Accessed 7/14/16.

Scott, James C. 2009. *The Art of Not Being Governed: An Anarchist History of Upland Southeast Asia*. New Haven, CT: Yale University Press.

———. 1998. *Seeing Like a State: How Certain Schemes to Improve the Human Condition Have Failed*. New Haven, CT: Yale University Press.

Scott, James Wesley. 2012. "European Politics of Borders, Border Symbolism and Cross-Border Cooperation." In Thomas M. Wilson and Hastings Donnan, eds., *A Companion to Border Studies*. Malden, MA: Blackwell, pp. 83–99.

———. 2000. "Transboundary Cooperation on Germany's Borders: Strategic Regionalism through Multilevel Governance." *Journal of Borderlands Studies* 15, 1, pp. 143–68.

Segal, Rafi, and Eyal Weizman. 2003. *A Civilian Occupation: The Politics of Israeli Architecture*. Tel Aviv: Babel Publishing.

Seidman, Gay. 2005. "Monitoring Multinationals: Corporate Codes of Conduct." In Joe Bandy and Jackie Smith, eds., *Coalitions Beyond Borders*. Lanham, MD: Rowman & Littlefield, pp. 163–83.

Semuels, Alana. 2016. "Upheaval in the Factories of Juárez." *The Atlantic*, January 21. http://www.theatlantic.com/business/archive/2016/01/upheaval-in-the-factories-of juarez/424893/. Accessed 1/22/16.

Shulman, David. 2016. "Israel: The Broken Silence." *New York Review of Books*, April 7, pp. 8–12.

Simmons, William Paul, and Carol Mueller, eds. 2014. *Binational Human Rights: The US-Mexico Experience*. Philadelphia: University of Pennsylvania Press.

Smith, Kirk R. 2006. "Women's Work: The Kitchen Kills More Than the Sword." In Jane S. Jaquette and Gale Summerfield, eds., *Women and Gender Equity in Development Theory and Practice: Institutions, Resources, and Mobilization*. Durham, NC: Duke University Press, pp. 202–15.

Sparke, Matthew B. 2006. "A Neoliberal Nexus: Economy, Security and the Biopolitics of Citizenship on the Border." *Political Geography* 25, pp. 151–80.

———. 2000. "Chunnel Visions: Unpacking the Anticipatory Geographies of an Anglo-European Borderland." *Journal of Borderlands Studies* 15, 1, pp. 187–220.

Spener, David. 2009. *Clandestine Crossings: Migrants and Coyotes on the Texas-Mexico Border*. Ithaca: Cornell University Press.

Staeheli, Lynn A., Eleonore Kofman, and Linda J. Peake, eds. 2004. *Mapping Women, Making Politics: Feminist Perspectives on Political Geography*. NY: Routledge.

Staudt, Kathleen. 1976. *Agricultural Policy, Political Power, and Women Farmers in Western Kenya*. Madison: University of Wisconsin, PhD Dissertation.

———. 2014. "The Border Performed in Films: Produced in Both Mexico and the US 'To Bring Out the Worst in a Country.'" *Journal of Borderlands Studies* 14, 4, pp. 465–80.

———. 2008. "Bordering the Other in the US Southwest: El Pasoans Confront the Local Sheriff on Immigration Enforcement." In Philip Kretsedemas and David Brotherton, eds., *Keeping Out the Other: Immigration Enforcement Today*. NY: Columbia University Press, pp. 291–313.

———. 1998. *Free Trade? The Informal Economic Sector at the US-Mexico Border*. Philadelphia: Temple University Press.

———. 2008. *Violence and Activism at the Border: Gender, Fear, and Everyday Life in Ciudad Juárez*. Austin: University of Texas Press.

———. 2009. "Violence at the Border: Broadening the Discourse to Include Feminism, Human Security, and Deeper Democracy." In Kathleen Staudt, Tony Payan, and Z. Anthony Kruszewski, eds., *Human Rights along the US-Mexico Border*. Tucson: University of Arizona Press, pp. 1–27.

Staudt, Kathleen, and Irasema Coronado. 2002. *Fronteras no Más: Toward Social Justice at the US-Mexico Border*. NY: Palgrave USA.

———. Forthcoming. "Gendering Border Studies: Biopolitics in the Elusive US Wars on Drugs and Immigration." *Eurasian Border Review*.

Staudt, Kathleen, and Pamela Cruz. 2014. "'Getting It': Business NGOs and Political Actors Talk about the Central US-Mexico Borderlands." Paper presented at the Association of Borderlands Studies Conference, April, Portland, Oregon.

Staudt, Kathleen, and Josiah Heyman. 2016. "Immigrants Organize Against

Everyday Life Victimization." In Rich Furman, Greg Lamphear, and Douglas Epps, eds., *The Immigrant Other: Lived Experiences in a Transnational World*. NY: Columbia University Press.

Staudt, Kathleen, and Zulma Méndez. 2015. *Courage, Resistance, and Women in Ciudad Juárez: Challenges to Militarization*. Austin: University of Texas Press.

Staudt, Kathleen, and Beto O'Rourke. 2013. "Challenging Foreign Policy from the Border: The Forty-Year War on Drugs." In Tony Payan, Kathleen Staudt, and Z. Anthony Kruszewski, eds., *A War That Can't Be Won: Binational Perspectives on the War on Drugs*. Tucson: University of Arizona Press.

Staudt, Kathleen, and David Spener. 1998. "The View from the Frontier: Theoretical Perspectives Undisciplined." In David Spener and Kathleen Staudt, eds., *The US-Mexico Border: Transcending Divisions, Contesting Identities*. Boulder: Lynne Rienner Publishers, pp. 3–34.

Staudt, Kathleen, Mosi Dane'el, and Guadalupe Márquez-Velarde. 2016. "In the Shadow of a Steel Recycling Plant in These Global Neoliberal Times: The Political Economy of Health Disparities among Hispanics in a Border *Colonia*." *Local Environment* 21, 5, March, pp. 636–52.

Staudt, Kathleen, César Fuentes, and Julia Monárrez Fragoso, eds. 2010. *Cities and Citizenship at the US-Mexico Border: The Paso del Norte Metropolitan Region*. NY: Palgrave.

Staudt, Kathleen, Tony Payan, and Timothy Dunn. 2009. "Closing Reflections: Bordering Human Rights, Democracy, and Broad-based Security." In Kathleen Staudt, Tony Payan, and Z. Anthony Kruszewski, eds., *Human Rights along the US-Mexico Border*. Tucson: University of Arizona Press, pp. 185–202.

Staudt, Kathleen, Tony Payan, and Z. Anthony Kruszewski, eds. 2009. *Human Rights along the US-Mexico Border:*
Gendered Violence and Insecurity. Tucson: University of Arizona Press.

Stevick, E. Doyle, and Bradley A. U. Levinson, eds. 2007. *Reimagining Civic Education: How Diverse Societies Form Democratic Citizens*. Lanham, MD: Rowman & Littlefield.

Stokłosa, Katarzyna. 2012. "Neighborhood Relations on the Polish Borders: The Example of the Polish-German, Polish-Ukrainian and Polish-Russian Border Regions." *Journal of Borderlands Studies* 27, 3, pp. 245–56.

———. 2014. "The Border in the Narratives of the Inhabitants of the German-Polish Border Region." In Katarzyna Stokłosa and Gerhard Besier, eds., *European Border Regions in Comparison: Overcoming Nationalistic Aspects or Re-Nationalization?* London and New York: Routledge, pp. 257–74.

Stone, Deborah. 2012. *Policy Paradox: The Art of Political Decision Making*. NY: W. W. Norton, 3rd edition.

Sur, Malini. 2014. "Divided Bodies: Crossing the India-Bangladesh Border." *Economic & Political Weekly* XLIX, 13, March 29.

Taub, Amanda. 2016. "The EU Is Democratic. It Just Doesn't Feel That Way." *New York Times*, June 30. http://www.nytimes.com/2016/06/30/world/europe/the-eu-is-democratic-it-just-doesnt-feel-that-way.html?hp&action=click&pgtype=Homepage&clickSource=story-heading&module=first-column-region®ion=top-news&WT.nav=top-news&_r=0. Accessed 6/30/16.

Tauman, Jessica. 2002. "Rescued at Sea, but Nowhere to Go: The Cloudy Legal Waters of the *Tampa* Crisis." *Pacific Rim Law and Policy Journal Association*. http://digital.law.washington.edu/dspace-law/bitstream/handle/1773.1/761/11PacRimLPolyJ461.pdf?sequence=1. Accessed 7/24/16.

Taylor, Alan. 2014. "Bhopal: The World's Worst Industrial Disaster, 30 Years Later." *The Atlantic*, December 2. https://www.theatlantic.com/

photo/2014/12/bhopal-the-worlds-worst-industrial-disaster-30-years-later/100864/. Accessed 4/19/2016.

Tchen, John Kuo Wei, and Dylan Yeats. 2014. *Yellow Peril!: An Archive of Anti-Asian Fear*. NY: Verso.

Theroux, Paul. 2013. *The Last Train to Zona Verde: My Ultimate African Safari*. Boston: Houghton Mifflin.

Tiano, Susan. 1994. *Patriarchy on the Line: Labor, Gender, and Ideology in the Mexican Maquila Industry*. Philadelphia: Temple University Press.

Tilly, Charles. 1985. "War Making and State Making as Organized Crime." In Peter Evans, Dietrich Rueschemeyer, and Theda Skocpol, eds., *Bringing the State Back In*. Cambridge: Cambridge University Press, pp. 169–91.

Torosyan, Tigran, and Arax Vardanyan. 2015. "The South Caucasus Conflicts in the Context of Struggle for the Eurasian Heartland." *Geopolitics* 20, 3, pp. 559–82.

Torpey, John. 1999. *The Invention of the Passport: Surveillance, Citizenship and the State*. NY: Cambridge University Press.

———. 2000. "States and the Regulation of Migration in the Twentieth-Century North Atlantic World." In Peter Andreas and Timothy Snyder, eds., *The Wall Around the West*. Lanham, MD: Rowman & Littlefield, pp. 31–54.

Trillo-Santamaria, Juan-Manuel. 2014. "Cross-Border Regions: The Gap Between the Elite's Projects and People's Awareness: Reflections from the Galicia-North Portugal Euroregion." *Journal of Borderlands Studies* 29, 2, pp. 257–73.

Tripathi, Dhananjay. 2016. "Creating Borders in Young Minds: A Case Study of Indian and Pakistani School Textbooks." *Regions & Cohesion* 6, 1, pp. 52–71.

———. 2012. "Energy Security: The Functional Area of Regional Cooperation for South Asia." *Eurasia Border Review* 3, 2, pp. 91–102.

UNDP (annual editions, from 1992 on). *Human Development Reports*. NY: United Nations Development Programme.

United States Conference of Catholic Bishops/Conferencia del Episcopado Mexicano. 2003. *Strangers No Longer: Together on the Journey of Hope*. Washington, DC: USCCB.

Valentine, Lisa Philips, and Allan K. McDougall. 2004. "Imposing the Border: The Detroit River from 1786 to 1807." *Journal of Borderlands Studies* 19, 1, pp. 13–22.

Vallet, Élisabeth, and Charles-Philippe David. 2012. "Introduction: The (Re) Building of the Wall in International Relations." *Journal of Borderlands Studies* 27, 2, pp. 111–20.

Van der Velde, Martin, and Szymon Marcińczak. 2007. "From Iron Curtain to Paper Wall: The Influence of Border Regimes on Local and Regional Economies—The Life, Death, and Resurrection of Bazaars in the Łódź Region." In Emmanuel Brunet-Jailly, ed., *Borderlands*. Ottawa: University of Ottawa Press, pp. 165–96.

Van Houtum, Henk. 2010. "Human Blacklisting: The Global Apartheid of the EU's External Border Regime." *Environment and Planning D: Society and Space* 28, pp. 957–76.

———. 2000. "An Overview of European Geographical Research on Borders and Border Regions." *Journal of Borderlands Studies* 15, 1, pp. 57–84.

Van Houtum, Henk, and Martin van der Velde. 2004. "De-politicizing Labour Market Indifference and Immobility in the European Union." In Olivier Kramsch and Barbara Hooper, eds., *Cross-Border Governance in the European Union*. London and NY: Routledge, pp. 41–55.

Van Schendel, Willem. 2005. *The Bengal Borderland: Beyond State and Nation in South Asia*. London: Anthem Press.

———. 2005. "Spaces of Engagement: How Borderlands, Illicit Flows, and Territorial States Interlock." In Willem Van Schendel and Itty Abraham, eds., *Illicit Flows and Criminal*

Things: States, Borders, and the Other Side of Globalization. Bloomington: Indiana University Press, pp. 38–68.

Van Schendel, Willem, and Erik de Maaker, eds. 2014. "Introduction to the Special Issue: Asian Borderlands: Introducing Their Permeability, Strategic Uses and Meanings." *Journal of Borderlands Studies* 29, 1, February, pp. 3–10.

Vélez-Ibáñez, Carlos. 2017. "Another Way of Looking at Things from the Prevailing Prisms." In Carlos Vélez-Ibáñez and Josiah Heyman, eds., *Anthropological Visions of the Mexico-US Transborder Region.* Tucson: University of Arizona Press.

Von Schreeb, Johan. 2015. "Medical NGOs." In Roger MacGinty and Jenny H. Peterson, eds., *The Routledge Companion to Humanitarian Action.* London and NY: Routledge, pp. 290–97.

Von Tunzelmann, Alex. 2007. *Indian Summer: The Secret History of the End of an Empire.* NY: Henry Holt and Company.

Vorrath, Judith. 2010. "On the Margin of Statehood? State-Society Relations in African Borderlands." In I. Zartman, et al., eds., *Understanding Life in the Borderlands: Boundaries in Depth and in Motion.* Athens: University of Georgia Press, pp. 85–104.

Walther, Olivier, and Bernard Reitel. 2013. "Cross-border Policy Networks in the Basel Region: The Effect of National Borders and Brokerage Roles." *Space and Polity* 17, 2, pp. 217–36.

Wassenberg, Birte, and Bernard Reitel. 2015. *Territorial Cooperation in Europe: A Historical Perspective.* Luxembourg: Publications Office of the European Union. http://www.ec.europa.eu/regional_polici/sources/information/pdf/brochures/interreg_25years_en.pdf.

Wasserman, Mark. 1984. *Capitalists, Caciques, and Revolution: The Native Elite and Foreign Enterprise in Chi-huahua, Mexico, 1854–1911.* Chapel Hill, NC: University of North Carolina Press.

———. 1997. *Persistent Oligarchs: Elites and Politics in Chihuahua, Mexico, 1910–1940.* Durham, NC: Duke University Press.

Wastl-Walter, Doris, and Andrea Ch. Kofler. 2000. "European Integration and Border-Related Institutions: A Practical Guide." *Journal of Borderlands Studies* 15, 1, pp. 85–106.

Weizman, Eyal. 2007. *Hollow Land: Israel's Architecture of Occupation.* London and NY: Verso.

Wesseling, H. L. 1996. *Divide and Rule: The Partition of Africa, 1880–1914.* Translated by Arnold J. Pomerans. Westport, CT: Praeger.

Wheatley, Christine, and Nestor P. Rodriguez. 2014. "With the Stroke of a Bureaucrat's Pen: US State 'Reforms' to Manage Its Undocumented Immigrant Population." In Lois Lorentzen, ed., *Hidden Lies and Human Rights in the United States.* Santa Barbara, CA: Praeger, vol. I, pp. 157–78.

Wilson, Thomas M., and Hastings Donnan, eds. 2012. *A Companion to Border Studies.* Malden, MA: Blackwell Publishing.

Winn, Peter. 2006. *Americas: The Changing Face of Latin America and the Caribbean.* Berkeley: University of California Press, 3rd edition.

Wright, Melissa. 2006. *Disposable Women and Other Myths of Global Capitalism.* NY: Routledge.

Wright, Robin. 2016. "How the Curse of Sykes-Picot Still Haunts the Middle East." *The New Yorker*, April 30. http://www.newyorker.com/news/news-desk/how-the-curse-of-sykes-picot-still-haunts-the-middle-east. Accessed 5/1/16.

Young, Gay. 2015. *Gendering Globalization on the Ground: The Limits of Feminized Work for Mexican Women's Empowerment.* NY: Routledge.

Young, M. Crawford. 1994. *The African Colonial State in Comparative Perspective*. New Haven, CT: Yale University Press.

Zabin, Carol. 1997. "Nongovernmental Organizations in Mexico's Northern Border." *Journal of Borderlands Studies* XII, 1–2, pp. 41–72.

Zartman, I. William, ed. 2010. *Understanding Life in the Borderlands: Boundaries in Depth and in Motion*. Athens: University of Georgia Press.

Index

5 *Broken Cameras*, 146, 209
7 *Soles*, 67, 157, 170
14 *Kilómetros*, 157, 207

Abraham, Itty, 178
Adichie, Chimamanda, 6, 13
Afghanistan, 38, 122, 141, 165, 209, 218
Africa, xxi, xxiii, xxiv, 3, 6 10, 15, 18, 20, 21, 23, 24, 26–9, 31, 47, 83, 131, 155, 181, 207; North Africa, 157, 170, 171. *See also individual countries*
African Borderlands Research Network (ABORNE), 6
African Union, 28, 224
Agnew, John, 4. *See also* territorial trap
al Assad, Bashar, 130, 167, 210
Al Qaeda, 130
Albahari, Maurizio, 168
alcohol, 179–80
Algeria, 22, 203
American Civil Liberties Union (ACLU), 159, 163, 170, 221
American Immigration Council, 239
Americas, xxiii, 56–78, 107, 203. *See also* Canada; Central America; North America; South America
Americas, 19, 59
Amnesty International, 73, 174n21, 217, 247n1
Anderson, Benedict, 15, 42, 118, 177
Anderson, Joan, 34, 186
Andreas, Peter, 51n13, 178, 182
Angola, 23
ant trade, 178. *See also* informal economies
Años de Bárbaros, 207
anthropology, xxi, xxiv, 4, 35
Annunciation House, 157, 221
Anzaldúa, Gloria, 112n6
Aquino, Corazon, 123
Arab Spring, 131, 171
Arabs, 202
Arendt, Hannah, 152–3, 247n1
Arai, Naok, 119
Argentina, 203, 204
Arizona, 61, 112n6, 160, 220, 224
Asia, xxi, xxiii, 3, 6, 12, 24, 155–6; Asian Tigers, 190; South, 5, 20, 24, 43, 46, 79, 93, 109, 116, 120–1, 180–3, 214, 218, 225, 237; South Asia Association for Regional Cooperation, 226; South-

east, 116, 120–1, 144, 155; Western, 5, 15, 20, 26, 30, 54, 96, 111, 148, 165, 166–9, 171, 205. *See also individual countries*
Asiwaju, A. I., 27
assimilation, 21, 91, 170–1, 203–4
Association for Borderlands Studies (ABS), xxv, 9–10, 95n21, 182
Association of Southeast Asian Nations (ASEAN), 12, 118, 242
Atwood, Margaret, 140
Australia, 12, 20–1, 116, 118, 121–2, 127n32, 128, 152, 164, 170, 203–4, 231, 245

Babel, 127n39
Balfour Declaration, 26
Balkans, 96, 98, 148, 153, 205
Bandy, Joe, 217–8
Banerjee, Paula, 89
Bangladesh, 10, 12, 45, 46, 47, 79, 81, 88–9, 90, 91, 92, 93, 120, 128, 134–5, 144, 153, 154, 156–7, 162, 177, 181–2
Baruah, Sanjib, 90–1
Battle of Algiers, 22, 203
Bauluz, Javier, 241, 244n5
Belgium, 25, 27, 136
Bell, Gordon, 229
Bengal, 46, 86–9, 93, 128, 154, 156–7, 181
Ben-Gurion, David, 202
Bergs, Rolf, 104–5
Berlin Conference, 27
Berlin Wall, 7, 50, 98, 99, 106, 143, 144, 172
Bhasin, Kamla, 84–5
Bhutan, 8, 89
Biafra, 6
biopolitics, 152–4, 158, 173n5
Blumberg, Renata, 219–20
bodies, 3, 85, 89–90
Boko Haram, 6
Bolívar, Simon, 59
Bolivia, 203
border bureaucrats, 1, 4, 47, 57, 67, 71, 80, 89, 115, 123–4, 141, 168, 169, 180–3, 190, 210, 215, 236, 238, 247n1. *See also* Border Patrol; Border Security Force

269

Norway, 122
Nugent, Paul, 21, 27
numeric metaphors, 40, 186. *See also* gross domestic product (GDP); methodologies

Obama, Barack, 66, 76n31
Ohmae, Kenichi, 11–2
O'Leary, Anna Ochoa, 170
Oman, 41, 97
O'Rourke, Beto, 185
Orwell, George, 11, 242
Ostrom, Elinor, 116, 125n2
Othering, 11, 15, 22, 23–5, 28, 30, 34, 45, 48–9, 67, 81, 85, 91, 104, 110, 128, 132, 145, 144, 147, 152, 158, 185, 200–1, 205–6, 211, 213, 231, 238
Ottoman Empire, 5, 25–6, 30, 131, 145, 203
Ovodenko, Alexander, 120

Pacific Century, 7, 118, 203
Pacific region, 116
Pakistan, 45, 47, 79, 83, 84, 86, 91–2, 144, 152, 156, 162, 165, 170, 181, 207, 208–9, 225
Palestine, 18, 25–6, 35, 41, 83, 97, 144–8, 165, 201–2, 204, 209–11, 221, 243n3
Palriwala, Rajni, 155–6
Panama, 144
Parovoz, 107
Partition, 12, 40, 46, 54, 80, 81, 83–6, 91–2, 128, 153, 181–2, 204, 211, 239; Partitioned Africans, 27
passports. *See* visas
patriotism. *See* nationalism
Payan, Tony, xxiv, 9, 71, 157, 227, 234n7
Peace Corps, xxiii
Peace Now, 145, 221
Peeking over the Wall, 231
People's Century, 28
Perkmann, Markus, 226–7
Peters, Arno, 18
Pew Research Center, 65
Philippines, xxiii, 12, 92, 116–19, 121–4, 154, 156, 188, 208
Philippou, Stavroula, 231
planned economies, 108–10
Plyler v. Doe, 69
Poland, xxv, 8, 12, 6, 50, 97, 99, 101, 105–11, 168, 178, 183, 208
police, 23, 73, 74, 78n56, 128, 131, 132, 157, 159, 172, 179, 206–9; costs of,

181, 183–4, 186. *See also* Border Patrol; Border Security Force; corruption
political parties, 28, 83, 92, 92, 139, 170, 191
political science, xxiv, xxvi, 3, 4, 80, 241
pollution, 120, 132, 134, 136, 187, 190
Pope Francis, 222–3, 239
Popescu, Gabriel, 122
popular culture, 38, 49, 48, 93, 102, 110, 114n47, 133, 138, 210, 240. *See also* films
Portugal, 25, 27, 104, 179, 208
postcolonial, xxiv, 2, 5, 33, 38, 40, 42, 43, 46, 47, 89, 111, 118, 129, 165, 177, 238
postcolonial South, xxv, 9
poverty, 39, 59, 61, 72, 89, 91, 93, 109, 110, 59, 61, 72, 129, 131, 132, 138, 188, 195n31, 203, 207, 209, 222, 239
power, 2, 4, 42–9, 51, 52n13, 91, 93, 103, 118, 120–1, 130, 214, 218, 237
Pratt, Mary Louise, 22, 24
Pray the Devil Back to Hell, 210
Prisoner of the Mountains, 26, 205
prohibition policies, 8, 63, 74, 157, 179. *See also* drugs
public policy, 4, 8, 12, 40, 43, 48–9, 128–9, 133. *See also specific policies such as* migration; security; trade
Punjab, 84–5, 182–3

Quartey, Kwei, 149n10

Rabbit-Proof Fence, 21, 204
racism, 22, 41, 179. *See also* White privilege
Radcliffe, Sir Cyril, 81, 83, 181
Rahman, Mirza Zulfiqur, xxv, 121
Rankin, Bill, 19, 30
rape, 6, 85. *See also feminicidio*; gender; sexual assault
Reagan, Ronald, 65
Rechilsky, Raphi, 219–20
Red Cross, 218
refugees, 3, 12, 54, 66, 74, 111, 121–2, 128, 130–1, 134, 145, 151, 156–7, 162–73, 201–2, 221, 245. *See also* migrants; Partition
Reitel, Bernard, 102, 104
religion, 83–4, 85, 92, 132, 142, 145, 146–7, 159, 161, 166, 170, 201, 205, 206, 210, 218, 230. *See also* faith-based activism
remittances, 93, 95n38, 183
Rensick, Brenden, 61
Rice University, 218